Globalisation, Economic Development and the Role of the State

UNIVERSITY COLLEGE WINCHESTER

Third
Pena

Globalisation, Economic Development and the Role of the State
is published by
Zed Books Ltd.,
7 Cynthia Street, London N1 9JF, UK and
Room 400, 175 Fifth Avenue, New York, NY 10010, USA
and Third World Network,
121-S Jalan Utama, 10450 Penang, Malaysia

Distributed exclusively in the US on behalf of Zed Books
by Palgrave,
a division of St Martin's Press, LLC
175, Fifth Avenue,
New York, NY 10010, USA

First Printing: 2003
Second Printing: 2004

Printed by Jutaprint,
2 Solok Sungai Pinang 3
11600 Penang, Malaysia

ISBN: 1 84277 142 6 Hb (Zed Books)
ISBN: 1 84277 143 4 Pb (Zed Books)
ISBN: 983 9747 87 8 (TWN)

A catalogue record for this book is obtainable from the British Library
US CIP is available from the Library of Congress

Contents

PART II. DOMESTIC POLICY ISSUES

PART III. POLICY ISSUES IN THE NEW GLOBAL CONTEXT

CHAPTER 7
GLOBALISATION, TRANSNATIONAL CORPORATIONS, AND
ECONOMIC DEVELOPMENT: CAN THE DEVELOPING COUNTRIES
PURSUE STRATEGIC INDUSTRIAL POLICY IN A GLOBALISING
WORLD ECONOMY?

CHAPTER 8
INTELLECTUAL PROPERTY RIGHTS AND ECONOMIC
DEVELOPMENT: HISTORICAL LESSONS AND EMERGING ISSUES 273

CHAPTER 9
INSTITUTIONAL FOUNDATIONS FOR EFFECTIVE DESIGN
AND IMPLEMENTATION OF SELECTIVE TRADE AND
INDUSTRIAL POLICIES IN THE LEAST DEVELOPED
COUNTRIES: THEORY AND EVIDENCE   305

ACKNOWLEDGEMENTS

Chapter 1: 'Theories of State Intervention in Historical Perspective' (with Robert Rowthorn) was originally published as 'The Role of the State in Economic Change – Introduction' (with Robert Rowthorn) in H.-J. Chang and R. Rowthorn (eds.), *The Role of the State in Economic Change* (1995, Oxford University Press). I thank the UNU/WIDER (United Nations University/World Institute for Development Economics Research) for its permission to reprint this article, with suitable modifications.

Chapter 2: 'State, Institutions and Structural Change' was published in *Economic Dynamics and Structural Change*, 1994, vol.5, no.2. I thank the Oxford University Press for its permission to reprint this article.

Chapter 3: 'An Institutionalist Perspective on the Role of the State', was originally published in L. Burlamaqui, A. Castro and H.-J. Chang (eds.), *Institutions and the Role of the State* (2000, Edward Elgar).

Chapter 4: 'The Political Economy of Industrial Policy', was originally published as Chapter 3 of *The Political Economy of Industrial Policy* (1994, Macmillan Press).

Chapter 5: 'The Economics and Politics of Regulation' was originally published in *Cambridge Journal of Economics,* 1997, vol.21, no.6. I thank Oxford University Press for its permission to reprint this article.

Chapter 6: 'Public Enterprises in Developing Countries and Economic Efficiency' (with Ajit Singh) is a shortened version of the article of the same title published in *UNCTAD Review*, 1993, no.4. I thank the UNCTAD (United Nations Conference on Trade and Development) for its permission to reprint this article in a shortened form.

Chapter 7: 'Globalisation, Transnational Corporations, and Economic Development' was originally published in D. Baker, G. Epstein and R. Pollin (eds.), *Globalisation and Progressive Economic Policy* (1998, Cambridge University Press). I thank Cambridge University Press for its permission to reprint this chapter.

Chapter 8: 'Intellectual Property Rights and Economic Development – Historical Lessons and Emerging Issues' was originally published in *Journal of Human Development,* July, 2001, vol.2, no.2. I thank the UNDP (United Nations Development Programme) for its permission to reprint this article.

Chapter 9: 'Institutional Foundations for Effective Design and Implementation of Selective Trade and Industrial Policies in the Least Developed Countries: Theory and Evidence' was originally prepared for the project, 'Economic Policymaking and Implementation in Africa: A Case Study of Strategic Trade and Selective Industrial Policies', sponsored by the International Development Research Center, Ottawa, Canada. I thank the IDRC for its financial support and permission to use this paper.

Introduction

THE role of the state in the economy has always been a controversial issue in public debate. However, during the last two decades or so, the debate has become particularly heated. During this period, we have seen the upsurge of neoliberal thinking that preaches the virtues of unregulated markets and recommends deregulation, opening-up, and privatisation. Indeed, many neoliberal commentators would argue that human nature and the nature of modern political institutions are such that the more constrained the state is the better it is for the economy. Over the last decade or so, this push for a minimal, pro-business state has been further intensified with the rise of the globalisation discourse that sees the nation-state at best as an anachronism and at worst as an obstacle to human progress.

Especially in developing countries, there have been many radical neoliberal 'reforms' since the mid-1980s. These reforms were implemented sometimes voluntarily but often under pressure from multilateral agencies (such as the International Monetary Fund (IMF), the World Bank, and the World Trade Organisation (WTO) and donor governments. What is notable is that, over time, the scope of such external intervention has been constantly widening, with serious implications for national sovereignty and the mandate of the multilateral institutions.

For example, before the adoption of the Structural Adjustment Programmes (SAPs) following the debt crisis of 1982, the IMF mainly concerned itself with short-term balance of payments problems. Under the SAPs, however, it started intervening in all areas of economic policy, especially monetary policy, budgetary policy, trade policy, and the management of state-owned enterprises. By the late-1990s, it was telling the Korean corporations what kind of corporate governance system and how much corporate debts they should have. Now many donor governments and multilateral institutions routinely attach so-called 'governance conditionalities' to their financial assistance, which require changes not just in economic policy but also in political, legal, and social institutions by the recipient country.[1]

Despite the continuous widening of their scope, neoliberal reform programmes have failed to produce expected results. Indeed, their record has been very poor. It is well known that neoliberal policies have increased income inequality and increased economic instability, which sometimes have even led to political instability and disintegration of society – as seen in many former Communist economies, Indonesia after the 1997 financial crisis, and Argentina in the recent period. However, the most damning failure of neoliberalism is in its failure to generate faster growth, in whose name we were asked to accept increased inequality, greater economic instability, and many other unpleasant things.

The world's *per capita* income was growing at 3.1% during the 'bad old days' of 1960-80, but it has been growing at only 2% during the neoliberal period of 1980-2000.[2] Growth of *per capita* income in developing countries has decelerated from 3% to 1.5% between these two periods. Even this 1.5% will not have been possible without the marked acceleration of growth in the distinctively non-neoliberal China and India. Without these two countries, this rate is reduced to around 1%. And even this paltry 1% masks the reality of growth collapse in many developing countries. *Per capita* income in Latin America virtually stood still in the 1980-2000 period, that in Sub-Saharan Africa has been shrinking, and those in many former Communist economies are still *half or less* of what they were before the fall of Communism.

1   A critique of the 'governance conditionality' from an international political economy point of view can be found in D. Kapur and R. Webber, 'Governance-related Conditionalities of the IFIs', G-24 Discussion Paper Series, no.6, 2000, Geneva, UNCTAD. A critique from a historical point of view can be found in Ch. 3 of H-J. Chang, *Kicking Away the Ladder – Development Strategy in Historical Perspective* (2002, London, Anthem Press).

2   All the figures in the paragraph are from Ch. 4 of H-J. Chang, *Kicking Away the Ladder – Development Strategy in Historical Perspective* (2002, London, Anthem Press).

This is a truly embarrassing record for a doctrine that has prided itself on its hard-nosed focus on efficiency and growth, and that has justified its policies on the ground that greater wealth needs to be generated before it can be redistributed. Given this, it is not a big surprise that there is now a widespread dissatisfaction with the neoliberal orthodoxy across the world, manifested in the increasingly frequent civil unrest in developing countries and 'anti-globalisation' demonstrations in developed countries. Those who are not completely beholden to neoliberal doctrine are beginning to accept that things cannot go on as they are.

But is there any viable alternative to neoliberalism? At one level, alternatives to neoliberalism have existed all along. The import-substitution policies pursued by many developing countries before the 1980s, the 'East Asian model' (pursued by countries like Japan, Korea, and Taiwan), or the unique mix of socialism and capitalism that China has been pursuing for the last decade-and-a-half are just some of the examples. However, not only do these alternative 'models' have their own problems but, more importantly, they also lack the robust theoretical foundations that they need if they are to challenge neoliberal orthodoxy at the ideological, as well as the practical, level.

The essays in this volume are some results of my attempt to construct a theoretical alternative to neoliberalism. They are a diverse collection in the sense that some are highly theoretical while some are focused on more empirical issues. And the issues covered concern a rather wide range of domestic and international policy issues. However, at another level, there are some important common theoretical threads running through them, which I call the institutionalist political economy approach.

In Part I, three essays provide the historical and theoretical backgrounds to the more concrete policy issues that are discussed in Parts II and III.

Chapter 1, 'Theories of State Intervention in Historical Perspective', co-authored with Bob Rowthorn, examines how the debate on the role of the state has evolved over the last two centuries, especially over the post-World War II period.

Following World War I, the old certainties of liberal capitalism (combined with imperialism) that dominated the world during the late-19th and the early-20th centuries were shattered by events like the

Great Depression and the Bolshevik Revolution. As a response, interventionist economic theories, especially welfare economics and Keynesian economics, as well as new policy practices, such as the New Deal and the Swedish social corporatism, emerged in some advanced capitalist countries, although the old order clung on until the Second World War in most countries.

Following the Second World War, there were dramatic theoretical and practical swings to state interventionism. The liberal *ancien regime* was discredited and Keynesian macroeconomic policy and the welfare state were established in the advanced capitalist economies, while socialism spread and was quite successful for a while. In particular, most developing countries embraced state interventionism as a reaction to the extreme free-market policy of colonialism, using insights from the emerging subject of development economics.

From the 1970s, however, there was a 'neoliberal' backlash to the interventionism of the early postwar years. The most important elements in this backlash include monetarist macroeconomic theories, theories of 'government failure' (as opposed to 'market failure' in welfare economics), and various attacks on import substitution industrialisation (ISI) in developing countries.

In this chapter, some common threads among these theories are identified and their theoretical premises are criticised. Most importantly, while rejecting the rather naive view of the state as the all-knowing, all-powerful agent devoted to social betterment (as in many earlier interventionist theories), the chapter argues that the neoliberal view of the state as no more than a collection of self-seeking agents that have no moral values (or, even worse, of agents that use moral values only as cynical 'marketing ploys') is equally, if not more, problematic. This theme is further extended in Chapter 3.

Chapter 2, 'State, Institutions and Structural Change', develops an 'institutionalist' theory of state intervention in the context of structural change, which is at the heart of any economic development process.

Chapter 2 starts by acknowledging some contributions that neoliberal theories of state intervention have made in their criticisms of traditional interventionist theories such as welfare economics. However, it is then pointed out, despite their differences, neoliberal theories and traditional interventionist theories share one important limitation, which is their belief in what I call the 'primacy of the market'. In this view, non-market institutions, including the state, are seen as second-best 'man-made' substitutes, which emerge only when the 'natural' order of the market fails to produce the promised outcomes. Neoliberalism fundamentally only differs from traditional interventionist theories in believing that the substitutes, especially state intervention, are likely to produce even worse results than failing markets.

The chapter then develops an explicitly 'institutionalist' approach to state intervention as an alternative that allows us to understand the market, the state, and other institutions within a unified and unbiased framework. This theoretical approach is more systematically developed in Chapter 3, but in Chapter 2 the focus is on the role of the state as the designer, defender, and reformer of many formal and informal institutions in the context of structural change. Two roles are highlighted – first, its role as an entrepreneur that provides the vision for the future and builds the necessary institutions, and, second, its role as the manager of conflicts which arise in the process of structural change. The role of political constraints and globalisation (or what is called 'multinationalisation of economic activities' in the chapter) in the performance of such functions is discussed.

Finally, Chapter 2 tries to affirm the value of the institutionalist approach with a brief comparative discussion of the 'industrial policy states' of East Asia and 'social corporatist states' of Scandinavia, both of which successfully played their dual roles as entrepreneur and conflict manager, albeit in very different political contexts and using very different policy tools and economic institutions.

Chapter 3, 'An Institutionalist Perspective on the Role of the State' tries to develop more fully the institutionalist approach that underlies the first two chapters of Part I.

Chapter 3 starts by pointing out some internal inconsistencies in neoliberal theories, stemming from the 'unholy alliance' between the neoclassical wing, which provides the technical tools, and the Austrian-Libertarian wing, which provides the philosophical basis and the political rhetoric. However, these are the least of the problems with neoliberal theories. The chapter argues that there are fundamental problems with the very way in which neoliberalism theorises the market and the state (and other institutions in those relatively rare occasions where they feature), as well as the relationship between the two. The chapter then asks four apparently simple questions, which expose the weaknesses in the theoretical foundation of neoliberalism and point us to an alternative theoretical approach.

First, the chapter asks 'what is a free market?' and points out how defining a free market (and thus state intervention) is an exercise that cannot be done without explicitly bringing in moral and political considerations. This means that the market and the state are not neatly separable, even at the theoretical level. In turn, this means that, contrary to the neoliberal claim, there is no reason to assume that the particular boundary between the market and the state that they prefer (that of a 'minimal state', although it must be said that in practice there is no one clear definition of it) is the 'correct' boundary.

Second, it is asked 'what does market failure mean and how much does it matter?'. The chapter argues that the definition of market failure is dependent on the underlying economic theory that defines the ideal market, of which neoliberal theory is only one (and not a very good one at that).

Third, I ask whether 'in the beginning, there were markets', as neoliberal theorists believe. This is the 'market primacy assumption' that I mentioned in Chapter 2, whose refutation has an important policy implication. If markets are 'natural' institutions that will flourish without state interference, those radical neoliberal reform programmes tried in the former socialist economies and many developing countries would not have been such resounding failures. That this was not the case is a corroboration of our contention in Chapter 2 that the state has to play an important role in engineering institutional changes.

Fourth, it is asked 'can we rid the market of politics?', as neoliberals want to do through shrinkage of the state and through restrictions on the discretion it has even in those 'minimal' functions. However, it is argued, all prices are at some level politically determined and therefore there cannot be such a thing as a 'pure market'. If this is the case, the neoliberal proposal for 'de-politicisation' of the market is a thinly-disguised attempt to rid the market of the kinds of politics that they do not like, such as trade unionism.

Chapter 3 concludes by laying out a research agenda that is necessary to further develop what I call an 'institutionalist political economy'.[3]

Part II of this book contains three chapters that deal with three key domestic policy issues for developing countries – industrial policy, regulation, and privatisation – explicitly and implicitly drawing on the theoretical approach developed in Part I.

Chapter 4, 'The Political Economy of Industrial Policy', discusses arguably the most controversial policy issue of our time. From the 1980s, there has been a heated debate on whether countries, especially, but not exclusively, developing countries, could benefit from adopting (selective) industrial policy, namely state intervention that promotes and winds down particular industries with an array of custom-designed policies (such as tariffs, subsidies, entry regulations, or technology supports) with a view to improving the productivity of the national economy in the long run.

After reviewing the debate on industrial policy up to the early-1990s, the chapter develops some economic theories of selective – as opposed to general or non-selective – industrial policy. On the static side, it is pointed out that coordination failure inherent in unregulated industries in a world with imperfectly-mobile resources can lead to social waste. Major policies to deal with this problem include investment coordination among potential competitors in expanding industries, state-supervision of recession cartels, and state brokerage in private sector negotiation regarding exit and capacity scrapping in declining industries. On the dynamic side, it is argued that 'socialising risk' through industrial policy can help the economy achieve faster structural change. Policies in this vein include coordination of investments in complementary projects and subsidisation of risky R&D projects.

After laying out these theories, the chapter examines a range of potential problems that may hamper the effectiveness of (selective) industrial policy such as: information problems (both insufficient and

3 This theory is further developed in H.-J. Chang, 'Breaking the Mould – An Institutionalist Political Economy Alternative to the Neo-Liberal Theory of the Market and the State', *Cambridge Journal of Economics*, September, 2002.

asymmetric information); possibility of rent-seeking; political problems (especially of legitimacy and democratic control); and the problems arising from the absence of certain institutions that are regarded as crucial for the success of industrial policy, such as high-quality elite bureaucracy. Suggestions are made as to how policies and institutions may be established to alleviate these problems.

Overall, Chapter 4 concludes that selective industrial policy of the kinds practised in East Asia during the postwar period – and also in a number of European countries such as France, Austria, Norway, and Finland – have ample theoretical justifications, some of which were not recognised until recently. It is acknowledged that there are potential pitfalls in the implementation of such policy, but it is argued that none of them are insurmountable, contrary to what its opponents like to argue.

Those commentators who are sceptical about the value of (selective) industrial policy almost invariably argue that what countries need is actually less, and not more, regulation of industries. Indeed, deregulation has been one of the key items in the neoliberal policy programme over the last couple of decades. Chapter 5, 'The Economics and Politics of Regulation', takes on this issue.

After a brief but necessary definitional clarification, the chapter surveys the evolution of perspectives on regulation during the postwar period, emphasising the interactions between intellectual changes and real world economic and political developments. The organisation of this theoretical review is similar to that adopted in Chapter 1, but the discussion here more specifically focuses on regulation, rather than state intervention in general. The chapter then looks at some themes that are neglected in the current literature on regulation but are critical in understanding the dynamics of regulatory change.

First, contrary to what many neoliberal economists suggest, deregulation should not be equated with a total withdrawal of the state. There are some regulations that are essential for the very existence, not to speak of the effective functioning, of many markets. Second, especially in the developing countries and the transition economies, the state needs to create markets, and not just regulate them. Therefore, the difficulty of drawing the boundary for the market and the difficulty of assigning property (and other) rights in creating the markets need to be considered (see Chapter 3 for further discussion). Third, we need to introduce distributional considerations more explicitly in our design of regulatory reform, especially if we want to increase its chance of success. Fourth, more attention needs to be paid to dynamic, as opposed to static allocative, implications of regulatory change. Fifth, we need to have a more sophisticated theory of the politics of regulation. Unlike what is assumed in the neoliberal literature, self-seeking is not the only motivation that determines people's actions, especially when they operate in the public domain. The designers of regulatory reform ignore the importance of 'moral' motives at their peril (see Chapters 1 and 3 for further discussions).

Chapter 6, 'Public Enterprises in Developing Countries and Economic Efficiency', a shortened version of the article co-authored with Ajit Singh, looks at another central element in the neoliberal policy reform package, that is, privatisation.

Neoliberal economists have put great emphasis on the privatisation of public enterprises in developing countries and especially in transition economies, on the ground that without private property ownership there is no incentive for anyone to improve enterprise performance. The chapter critically examines the theories underlying this contention and the empirical evidence that is supposed to back it up.

The neoliberal belief in the inefficiencies of public ownership is founded on two theoretical planks. The first of this is the view that without the ability that comes from property ownership to appropriate the efficiency gains from better management, managers do not have the incentive to improve enterprise efficiency. The problem with this view becomes immediate when we recognise that most large private enterprises are not run by owners either.

Against this, neoliberal economists invoke the second plank of their argument, namely that public enterprises are certain to be poorly managed because they are not subject to the disciplines of product markets (usually being statutory monopolies) or the capital market (as they are immune to the threats of bankruptcy and takeover). This claim, however, is exaggerated, as most public enterprises are subject to some degree of product-market competition and as they are also subject to changes in management (public sector equivalent of take-over) and liquidation (public sector equivalent of bankruptcy). Moreover, in reality capital market discipline does not work as well as it is supposed to. For example, empirical studies show that size, rather than efficiency, is the most important determinant of a takeover. More importantly, stock markets can create perverse incentives in the form of 'short-termism', which makes the managers focus on short-term profit, often at the cost of long-term prospect of the enterprise.

On the empirical front, there is no systematic evidence that public enterprises are inherently less efficient than private sector enterprises. Statistical studies trying to find negative correlation between the size of an economy's public enterprise sector and its growth have produced inconclusive results. Across the world, there are many examples of efficient public enterprises – we do not get to hear about them often because they are less studied than the problematic ones. There are also countries like France, Austria, and Taiwan which have done very well economically, despite (or rather, some would say, because of) having some of the largest public enterprise sectors in the world.

Next, the chapter discusses the practical problems of privatisation, especially in developing countries. Even when public ownership is the main cause of poor enterprise performance, it is costly to privatise – it is difficult to find buyers in countries with an underdeveloped private sector and sales through the stock market are costly to organise (you need valuation and floatation, if not anything else). It is then suggested that there are other ways to improve public enterprise performance, such as organisational reform, increased competition, and political reform.

Part III of the volume is made up of three essays that explore the issue of state intervention and economic development in the context of globalisation. The recent advance of globalisation – not only in terms of the relative importance of cross-border economic activities but also in terms of conscious lowering of policy-induced barriers to such activities – has added another dimension to the debate on the role of the state. Now it is frequently argued that the forces of globalisation are such that any policy that impedes the process should be abolished. The chapters in this part critically examine such a contention.

The first essay in Part III, Chapter 7, 'Globalisation, Transnational Corporations, and Economic Development', critically examines the currently popular view that, given the process of globalisation, and especially given the increasing flows of foreign direct investment

(FDI), developing countries need to liberalise their policies towards FDI and other activities of the transnational corporations (TNCs). Against this view, the chapter first points out that globalisation has not progressed to the extent that it makes all national policy variations meaningless or harmful. It is then shown that FDI flows remain highly concentrated and most developing countries are left out. Roughly speaking, more than two-thirds of FDI flows occur between the developed countries, and of the remaining amount, a dozen or so countries take around three-quarters (China alone takes one-third of this developing country total, or about 10% of the world total). Finally, the chapter points out that, contrary to what neoliberal commentators want us to believe, the successful East Asian countries have not in general relied heavily on FDI. Even among the countries that have, it was only Hong Kong, and Malaysia to a lesser extent, that can be described as having had liberal policies towards FDI. Singapore, while relying heavily on TNCs, directed them into particular directions through strategic use of infrastructural development, skill formation, and targeted subsidies.

Unless we agree with the naive neoliberal belief in the congruence of interests between TNCs and host countries, the critical question is whether TNCs have become so mobile that any attempt by national governments to regulate them in their national interests will only harm the potential host economies by reducing FDI flows. The answer to this question, the chapter argues, very much depends on the country and the industry in question. In certain industries where the capital equipment involved is small and where there are a large number of potential production sites (e.g., garments, stuffed toys, shoes), TNCs are indeed very mobile and heavy regulation is likely to lead to their relocation. However, in other industries, where production facilities are difficult to move (e.g., chemical, steel) or where there are relatively few alternative production sites (e.g., industries that require skilled workers), TNCs are not as mobile and there is much more room for national policy intervention.

Most importantly, the chapter points out that the 'liberality' of the regulatory regime is actually not one of the key determinants of FDI. In making their investment decisions, TNCs tend to look for things like large and/or growing markets, good infrastructure, and good-quality labour force, before they look at the regulatory regime.

In other words, they tend to follow, rather than create, good national economic environment, which is in large part created by good (but not neoliberal) economic policy.

The chapter concludes that, contrary to what neoliberal commentators recommend, developing countries should not have a uniformly liberal policy across all areas of FDI. They should, rather, design the regulatory regime for each industry according to its particular needs and with reference to its place in the national economic strategy.

Chapter 8, 'Intellectual Property Rights and Economic Development – Historical Lessons and Emerging Issues', looks at the issue of policies towards intellectual property rights, which has become particularly important following the TRIPS (Trade-Related Intellectual Property Rights) Agreement of the WTO.

The TRIPS Agreement requires that all countries accord 'global standard' protection to the owners of intellectual property. The agreement is not another of those toothless international declarations, because it allows countries to punish trading partners that violate the intellectual property rights of their citizens through trade sanctions. Such an approach is adopted on the ground that TRIPS will benefit not only the developed countries that own most of the world's patents and other intellectual properties (trademarks, copyrights, etc.) but also the developing countries. It is argued that stronger protection of property rights in developing countries will encourage innovation within them and also promote inflow of advanced technologies by giving their owners greater assurance of protection. The proponents of TRIPS argue that the history of the developed countries shows that economic development is promoted by strong protection of intellectual property rights.

Against this view, the chapter argues, first of all, that today's developed countries did not develop on the basis of strong protection of intellectual property rights. Although most of them had introduced patent laws by the late-19th century, these laws initially fell well short of the standards demanded of the developing countries through TRIPS. In particular, in many of these countries patenting of foreign inventions was explicitly allowed. Switzerland and the Netherlands did not have a patent law until the early-20th century.

The chapter then goes on to argue that private intellectual property rights, such as patents, are not always necessary in motivating investments in the generation of new knowledge. New knowledge is often pursued for its own sake. In most industries, there is a 'natural' imitation gap, which allows the innovators to enjoy monopoly positions (and therefore extra profits) long enough to recoup their investments in innovation. Indeed, Schumpeter's famous theory of innovation was built on this very premise. Economic theories and empirical evidence also show that patents can be 'wasteful' (especially as efforts are duplicated because of their 'winner-takes-all' nature) and can even become an obstacle to technological progress in related areas.

The final section of the chapter examines the costs and benefits of the TRIPS Agreement for developing countries. First of all, it is argued that the alleged benefits of TRIPS – greater innovation and more technology transfer – are in reality likely to be minimal. On the other hand, it is argued, TRIPS will impose a lot of additional costs on developing countries in the forms of increased royalty payments, greater chance of monopoly abuse, diversion of the scarce high-quality human resources into running the patent system, and even the theft of traditional knowledge (see the cases of turmeric and basmati rice discussed in the chapter). These costs are likely to overshadow the benefits by a large margin.

In the end, private intellectual property rights, like any property right, are a form of monopoly created because it is believed that its social usefulness outweighs its costs. Therefore, if and when it is judged that the net benefit from it is negative, societies have the right to revoke that right. Indeed, the US government, which fully supported its pharmaceutical companies trying to prevent the exports of cheap HIV/AIDS drugs by some developing country producers by invoking TRIPS, extracted a 50% discount on its purchase of anti-anthrax drugs from the German company Bayer with a threat of revocation of its patent, because it decided, rightly or wrongly, that the costs of this particular patent could well outweigh its benefits.

Chapter 9, the last chapter in this book, 'Institutional Foundations for Effective Design and Implementation of Selective Trade and Industrial Policies in the Least Developed Countries: Theory and Evidence', revisits the issue of selective industrial (and trade) policy that is discussed in Chapter 4 with a more specific reference to globalisation.

The chapter starts its discussion by criticising the presumption underlying the neoliberal argument that selective industrial and trade policies (or SIT policies) can work only under exceptional conditions while market-oriented policies are 'universal' and therefore can work anywhere. It is argued that, in the same way in which the SIT policies used in East Asia required certain 'special conditions' (such as good bureaucracy), the Anglo-American-style market-oriented policies need certain special institutions (such as good contract laws or a developed financial system), if they are to work well. The fact that, during the last few decades, many countries have tried to copy the Anglo-American model with little success is a testimony to the difficulty of building the 'special' institutions that are required for an effective functioning of market-oriented trade and industrial policies. The chapter then examines one by one the internal institutional conditions that are supposed to have been indispensable for the success of SIT policies in East Asia. They are: the bureaucracy; the institutions that provide control over resource flows (such as state-owned enterprises and financial controls); and 'intermediate institutions', namely, the institutions that link the state bureaucracy with individual firms (such as industry associations). It is pointed out that the roles of these institutions are very much misunderstood in the current debate, both theoretically and empirically, and corrective arguments are provided.

The final section of the chapter addresses the implications of globalisation for the conduct of SIT policies by examining the currently popular argument that the launch of the new global free trade regime of the WTO has made the use of these policies, whatever their merits may have been in the past, virtually impossible. Those who propagate this view point out that the WTO regime has drastically reduced tariffs, virtually eliminated quotas and other forms of quantitative restrictions, and banned the use of most subsidies – all tools that were used by the East Asian countries that practised SIT policies.

However, the chapter argues, while the WTO has brought about significant changes to global trading rules, it does not spell the end of SIT policies. To begin with, the WTO rules are still in the formative stage and need, like any legal framework, active interpretation, which gets influenced by international politics. The recent moderation of developed country attitudes *vis-à-vis* TRIPS in the face of the international criticisms regarding their HIV/AIDS drugs policy is a good example. Moreover, while the rules regarding the use of tariffs and subsidies may have been tightened, there is still room for manoeuvre. For example, tariffs for infant industry protection, emergency tariffs (in the face of sectoral or overall balance of payments problems), and a range of subsidies (e.g., regional development, agriculture, basic R&D) are still allowed. In addition, while the Agreement on TRIPS (see Chapter 8) and TRIMs (Trade-Related Investment Measures) are likely to make selective and industrial policies more difficult, there is still some room for manoeuvre even in these areas.

Despite what their supporters say, neoliberal policies have spectacularly failed, especially in developing countries. As discussed in the essays in this volume, the failure of neoliberalism stems ultimately from its failure to base its discourse on a balanced and sophisticated theory of the inter-relationship between the market, the state, and other institutions. It is also informed by very biased and partial reading of the empirical evidence, which reinforces its theoretical flaws.

In this book, I have tried, in a number of different ways and in relation to a range of issues, to expose the intellectual bankruptcy of neoliberalism and construct an alternative theoretical framework informed by a balanced understanding of empirical evidence. I hope this book helps those who are trying to construct, either at the theoretical level or at the practical level, some credible alternatives to neoliberalism – even if their alternatives are significantly different from mine.

Chapter 1

Theories of State Intervention in Historical Perspective

AS Deane (1989) shows in her masterpiece on the history of economic thought, the role of the state has occupied the central stage in the development of economics as an independent discipline. As the early names of the discipline like 'political arithmetic' or 'political economy' suggest, the very inception of the discipline was prompted by the growing need for policy advice to the rulers of the emerging nation states whose role was growing with the development of capitalism in Western Europe. Although attempts to purge the discipline of those awkward 'political' elements culminated in the re-christening of the subject as 'economics' around the turn of the 20th century, the state was brought back into economic theory and policy making in a rather dramatic fashion during the interwar period.

One development which brought the state back into economics was the birth of welfare economics, pioneered by Arthur Pigou. By explaining why the free market system purely based on individual maximising behaviour may not achieve socially 'optimal' resource allocation as predicted by the then new orthodoxy of neoclassical economics, welfare economics provided justification for the manipulation of price signals by the state. Although during the interwar period itself welfare economics remained a rather esoteric exercise detached from practical policy questions, its use of the orthodox language of marginalist analysis made it possible for later policy makers to break away from the *laissez-faire* policies without being accused of unscientific behaviour.

Another, more important, development which produced the comeback of the state was the birth of Keynesian economics. By showing that the free market economy may not be able to achieve an optimal resource allocation at the full employment level of output, the Keynesian 'revolution' justified the new practice of active budgetary policy to fight unemployment and business cycles, which was developing simultaneously in the USA (the New Deal), Germany (Fascist armament programmes), and Sweden (the incipient Corporatist Compromise) (for an excellent account of interwar economic development in the USA and Germany, see essays in Maier 1987; on Sweden, see Wright 1991). As we shall see later, the goals of full employment and smoothing business cycles were unchallenged as objectives of state intervention during the quarter-century after World War II, and consequently Keynesian ideas achieved a pre-eminent status in government policy making.

The consolidation of the socialist central planning system in the USSR was another major interwar development. The rapid industrialisation of the USSR, whose achievement was later proven by its success in halting the Nazi advance on the Eastern Front during World War II, provided credentials to certain non-orthodox interventionist measures such as nationalisation of industry and investment planning, adopted even by many non-socialist countries after the war (for the exposition of these theories, see Ellman 1989) – for example, nationalisation in the UK and France, medium-term (usually five-year) planning in Japan, France, and many developing countries.

These interwar developments culminated in a dramatic swing of economic theory and practice towards interventionism in the immediate postwar years. With the urgent need for postwar reconstruction in the advanced capitalist countries (henceforth ACCs), the establishment of socialism in parts of Asia and Eastern Europe, and the liberation of many developing countries from colonialism, the states in almost all countries in the world were forced to and willing to assume highly interventionist positions in the immediate postwar years. And during the quarter-century after World War II – the period commonly known as the 'Golden Age' of capitalism, interventionist policies were highly successful across the world, firmly establishing the state as an important and often the leading actor in the functioning of the economy (see Marglin and Schor 1990 and Armstrong *et al.* 1991).

If this rise of the state in theory and practice in the Golden Age was dramatic, its fall after the Golden Age was equally, if not more, dramatic. The collapse of the Golden Age has produced a virulent attack on the state both at the theoretical and at the practical levels, starting from the discrediting of welfare statism in the ACCs, being amplified with the spread of liberalisation programmes among developing nations during the 1980s and culminating in the dismantling of socialist central planning since 1989 and the attempt to establish capitalism in Eastern Europe and what used to be the USSR. Although the 'rolling back' of the state has not proved to be straightforward as many anti-interventionists had initially thought, this reversal of trend has had a significant impact on the theory and practice of state intervention.

In this chapter, we survey these developments and provide some critical comments on the major contemporary anti-interventionist theories, which we classify under the general heading of 'neoliberalism'. After presenting an account of the rise of the state in the Golden Age in the first section, we move to an account of the fall of the state after the Golden Age, then we present criticism of some major theoretical underpinnings of neoliberal theories, using both some new theoretical developments and empirical evidence which question the wisdom of this new orthodoxy.

1.   THE GOLDEN AGE AND THE RISE OF THE STATE

In this section, we review the political, intellectual, and economic factors responsible for the widespread extension of state activity during the Golden Age following World War II.

1.1 Advanced Capitalist Countries

World War II produced new political coalitions in the advanced capitalist countries with a strong representation of organised labour – often described as 'corporatist' coalitions. The prominent role of the left in the struggle against Fascism during World War II meant that, in the postwar society of class compromise, full employment and social welfare – the overriding objectives of the working class – were to be on the top of the political agenda. Moreover, given the belief that the rise of Fascism had owed a lot to the Great Depression, active state intervention to smooth the business cycle through the use of new-found Keynesian policy tools was deemed imperative. Although the dominance of Cold War politics put strict limits on more radical forms of labour and other political movements, the new regime incorporated the interests of the working class in national policy making to an unprecedented degree.

As the theoretical possibility of avoiding recession by deliberately injecting purchasing power into the economic system was confirmed by the successes of proto-Keynesian policies during the interwar period (using budget deficits) and of the Marshall Plan in the immediate postwar period (using foreign aid), the state now actively assumed a new role of 'fine tuning' the economy through budgetary policy (on the Marshall Plan, see Panic 1990). The old dogma of balancing the budget at all costs was abandoned, and budgetary policy was given the role of coordinating investment and savings so that the economy could stay at full employment level. Social welfare systems, which existed in rudimentary form before the war, were vastly extended following the rise of the 'corporatist' political coalitions, and the state was also expected to help stabilise the economy by automatically increasing (reducing) spending in the recessionary (boom) phase of the business cycle.

In many countries, the role of the state expanded much further than the simple maintenance of the level of activity through aggregate demand management. Helped by the success of wartime planning, the old liberal dogma that centralised coordination of economic activities is unworkable was now rejected, and many states started intervening with a view to changing the structure of their economies. Japan and France combined sectoral industrial policy with centralised investment coordination through five-year indicative planning (see Cohen 1977, on France; see Johnson 1982, on Japan). Scandinavian countries operated in a 'social corporatist' framework, where centralised wage bargaining and active labour market policy were combined to produce structural change towards high-productivity industries at a speed and orderliness beyond what would have been possible through a pure market mechanism (see Pekkarinen *et al.* (eds.) 1992). Even in the UK and the USA, countries which were least open to the idea of industrial policy, the state involvement in industrial development was substantial (see Thompson (ed.) 1989). The evolution of the European Coal and Steel Community (ECSC) and European Economic Community (EEC) during this period even established some grounds for an international coordination of national industrial policies.

1.2 Less Developed Countries

During the Golden Age, the state took an even more active role in many less developed countries (henceforth LDCs) than in the advanced capitalist countries. The desire of the newly independent nations to acquire not only political but also economic independence from their former colonial masters put rapid economic development at the top of the political agenda. And, in this period, it was widely accepted that state-led industrialisation was the fastest and surest way to achieve the aim (see Toye 1987).

The traditional reliance of LDCs on primary commodity exports to finance the manufactured imports was thought to be a dead end, given (i) the volatile and apparently falling terms of trade for primary commodity exports; (ii) the fragility of the international economy, as testified by the collapse of international trade following the Great Depression; and (iii) the low income elasticities of primary commodities, which limited the scope for increase in their exports in the future. Also it was thought that primary commodity production lacked the self-reinforcing growth mechanism observed in manufacturing, where faster output growth leads to faster productivity growth (the so-called Verdoorn's Law, promoted by Kaldor 1966). Therefore, it was thought, the LDCs should move out of their role in the traditional international division of labour as the suppliers of primary products and develop manufacturing industries.

In order for the LDCs to start industrialisation, however, it was thought to be necessary to have an active state intervention. Not only was the traditional infant industry argument evoked to justify the strategy of state-led industrialisation based on heavy import protection and subsidies, but also an array of new theories justifying the centralised coordination of industrial investments were developed within the emerging sub-discipline of 'development economics'.

The 'big push' models of Rosenstein-Rodan (1943), Nurkse (1952), and Scitovsky (1954) emphasised the demand complementarity between different industries, which called for an *ex ante* investment coordination by the state. Hirschman (1958), while criticising the 'balanced growth' models, used the same idea of sectoral interdependence in order to develop an 'unbalanced growth' model, where the state-prompted development of the sectors with the most widespread interdependences (what he called linkages) would create imbalances in the economy, which would induce the development of other sectors. Gerschenkron (1966), basing his case on the experiences of earlier European industrialisations, provided a further justification of state intervention based on the interaction of technological (the growing minimum efficient scale of production) and institutional factors (the underdevelopment of financial institutions). Gerschenkron suggested that as a country embarks on a developmental process later and later, it needs to raise proportionally bigger and bigger amounts of savings (as the minimum efficient scale of production grows larger), and therefore needs a more and more powerful institution for industrial financing, the state being the most powerful of such institutions.

These new theories were greeted with enthusiasm by the political leaders and state officials in many post-independence nations of Asia and Africa. In these countries, there existed strong feelings against capitalism, if only for the simple reason that all colonial powers were capitalist. As a result they exhibited preference for more state ownership and central planning, if not outright socialism. On a more practical level, the states in these nations were often compelled to take the role of an entrepreneur, because these nations lacked a well-developed capitalist class which could take over the economic organisations left behind by the colonisers, and whatever little capitalist class there was, it was often politically discredited as the collaborator with the colonial power. Even in the East Asian newly industrialising countries (NICs), where the Cold War consolidated the staunchest anti-communist regimes, vigorous state intervention was regarded as legitimate and necessary, and paradoxically functioned much more efficiently than in other Less Developed Countries (LDCs). Even in Latin American countries, where independence was achieved much earlier and where socialist tendencies were weaker, the political tide was turning for state-led industrialisation. The success of state-led import substitution industralisation during the interwar period produced new social coalitions that could challenge the landed oligarchy – that is, the alliance between the incipient industrial capitalist class and the urban working class (Peronism being the best example) – and gave them the confidence and power to push further the state-led industrialisation programme.

The result was the emergence of a variety of new industrialisation strategies in LDCs, in which 'the state played the leading role in manufacturing and infrastructure through its control over state-owned enterprises and/or financial resources. As most LDCs experienced rates of growth more vigorous than the rest of the world during the Golden Age (see Singh 1992a), these strategies – which are usually (and somewhat misleadingly) known as the import substitution industrialisation (ISI) strategies – acquired the status of 'the' development strategy.

1.3   Socialist Countries

In addition to the independence of the former colonies, the end of World War II produced another dramatic change in the world political map. The USSR and Mongolia were no longer the only socialist countries in the world. Between the end of World War II and the early-1950s, socialist regimes had been established in Eastern European and some Asian countries (China, North Korea, and North Vietnam), and this meant, largely thanks to China, that now about one-third of the world's population was under socialist rule. The advance of socialism into other poorer, especially Asian, nations seemed inevitable unless an active policy to 'roll back' Communism was adopted.

In the immediate postwar years, the socialist countries, mostly as the victorious parties either in World War II or in their own anti-imperialist struggle, were full of confidence and hope. The rise of the USSR from one of the most backward nations in Europe to a nation which played a crucial role in saving the world from Fascist takeover convinced many people, except some fierce anti-communists, that central planning was as least as viable as the market mechanism in running the economy. The victory of the USSR over the USA in the early space programme suggested to many that, for large projects requiring concerted efforts on the national scale, central planning was probably superior. The fact that even the most backward socialist countries like North Korea and China made very impressive progress in industrialisation in the 1950s seemed to prove that central planning was an effective way to achieve rapid industrialisation and massive structural transformation.

To be sure, it was obvious that central planning had its own problems, as revealed in the (largely unsuccessful) attempts by Hungary (1956) and Czechoslovakia (1968) to liberalise their economies. However, many advocates of central planning believed that the relentless development of computers, input-output analysis, mathematical programming techniques, and other tools of planning would eventually ensure that the rational order of socialism would triumph over the irrational anarchy of capitalism. Moreover, the supposed 'classless' nature of their societies made their policy makers believe that policy making in socialist societies can be treated as a 'technocratic' rather than a political exercise. With the beliefs in the perfectibility of tools of forecast and computation, on the one hand, and in the absence of fundamental political conflicts, on the other hand, it was not surprising that many saw the seeds of a truly rational and egalitarian society in the existing societies during this period.

2.   THE FALL OF THE GOLDEN AGE AND THE NEOLIBERAL UPSURGE

A series of events which started emerging from the late-1960s began to create growing difficulties for the interventionist models of economic management established during the Golden Age, especially once the political consensus which buttressed the interventionist regimes started breaking down (see later). Policy makers found it increasingly difficult to mediate the growing conflicts while the theorists could no longer assume political neutrality and ignore the considerations of 'political economy'. To the policy maker, this meant that more and more policies would have to accommodate demands from specific interest groups, and to economics theorists, it meant that it was increasingly difficult for them to remain technocratic. It is no coincidence that the post-Golden Age period witnessed the revival of political economy, both from the right and left.

In this section, we review major contemporary anti-interventionist theories under the broad heading of neoliberalism, without necessarily implying the existence of a unified political philosophy underlying all the theories we examine. In spelling out these theories, we do not attempt to discuss all the details of individual theories, as our purpose here is to provide a broad overview of the changes in the intellectual climate of the post-Golden Age era (interested readers can go back to the originals or reviews contained in Cullis and Jones 1987, and Mueller 1979, for the advanced capitalist countries; Toye 1987, and Shapiro and Taylor 1990, for LDCs; Ellman 1989, and Brus and Laski 1989, for the socialist countries).

2.1 Advanced Capitalist Countries

The long postwar boom in Europe and North America was brought to an end by a variety of factors, including a profit squeeze due to the depletion of surplus labour in the rural area and over-accumulation, growing competition from Japan and the NICs, and the growing globalisation of capital which made national macroeconomic management much less effective (see Glyn *et al.* 1990). With the growing intensity of distributional conflicts in the face of massive structural change and decelerating economic growth, the existing political consensus on the welfare state based on corporatist bargaining and Keynesian macroeconomic management broke down and, with it, the theoretical consensus on the role of the state.

2.1.1 Monetarism

The best-known attack on the theoretical consensus underlying the Golden Age is the monetarist onslaught on Keynesianism. Basing themselves on the assumption of adaptive or rational expectations, and Walrasian market clearing, the monetarists comprehensively rejected the effectiveness of macroeconomic demand management by the state (for a critique, see Kaldor 1985). This exposed a fundamental weakness in the theoretical structure known as the Keynesian compromise. Under this compromise, the role of the state was confined to the regulation of macroeconomic aggregates, leaving the question of resource allocation to the neoclassical doctrine of free markets (Deane 1989). In political terms, the monetarist rendering of its argument in populist anti-inflationary rhetoric – 'inflation erodes the incomes of honest working families and the savings of poor old grannies on pensions' – proved especially effective in making the potentially unpopular recessionary policies widely accepted. (On this topic, see the essays in Lindberg and Maier (eds.) 1985.)

2.1.2 Institutional Sclerosis

This is a line of argument which emphasises that institutions designed to guarantee politically-negotiated economic benefits to certain groups (e.g., welfare provisions, trade protection, labour laws) are bound to create rigidities which are harmful to economic development in the long run. Developed particularly in the European context where the corporatist institutions were strong, the argument is often presented under the heading 'Eurosclerosis' (see Giersch 1986), but it has also seen application in the American context by Olson (1982).

The implications of the sclerosis theory for the role of the state were probably more far reaching than those of monetarism. At the political level, it undermined the credibility of state intervention by identifying the very corporatist institutions upon which such intervention is based as the source of sluggish growth and high inflation. At a more fundamental level, the theory challenged belief in collective institution building of any kind by stressing the inevitability of degeneration to which all institutions are subject.

2.1.3 New Contractarianism

Related to the sclerosis argument, with possibly Hayek as the link between the two, is the new contractarianism of libertarian authors like Buchanan and Tullock (1962) and Nozick (1974). The new contractarians argued that any form of state beyond the old liberal minimalist state, which does no more than provide law and order (including, among other things, the protection of property rights), cannot be justified in the eyes of those who believe in the sanctity of individual freedom. A major source of popularity of these writings lay in their emphasis on individual freedom and their articulation of modern discontent with the welfare state and its alleged restrictions on personal choice. The welfare state was no longer to be seen as a benign, if paternalistic, institution, but as a leviathan which must be restrained to preserve our liberties and the vitality of civil society.

2.1.4 Principal-Agent Models of Bureaucracy

Another important development along the anti-interventionist line was the emergence of various types of principal-agent models of bureaucracy developed by authors like Niskanen (1973), Peacock (1979), and Rowley (1983). These models see the root of many of the problems of the contemporary capitalist countries – for example, the over-extension of the bureaucracy, the waste of resources in government administration, the inefficiency of the public enterprises – in the inability of the principals (the public) to monitor the self-seeking behaviours of their agents in public affairs (the bureaucrats). These models were usually presented as neutral efficiency arguments, but have had much deeper political impacts. By arguing that the same assumption of self-centred behaviours should be applied to both the private sector agents and the public sector agents, they not only questioned the public's trust in the benign paternalism of the welfare state but also undermined the self-confidence of government officials and their commitment to a public service ethic.

2.2 Less Developed Countries

For the LDCs, the end of the Golden Age arrived slightly later than for the advanced capitalist countries, that is, in the 1980s. Although there were growing criticisms of their import substitution strategies, the 1970s was a period of relatively rapid progress for many developing countries, especially for those willing to borrow heavily in the international capital market awash with the so-called petrodollar (see Singh 1992a). However, with the beginning of the monetarist policies in the advanced capitalist countries, industrialisation in most LDCs ran into trouble because of the critical shortage of foreign exchange, promoted by high interest rates, falling world demand, and the debt crisis (Hughes and Singh 1991). The fragile ruling coalitions in most of these countries could not survive the massive external shocks to systems which were already finding it increasingly difficult to cope with the growing population and the increasing diversification of interests. In the face of severe foreign exchange constraints, most LDCs ended up launching (often unsuccessful) dramatic liberalisation programmes along the lines demanded by the Bretton Woods institutions (i.e., the World Bank and the IMF), whose endorsement suddenly became critical in the continuation of foreign exchange inflow.

2.2.1 Attack on Import Substitution Industrialisation

Usually associated with the Bretton Woods institutions, this critique reasserts the wisdom of neoclassical doctrines, especially the Heckscher-Ohlin-Samuelson theory of comparative advantage, which were rejected by the proponents of the import substitution industrialisation (ISI) strategy (see World Bank 1987 and 1991; for criticism see Weiss 1990 and Singh 1992b). The argument is that, by producing goods which could be produced more cheaply (in relative terms) in other countries, countries trying to substitute imports forgo the gains from trade. Moreover, given their small market sizes, the protected industries in the LDCs end up being monopolists or oligopolists producing at suboptimal scales and/or under full capacity and having no compulsion to improve their productivity. Finally, it is argued that the artificially cheap price of 'capital' (i.e., artificially low interest rates) created by 'financial repressions' associated with ISI leads to lower savings and to the adoption of excessively capital-intensive technologies, which adds to unemployment and income inequality.

2.2.2 Rent-Seeking and the New Political Economy

First developed by Krueger (1974) and Posner (1975), the rent-seeking argument asserts that the creation of entry barriers by the state leads not only to the standard deadweight welfare losses but also to additional 'waste' from expenditures on 'unproductive' political activities intended to influence the state in its capacity as the creator of entry barriers (and the accompanying property rights). In the context of LDCs where the rules of contesting property rights are not as well established as in the advanced capitalist countries, the scope for rent-seeking associated with those state interventions associated with import substitution was seen to be much wider. Associated with this view is the so-called New Political Economy, which shows how a 'predatory' state in LDCs can create a property rights structure which maximises its revenues rather than social welfare (North 1981; Findlay 1990). An especially influential recent development has been the extension of these theories to what is similar to the 18th century liberal attack on mercantilism (see e.g., de Soto 1989).

2.2.3 Attack on Public Enterprises

The late-1970s and the early-1980s saw the proliferation of reassessments of the performance of the public enterprises across the world, especially in the LDCs. While there were many balanced studies (see Baumol (ed.) 1980; Vernon and Aharoni (eds.) 1981; and Jones (ed.) 1982), there were also some damning indictments of public enterprise as the major source of economic inefficiency and stagnation of the LDCs (see e.g., World Bank 1983). Identifying the source of these inefficiencies as emanating from the lack of profit incentives, competition, and financial discipline imposed by the capital market, the neoliberal arguments for privatisation became a centre-piece of their attack on the interventionist economic managements of the Golden Age (for some criticisms of these theories, see Chang and Singh 1993; Rowthorn and Chang 1993). In many LDCs, where the frequent inefficiency of public enterprises was especially damaging, given their weight in the manufacturing and infrastructural sectors of the economy, the support for privatisation spread like wildfire.

2.3 Socialist Countries

Following a period of impressive achievement after the war, the socialist countries underwent a prolonged economic stagnation associated with lagging technical progress, institutional sclerosis, and growing political disillusionment (see Bleaney 1988; Brus and Laski 1989). Although the sudden collapse of the socialist system in the late-1980s has made the understanding of their experience less important than previously, it is still the case that some of the theories developed in the context of socialist experience have left us with interesting insights into the role of the state.

2.3.1 The Shortage Economy

Based on an economic situation which is almost the polar opposite of what Keynes faced in the interwar period, that is, a situation where the problem of excess demand is institutionalised through a peculiar incentive system, Kornai invented the concept of the 'shortage economy' and developed it into the foundation of his institutionalist critique of socialism (see e.g., Kornai 1979). The fundamental message is that the lack of financial discipline (the so-called 'soft budget constraints') associated with the lack of private property leads to a situation where not only a substantial part of national income is wasted in 'unproductive' activities such as hoarding of material and human inputs but also there is no incentive to improve the productive efficiency. Moreover, when associated with the absolute political commitments to zero unemployment, the need for the stockpiling of labour inputs produces some perverse effects on labour discipline, originally stressed in a capitalist context by Marxian writers but generalised more recently by efficiency wage theorists (Bowles 1985; Akerlof and Yellen (eds.) 1986).

2.3.2 Property Rights Approach

Although it is difficult to suggest that the property rights approach sprang entirely from the research on socialist economies, some critical initial contributions to the development of the approach originated there (for a survey, see Furubotn and Pejovich 1972). The argument basically is that the lack of private property institutions in the socialist societies eliminates the individual incentive to remain efficient and improve productivity. This was a particularly damning indictment for the socialist countries, as they traditionally saw their distinct system of property rights as the source of their supposed economic superiority over the capitalist countries. The recognition that the defining characteristic of their system, namely, state ownership of the means of production, might be the root cause of their economic troubles had a profound impact on popular consciousness, as is well proven by the almost irrational obsession with privatisation issues in the post-communist reforms in Eastern Europe.

2.3.3 The Austrian Attack on Central Planning

The oldest, but possibly the most fundamental, attack on socialism is the Austrian attack on central planning. Starting from the interwar debate between Mises and Hayek on one side and Lange and Taylor on the other side, the Austrians have constantly asserted the unviability of central planning (for a good survey of the debate, see Lavoie 1985). They argued that the completely centralised coordination of activities in a complex and constantly changing modern economy would require the collection and processing of information on a scale far beyond the capability of any present or future state. More importantly, they argued that only competitive rivalry amongst genuinely independent, profit-seeking agents can generate and utilise the accurate and detailed information required to run a modern economy. Although quite unacceptable in its extreme form – that all forms of state intervention, and not just central planning, are bound to fail or threaten liberty – the power of this argument is now widely accepted even by many who favour an interventionist state.

3.   CRITICAL EVALUATION OF THE NEOLIBERAL THEORIES

As may be seen, different anti-interventionist theories developed in different historical, political, and institutional contexts, on the one hand, and from different theoretical traditions, on the other. Some draw heavily on the neoclassical legacy (e.g., the Bretton Woods critique of import substitution), while others draw on more heterodox traditions like Austrian or institutional economics. However, one thing which is common to most of these theories is that they lay more emphasis on the 'political' rather than 'technocratic' aspects of economic problems, i.e., by questioning the very political foundation of interventionist models of economic management, neoliberal theories have brought issues of morality, justice, and power – although in their own peculiar ways – back into economics. In this section, rather than trying to criticise theories in the neoliberal tradition individually, we make some general comments on their central theoretical underpinnings.

3.1 Principal-Agent Framework

Common to many neoliberal theories is the principal-agent framework, where the limited scope for monitoring by the principal creates problems of designing incentives for agents who pursue their own self-interests. Major examples will be the problem of designing optimal welfare or social insurance programmes due to the difficulty of identifying the true 'type' of the potential subscribers (for a survey of related issues, see Barr 1992), and the problem of designing optimal industrial subsidy schemes or optimal public enterprise management rules due to the difficulty of identifying the source of bad performance (e.g., external shock or bad management).

For certain individual problems, the principal-agent framework is a fruitful approach, since it questions the naivety of traditional welfare economics and its assumption that state officials always have the incentive to correct market failures once these are identified. However, at a more general level, this framework posits an awkward question – who is the principal and who is the agent, especially in a modern mass democracy? For example, in relation to social welfare programmes, we can argue that 'the state' is the principal, but from the points of view of the principal-agent models of bureaucracy or of contractarian political philosophy, the state is an agent of 'the public'. Thus seen, there are inconsistencies in the ways in which different principal-agent models characterise the process of state intervention.

We are not arguing that there is only one correct way of deciding who is the principal and who is the agent. Indeed, the very existence of different ways of envisaging principal-agent problems in our society reflects the complexity of modern polity. Our point is that, without an adequate understanding of the complex political process in a modern society, the use of principal-agent models may end up obscuring major issues rather than clarifying them. The political process in a modern society involves collective action and bargaining problems at many different levels (local, industry, or national levels), whose solutions are strongly influenced by social norms (working class solidarity, work ethic, abstinence), political institutions (dictatorial, corporatist, or liberal institutions), and socio-politico 'visions' (socialism, nationalism, welfare statism, free enterprise). The principal-agent model, given its sole emphasis on wealth-maximising behaviour of selfish individuals, cannot take such complexity of political-economic process into account. Thus seen, there are serious dangers in accepting the radical proposals for rolling back the state derived from such models.

3.2 Mistrust of the State

Another common feature of the neoliberal theories is their deep mistrust of the state. The new contractarians see the state as a necessary evil with a natural tendency to expand, which has to be put under constant surveillance by sovereign individuals as partners in a social contract. The principal-agent model of bureaucracy is another well-known manifestation of this belief. If somewhat less obvious, the monetarist argument for a constitutionally binding money growth target is also symptomatic of the belief that the state cannot be trusted to withstand the demands of 'special interest' groups. Similar to this is the 'regulatory capture' argument propagated by Stigler (1975) that the regulatory agencies may be set up in order to serve public interests but end up serving the interest groups which they are supposed to regulate.

One serious problem with the neoliberal mistrust of the state is that it uncritically (or intentionally?) assumes that the state (or the bureaucrats as its components) always acts in its (their) own interest. Apart from the obvious observation that individuals and institutions do not always act in their own interest, there are too many facts of life which make this simple self-centredness assumption problematic. Even the most casual observation confirms that different states have different degrees of commitment to the public interest, that the boundaries of the public domain are different in different countries and constantly changing even in the same country, that people operating in different environments (e.g., civil servants and businessmen) have different rules of behaviour, and that even the same individual may apply different rules of behaviour in different circumstances (e.g., a civil servant during and outside his office hours). Policy conclusions drawn from models ignoring these facts are at best misleading and at worst pseudo-scientific renderings of the model-builder's ideological conviction against the state.

More fundamentally, we argue that the more generalised mistrust of collective action, on which the neoliberal mistrust of the state is based, is problematic. First of all, it is not correct to argue that institutions (e.g., the state, labour unions) are always (or even predominantly) products of social contracts among free-contracting individuals. Human beings have always existed as members of certain collectivities, and the notion of the free contracting individual is a product of the capitalist order (Polanyi 1957). Individuals are perhaps more a product of institutions than the latter are the products of contracts among individuals. Secondly, the neoliberal preference for individual actions over group actions has some awkward political implications. Neoliberals often attack 'interest groups', but after all, those interest groups are associations of individuals whom the neoliberals regard as absolutely sacred. How can a consistent liberal deprive individuals of the freedom to join a collectivity he/she likes? And, indeed, the neoliberals do endorse certain interest groups such as private firms. If some interest groups are legitimate and others are not, what is the criterion to decide which groups belong to which category? The anti-collectivist rhetoric of the neoliberals merely obscures the existence of a hidden political agenda against certain particular groups.

3.3   Trust in Individual Entrepreneurship

The other side of the coin of the neoliberal mistrust of the state is the trust in individual entrepreneurship. While all pro-market theories believe that 'wrong' institutions and state policies lead to allocative inefficiency, many neoliberals would go even further and argue that state intervention impairs the ability of individuals to improve the productive capacity of the economy by generating new knowledge (i.e., innovation) in their attempts to capture profit.

One problem with this position is that it sees entrepreneurship as essentially an individual activity. This view stems from the belief that knowledge is always deposited in individuals, but it ignores the fact that, at least in modern economies, institutions and organisations are also depositories of knowledge. Contrary to what Schumpeter (1987) predicted, institutionalisation of R&D did not decelerate innovation in modern economics, but,if anything, accelerated it. This is because, as the recent literature on technical change shows (see e.g., Dosi *et al.* (eds.) 1988), innovative activities often are facilitated by collective effort, including, among other things, state support. This means that the old concept of entrepreneurship based entirely on individuals is no longer valid (Chang and Kozul-Wright 1994), i.e., entrepreneurship has increasingly become a collective effort.

Equally problematic is the argument that state intervention creates an incentive to divert entrepreneurship into 'wasteful' activities of securing property rights through political means (e.g., Krueger 1974; Bhagwati 1982; de Soto 1989). Although this position is not necessarily wrong, this brings back something the mainstream economists tried so hard to eliminate from the discipline, i.e., value judgements. As the definition of productive and unproductive activities needs some criteria to tell whether a certain activity is 'necessary' for the functioning of the economy, it is impossible to come up with a viable concept of unproductive labour without calling in some political and moral value judgements (Driver 1980; Boss 1990). Many of those who condemn political competition (e.g., rent-seeking) as wasteful do not recognise this dilemma, but implicitly assume that a simple deregulation of the present economy will eliminate all 'unproductive' activities, which is not necessarily the case (see Chang 1994: Chapter 2).

3.4   Anti-Utilitarianism

Strong anti-utilitarianism, or more broadly anti-consequentialism, runs through most neoliberal theories (for some philosophical debates on consequentialism, see essays in Scheffler (ed.) 1988). Of course, there exists a well-known tension between utilitarianism and political liberalism (on this, see Berlin 1969), and those neoliberal theorists who have been brought up in a strongly utilitarian tradition of neoclassical economics would find it difficult to totally abandon the utilitarian legacy in their thinking. However, many neoliberal positions – such as the new contractarian defence of the rule of law, the Austrian adherence to free competition, and the monetarist insistence on constitutional limits on the formulation of monetary policy – are all based on the idea that there are certain fundamental rules that have to be abided by regardless of their consequences (i.e., individual freedom, freedom of entry, zero inflation). Indeed, many neoliberals claim to be willing to 'trade off economic efficiency for individual freedom where such a policy conflict becomes apparent' (Peacock and Rowley 1979: Chapter 26).

However, is this really a tenable position? We think not, because any defence of a certain rule (or procedure) assumes a preference for a certain consequence. Otherwise, we would have to assume that the rule is God-given or totally randomly chosen, which would not be acceptable, even to most neoliberal theorists. For example, we may say that we value the principle of majority rule and therefore are willing to accept certain 'suboptimal' outcomes if they are the results of that rule, but why did we decide to value majority rule in the first place? Was it not essentially because we thought that it, on average, would produce the 'best' outcome in some sense? If this is the case, the neoliberals are calling for no more than a higher-order utilitarianism, so to speak, based on the recognition of human fallibility (e.g., imperfect foresight, imperfectly transferable knowledge, weakness of will, whim, etc.), which makes it impossible to custom-design rules for every contingency in order to produce the optimal outcome. Of course, it is possible to get out of this dilemma by arguing that the neoliberal rules are beyond dispute and therefore cannot be interpreted as a product of a higher-order utilitarianism. However, for those who do not dogmatically accept these rules, it is not clear how any man-made rule can be totally devoid of consequentialist thinking.

4.   CONCLUSION

The neoliberal revival represents a partial return to the 19th century *laissez-faire* tradition, supplemented by an Austrian emphasis on the limited transferability of knowledge and the role of entrepreneurship. The neoliberal approach stresses the efficacy of the free market, and insists on the inefficiency and/or counter-productiveness of state intervention. It blames the past and present state interventions for most recent economic ills, and its prescriptions for most economic problems consist largely of deregulation and reducing the economic role of the state to that of a 'night-watchman'. The failings of state intervention are ascribed either to an inherent shortage of information (the Austrians) or to the self-seeking behaviours of the bureaucrats (Niskanen, Peacock, and Rowley) and/or organised interest groups (rent-seeking, institutional sclerosis).

From the mid-1970s onwards, neoliberal doctrines gained a wide following throughout the world. They inspired liberalisation and privatisation in many developed and developing countries, and even political revolution in many socialist countries. Amongst the advanced capitalist countries, neoliberal programmes were implemented vigorously in the UK and the USA, and somewhat less vigorously in most of the rest. Many developing countries have also implemented neoliberal programmes in the areas of trade, industry, and labour market policy – sometimes by choice and sometimes under pressure from external creditors. As a rule, the promise of these programmes has been that the freeing up of markets and the reduction in direct state intervention would make economies more flexible and creative, helping to solve their immediate economic problems and contribute to their long-run economic dynamism.

It is now frequently, though by no means universally, accepted that the neoliberal programmes have mostly failed to live up to their promise. The problems of the world economy remain formidable; many developing countries which have followed this programme are still in great difficulty; in the advanced capitalist world, the Thatcherite experiment in the UK was conspicuously unsuccessful in making the economy more competitive, and the Clinton administration in the USA overtly refuted the ideas associated with Reaganomics. As a result of these experiences, there is growing disenchantment with the neoliberal programme. One partial exception to this new trend is perhaps Eastern Europe and the Soviet Union, but even there the initial optimism in the efficacy of the free market is fading fast.

In this chapter, we have provided some criticism of the neoliberal theories. We have pointed out that most neoliberal theories do not take into account the complexity of human motivation (which differs across agents, societies, and time), the complexity of modern polity (who is the principal and who is the agent?), the importance of the legitimisation process in policy making and implementation, the inevitability of collective managements, in one form or another, of complex modern economy, and so on. Their simplistic notion of politics makes the neoliberal arguments at best misleading and at worst deceitful. To be consistent, neoliberals must either be so naive as to believe that a rewriting of the constitution to ban virtually all collective action (except the minimal state) is possible, or else have a hidden agenda behind their populist rhetoric, whose aim is simply to roll back the gains made by working class and other 'progressive' movements during the 20th century.

Neoliberals, especially those with Austrian influence, are correct in saying that central planning is not the most rational way to run a complex and constantly changing modern economy as its advocates thought it would be. However, it is erroneous to jump from this to the conclusion that all forms of state intervention are doomed to failure. For one thing, even central planning works better than the market for situations where there is one overriding objective, as in wartime or in a space programme. Moreover there are other types of state intervention which are not as informationally demanding as central planning and at least equally effective, for example East Asian-style industrial policy (see Chang 1994: Chapter 3). Contrary to what Hayek says, there is a third way, or rather, there are many third ways.

More broadly, the neoliberal belief that no collective organisation, other than the minimalist state, has any positive economic role to play is not acceptable. For one thing, the firm is after all not a purely individualistic organisation made up only of arms-length contracts, but has a lot of 'hierarchical' and 'relational' elements (Williamson 1975; Pagano 1985). Moreover, there exist extensive 'networks' in the modern economy, which are not pure contractual relationships but are based on trust and solidarity (see Thompson *et al.* (eds.) 1991). In other words, the world as envisaged by the neoliberals, which is populated by lone individuals whose interactions with each other are only ephemeral, has never existed and probably will never exist (among others, see Polanyi 1957).

Having made the above criticisms, we should point out that even the most ardent critics of neoliberalism would now recognise that it contains some important insights about the economic role of information, the importance of competition, and the like. There is now a widespread agreement that the management of a complex modern economy requires a market which is independent from the state to a considerable degree, although there is still a considerable amount of disagreement regarding to what extent a well-functioning market needs private property (see essays in Pagano and Rowthorn (eds.) 1996). The more important point is that the nature and extent of intervention will vary with circumstances. This means that, although one can talk of certain general principles, there is no hard and fast rule to determine the optimal degree and the desirable areas of state intervention, and that it can only be determined in the concrete historical, institutional, and geographical context.

The neoliberals have served the useful historical function of questioning the viability of the existing forms of state intervention, some of which clearly had serious problems, and of opening lines of inquiry leading to the basis for new forms of intervention. Nevertheless, they have failed to provide an intellectually successful and politically workable programme for comprehensively rolling back the state and achieving their vision of the 'brave new world'. Few now believe that it is either possible or desirable to turn the intellectual clock back to the time before the neoliberal upsurge. Not only has the world economy changed considerably, but both practical experience and the neoliberal critique have revealed some of the flaws in old ways of thinking. The challenge, therefore, is not simply to return to some previous intellectual golden age, but to form a new synthesis in which the valid insights of neoliberalism are stripped of their ideological baggage and integrated into a wider and more objective intellectual framework.

BIBLIOGRAPHY

Akerlof, G. and Yellen, J. (eds.) (1986). *Efficiency Wage Models of the Labour Market.* Cambridge: Cambridge University Press.

Armstrong, P., Glyn, A. and Harrison, J. (1991). *Capitalism since 1945.* Oxford: Blackwell.

Barr, N. (1992). 'Economic Theory and the Welfare State: A Survey and Interpretation', *Journal of Economic Literature,* vol.30, no.2.

Baumol, W. (ed.) (1980). *Public Enterprise in a Mixed Economy.* London and Basingstoke: Macmillan.

Berlin, I. (1969).'Two Concepts of Liberty', in *Four Essays on Liberty.* Oxford: Oxford University Press.

Bhagwati, J. (1982).'Directly Unproductive Profit-Seeking (DUP) Activities', *Journal of Political Economy,* vol.90, no.5.

Bleaney, M. (1988). *Do Socialist Economies Work?* Oxford: Blackwell.

Boss, H. (1990). *Theories of Surplus and Transfer.* Boston: Unwin Hyman.

Bowles, S. (1985). 'The Production Process in a Competitive Equilibrium: Walrasian, Neo-Hobbesian, and Marxian Models', *American Economic Review,* vol.75, no.1.

Brus, W. and Laski, K. (1989). *From Marx to the Market.* Oxford: Clarendon Press.

Buchanan, J. and Tullock, G. (1962). *The Calculus of Consent: Logical Foundations of Constitutional Democracy.* Ann Arbor: University of Michigan Press.

Chang, H.-J. (1994). *The Political Economy of Industrial Policy.* London and Basingstoke: Macmillan.

Chang, H.-J. and Kozul-Wright, R. (1994). 'Organising Development: Comparing the National Systems of Entrepreneurship in Sweden and South Korea', *Journal of Development Studies,* vol.30, no.4.

Chang, H.-J. and Singh, A. (1993). 'Public Enterprises in Developing Countries and Economic Efficiency', *UNCTAD Review,* no.4.

Cohen, S. (1977). *Modern Capitalist Planning: The French Model,* 2nd edn. Berkeley: University of California Press.

Cullis, J. and Jones, P. (1987). *Microeconomies and the Public Economy: A Defence of Leviathan.* Oxford: Blackwell.

Deane, P. (1989). *The State and the Economic System.* Oxford: Oxford University Press.

de Soto, H. (1989). *The Other Path.* New York: Harper and Row.

Dosi, G., Freeman, C., Nelson, R., Silverberg, G. and Soete, L. (eds.) (1988). *Technical Change and Economic Theory.* London: Pinter Publishers.

Driver, C. (1980). 'Productive and Unproductive Labour: Uses and Limitations of the Concepts', Thames Papers in Political Economy.

Ellman, M. (1989). *Socialist Planning,* 2nd edn. Cambridge: Cambridge University Press.

Findlay, R. (1990). 'New Political Economy', *Economics and Politics*, vol.2, no.2.

Furubotn, E. and Pejovich, S. (1972). 'Property Rights and Economic Literature: A Survey of Recent Literature', *Journal of Economic Literature*, vol.10, no.4.

Gerschenkron, A. (1966). 'Economic Backwardness in Historical Perspective', in *Economic Backwardness in Historical Perspective*. Cambridge, MA: Belknap Press.

Giersch, H. (1986). 'Liberalisation for Faster Economic Growth', *IEA Occasional Paper, no.74*. London: Institute of Economic Affairs.

Glyn, A., Hughes, A., Lipietz, A. and Singh, A. (1990). 'The Rise and Fall of the Golden Age', in S. Marglin and J. Schor (eds.), *The Golden Age of Capitalism*. Oxford: Clarendon Press.

Hirschman, A. (1958). *The Strategy of Economic Development*. New Haven: Yale University Press.

Hughes, A. and Singh, A.(1991). 'The World Economic Slowdown and the Asian and Latin American Economies: A Comparative Analysis of Economic Structure, Policy and Performance', in T. Banuri (ed.), *Economic Liberalisation: No Panacea*. Oxford: Clarendon Press.

Johnson, C. (1982). *MITI and the Japanese Miracle*. Stanford, California: Stanford University Press.

Jones, L. (ed.) (1982). *Public Enterprise in Less-developed Countries*. Cambridge: Cambridge University Press.

Kaldor, N. (1966). *Strategic Factors in Economic Development*. Ithaca, NY: Cornell University Press.

Kaldor, N. (1985). *The Scourge of Monetarism,* 2nd edn. Oxford: Oxford University Press.

Keynes, J. M. (1926). 'The End of Laissez Faire', in *Essays in Persuasion*. London and Basingstoke: Macmillan.

Kornai, J. (1979). 'Resource-Constrained versus Demand-Constrained Systems', *Econometrica*, vol.47, no.4.

Krueger, A. (1974). 'The Political Economy of the Rent-Seeking Society', *American Economic Review*, vol.64, no.3.

Lavoie, D. (1985). *Rivalry and Central Planning*. Cambridge: Cambridge University Press.

Lindberg, L. and Maier, C. (eds.) (1985). *The Politics of Inflation and Economic Stagnation*. Washington, D.C.: The Brookings Institution.

Maier, C. (1987). *In Search of Stability*. Cambridge: Cambridge University Press.

Marglin, S. and Schor, J. (eds.) (1990). *The Golden Age of Capitalism*. Oxford: Clarendon Press.

Mueller, D. (1979). *Public Choice*. Cambridge: Cambridge University Press.

Niskanen, W. (1973). *Bureaucracy: Servant or Master?* London: Institute of Economic Affairs.

North, D. (1981). 'Neoclassical Theory of the State', in *Structure and Change in Economic History*. New York: W.W. Norton and Company.

Nozick, R. (1974). *Anarchy, Utopia and the State*. Oxford: Blackwell.

Nurske, R. (1952). 'Some International Aspects of the Problem of Economic Development', *American Economic Review*, vol.42, no.2.

Olson, M. (1982). *The Rise and Decline of Nations*. New Haven: Yale University Press.

Pagano, U. (1985). *Work and Welfare in Economic Theory*. Oxford: Blackwell.

Pagano, U. and Rowthorn, B. (eds.) (1996). *Democracy and Efficiency in the Economic Enterprise*. London: Routledge.

Panic, M. (1990). 'Managing Reform in the East European Economies: Lessons from the Postwar Experience of Western Europe', paper presented for the United Nations Economic Commission for Europe.

Peacock, A. (1979). 'Appraising Government Expenditure: A Simple Economic Analysis', in A. Peacock, *The Economic Analysis of Government*. Oxford: Martin Robertson.

Peacock, A. and Rowley, C. (1979). 'Pareto Optimality and the Political Economy of Liberalism', in A. Peacock, *The Economic Analysis of Government*.

Pekkarinen, J., Pohjola, M. and Rowthorn, R. (eds.) (1992). *Learning from Corporatist Experience*. Oxford: Clarendon Press.

Polanyi, K. (1957). *The Great Transformation*. Boston: Beacon Press.

Posner, R. (1975). 'The Social Costs of Monopoly and Regulation', *Journal of Political Economy*, vol.83, no.4.

Rosenstein-Rodan, P. (1943). 'Problems of Industrialisation of Eastern and South-Eastern Europe', *Economic Journal*, vol.53, no.3.

Rowley, C. (1983). 'The Political Economy of the Public Sector', in B. Jones (ed.), *Perspectives on Political Economy*. London: Frances Pinter.

Rowthorn, R. and Chang, H.-J. (1993). 'Public Ownership and the Theory of the State', in T. Clarke and C. Pitelis (eds.), *The Political Economy of Privitisation*. London: Routledge.

Scheffler, S. (ed.) (1988). *Consequentialism and its Critics*. Oxford: Oxford University Press.

Schumpeter, J. (1987). *Capitalism, Socialism and Democracy*, 6th edn. London: Unwin Paperbacks.

Scitovsky, T. (1954). 'Two Concepts of External Economies', *Journal of Political Economy*, vol.62, no.2.

Shapiro, H. and Taylor, L. (1990). 'The State and Industrial Strategy', *World Development*, vol.18, no.6.

Singh, A. (1992a). 'The Actual Crisis of Economic Development in the 1980s: An Alternative Policy Perspective for the Future', in A.K. Dutt and F. Jameson (eds.), *New Directions in Development Economics*. Aldershot: Edward Elgar.

Singh, A. (1992b). '"Close" vs. "Strategic" Integration with the World Economy and the "Market-Friendly Approach to Development" vs. an

"Industrial Policy": A Critique of the *World Development Report 1991* and an Alternative Policy Perspective', mimeo, Faculty of Economics and Politics, University of Cambridge.

Stigler, G. (1975). *The Citizen and the State.* Chicago: University of Chicago Press.

Thompson, G. (ed.) (1989). *Industrial Policy: USA and UK Debates.* London: Routledge.

Thompson, G., Frances, J., Levacic, R. and Mitchell, J. (eds.) (1991). *Markets, Hierarchies and Networks.* London: Sage.

Toye, J. (1987). *Dilemmas of Development.* Oxford: Blackwell.

Vernon, R. and Aharoni, Y. (eds.) (1981). *State-Owned Enterprises in the Western Economies.* London: Croom Helm.

Weiss, J. (1990). *Industry in Developing Countries.* London: Routledge.

Williamson, O. (1975). *Markets and Hierarchies.* New York: The Free Press.

World Bank (1983). *World Development Report 1983.* New York: Oxford University Press.

World Bank (1987). *World Development Report 1987.* New York: Oxford University Press.

World Bank (1991). *World Development Report 1991.* New York: Oxford University Press.

Wright, R. (1991). 'Three Essays in Comparative Institutional Economics', unpublished Ph.D. dissertation. Faculty of Economics and Politics, University of Cambridge.

Chapter 2

State, Institutions and Structural Change

1. INTRODUCTION

SINCE the end of the so-called 'Golden Age' of capitalism, the industrial countries of Western Europe and North America have experienced a marked slowdown in their capital accumulation and productivity growth (Marglin and Schor (eds.) 1990; Armstrong *et al.* 1991). When combined with the changing international division of labour following the rise of Japan and the newly industrialising countries (NICs), this meant that they have had to go through massive industrial adjustments. In dealing with such 'industrial crises', different countries have exhibited markedly different abilities to restructure their economies in terms of speed, effectiveness and equality of the restructuring process. To many commentators, this came as a surprise, since these countries were previously thought to be very similar (if not identical) to each other as 'market' economies.

The most popular interpretation of such differential performance across countries, until recently, has been the neoliberal one which emerged in the late-1970s. This view sees all rules, regulations and institutions other than the ones which are necessary for market exchange to occur at all (e.g., property rights, contract laws) as rigidities which prevent the smooth operation of market forces. The proponents of this view hold that the sluggish industrial adjustments of certain, especially European, industrial countries are the results of institutional rigidities created by state intervention under pressures from interest groups (e.g., see Olson 1982; Giersch 1986). They argue that such institutional rigidities prevent the movement of factors of production into more profitable (and with some minor qualifications, socially

desirable) activities. Thus, to them, countries with less state intervention and other institutional rigidities are likely to have better records of
growth and structural change.

However, more recently, an alternative type of interpretation,
referred to here as 'institutionalist', has been gaining ground. The
institutionalists try to explain the differential abilities of different
countries to engineer an effective and equitable restructuring process
by their differences in economic and political institutions. They argue
that the success or otherwise of an economy depends on an array of
institutions, of which the market is only one, if a very important,
component. Many of them put particular emphasis on the role of the
state as a component in and as the manager of such an institutional
matrix, although they also recognise the importance of non-state
institutions such as enterprise networks, trade unions and large-scale
enterprises. Prominent examples include the debates on social corporatism (Goldthorpe 1984; Katzenstein 1985; Pekkarinen *et al.* (eds.)
1992), industrial policy (Johnson (ed.) 1984; Thompson (ed.) 1989;
Chang 1994), post-Fordism and flexible specialisation (Piore and
Sabel 1984; Boyer (ed.) 1988; Jessop *et al.* (eds.) 1991) and national
systems of innovation (Dosi *et al.* (eds.) 1988; Lundvall (ed.) 1992;
Nelson (ed.) 1993).

This chapter aims to develop a theory of state intervention
relating to the issue of large-scale economic change which involves
substantial changes in technology and institutions (which from now on
will be called *structural change* as a shorthand) from what is known
as the institutionalist perspective. After providing a comparison of
three alternative ways to understand the role of the state, namely,
welfare economics, neoliberalism and institutionalism (Section 2),
this chapter goes on to develop its own theory. Two roles that a state
should play in order to facilitate the process of structural change are
identified, namely, entrepreneurship in the sense of providing the
'vision' for the future and building new institutions (Section 3) and the
management of conflicts which arise during the process of structural
change (Section 4). Then, in Section 5, this chapter shows how the
theory can help us to understand the different ways in which different
'market' economies have managed the process of structural change,
using the examples from the two varieties of market economy which
have recently been suggested as potentially superior alternatives to the

Anglo-Saxon *laissez-faire* variety, namely, the 'industrial policy states' of East Asia (Japan, Korea and Taiwan) and France, on the one hand, and the 'social corporatist' economies of Scandinavia (Sweden, Norway and Finland) on the other. This chapter concludes with Section 6.

2. WELFARE ECONOMICS, NEOLIBERALISM AND INSTITUTIONALISM

Welfare economics or the 'market failure' approach has dominated the postwar discussion on the role of the state. This approach sees state intervention as necessary because of the inability of decentralised agents, in their pursuit of self-interest, to produce outcomes which would fulfil the 'efficiency' conditions of a competitive equilibrium. Conditions such as indivisibility, lack of exclusive property rights and strategic behaviour lead to discrepancies between private and social costs and benefits, which are manifested in problems such as public goods, externalities and monopolies. When the market mechanism 'fails' to produce the socially optimal outcome, the state, as the all-knowing and all-powerful social guardian (the modern equivalent of Plato's Philosopher King), is expected to step in to correct such failures, using means such as public production, regulation of pricing, franchise bidding, taxes, subsidies and reallocation of property rights. Hence the name, market failure approach. This view, however, has been subject to severe criticisms with the rise of neoliberalism (see Chang 1994: Chapters 1 and 2).

As far as the role of the state is concerned, the neoliberal view has three major components in it, which are all critical of the welfare economics approach. Firstly, its subscription to contractarian political philosophy (Nozick 1974; Buchanan 1986) leads to the view that any extension of the role of the state beyond the 'night-watchman' role is morally unacceptable. Criticising welfare economics for its 'utilitarian' view, many neoliberal thinkers argue that economic efficiency should be sacrificed for the sake of individual freedom, should the two clash (e.g., Peacock and Rowley 1979). Secondly, most (if not all) neoliberal economists concur with the Austrian economists (Mises 1929; Hayek 1949) in arguing that state intervention in a complex

modern economy is doomed to failure due to problems of informational costs and, more fundamentally, uncertainty. They believe that
the only feasible order in such an economy is the 'spontaneous' order
of the market and therefore an attempt by the state to substitute it
through 'planning' is misguided (e.g., Burton 1983). Thirdly, the
neoliberals subscribe to the new political economy or the 'government
failure' approach, which rejects the welfare economics view of the
state as a benign and omnipotent social guardian which maximises
social welfare. They argue that the state should be seen as an agent
which serves the interests of politically influential groups inside and
outside the state apparatus (politicians, bureaucrats, interest groups),
which means that state intervention is likely to create allocative
inefficiencies, organisational slacks (or x-inefficiencies) and rent-
seeking 'wastes', rather than correct for 'market failures' (see e.g.,
essays in Alt and Shepsle (eds.) 1990).

Even if we do not accept the first component of the neoliberal
argument, namely the contractarian political philosophy, and reject the
'moralistic' critique of interventionism, the latter two components
provide a formidable platform from which to criticise the conventional
interventionist position based on welfare economics. Firstly, if we
accept the Austrian argument that neoclassical economics (of which
welfare economics is a branch) takes things such as technologies and
institutions as 'data' when they are in fact in constant flux of the
'market process' (Kirzner 1973), the very notion of market failure
becomes difficult to sustain. If the fundamental uncertainties pervading the market process do not allow us to identify the ideal against
which market failures are to be identified, namely, the neoclassical
competitive equilibrium, the whole exercise in welfare economics
becomes pointless. Secondly, if we agree that the depiction of the state
as the all-knowing and all-powerful social guardian in welfare economics is too idealistic and accept the (more realistic, if biased) new
political economy argument that it is mainly an instrument with which
politically influential groups advance their sectional interests, we may
see a less interventionist state as more desirable. If we take this view,
limiting the involvement of the state in the economy seems to be the
only certain way to insulate economic management from the 'corrupting' forces of politics.

These two elements of the neoliberal critique (namely, the

Austrian element and the new political economy element) have provided us with some enormously valuable insights, which have fundamentally changed the way we understand state intervention. Many would accept that, however sophisticated the analyses of market failures may become, they will never be able to provide us with a fully satisfactory solution, given the constantly changing and uncertain nature of the world. Similarly, most supporters of state intervention would not deny that state intervention can and did lead to highly undesirable outcomes in some cases, due to things like 'predatory' states or 'captured' states by certain interest groups.

However, recent researches have shown that the state has often played a positive role in the development experience of many countries (for some examples, see Section 5). We are still some way away from understanding exactly why different countries have different records of state intervention, but this suggests that the neoliberal aversion to state intervention is as unwarranted as the welfarist belief in it. Therefore, what is needed is to identify the factors which determine the success or otherwise of state intervention.[1] Moreover, recent developments in the institutionalist approach to political economy (which is broader than what is usually understood by terms such as new institutional economics) have shown that the neoliberal views have

---

1 A satisfactory discussion of these factors is beyond the scope of this chapter, although later sections of this chapter discuss some of them in a tentative way. Here we merely provide basic thoughts. First of all, what disciplines the state? Domestic politics (e.g., through elections, through interest group pressures) is an obvious candidate, but the role of external pressures (e.g., being an open economy, hostile neighbours) should not be underestimated (see Section 5). Secondly, how does the development of an economy affect the effectiveness of state intervention? Development may, for example, make the economy more complex and, therefore, makes it increasingly difficult for the state to intervene, but it may also increase the capability of the state through a kind of 'learning by doing' process in administration. Thirdly, how is legitimacy of state intervention, which is critical for effective intervention, secured? For example, does a more 'participatory' political regime provide more legitimacy to the state or does it merely weaken the legitimacy by overburdening the state and reducing its credibility? Does a more or less 'politicised' economic management enhance state legitimacy? Fourthly, how does the form of interest representation affect the success or otherwise of state intervention? Do we need an aggregation of interest groups at the national level as, say, in Scandinavia? Or are there different forms of interest representation which fit different areas? Is there any conflict between them? The author wishes to thank Michael Landesmann for his helpful comments on these issues.

some fundamental theoretical problems. Remedying them is one of the main purposes of this chapter.

Firstly, contrary to the Austrian argument, 'constructed' orders associated with organisations, networks and state intervention play an equally important role as the spontaneous order of the market (Simon 1991). The fact that the world is full of uncertainties does not necessarily mean that, therefore, we cannot do anything about it. After all, all institutions can be seen, to an extent, as devices to overcome uncertainties by providing some man-made (and therefore necessarily imperfect) order (more on this in Section 3). Moreover, historically, the very emergence of the apparently 'spontaneous' market order owed a lot to an active role of the state in establishing property rights and other market institutions. This is more obvious in many 'late-developing' countries where the state practically had to create the capitalist class and start modern financial and productive organisations (Gerschenkron 1966), but even in the early developers like Britain, the state played an important role in this regard (Polanyi 1957; Coase 1988). As we shall argue later, the recognition of this point opens up a whole new field of inquiry, namely, the role of the state as an entrepreneur whose task is to provide a vision for the society and create new institutions required to achieve the vision (see Section 3).

Secondly, the new political economy view that the withdrawal of the state is necessary to prevent the corrupting influence of politics on the management of the economy is problematic. While it is true that an 'abdication' (voluntary or not) of power by the state could be a good way of insulating it from certain undesirable political pressures under certain conditions, this does not mean that a less 'politicised' management of the economy is necessarily better. Recent researches show that an explicitly political management of the economy may or may not produce a desirable outcome depending on things such as the influence of institutions and ideologies on the determination of the public agenda, the autonomy of the state *vis-à-vis* interest groups in setting and executing such an agenda, and the forms of interest group representation and its impact on the process and outcome of state intervention (Zysman 1983; Evans *et al.* (eds.) 1985; Maier 1987; Hall (ed.) 1989). In fact, there are studies which show that certain 'politicised' varieties of economic management did result in effective or equitable structural changes, as in the cases of the industrial policy states (of East Asia and France) or the social corporatist economies (of Scandinavia), which we shall discuss later (in Section 5).

The institutionalist view is different from both the welfare economics view and the neoliberal view of the state. It rejects the institutional primacy accorded to the market by the latter two views and believes that there is nothing 'natural' about the market order. Welfare economics sees the non-market institutions as second best man-made substitutes, which arise when the natural order of the market fails to produce the promised outcome. According to Arrow (1974), who represents this view, non-market institutions, which he calls 'organisations' as a shorthand, are simply 'means of achieving the benefits of collective action in situations in which the price system fails' (p.33). The new political economy strand of neoliberalism fundamentally shares the same view, but only differs in pointing out that the substitute (i.e., the 'government') may also fail and is likely to be even worse. The Austrian strand of neoliberalism differs from welfare economics and the new political economy in not seeing the market as a mechanical device whose movements can be clearly predicted, but as something which spontaneously emerges, while regarding other man-made institutions as the doomed products of a futile exercise in 'rational constructivism' (the term is due to Hayek 1988).

Thus seen, despite its fundamentally pro-interventionist tone, welfare economics shares a belief in the institutional primacy of the market with neoliberalism which is anti-interventionist. This apparently paradoxical observation will make sense when we realise that giving institutional primacy to the market is not equivalent to believing in less state intervention, as the extent of intervention may turn out to be absolutely gigantic due to the pervasiveness of market failure. The institutionalist view, in contrast, does not believe in the institutional primacy of the market. It believes that the market is only one of the many economic institutions and not necessarily the primary one (e.g., Williamson 1985; Simon 1991). Moreover, it argues that there is no reason to believe that there are 'scientifically' given boundaries between different institutions – especially the kind of boundary depicted in the market-state dichotomy upheld by welfare economics and neoliberalism. As we argued earlier, this view explicitly recognises the role of the state as the designer, defender and reformer of many formal and informal institutions, while taking seriously the political constraints on the effective exercise of such a role (as pointed out by the new political economy). In the following two sections, a theory of the role of the state which develops these points with a special reference to the process of structural change is outlined.

3.   THE STATE AS AN ENTREPRENEUR

In a modern economy, where the factors of production are 'interdependent in use but dispersed in ownership' (Abramovitz 1986: p.402), effective structural change may require coordinated changes in many components of the economy. This is because those who control individual components may be unable to initiate and achieve the change, as they may suffer from a lack of 'systemic' vision and/ or from strategic uncertainty as to the behaviour of the other relevant agents. Hence, the need for coordination by some central agent (be it the state or not) for an economy-wide change to happen.[2] Such coordination, however, should not be seen as merely coordinating a shift from one equilibrium position to a higher-level one (e.g., Stiglitz 1992), although such a formulation may be useful for certain purposes. This view assumes that all the relevant agents know all the possible equilibria and can find out which of them is the best outcome (at least in the probabilistic sense). In such a formulation, the only obstacle to change is the difficulty of simultaneous movement. However, as the Austrians have persuasively argued, the problem of our economic life is exactly that we are not aware of the full range of possibilities, not to speak of being unable to tell which of them is the best.[3]

---

2   This reasoning formed the basis of certain earlier theories of industrialisation such as the so-called 'big push' or 'balanced growth' model (Rosenstein-Rodan 1943; Scitovsky 1954) and, more recently, has also been applied to the study of technical progress (David 1985; Dosi et al. (eds.) 1988).
3   Similarly, Hirschman (1958) argued in his celebrated critique of the balanced growth approach that economic development 'depends not so much on finding optimal combinations for given resources and factors of production as on calling forth and enlisting for development purposes resources and abilities that are hidden, scattered, or badly utilised' (p.5).

Thus seen, structural change, as defined here, requires much more than choosing from a pre-existing choice set. It requires formulating the choice set itself, namely, providing a vision for the future. And the state, as the central agent, can play an important role in providing such a vision. By providing such a vision at the early stage of the change, the state can drive private sector agents into a concerted action without making them spend resources on information gathering and processing, bargaining and so on. In engineering a structural change the state is providing a vision rather than merely coordinating a move to a higher equilibrium; this means that there is an important entrepreneurial element in the exercise. Be it private or public (state), entrepreneurship requires the ability to provide a new vision, however grand (as in the case of Henry Ford's vision of mass production or the Japanese state's vision of a highly skilled, software-based economy) or limited (as in numerous cases of incremental innovation) its scope may be.[4]

Note that this chapter is not asserting that the state necessarily has a superior ability to identify a better future course for the national economy (although this may well be the case, as in the case of some Japanese high-tech industries; see Okimoto 1989), but only that the provision of a 'focal point' around which economic activities may be organised in times of major economic change can be extremely useful (on the notion of focal point, see Schelling 1960).[5] Our case for state entrepreneurship, then, is mainly based on its strategic position – the

---

4 Another critical element of entrepreneurship is the ability to mobilise resources, to implement the vision. In the existing literature, the role of the state in resource mobilisation is widely discussed (e.g., Gerschenkron 1966), but it has rarely been combined with the analysis of its role as a provider of 'vision'.

5 In this connection, note the observation that the economic bureaucracy in certain East Asian countries with successful interventionist records has been manned by lawyers and engineers rather than economists. This suggests that what makes successful intervention may not be 'specialist' knowledge about economics but the ability to formulate a vision and to coordinate decisions. See Johnson (1982) and Dore (1986) on Japan, Wade (1990) on Taiwan and Korea, and Chang (1994) on Korea and Japan.

state, by definition, is the only agent which may represent the interest of the whole society,[6] although it will be naive to assume that all existing states have the organisational coherence, the political desire or the power to exploit such strategic position to national advantage.

Moreover, we accept the possibility that the vision provided by the state as an entrepreneur can be wrong from the beginning or become so due to a failure to modify it according to changes in the environment. However, this possibility cannot, in itself, provide a definitive case against state entrepreneurship. This is because all entrepreneurial visions, private or public, run the risk of being wrong. In a world where this is not the case (i.e., in a world with perfect foresight), entrepreneurship would, in fact, not be necessary to begin with. As there are kinds of entrepreneurial decisions which can only be sensibly made and coordinated at the national level, abandoning the attempts at state entrepreneurship altogether on the grounds that it can go wrong will be undesirable. The possibility of the state promoting a wrong vision should be minimised by building a mechanism to put together and compare different visions extant in the society, including the one held by the state, and to create a consensus out of them.[7]

State entrepreneurship does not stop at providing a vision for the future. If its vision is to be realised, the state has to provide an institutional reality to it. In fact, the success or otherwise of private entrepreneurship itself also critically depends on the construction of new institutional vehicles for the realisation of its vision – as seen in

---

6   This point is essentially what Marxists had in mind when they argued that the growing socialisation of production leads to more centralised forms of coordination, starting from the rise of the factory system, leading to growth of monopoly and expansion of state intervention and culminating in central planning under socialism. A similar reasoning lies behind the theory of 'encompassing' organisations (Olson 1982) and theories of centralised wage bargaining and social corporatism (Schott 1984; Bruno and Sachs 1985; Pekkarinen et al. (eds.) 1992). The common theme here is how the centralisation of the decisions of subsocietal groups whose actions have economy-wide impact may be beneficial for the society.

7   Consensus should not be interpreted as an outcome of a harmonious decision-making process involving all relevant agents. In the real world, consensus typically emerges out of a conflict-ridden process which often excludes many agents who are relevant at least from certain points of view. In fact, a large part of politics is deciding about who is going to be included in or excluded from the decision-making process.

the cases of British railway companies, Carnegie's US Steel and Toyota's 'lean manufacturing' (also see Chandler 1990; Lazonick 1991). This means that we need to look at the role of the state as an institution builder.

During the process of structural change, new interdependencies will appear and old ones disappear. The rise of the new patterns of interdependence makes it necessary to establish a new coordination structure or new 'principles of efficient coordination' as Loasby (1991: p.11) refers to it. Note here that what is required is a set of coordination *principles or rules* rather than individually optimal decisions, as the coordination of the growth of knowledge 'depends on rational structures and rational procedures rather than on rational choice' (Loasby 1991: p.101).[8]

The establishment of a new coordination structure necessarily requires state involvement, even if the particular government in power does not want it. This is because only the state has the power to legalise (or at least give implicit backing to) the new property rights and the new power relations (both at the societal level and at the enterprise level) which provide an institutional reality to the new coordination structure. In other words, by giving the emergent coordination structure an institutional reality, the state will help agents with bounded rationality to establish quickly new organisations, new productive routines and new contracts which would enable them to deal with the 'new world' with less informational burden. In this process of institution building, the state is not merely responding to changes but also leading them, as it cannot grant property (and other) rights to people in a coherent way, unless it has a certain vision of what it regards

---

8   There is a tremendous difference between the principles of efficient coordination applied to 'a rational choice of specialisation in order to gain access to the well-
specified benefits of a superior production function' and the ones applied to 'the
attempt to create a superior system for generating new knowledge, the content of
which, and therefore the benefit of which, cannot be known before it has been
discovered' (Loasby 1991: p.11). Of course, 'even though future knowledge cannot
be predicted if it is to remain future knowledge, it may often be possible to set limits
on it – to say what cannot be done. Even that kind of prediction may be wrong,
because ... there is no way of proving any general proposition to be true' (p.103).
Nevertheless, this is the kind of world we are living in and we have to make the best
of it.

as the desirable future. In the words of Matthews (1986), it 'has to decide what kinds of rights and obligations it is prepared to recognise and enforce' (p. 910). In this sense, the state is both responding to *and* shaping the course of changes, as any good entrepreneur would do.

Establishing a new coordination structure is easier said than done, for several reasons. For one thing, it is not simple to identify the optimal timing of such institutionalisation.[9] Moreover, given that most laws are enforced only within the borders of nation states, establishment of a new coordination structure may be constrained by internationalisation of economic activities.[10] The question of feasibility also arises because of the resistance of certain groups which may lose out under the new coordination structure. A new coordination structure requires a new property rights structure, which may result in an unacceptable reduction in the incomes of certain groups. And if this is the case, those who are to lose out will try to mobilise against the new institutional arrangements and sometimes succeed in doing so. Indeed, the resistance from such vested interests has traditionally been identified, by economists both on the right and the left, as the reason for 'sclerosis' of certain mature economies (Olson 1982; Giersch 1986; Hodgson 1989). However, the role of the state in speeding up structural change by reducing such resistance has rarely been discussed and this is what we intend to discuss in the next section of the chapter.

Let us sum up the discussion in this section. The co-existence of widespread interdependencies and private control of means of production means that efficient structural change requires concerted efforts coordinated by the state. However, because of the fundamental uncer-

---

9 For example, sometimes an early institutionalisation of new practices (e.g., standardisation of technology) boosts change, while at other times prevention or premature privately-initiated institutionalisation – which, if allowed, the state will eventually be compelled to ratify – may be more desirable (see Chang 1994: Chapter 3).

10 Examples include the difficuly of regulating trade flows due to the constant emergence of new products and new sources of supply from abroad, the difficulty of macroeconomic management in a world of internationalised financial markets and the difficulty of affecting the pattern of production and employment through policy variables in a country dominated by large multinational corporations (MNCs) (see Rowthorn 1971; Banuri and Schor (eds.) 1991).

tainties pervading our economic life and especially the dynamic process of structural change, this exercise is much more than choosing between multiple equilibria (a simple coordination) but involves an important entrepreneurial element, namely, the provision of a vision for the future by the state, around which the concerted efforts can be organised. The role of the state as an entrepreneur does not stop at providing a vision. As in many cases of private entrepreneurship, it requires institution building, which gives an institutional reality to the vision held by the entrepreneur by shaping the emergent coordination structure. This task of institution building is made complicated by the difficulty of identifying the ideal timing of such activity, the existence of international interdependence in a world of nation states and the resistance from vested interests. However, such complications should not detract us from the enormous potential gains from good state entrepreneurship.

4.   THE STATE AS THE MANAGER OF CONFLICTS

As Kuznets (1973) eloquently argued, technological innovations which characterise the modern growth and structural change process inevitably lead to dislocation of productive factors, thus making the process extremely conflictual. With perfectly mobile factors of production, this should not cause a problem, as the owners of those productive assets which need to find alternative employment will easily be able to switch to the next best option, whose return will be only marginally lower (in a perfectly competitive economy). However, when the mobility of certain physical and human assets is limited their owners will face the prospect of 'obsolescence, unemployment and income differentials', *if* they accept the market outcome (Kuznets 1973: p.204). When the owners of the affected productive assets do not accept such an outcome, they will take non-market or political actions to redress the situation (e.g., petition, strikes, bribing, horse trading), which will make the process of structural change very conflictual and generate pressures for an explicitly political management of the economy by the state.

Needless to say, certain governments, especially those with an ideological commitment to a free market, may not wish to be involved in the management of such conflicts, but the state can never remain a spectator. The fact that it is the ultimate guarantor of property (and other) rights and (normally) the most important actor in setting and executing the public agenda for changes in rights and institutions makes it the ultimate manager of conflicts. Obviously, there are many ways for the state to manage conflicts which arise during the process of structural change, each of which will have different implications for objectives like efficiency, productivity and equality, to name just a few. In the following, let us discuss some major ways of managing conflict and their economic and political implications.

Let us begin with the classic method of conflict management in the capitalist economy, that is, accepting the market solution. Most mainstream economists (especially the ones with neoliberal tendencies) regard this as the most 'natural' and the most efficient way to manage conflict in a capitalist economy. However, as we shall argue later, there is nothing natural or inevitable about a certain market outcome. Moreover, accepting the market solution is not even the most efficient way of managing conflicts. This method can create a lot of tension when the costs that have to be paid by the losers are large and, therefore, is usable only when the state can prevent the losers from organising countervailing political action. Hence, the paradox that a free market requires a strong state (Gamble 1987). And when there are many such losers (as, for example, in a time of industrial crisis), even a very strong state may find it difficult to manage conflict in this way. This method may also result in the unnecessary writing off of many specific assets, a point powerfully conveyed by the image of a middle-aged redundant steel worker flipping hamburgers in McDonald's (on the notion of asset specificity, see Williamson 1985; this will be discussed further).

Secondly, the state may reduce conflicts by openly defying the market outcome, in the sense that it takes actions which clearly reveal who is getting protection from what. The examples will include the imposition of trade restrictions on specific products (e.g., quotas on Japanese cars in many European countries), the restructuring of the losers through an outright state takeover of technically bankrupt private enterprises (e.g., the nationalisation of the Swedish shipbuilding industry or of Volkswagen in West Germany in the late-1970s) and the political re-negotiation of prices (e.g., the early-1990s coal crisis in the UK).[11] Openly defying the market logic is likely to allow the state to resolve the conflicts in a less adversarial manner, but it can open the door for what the neoliberals call an 'unmanageable politicisation of the economy' (this will be discussed further).

Thirdly, there will be a group of methods which do not openly defy the market outcome, but try to modify it in less visible ways. One example is monetary policy. Monetary policy is often regarded as neutral in terms of distributional consequences, but as the conflict theories of inflation tell us, it is not neutral to the outcome of distributional conflicts manifested in inflation (Rowthorn 1977; Lindberg and Maier (eds.) 1985). Thus seen, monetary policy may be used as a means to promote the interests of certain groups with the appearance of impartiality. Also, there are methods which explicitly compensate the losers in general, but without specifying their identities. The examples will include automatic fiscal transfers through things such as unemployment benefits, income support and tax reductions following falls in incomes.

Lastly, the state may try to solve conflict by resetting the public agenda and thereby changing the accepted boundary between the economic and the political (for the importance of agenda setting in general, see Skocpol 1985). The resetting of the public agenda, of course, can mean more politicisation or less, depending on the purpose of such action. Moreover, the same issue may be put on and taken off the public agenda under different circumstances. The best example of this is provided by the fate of employment as a public issue in OECD economies. Employment in the early days of capitalism was a vital issue on the public agenda (as seen by the importance of the Poor Law), until it was struck off the agenda by liberal governments with the establishment of a working labour market and the rise of free market ideology (Polanyi 1957). It came back onto the public agenda as the top priority item after the Second World War with the rise of corporatist

---

11 The fact that many of our examples of the state's defiance of the market logic involve avowed 'free-marketeer' governments – the conservative coalition in Sweden and the Conservative government in the UK – shows the inevitability of state involvement in conflict management.

ruling coalitions, but has almost disappeared again with the right-wing government emphasis on the importance of labour market flexibility in the 1980s (Boyer (ed.) 1988). When the issue was taken off the public agenda, the state could resolve a lot of employment-related conflicts through the market logic by declaring them basically non-political issues which are beyond its power.

Our preceding discussion immediately reveals a major problem with the neoliberal call for the depoliticisation of economic management on the grounds that political determination of prices goes against the objective laws of the market. This position has a long intellectual history, as documented by Polanyi (1957), and, indeed, has some justification. Politicisation of everything, as in the former socialist countries, may create all sorts of problems, for example, the waste of time and resources in bargaining, the difficulty of setting objective performance standards, the difficulty of containing certain redistributive demands and so on. And one may argue that a well-functioning economy needs a substantial degree of depoliticisation of production and distribution of goods and services through the use of the market mechanism.

However, contrary to what the neoliberals lead us to believe, the boundary between the economic and the political is *not* something naturally given *but* something which can vary across time and places.[12] As Oskar Lange pointed out a long time ago, all prices are *potentially* political and there is no scientific rule that will tell us which prices are (or should be) political or not. This point becomes more obvious when considering the fact that a few critical prices which affect almost every sector, namely, wages (especially when considering immigration control) and interest rates, are politically determined to a very large degree. If this is the case, there is no reason to assume any inherent supremacy of the market solution over other methods of conflict resolution.

Of course, at any point in time, for the purpose of policy prescription, some prices may be approximately treated as largely economic (political) and therefore more market-oriented (political)

---

12 For example, in many developing countries, strikes are banned and therefore striking, an activity which will be regarded as 'economic' in most OECD economies, becomes a political act.

means may be applied in resolving conflicts relating to them. However, in the longer run, changes in ideologies and institutions of a society will change the society's perception of what is legitimate and therefore affect the way the boundary between the economic and political is drawn. For instance, as we mentioned earlier, during the 19th century, unemployment was regarded as the outcome of 'imperatives of the market', but with the rise of corporatist ideology and with the development of the Keynesian institutions of demand management (and of the institutions of active labour market policy in the social corporatist economies), it has become something that can be legitimately negotiated and sanctioned in the domain of politics.

Another important point regarding conflict management is that it should *not* be seen merely as taking care of the social or human dimension of an essentially economic adjustment – as the talk of 'safety net' in Eastern European reform or of 'adjustment with a human face' in IMF stabilisation programmes in LDCs implies. This chapter argues that conflict management also has an extremely important 'economic' role, which seems to go a long way in explaining the differential performances between economies with different regimes of conflict management.

The state in its role as conflict manager can be seen as providing insurance to the members of the society, by providing a governance structure which will guarantee some fair level of income to all, under even the most adverse circumstances. This insurance function of the state is related to, but by no means the same as, the notion of the welfare state as improving allocative efficiency through the pooling of risk (e.g., see Barr 1992). For one thing, a state pooling risk through the welfare state is dealing with calculable risks, while a state providing governance through conflict management is dealing with uncertain contingencies, which do not permit probabilistic calculation. Moreover, our insurance function of the state can improve the productivity of the economy in the medium to long run by encouraging risk taking in general (the good old 'socialisation of risk' of investment activities) and investments in *specific* assets (a point that has hardly been discussed before), although it can harm the economy when it creates too much room for 'moral hazard'.

In societies where the state fails to manage conflict in an appropriate way, people will be reluctant to take risks or commit their resources in specific investments and therefore the dynamism of the economy may suffer. Examples of such cases are some developing countries where the lack of a reliable mechanism for conflict resolution discourages industrial investments (which would normally involve specific investments) and encourages the holding of liquid assets such as gold, foreign currency and (if the government is expected to last at least in the foreseeable future) money. Another example of the adverse effect of a deficient conflict resolution mechanism on the dynamic efficiency of the economy is given by the British economy in the 20th century. There is a popular argument that the British industrialists have been slow in introducing new technology (and, hence, new work practices) as they have had to worry about the possible resistance of the workers, while their workers have been unwilling to accept new technology and adopt new work practices because it has often meant unemployment and/or substantial reductions in the value of their existing skills. In the absence of a more comprehensive industrial policy with a functioning conflict management regime, the traditional craft divisions have survived as a means of defending the specific investments made by workers in their skills, discouraging the capitalists from introducing new technology and/or making it inevitable for them to write off a whole lot of human capital if they want to introduce a major technical change.

Conflict management by the state becomes much more difficult when it involves agents who do not fall within the jurisdiction of a particular state, that is, the multinational corporations (MNCs). As the consequences of state actions to restrict their gains or to compensate for their losses will easily spill over the national boundary, the involvement of the MNCs in a conflict gives rise to certain fundamental property right questions. In particular, in the case of small countries where individual MNCs may account for a significant portion of industrial output, the state may be reluctant to 'aid business' or 'help an industry', as the positive effects of such actions may not be contained within its own national boundary. This may require at least one of the following two outcomes, both of which do not seem politically feasible in many countries at present. One is the attitude of the state towards MNCs may have to become more explicitly contractual ('We will give you this. You do that in return'). However, such explicitness may not be acceptable for various political reasons.

Alternatively, we may want an international body (or even a world state) to deal with such multinational externality problems. This, however, does not seem politically feasible outside the EU in the near future.

Let us sum up our argument in this section. Structural change involves 'creative destruction' of existing productive routines and institutions. In the presence of asset specificity and other sources of factor immobility, this may lead to a substantial deterioration in certain groups' absolute and relative positions. As these groups will try and sometimes succeed to resist the change and as other groups may take countermeasures, the process of structural change can become extremely conflictual. The state may manage the conflicts in many different ways, many of which will be defying the market logic and are thus political. Although an excessive politicisation of the economy may be undesirable, there is no reason to assume that a more or less politicised variety of conflict management is more desirable. It was argued that the establishment of a well-functioning conflict management regime has an important implication for the dynamism of the economy, as it provides a governance structure which will encourage people to invest in long-term specific assets. Without the provision of a well-functioning regime of conflict management by the state, the economic dynamism of the economy may suffer. As in the case of state entrepreneurship, multinationalisation of economic activities may challenge the functioning of such a regime.

5. UNDERSTANDING THE ROLE OF THE STATE IN DIFFERENT TYPES OF CAPITALISM: 'INDUSTRIAL POLICY' STATES VERSUS SOCIAL CORPORATISM

In this section, it will be illustrated how the theory developed in this chapter may help us understand the role of the state in different types of capitalism. This is done by comparing the role of the state in two very different groups of successful capitalist countries, namely the industrial policy states of East Asia (Japan, Korea and Taiwan) and France, on the one hand, and social corporatist countries in Scandinavia (Sweden, Finland and Norway), on the other. In recent debates on industrial policy and on social corporatism, their systems of political economy have both been discussed a lot as potentially superior alternatives to the *laissez-faire* capitalism of the Anglo-Saxon countries (for references, see below). In these debates, it is widely recognised that in both these groups of countries, the state has played an important role in engineering structural change, but practically no attempt has been made to discuss them from a comparative perspective (for an exception, see Vartiainen 1995). This is partly because of the lack of cross-fertilisation between the participants in the two debates, but it is also because people usually perceive the states in each of the groups as being too different to warrant a comparison.

At one level, such a perception is correct. In the industrial policy states, the states have been dominated by right-wing coalitions which are often described as 'authoritarian' (and worse, in the cases of Korea and Taiwan), the bureaucracy had dominated the policy-making process, and heavy-handed and precisely targeted (often at the firm level) industrial policies were used as the major tools to engineer structural change (see Johnson (ed.) 1984; Thompson (ed.) 1989; Chang 1994).[13] In contrast, in the social corporatist countries, the state apparatus has been mainly occupied by 'social democratic' coalitions (with the partial exception of Finland), centralised trade unions and employers' associations have played central roles in policy formulation, and macroeconomic policies combined with active interventions in the labour market were the major tools of structural transformation (Goldthorpe 1984; Katzenstein 1985; Pekkarinen *et al.* (eds.) 1992).[14] However, at another level, we can argue that the states in these two apparently very different types of capitalism have both played the crucial roles of entrepreneur and conflict manager equally well, albeit in very different ways.

The industrial policy states, as is well known, have played a prominent entrepreneurial role. These states were manned by politi-

---

13 See Cohen (1977), Zysman (1983) and Hall (1987) on France. See Johnson (1982), Dore (1986) and Okimoto (1989) on Japan. See Amsden (1989) and Chang (1993) on Korea. See Amsden (1985) and Wade (1990) on Taiwan.
14 Among the Scandinavian countries, Sweden, being the quintessential social corporatist economy, has attracted the largest amount of research. On Sweden, see LO (1963), Korpi (1983), Lundberg (1985) and Pontusson (1987). Salmon (1990), Pekkarinen (1992), Landesmann (1992) and ELTA *et al.* (1987) provide comparative accounts of the postwar developments in Scandinavian countries.

cians and bureaucrats who were imbued with nationalist ideologies, which called for rapid industrialisation and structural change. The vision which guided their industrial policies is summarised as industrial upgrading, namely, structural shifts to high technology and high-value-added industries, which provide good prospects for demand expansion and technical progress. How this shift was to be achieved was set out in their medium-term (usually five years) indicative planning documents (which, contrary to what the name suggests, involved a lot of coercive elements) and other complementary policy documents such as 'white papers'. Although there was a substantial and often close consultation with the employers' organisations (but not the unions), the state was a clear leader in the formulation of such a vision.[15]

The states in these countries were all able and willing to realise the visions they formulated by using their enormous economic powers. These powers were based on their control over public enterprises and the banking sector (the state has owned at least a substantial part 'or even all' of the banking sector except in Japan), on the one hand, and on their direct and indirect influences on oil industry associations, employers' organisations and the unions (as far as they mattered), on the other. As rapid capital accumulation was seen by the policy makers in these countries as a prerequisite of rapid structural change, interest rates were often kept under the market rates (financial repression) and various tax incentives were provided to encourage certain types of investments (e.g., equipment investments in certain industries). Trade protection, subsidies and other means of modifying market prices have been used to provide the industries concerned with the extra time and resources to learn, develop and reorganise themselves (see Chang 1994, 1995). Moreover, the states in these countries also exercised direct influence on the patterns of the trajectory of technical progress

---

15 Thus Renshaw (1986), writing on Japan, points out that 'a sense of overall direction to the overall evolution of the economy has been provided by the annual economic white papers of the Economic Planning Agency with their thematic titles and by the forward looks or "visions" published every two or three years by the MITI, via the Structure Council.... In practical terms, these documents provide criteria or orientation against which countless individual decisions by private and public officials can be tested and hence *given order and coherence which could otherwise only be achieved by a higher degree of centralisation'* (italics added) (p.144).

not only through their support of R&D but also through controls over importing technology (especially with regard to multinational investments and licensing) and financial incentives for the users of certain kinds of technology over others (e.g., domestic technologies and more modern technologies) (see essays in Nelson (ed.) 1993).

The conflict management side of state intervention in the industrial policy states is less frequently discussed than its entrepreneurial side for good reasons, but should not be ignored. The main thrust of conflict management in these countries can broadly be described as the strong state suppressing the reaction of the losers from structural change, while buying off some of them (in particular, the farmers and small shopkeepers) with resources channelled from the efficient manufacturing sector (Zysman 1983). Although high growth of these economies made it easier for the dismissed workers to find alternative employment, the industrial workers in these countries have been bearing an unequally large share of the burdens of adjustment, in particular when compared with their counterparts in the more egalitarian social corporatist countries of Scandinavia.

Moreover, industrial policy as practised in these countries has helped, if unwittingly, their states to manage conflicts more easily. The *ex ante* investment coordination by the state which was intended to reduce the possibility of price wars under adverse demand conditions reduced the possibility of conflict arising out of mass bankruptcy and redundancy during recession in industries with large sunk costs (for details of such investment coordination, see Chang 1994, Chapter 3). More importantly, in times of industrial crises, the states in these countries were willing to facilitate and often even impose deals on mergers, takeovers and negotiated capacity scrapping to resolve the adjustment problems. This enabled these countries to restructure with less prolonged conflicts than would have been otherwise (Zysman 1983; Dore 1986; Chang 1995). In Japan, the process was further facilitated by the lifetime employment schemes, which, by guaranteeing jobs for the 'core' workers (approximately one-third of the workforce), reduced their resistance to the introduction of new (usually labour-saving) technologies (for details, see Koike 1987).

The Scandinavian countries are known for their excellent systems of conflict management, which enabled them to restructure their economies with an orderliness and equity (if not speed) hard to find elsewhere. The basis of such systems is to be found in their tripartite bargaining systems between organised labour, organised capital and the state, under a social democratic hegemony based on class compromise between highly organised labour and highly organised capital. In this bargaining system, the three parties sit together to determine wage demands, employment levels (significantly affected by public sector employment policies) and investment plans, in order to maintain full employment and sometimes even to reduce wage dispersion, which, in turn, reduces social conflicts (Pekkarinen 1992).

While there was a clear recognition in the minds of all three parties involved that employment should not be preserved at the cost of international competitiveness and therefore there was a willingness to let redundancies occur, the social corporatist states actively intervened in the labour market in order to provide unemployment benefits, relocation assistance and retraining for the displaced workers. Public sector employment was also frequently used to absorb some of the displaced workers. In general, the Scandinavian countries were much more willing than other capitalist countries to temporarily slow down the pace of adjustment to preserve full employment, income equality and, consequently, social peace. Such policy may be costly in the short run, but in the long run, it has served an important productive function, as it reduces the resistance to structural change in the future, by making people accept that structural change need not mean unemployment, dislocation and a drastic fall in living standards.

When it comes to entrepreneurship, the states in the social corporatist countries have played a much less prominent role than their counterparts in the industrial policy states. However, it does not mean that they played no such role and just let the market run its course. Like the policy makers in the industrial policy states, the Scandinavian policy makers in the immediate postwar period strongly wanted to modernise and 'rationalise' their economies – in other words, diversify their industrial (and export) structures away from primary commodities and natural-resource-based industries (e.g., timber, iron ore and the related industries) to high-skill, high-value-added industries producing high-quality (often niche) products using highly skilled labour (LO 1963 is a classic statement; also see Edquist and Lundvall 1993: p.274).

In realising such a vision of structural change, the Scandinavian states have also played an important role. However, they did not use as much 'industrial policy' measures as the industrial policy states did. This was at least partly because the inherently specific nature of industrial policy measures made them less than fully compatible with the egalitarianism of social corporatism (Landesmann 1992). In Sweden at least until the 1970s, instead of industrial policy measures, labour market measures were used as the main tool to upgrade the economy. Solidaristic wage policy, which explicitly aimed to equalise wages across industries for same types of workers, was used in order to generate pressure on the firms in low-wage sectors to upgrade their capital stock or shed labour, while allowing the firms in high-wage sectors to retain extra profit and expand faster than would otherwise have been possible. As a good conflict manager, the Swedish state used active labour market policies, in order to soften the consequences of such a policy. In the cases of Norway and Finland, more active use was made of industrial policy measures (Landesmann 1992). In particular, in Finland, where the private sector was much less developed, public enterprises were used as vehicles for the modernisation of the economy (Salmon 1990).

One interesting commonality between the two groups of countries is the existence of a political and/or bureaucratic elite which had a stronger commitment to social goals such as industrialisation and structural change than is usually regarded as possible by the neoliberals. In the case of the industrial policy states, historical experiences of national humiliation through events such as defeat in war (Japan, France and Taiwan) and colonisation (Korea and Taiwan), on the one hand, and the sense of national vulnerability due to confrontation with a hostile enemy (Korea and Taiwan), on the other, are often thought to have contributed to the emergence of such an elite. In the case of the social corporatist countries, elites did not need such catastrophes to reach their historic compromises (namely, the Norwegian Basic Agreement in 1935 and the Swedish Saltsjobaeen Pact in 1938), but such compromises were achieved after experiencing a period of bitter class struggle (Korpi 1983; Salmon 1990).[16] Also, the sense of national vulnerability from being small, open economies is regarded as having

---

16   For example, Sweden had the highest incidence of industrial actions in Europe during the 1920s (Korpi 1983).

been instrumental in the emergence of class compromise in those countries (Katzenstein 1985; Vartiainen 1995). However, as the above-mentioned conditions were also present in many other countries which did not produce such elites, they are by no means enough to explain the emergence of a ruling elite committed to industrialisation and structural change. We need to accept that some elite groups are more willing and able to learn from their own history and from the experience of other countries.

6. CONCLUSION

This chapter has pointed out the limitations of two dominant theories of state intervention, namely, welfare economics and neoliberalism, and developed an institutionalist theory which can overcome these limitations, especially in relation to the process of structural change in a modern economy with interdependent and specific assets. The theory singles out two roles for the state as being especially important in the process of structural change, namely, entrepreneurship and conflict management. Its role as entrepreneur has two components. Firstly, its position as the central agent imparts it with a crucial role of providing a vision for the future in a period of transformation. Secondly, its role as an institution builder allows it to give institutional reality to its vision as well as institutionalising the emergent coordination structure. Its roles as the guarantor of property rights and as the designer and executioner of a public agenda make it the ultimate conflict manager, a role which also has a very important productive function of providing a governance structure through which risk can be socialised. Using this theory, we discussed the experiences of two groups of capitalist economies which are currently receiving attention as possibly superior alternatives to the Anglo-Saxon variety of capitalism, namely, the industrial policy states of East Asia and France on the one hand, and the social corporatist countries of Scandinavia on the other. We argued that, despite the very different configurations of political economy, the states in these two groups of countries have been engaged in both state entrepreneurship and conflict management. The former group have had a particularly good record in state entrepreneurship and the latter group in conflict management, but both of them have had more than respectable records in the other area.

As we noted in our discussion, the role of the state as the entrepreneur and the conflict manager will be constrained by many factors, even if the state possesses the administrative capacity to perform such functions (obviously, some states do not possess such capacity). Its autonomy *vis-à-vis* interest groups will determine how effectively it can institute a new property rights structure and manage conflicts in the way it wants. Many states certainly are lacking such autonomy. Even for a highly autonomous state, the prevailing ideologies, institutions and political agenda of the society will set a limit to its innovativeness in the design of a coordination structure and of a conflict management system. No state, however 'strong' it may be, works with a clean slate and therefore is free from history. Moreover, increasing multinationalisation of economic activities in many areas is making it more difficult for the nation states to devise policies.

However, whether the state (or anyone else) likes it or not and whether it is difficult or easy, the state is bound to play critical roles as the ultimate entrepreneur and the conflict manager in modern economies with complex interdependencies and (radical and incremental) innovations in technologies and institutions. To pretend otherwise will only delay the emergence of a coherent coordination structure and a functioning regime of conflict management and, consequently, make the economy unable to change without considerable waste and/or social division.

BIBLIOGRAPHY

Abramovitz, M. (1986). 'Catching Up, Forging Ahead, and Falling Behind', *Journal of Economic History*, vol.46, pp.385-406.

Alt, J. and Shepsle, K. (eds.) (1990). *Perspectives on Positive Political Economy*. Cambridge: Cambridge University Press.

Amsden, A. (1985). 'The State and Taiwan's Economic Development', in P. Evans, D. Rueschemeyer and T. Skocpol (eds.), *Bringing the State Back In*. Cambridge: Cambridge University Press.

Amsden, A. (1989). *Asia's Next Giant*. Oxford University Press.

Armstrong, P., Glyn, A. and Harrison, J. (1991). *Capitalism since 1945*. Oxford: Basil Blackwell.

Arrow, K. (1974). *The Limits of Organisation*. New York and London: W.W. Norton and Company.

Banuri, T. and Schor, J. (eds.) (1991). *Financial Openness and National Autonomy*. Oxford: Clarendon Press.

Barr, N. (1992). 'Economic Theory and the Welfare State: A Survey and Interpretation', *Journal of Economic Literature*, vol.30, pp.741-803.

Boyer, R. (ed.) (1988). *The Search for Labour Market Flexibility*. Oxford: Clarendon Press.

Bruno, M. and Sachs, J. (1985). *Economics of Worldwide Stagflation*. Cambridge, MA: Harvard University Press.

Buchanan, J. (1986). *Liberty, Market and State*. Brighton: Wheatsheaf Books Ltd.

Burton, J. (1983). *Picking Losers ... ?: The Political Economy of Industrial Policy*. London: Institute of Economic Affairs.

Chandler, A. (1990). *Scale and Scope*. Cambridge, MA: Belknap Press.

Chang, H.-J. (1993). 'The Political Economy of Industrial Policy in Korea', *Cambridge Journal of Economics*, vol.17, no.2, pp.131-57.

Chang, H.-J. (1994). *The Political Economy of Industrial Policy*. London and Basingstoke: Macmillan.

Chang, H.-J. (1995). 'Explaining "Flexible Rigidities" in East Asia', in T. Killick (ed.), *The Flexible Economy*. London: Routledge.

Coase, R. (1988). 'The Firm, the Market and the Law', in *The Firm, the Market and the Law*. Chicago: The University of Chicago Press.

Cohen, S. (1977). *Modern Capitalist Planning: The French Model*, 2nd edn. Berkeley, CA: University of California Press.

David, P. (1985). 'Clio and the Economics of QWERTY', *American Economic Review*, vol.75, pp.332-7.

Dore, R. (1986). *Flexible Rigidities: Industrial Policy and Structural Adjustment in the Japanese Economy 1970-80*. London: The Athlone Press.

Dosi, G., Freeman, C., Nelson, R., Silverberg, G. and Soete, L. (eds.) (1988). *Technical Change and Economic Theory*. London: Pinter Publishers.

Edquist, C. and Lundvall, B.-A. (1993). 'Comparing the Danish and Swedish Systems of Innovation', in R. Nelson (ed.), *National Innovation Systems.* New York: Oxford University Press.

ELTA, IFF, IUI and IØI (1987). *Growth Policies in Nordic Perspective.* Helsinki, Copenhagen, Stockholm and Bergen: ELTA, IFF, IUI and IØI.

Evans, P., Rueschemeyer, D. and Skocpol, T. (eds.) (1985). *Bringing the State Back In.* Cambridge: Cambridge University Press.

Gamble, A. (1987). *The Free Market and the Strong State.* London and Basingstoke: Macmillan.

Gerschenkron, A. (1966). 'Economic Backwardness in Historical Perspective', in *Economic Backwardness in Historical Perspective.* Cambridge, MA: Belknap Press.

Giersch, H. (1986). 'Liberalization for Faster Economic Growth', *IEA Occasional Paper*, no.74. London Institute of Economic Affairs.

Goldthorpe, J. (1984). *Order and Conflict in Contemporary Capitalism.* Oxford: Oxford University Press.

Hall, P. (1987). *Governing the Economy.* Cambridge: Polity Press.

Hall, P. (ed.) (1989). *The Political Power of Economic Ideas: Keynesianism across the Nations.* Princeton: Princeton University Press.

Hayek, F. (1949). *Individualism and Economic Order.* London: Routledge & Kegan Paul.

Hayek, F. (1988). *The Fatal Conceit.* London: Routledge.

Hirschman, A. (1958). *The Strategy of Economic Development.* New Haven: Yale University Press.

Hodgson, G. (1989). 'Institutional Rigidities and Economic Growth,' *Cambridge Journal of Economics*, 13, pp.79-101.

Jessop, B., Kaastendiek, H., Nielsen, K. and Pedersen, P. (eds.) (1991). *The Politics of Flexibility – Restructuring State and Industry in Britain, Germany and Scandinavia.* Aldershot: Edward Elgar.

Johnson, C. (1982). *MITI and the Japanese Miracle.* Stanford: Stanford University Press.

Johnson, C. (ed.)(1984). *The Industrial Policy Debate.* San Francisco: Institute of Contemporary Studies.

Katzenstein, P. (1985). *Small States in World Markets.* Ithaca and London: Cornell University Press.

Kirzner, I. (1973). *Capitalism and Entrepreneurship.* Chicago: University of Chicago.

Koike, K. (1987). 'Human Resource Development and Labour- Management Relations', in K. Yamamura and Y. Yasuba (eds.), *The Political Economy of Japan,* vol.1. Stanford: Stanford University Press.

Korpi, W. (1983). *The Democratic Class Struggle.* London: Routledge and Kegan Paul.

Kuznets, S. (1973). 'Innovations and Adjustment in Economic Growth', in *Population, Capital and Growth.* London: Heinemann.

Landesmann, M. (1992). 'Industrial Policies and Social Corporatism', in J. Pekkarinen, M. Pohjola and B. Rowthorn (eds.), *Social Corporatism*. Oxford: Clarendon Press.

Lazonick, W. (1991). *Business Organisation and the Myth of the Market Economy*. Cambridge: Cambridge University Press.

Lindberg, L. and Maier, C. (eds.) (1985). *The Politics of Inflation and Economic Stagnation*. Washington, D.C.: The Brookings Institute.

LO (LANDSORGANISATIONEN I SVERUGE) (1963). *Economic Expansion and Structural Change*. Edited and translated by T. Johnson. London: George Allen and Unwin.

Loasby, B. (1991). *Equilibrium and Evolution*. Manchester: Manchester University Press.

Lundberg, E. (1985). 'The Rise and Fall of the Swedish Model', *Journal of Economic Literature*, vol.23, pp.1-36.

Lundvall, B.-A. (ed.) (1992). *National Systems of Innovation: Towards a Theory of Innovation and Interactive Learning*. London: Pinter.

Maier, C. (1987). *In Search of Stability*. Cambridge: Cambridge University Press.

Marglin, S. and Schor, J. (eds.)(1990). *The Golden Age of Capitalism*. Oxford: Clarendon Press.

Matthews, R. (1986). 'The Economics of Institutions and the Source of Growth', *Economic Journal*, vol.96, pp.903-18.

Mises, L. (1929). *A Critique of Interventionism*. Translated by H.Sennholz (1977). New Rochele, New York: Arlington House.

Nelson, R. (ed.) (1993). *National Innovation Systems*. New York: Oxford University Press.

Nozick, R. (1974). *Anarchy, Utopia and the State*. Oxford: Basil Blackwell.

Okimoto, D. (1989). *Between MITI and the Market: Japanese Industrial Policy for High Technology*. Stanford: Stanford University Press.

Olson, M. (1982). *The Rise and Decline of Nations*. New Haven: Yale University Press.

Peacock, A. and Rowley, C. (1979). 'Pareto Optimality and the Political Economy of Liberalism', in A. Peacock (ed.), *The Economic Analysis of Government*. Oxford: Martin Robertson.

Pekkarinen, J. (1992). 'Corporatism and Economic Performance in Sweden, Norway, and Finland', in J. Pekkarinen, M. Pohjola and B. Rowthorn (eds.), *Social Corporatism*. Oxford: Clarendon Press.

Pekkarinen, J., Pohjola, M. and Rowthorn, B. (eds.) (1992). *Social Corporatism*. Oxford: Clarendon Press.

Piore, M. and Sabel, C. (1984). *The Second Industrial Divide*. New York: Basic Books.

Polanyi, K. (1957). *The Great Transformation*. Boston: Beacon Press.

Pontusson, J. (1987). 'Radicalism and Retreat in Swedish Social Democracy', *New Left Review*, Sept-Oct, pp.5-33.

Renshaw, J. (1986). *Adjustment and Economic Performance in Industralised Countries*. Geneva: ILO.

Rosenstein-Rodan, P. (1943). 'Problems of Industrialisation of Eastern and South-Eastern Europe', *Economic Journal*, vol.53, pp.202-11.

Rowthorn, R. (1971). 'Imperialism in the Seventies – Unity or Rivalry?', *New Left Review*, Sept-Oct, pp.31-54.

Rowthorn, R. (1977). 'Inflation and Crisis', *Marxism Today*, November.

Salmon, P. (1990). 'Scandinavia', in A. Graham and A. Seldon (eds.), *Government and Economies in the Postwar World – Economic Policies and Comparative Performance, 1945-85*. London: Routledge.

Schelling, T. (1960). *The Strategy of Conflict*. Cambridge, MA: Harvard University Press.

Schott, K. (1984). *Policy, Power and Order*. New Haven and London: Yale University Press.

Scitovsky, T. (1954). 'Two Concepts of External Economics', *Journal of Political Economy*, vol.62, pp.143-51.

Simon, H. (1991). 'Organisations and Markets', *Journal of Economic Perspectives*, vol.5, pp.25-44.

Skocpol, T. (1985). 'Bringing the State Back In', in P. Evans, D. Rueschemeyer and T. Skocpol (eds.), *Bringing the State Back In*. Cambridge: Cambridge University Press.

Stiglitz, J. (1992). 'Alternative Tactics and Strategies in Economic Development', in A.K. Dutt and K. Jameson (eds.), *New Directions in Development Economics*. Aldershot: Edward Elgar.

Thompson, G. (ed.) (1989). *Industrial Policy: USA and UK Debates*. London: Routledge.

Vartiainen, J. (1995). 'The State of Structural Change: What Can Be Learnt from the Successful Late Industralisers?', in H.-J. Chang and B. Rowthorn (eds.), *Role of the State in Economic Change*. Oxford: Oxford University Press.

Wade, R. (1990). *Governing the Market*. Princeton: Princeton University Press.

Williamson, O. (1985). *The Economic Institutions of Capitalism*. New York: The Free Press.

Zysman, J. (1983). *Governments, Markets and Growth*. Oxford: Martin Robertson.

Chapter 3

An Institutionalist Perspective on the Role of the State: Towards an Institutionalist Political Economy

1. INTRODUCTION

WHAT is the appropriate role of the state? This has been one question that has constantly occupied economists for the last two or three centuries since the birth of the subject (for some excellent historical reviews, see Deane 1989, and Shonfield 1965). During this period, there have been a number of swings in the dominant opinion on the subject, but the two major swings that have occurred during the last half-century after the Second World War are particularly remarkable in their scope and suddenness (Chang and Rowthorn 1995a, Spanish translation appears in Chang 1996).

The early postwar years witnessed the worldwide rejection of the *laissez-faire* doctrine that had failed so spectacularly during the interwar period, and the resulting emergence of a widespread consensus on state activism. By the 1960s, the end of *laissez-faire* capitalism was announced in many quarters and there was a widespread consensus that we were now living in the 'mixed economy'(alternatively, 'modern capitalism' or 'organised capitalism'). However, this new consensus has been dramatically overturned since the mid-1970s, following the neoliberal counter-offensive, which sought to end the mixed economy and reintroduce market principles to an extent that would have been unimaginable during the early postwar years.

The upsurge of neoliberalism during the last two decades or so has fundamentally changed the terms of debate on the role of the state (Chang 1994a: Chapters 1-2). The state is no more assumed to be an impartial, omnipotent social guardian and is now analysed either as a 'predator' or as a vehicle for politically powerful groups (including the politicians and the bureaucrats themselves) to advance their sectional interests. No other motives than maximisation of material self-interests are accorded to any agent even in the 'public' domains of life, denouncing the role of politics as a legitimate way to correct market outcomes according to the 'collective will'. The resulting 'minimalist' bias in the terms of debate means that those who want to make a case for state intervention have to fight their adversaries at each and every step of their arguments, whatever the merits of their arguments may be, whereas those who want to discredit state activism can often do so with a very simplistic logic supported by often unrepresentative anecdotes.

Although the neoliberal agenda itself has a lot of intellectual limitations and biases, as we will discuss in the rest of the chapter, the legacy of the neoliberal counter-offensive has not been entirely negative. For one thing, it exposed fundamental problems with the 'technocratic' view of the role of the state that prevailed in the heyday of welfare economics (1950s and 1960s) and brought politics back into economics (although it ultimately aimed to abolish politics – see Section 3.4). And more importantly, its explicit engagement in 'political economy' discussions opened the door for the subsequent rise of 'institutionalist' criticisms (e.g., Evans, Rueschemeyer and Skocpol (eds.) 1985; Hall (ed.) 1989; Toye 1991; Evans 1995; Chang and Rowthorn 1995b).[1] And following the institutionalist criticisms, even some proponents of neoliberal doctrine have recently come to admit (but without necessarily recognising the contributions of their critics) the importance of institutional factors in understanding the role of the state (North 1994; World Bank 1997).

However, having achieved that important, if unfairly unacknowledged, victory over the neoliberals, the institutionalists, I think it is fair to say, still lack a full-blown political economy that can replace the neoliberal political economy. In this chapter, I will make some suggestions as to what I think should be the building blocks of what may be called an institutionalist political economy. For this purpose,

---

1 A Spanish translation of Chang and Rowthorn (1995b) appears in Chang (1996).

I will dissect the neoliberal research agenda on the role of the state from an explicitly institutionalist perspective and identify what I think are the fundamental flaws in it, and in that process suggest what should be the elements in the institutionalist theory of state intervention that can overcome these flaws.

2.   DISENTANGLING THE NEOLIBERAL AGENDA

The messianic convictions with which many proponents of neoliberalism have delivered their messages have created the impression that it is a very coherent doctrine with clear conclusions. However, contrary to this popular belief, the neoliberal doctrine is in fact a very heterogeneous and internally inconsistent intellectual edifice. So before going into the detailed criticisms of this doctrine, it will be useful to delineate the basic fault lines in the neoliberal intellectual agenda and reveal some of its obvious weaknesses.

2.1   The Unholy Alliance: Neoclassicism and the Austrian-Libertarian Tradition

The biggest contradiction in the neoliberal research programme comes from the fact that it was born out of a marriage of convenience between neoclassical economics as the source of intellectual legitimacy (given its dominance in academia) and what may be broadly called the Austrian-Libertarian tradition as the source of political rhetoric. The gap between these two intellectual traditions is not a minor one, as those who are familiar with, for example, Hayek's scathing criticism of neoclassical economics would know (e.g., Hayek 1949). However, the marriage of convenience goes on, because the Austrian-Libertarian tradition supplies the popular appeal that neo-classical economics can never dream of supplying itself (who are going to risk their lives for 'Pareto optimality'? – but many have been willing to for 'liberty' and 'entrepreneurship'), while the Austrian-Libertarian tradition, given its lack of intellectual legitimacy in 'respectable' circles, needs the aura of 'science' that neoclassical economics carries around.[2]

But in return for the increased power of persuasion that it acquired by allying with the Austrian-Libertarian tradition, neoclassical economics had to pay a heavy price. In order to maintain the alliance, it has had to suppress its interventionist streak, given the strong anti-statism of the latter. So how is this done?

One such method of suppression is to accept the logic of 'market failure' behind welfare economics but then not to extend it beyond the set of 'politically acceptable' areas. So, for example, the externality argument is often applied to politically less controversial areas such as the environment or education, but is rarely applied to such politically more controversial areas as 'selective' industrial policy à la East Asia, which can be justified by the same logic equally well. Given that there is no theoretical way in neoclassical economics to determine what is the 'correct' boundary for state intervention, it becomes necessary to argue that market failures exist as logical possibilities, but rarely occur in reality – naturally without providing much evidence (Friedman 1962 is a good example).[3]

The second method of suppressing the interventionist instinct of neoclassical economics is to separate, partly deliberately and partly subconsciously, the 'serious' academic discourse from the 'popular' policy discourse and compartmentalise them. So neoclassical econo-

---

2   This point is best illustrated by the experiences during the early days of reform in the former Communist countries. What captured people's imagination in those days was the Austrian-Libertarian languages of freedom and entrepreneurship,. and not the arid neoclassical languages of Pareto optimality and general equilibrium. However, when the post-Communist governments in these countries chose their foreign economic advisers, it was largely according to how high a standing they had in the Western academic 'hierarchy', which was determined by how good they were in handling the concepts and tools of neoclassical economics.

3   Friedman's list of legitimate functions of the state is as follows: maintenance of law and order; definition of property rights; service as a means whereby people modify property rights and other rules of the economic game; adjudication of disputes about the interpretation of the rules; enforcement of contracts; promotion of competition; provision of a monetary framework; engagement in activities to counter technical monopolies and to overcome 'neighbourhood effects' (his term for externality) widely regarded as sufficiently important to justify government intervention; supplementation of private charity and the private family in protecting the irresponsible, whether madman or child (Friedman 1962: p.34).

mists in universities may be doing research justifying stringent anti-trust policy, but the 'lax' anti-trust policy of government may be justified in terms of some other logic which has no place in neoclassical economics – say, by citing the need 'not to discourage entrepreneur-ship', etc. The recent 'reform' experiences in the former Communist countries mentioned above are the most poignant example of such practice.

The last method of suppression is to accept fully the logic of market failure and build models that may have strong interventionist conclusions, but later dismiss them on the ground that 'real life' states cannot possibly be entrusted with such policies that are technically difficult (due to informational asymmetry) and politically dangerous (due to the possibility of bureaucratic abuse and/or interest group capture). Various writings by the American trade economist Krugman provide the best example, where frequently a few paragraphs of 'pop political economy' analysis dismissing the integrity of the state at the end of an article would be used to discredit his own elaborate 'strategic trade theory' model endorsing state intervention that went on in the rest of the article.[4] To put it bluntly, the name of the game is that a neoclassical economist may build a model that recommends state intervention as far as it is 'technically competent', but he/she has to prove his/her political credentials by rubbishing his/her own model on political grounds.

2.2   The Indeterminacy of the Neoclassical Position on State Intervention

Even when we ignore the above-mentioned tension between the neoclassical element and the Austrian-Libertarian element in the neoliberal intellectual edifice, there are still disagreements amongst the neoclassical economists themselves on exactly what the role of the state should be, as we implicitly suggested above.

---

4   A well-known neoliberal economist, Robert Lucas, reviewing Krugman's book with Helpman, asked why they had written the book in the first place if they were going to say in the end that the interventionist policies that follow from their models cannot be recommended because of the political dangers that they carry. See Lucas (1990).

As I indicated above, neoclassical economics has a strong interventionist streak that is best manifested in welfare economics. Especially, as Baumol (1965) and others have pointed out, once we begin to follow the logic of externality faithfully, it seems doubtful whether we should have any market transaction at all. Most goods create some negative externalities in their production processes in the form of pollution, except in those few cases where proper compensation is actually made. When considering 'linkage effects' (Hirschman 1958, Chapter 6) or 'pecuniary externalities' (Scitovsky 1954), many goods may additionally be classified as having positive externalities. Some economists even argue that some goods which have conventionally been treated as lacking externalities, say basic foodstuffs, can be seen as creating externalities when they are not consumed in the proper amount and therefore induce crime (Schotter 1985: pp.68-80). Moreover, there exist interdependencies between individual preferences. For example, people have what Elster (1983: Chapter 2) calls counter-adaptive preferences – 'the grass is always greener on the other side of the fence'. The psychology of luxury goods consumption – part of one's pleasure derives from the very fact that one consumes what others do not – is another example of interdependent consumer preference.

The list can go on, but the point here is that, even using a purely neoclassical logic, one can justify an enormous range of state intervention. Indeed, in the 1920s and 1930s people like Oskar Lange were trying to justify socialist planning on the basis of essentially neoclassical models (Lavoie 1985; Pagano 1985). Thus seen, whether a neoclassical economist is an interventionist or not depends more on his/her political preference rather than the 'hard' economics that he/she practises. Therefore, it is important to reject the myth propagated by neoclassical economists that the boundary between 'good' and 'bad' interventions can be drawn according to some 'scientific' rules.

2.3 Concluding Remarks

Neoliberalism is based on an unholy alliance between neoclassical economics, which provides the intellectual legitimacy, and the Austrian-Libertarian tradition, which provides the political rhetoric. This, in turn, means that the interventionist streak of neoclassical economics has to be suppressed. Such suppression involves, we pointed out, intellectually and morally indefensible practices like drawing an 'arbitrary' boundary around the state without acknowledging its arbitrariness, using different discourses for 'serious' academic research and for 'popular' policy discussion (again without acknowledging such compartmentalisation), and denouncing the interventionist conclusions of formal models with unsubstantiated 'pop' political economy. We then argued that even neoclassical economics itself does not provide us with any unambiguous 'scientific' criterion to draw the boundary between 'good' and 'bad' interventions. Thus seen, despite its pretence of intellectual coherence and clear-cut messages, neoliberalism is an internally heterogeneous and inconsistent intellectual doctrine with confused and confusing messages.

3.   SOME INSTITUTIONALIST CRITICISMS OF THE FOUNDATIONS OF THE NEOLIBERAL ANALYSIS OF MARKET, STATE, AND POLITICS

Having pointed out the fundamental fractures in the very set-up of the neoliberal doctrine, let us now make some detailed criticisms of it from an institutionalist perspective, questioning the very way it envisages the market, the state, and other institutions, as well as the relations between them.

3.1   What is a Free Market?: Defining and Measuring State Intervention

3.1.1 Defining State Intervention

The neoliberal discourse on the state is basically about whether 'free' markets produce socially optimal results, which it thinks is the case most of the time, and whether therefore state intervention may be able to improve the free market outcomes, which it thinks is rarely the case. Whether or not we agree with the conclusion, the discourse seems straightforward enough, but is it?

This question may look stupid. Surely we know that a 'free' market is a market without state intervention? Of course, the argument may go, we may have disagreements on which is a 'good' state intervention and which is a 'bad' one, but surely we all know what state intervention means? I am not actually sure that we do. The trouble is that the same state action can be, and has been, considered an 'intervention' in one society but is not in another (which could be the same society at a different point of time). Why is this? Let me answer this question with a few examples.

First, let us take the case of child labour. Few people in the OECD countries at present would consider the ban on child labour as a state intervention 'artificially' restricting entry into the labour market, whereas many Third World capitalists (and indeed the capitalists in the now-OECD economies in the late-19th and the early-20th centuries) regard it as just that. In developed countries, the rights of the children not to toil but to be educated are totally accepted, and have been incorporated into the structure of (property and other) rights and obligations underlying the labour market (as the right to self-owner-ship has been, since the abolition of slavery); they are *not* a matter of policy debate (i.e., there is no debate on whether the ban on child labour is 'efficient' in some sense). In contrast, in the developing countries (of today and yesterday), such rights of children are not so totally accepted, and therefore state action regarding child labour is consid-ered an 'intervention', whose impact on 'efficiency' is still a legitimate subject of policy debate.

To give another example, many environmental standards (e.g., automobile emission standards), which were widely criticised as unwarranted intrusions on business and personal freedom when they were first introduced in the OECD countries not so long ago, are these days rarely regarded as 'interventions'. Therefore there would be few people in the OECD countries who would say that their country's automobile market is not a 'free' market because of these regulations. In contrast, some developing country exporters who do not accept such stringent environmental standards as 'legitimate' may consider them as 'invisible trade barriers' that 'distort' the market.

In yet another example, many neoclassical economists who criticise minimum wages and 'excessively' high labour standards in the advanced countries as unwarranted state interventions that 'artifi-cially' set up entry barriers into the labour market, do not even regard the heavy restrictions on immigration that exist in these countries as a state intervention (not to speak of supporting them), although immigration controls set up an 'artificial' entry barrier into the labour market as much as the above-mentioned 'interventions' do. This contradictory attitude is possible only because these economists believe in the right of the existing citizens of a country to dictate the terms of the non-citizens' participation in 'their' labour market, without explicitly stating their 'political' position on this matter.

The examples can go on, but the point is that, depending on which rights and obligations are regarded as 'legitimate' by the members of the society, the same action could be considered an 'intervention' in one society and not in another. And once something is not even considered to be an 'intervention' in a particular society at a given time (e.g., the ban on child labour or slavery in the OECD countries), debating their 'efficiency' becomes politically unacceptable – although there is no God-given reason why this should be the case. The corollary is that, depending on the rights-obligations structure, the same market with the same state 'intervention' in the same area – for example, regarding child labour – can be seen as 'free' (from state intervention) in one society and not in another.

So, therefore, if we want to decide whether a particular market is 'free' or not, we need to understand the underlying institutions which define the rights-obligations structure for the participants in the relevant market (and indeed certain non-participants, when it involves 'externalities'). The institutions that need to be understood in this context will include, among other things: (i) the formal and informal rules that govern the way in which interests are organised and exercised (e.g., rules on political associations, rules on incorporation, rules on lobbying); (ii) the formal and informal 'ideologies' relating to notions such as 'fairness' and 'natural rights' that prevail in the society (e.g., rights of everyone to self-ownership, rights of children to education); (iii) the formal and informal institutions that determine how the rights-obligations structure could be changed (e.g., procedures for legal changes, social customs about when and how some *de facto* rights/obligations can become 'legitimate', if not necessarily legalised).

Thus, the apparently simple exercise of defining what is a 'free' market (and what constitutes 'state intervention') is not so obvious anymore – and this is, to repeat, even before we can discuss whether some markets are 'failing' and therefore state intervention may make them 'more efficient'. From the institutionalist perspective, we may even say that defining a free market is at the deepest level a pointless exercise, because no market is in the end 'free', as all markets have some state regulations on who can participate in which markets and on what terms. It is only because some regulations (and the rights and the obligations that they are creating) can be so totally accepted (by those who are making the observation as well as by the participants in the market) that some markets appear to have no 'intervention' and therefore be 'free'.

3.1.2 How Do We Measure State Intervention and Why Does It Matter?

For the purpose of international and historical comparison, people have used some quantitative measures of state intervention. At one level, this seems a straightforward exercise. However, how good a measure of state intervention is depends on the theory (of state intervention) that underpins it. Therefore, we need to look beyond the 'numbers' that are supposed to measure the extent of state intervention and analyse the theories that lie behind those numbers. Let us explain what we mean by this.

Traditionally, the most popular measures of the degree of state intervention have been the total government budget as a ratio of GDP and the share of the public enterprise (PE) sector in GDP (or total investment). It may be true that these measures give us a good idea of how 'big' the state sector is but it is not true that they are good indicators of the degree of state intervention. This is because a 'big' government is not necessarily a more 'interventionist' government. The point is very well illustrated by the East Asian countries of Japan, Korea, and Taiwan.

On the basis of these traditional measures, until recently many people believed that we could 'objectively' establish that the East Asian countries are 'non-interventionist' (e.g., World Bank 1991: p.40, Table 2.2). And except for the (conveniently ignored) fact that Taiwan has one of the largest PE sectors in the non-socialist, non-oil-producing world, this observation does not seem to be too far from the truth – that is, as far as we accept that the 'vision' of the role of the state that lies behind these measures correctly reflects the actual role of state intervention in these countries.[5] However, the mode of state intervention in East Asia has been quite different from what is envisaged in the 'vision' that lies behind these traditional measures, and thus they 'wrongly' measure the extent of state intervention in East Asia.

In the 'traditional' vision, the state exercises its control basically through the ownership of the means of production, which is (wrongly) equated with the control over their use, and the reallocation of resources via taxes and subsidies, for example, in the manner prescribed in welfare economics. However, state intervention in East Asia has been conducted less through state ownership and budgetary outlays, but more through measures which need little state ownership or budgetary outlays. They include: (i) regulatory measures (on entry, capacity, price, technology, etc.); (ii) the state's influence on bank lending decisions (especially in Korea and Taiwan, the majority of the

---

5   The ratio of government expenditure to GDP for Japan in 1985 was 33%, far lower than those in other industrial nations except the US (37%). Corresponding figures include 47% for Germany, 48% for the UK, 52% for France, and 65% for Sweden (World Bank 1991: p.139, Table 7.4). In the case of Korea, the ratio of central government expenditure to GNP in 1989 was 16.9%, a figure substantially lower than those for other semi-industrialised countries. Corresponding figures were 21.2% for Mexico, 30.6% for Brazil, 32.5% for Chile, and 33% for South Africa (World Bank 1991: pp. 224-5, Table 11). Comparable data for Taiwan is not readily available. As of the mid-1970s (1974-77), the share of public enterprise output in GDP in Korea was around 6.4% and that in Taiwan around 13.6%. The average for developing countries was 8.6%. Korea, then, was somewhat less interventionist than the average on this account (but higher than Pakistan (6.0%), the Philippines (1.7%), Argentina (4.8%), which are all regarded to be cases of failed state intervention), and Taiwan substantially above-average interventionist. The corresponding figure for Japan is not available, but on the basis of the share of the public enterprise sector in gross fixed capital formation, Japan (11.6%) as of the mid-1970s was of about average interventionism amongst industrialised countries – the average being 11.1 % (see Short 1984: Table 1). A more recent estimate by the World Bank puts the share of the public enterprise sector in GDP for the 1978-91 period at 6.9% for Taiwan and at 10.6% for Korea, when the unweighted average of the corresponding figures for 40 developing countries in the sample was 10.9% (World Bank 1995: Table A.1). However, in the light of other qualitative evidence, the World Bank figures seem to underestimate grossly the importance of public enterprises in Taiwan. In my view, this may be due to the fact that there are many 'public' enterprises that are owned by the ruling Kuomintang Party which may be officially classified as 'private' enterprises. Unfortunately, I have not been able to acquire any systematic data on this.

banks have been state-owned); and (iii) various 'informal' channels of influence on the business sector (a manifestation of what Evans describes as the 'embeddedness' of these states; see Evans 1995).

The example does not, in fact, stop in East Asia. For example, some commentators point out that the US federal state, despite its *laissez-faire* rhetoric, has strongly influenced the country's industrial evolution through defence procurement programmes and defence-related R&D contracts – especially in industries like computers, telecommunication, and aviation (Johnson 1982).[6] So, again, the prevailing vision of the role of the state, where 'defence' is accepted as one of the 'minimum' functions of the state (almost shading into 'non-intervention'), makes people underestimate the importance of the US federal government in the country's industrial development.

The point that we are trying to illustrate with the above examples is that how we measure state intervention matters, because the particular measures that we use embody a particular vision of the role of the state which may not be universally applicable because the institutional assumptions behind that vision may not hold in contexts other than the one from which that vision emerged. Unless we recognise that different measures of state intervention are based on different theories of the role of the state, which embody different assumptions about the institutions and political economy of state intervention, our empirical investigation of the role of the state will be constrained by the limitations of the theoretical perspective that lies behind the 'measures' of intervention that we use.

3.2   What Does Market Failure Mean and How Much Does It Matter?: Rival Views of Market Society

3.2.1 When Does the Market Fail?

The term 'market failure' refers to a situation when the market does not work in the way expected of the 'ideal' market. But what is

---

6   The most recent and striking example of this comes from the aviation industry. The repeated rejections by the US federal government of applications from McDonnell Douglas for a number of critical defence projects have damaged the latter's profits so badly that it had to merge with its major rival, Boeing, changing the fate of the country's, and indeed the world's, civil aviation industry.

the ideal market supposed to do? Given the current domination of neoclassical economics, the ideal market is usually equated with the 'perfectly competitive market' in neoclassical economics. However, the neoclassical theory of the market is only one of the many legitimate theories of how the market works (and therefore what we can expect from the ideal market and therefore when we can say a market has 'failed') – and not a particularly good one at that. In other words, there are, to borrow Hirschman's phrase, many different 'rival views of market society' (Hirschman 1982a). Therefore, the same market could be seen as 'failing' by some people while others regard it as 'normal' or even 'succeeding', depending on their respective theories of the market. Let us illustrate this point with some examples:

1.   Many people think that one of the biggest 'failures' of the market is to generate 'unacceptable' levels of inequality (whatever the criteria for 'acceptability' may be). However, in neoclassical economics, this is not a market 'failure', because the 'ideal' neoclassical market is not assumed to generate equitable income distribution in the first place. This is not to deny that many well-intentioned neoclassical economists may dislike the income distribution prevailing in, say, Brazil, and may support some 'non-distortionary' lump-sum income transfers, but to point out that even they would argue that an equitable income distribution is simply not something that the market should be expected to generate and therefore the issue is beyond economic 'science'.

2.   A 'non-competitive' market is one of the most obvious examples of a 'failing' market for neoclassical economics, while the Schumpeterian theory (and before it the Marxist theory) argues that the existence of 'non-competitive' (in the neoclassical sense) markets is an inevitable, if secondary,[7] feature of a dynamic economy driven by technological innovation. Thus, a classic example of market failure in the neoclassical framework,

---

7   Recall Schumpeter's famous metaphor that the relationship between the efficiency gains from competition through innovation and that from (neoclassical) price competition was 'as a bombardment is in comparison with forcing a door' (Schumpeter 1987: p.84).

namely, the non-competitive market, is regarded as an inevitable feature of a 'successful' dynamic economy, according to the Schumpeterian perspective.[8] Or to put it differently, a market which is 'perfect' in the neoclassical sense (e.g., no participant in the market has any market power) may look like an absolute 'failure' to a Schumpeterian because it lacks technological dynamism.

The point that we have just tried to illustrate with our examples is that, when we talk about 'market failures', we need to make it clear what we think the 'ideal' market is capable of doing. Otherwise, the concept of market failure can become so elastic that it means a hundred different things to a hundred different people. Thus, where one person sees 'perfection', another person can see a miserable 'failure' of the market, and vice versa (the above example about monopoly illustrates this point very well). Only when we make our 'theory of the market' clear, can we make what we mean by 'market failure' clear.

3.2.2 How Much Does Market Failure Matter?

Now, how much does 'market failure' matter, however we may define it? The short answer is that it would matter greatly for the neoclassical economists, while it may not matter so much for other people, especially the institutionalist economists. Neoclassical economics is an economics about the market or more precisely not even that – it is really about the barter exchange economy, where there are, to borrow Coase's analogy, 'lone individuals exchanging nuts and berries on the edge of the forest' (Coase 1992: p.718). In neoclassical theory, even the firm exists only as a 'production function', and not as an 'institution of production'. Other forms of institutions that make up the modern capitalist economy (e.g., formal producer associations, informal 'networks', trade unions) figure, if they do, only as 'rigidities' that prevent the proper functioning of markets (for a criticism of the view of non-market institutions as 'rigidities', see Chang 1995, whose Spanish translation appears in Chang 1996).

---

8 This, needless to say, does not exclude the possibility (which is often realised) that an economy may be full of monopolies but undynamic.

Therefore, for the neoclassical economists, for whom 'the market' is essentially 'the economy', if the market fails, the economy fails. And if the economy fails, the state has to step in, as no intermediate institutions or organisations have a legitimate place in their scheme. In contrast, for the institutionalist economists, who regard the market as only one of the many institutional mechanisms that make up the capitalist economic system, market failures may not matter as much, because they know that there are many institutional mechanisms other than markets through which we can organise, and have organised, our economic activities. In other words, when most economic interactions in the modern industrial economy are actually conducted within organisations, and not between them through the market (Simon 1991), the fact that some (or even many) markets are 'failing' according to one (that is, neoclassical) of many possible criteria may not really make a big difference for the performance of the capitalist system as a whole.

For example, in many modern industries where there are high incidences of monopoly and oligopoly, the market is 'failing' all the time according to the neoclassical criterion, but at the same time these industries were often very 'successful' in the Schumpeterian sense in that they generated high productivity growth and consequently high standards of living. Such an outcome was due to the 'success' of modern business organisations which enabled the coordination of a most complex division of labour – so, where neoclassical economists see a 'market failure', other economists may see an 'organisational success' (Lazonick 1991). And if this is indeed the case, state intervention in these markets, especially of the neoclassical anti-trust variety, may not be very necessary, and indeed under some circumstances may actually harm the economy.

The point is not that market failures do not exist or that they do not matter at all – on the contrary, the real world is full of market failures even by neoclassical standards (see Section 2.2) and they do matter. The real point is that the market is only one of the many institutions that make up what people call 'the market economy', or what we think is better called 'capitalism'. The capitalist system is made up of a range of institutions, including markets as institutions of exchange, firms as institutions of production, and the state as the creator and regulator of the institutions governing their relationships.

Thus, focusing on the market (and market failure), as neoclassical economics does, really gives us a wrong perspective in the sense that we lose sight of a large chunk of the economic system and concentrate on one part only.[9]

3.3 'In the Beginning, There Were Markets': The Market Primacy Assumption

One thing that distinguishes even the most enlightened and open-minded neoclassical economists from the truly institutionally-conscious economists is their belief in what I call the market primacy assumption. In their view, 'in the beginning, there were the markets' (Williamson 1975: p. 20),[10] and state intervention, organisations, and other institutions are seen as man-made substitutes which emerged only after the defects in the market ('market failure') became unbearable (Arrow 1974 is the most sophisticated example of this view).

The most obvious example of this market primacy assumption is the contractarian 'explanation' of the origin of the state. In this view, the state has emerged as a solution to the 'collective action problem' of providing the 'public good' of law and order (especially the security of property), which is seen as necessary (and often sufficient) for markets to function at all (Nozick 1974; Buchanan 1986). Thus, in this view, even the very existence of the state is explained according to the logic of 'market failure' in the sense that it is seen as having emerged only after the market has failed to provide law and order due to the 'public goods' problem – an explanation which is obviously contrary to historical truth and therefore can only be seen as an 'ideological'

---

9   More recently, the neoclassical economists have started to discuss the workings of non-market institutions, especially the firm (transaction cost economics, e.g., Williamson 1975) and the state (the 'government failure' literature, e.g., Krueger 1990). However, these analyses have important shortcomings as these institutions are analysed as 'quasi-markets' ultimately based on voluntary contracting (see Vira 1998).

10 Williamson defends this starting assumption on the ground of 'expositional convenience', arguing that the logic of his analysis would be the same even if the starting assumption was that 'in the beginning, there was central planning' (pp.20-1). However as we shall see below, this apparently innocuous assumption has a lot of important theoretical ramifications and policy implications.

defence of an 'unjust' system (for a criticism, see Chang 1994a: Chapter 1).

At this point, we must emphasise that the fact that someone attributes institutional primacy to the market does not necessarily mean that he/she endorses a minimal state view, as the problem here is not really about where the right 'boundary' between the state and the market should lie. There are many who start (at least implicitly) from the market supremacy assumption but are keenly aware of the failings of the market and willingly endorse a relatively wide range of interventions. Indeed, as we pointed out earlier (Section 2.2), if these open-minded neoclassical economists began to take their own logic to the limit, they could end up endorsing all kinds of state intervention.[11] However, they would still see state intervention, or for that matter any other solution based on non-market institutions (e.g., hierarchical organisations like firms), as 'man-made' substitutes for the 'natural' institution called the market.

The point is that, in the beginning, there were no markets. Economic historians have repeatedly shown us that, except at the very local level (in supplying basic necessities) or at a very international level (in luxury trade), the market mechanism was not an important part of human economic life until recently. In fact, although even Joseph Stiglitz, one of the most enlightened neoclassical economists of our generation, says that 'markets develop naturally' (Stigiltz 1992: p.75), the emergence of markets was almost always deliberately engineered by the state, especially in the early stage of capitalist development. Karl Polanyi's classic work shows how even in the UK, where the market economy is supposed to have emerged 'spontaneously', state intervention played a critical role in the process. He argues that:

'[t]he road to the free market was opened and kept open by an enormous increase *in continuous, centrally organised and controlled interventionism* (italics added). To make Adam Smith's "simple and

---

11 Lange's defence of socialist planning may be an extreme example, but Schotter's argument for state provision of basic goods (on the ground that an inadequate amount of consumption of such goods can create 'externality' in the form of crime), which we cited earlier, is a less extreme example of how the logic can be carried much beyond where most neoclassical economists are currently willing to take it.

natural liberty" compatible with the needs of human society was a most complicated affair. Witness the complexity of the provisions in the innumerable enclosure laws; the amount of bureaucratic control involved in the administration of the New Poor Laws which for the first time since Queen Elizabeth's reign were effectively supervised by central authority; or the increase in governmental administration entailed in the meritorious task of municipal reform....' (Polanyi 1957: p.140).[12]

Also in the case of the US, the early interventions by the state in establishing property rights, providing critical physical infrastructure (especially railways and telegraphy), the funding of agricultural research, and so on, were critical for its success in early industrialisation (Kozul-Wright 1995; even the World Bank now recognises this – see World Bank 1997: p.21, Table 1.2). Most importantly, the US was the home of the idea of infant industry protection (Freeman 1989), and was indeed the most heavily protected economy among the industrial countries for around a century until the Second World War (see World Bank 1991: p.97, Table 5.2; Kozul-Wright 1995: p.97, Table 4.8).[13]

Moving beyond the UK and the US, we realise that there is virtually no country, except Hong Kong, which achieved the status of an industrialised country without at least some periods of heavy state involvement in the development effort. The exact forms of intervention varied – the 'pre-emptive' welfare state in Bismarckian Germany, postwar French industrial policy, early Swedish state support of research and development, the transformation of the Austrian manu-

---

12 And he continues: 'Administrators had to be constantly on the watch to ensure the free working of the system. Thus even those who wished most ardently to free the state from all unnecessary duties, and whose whole philosophy demanded the restriction of state activities, could not but entrust the self-same state with the new powers, organs, and instrument required for the establishment of *laissez-faire*' (p.140).

13 During this period few countries had tariff autonomy either because of outright colonial rule or because of 'unequal treaties' – for example, Japan got tariff autonomy only in 1911 when all its unequal treaties expired. Of the countries with tariff autonomy, the US had by far the highest tariff rates. Its average tariffs since the 1820s were never below 25%, and usually around 40%, when those in other countries for which the data are available, such as Austria, Belgium, France, Italy, and Sweden, were rarely over 20%. For detailed figures, see World Bank 1991: p.97, Table 5.2.

facturing sector since the Second World War through the public enterprise sector, the well-known state-led development of the East Asian countries – but the fact remains that all successful development efforts involved substantial state intervention. So if virtually all now-advanced countries, with the possible exceptions of Britain at certain phases and Hong Kong, developed in some 'unnatural' way which involved heavy state intervention, it seems questionable whether there is any point in calling the market a 'natural' phenomenon.

What we have just discussed is not simply of historical interest. Whether or not we accord primacy to the market institution makes a critical difference to the way we design development policies. For example, many former Communist countries which opted for a 'big bang' reform have experienced severe economic crises during the last several years; this is one striking example which shows how the establishment of a well-functioning market economy is impossible without a well-functioning state (see Chang and Nolan 1995, whose Spanish translation appears as Chang and Nolan 1996). In fact, if markets evolve so 'naturally' as the neoclassical economists believe, these countries would not be in such trouble now. Likewise, the developmental crises that many developing countries have gone through during the last two decades or so also show how dangerous it is to assume the primacy of market institutions and believe that a market will naturally develop as long as the state does not 'interfere' with its evolution. The assumption of market primacy has a lot more serious implications than are first apparent.

3.4   Can We Rid the Market of Politics?: The Disguised Revival of the Old Liberal Politics

One major assumption behind neoliberal doctrine is the belief that politics allows 'sectional' interests to 'distort' the 'rationality' of the market system and therefore this is something that has to be purged from the market. Criticising the naivety of welfare economics which assumed the state to be the all-knowing, all-powerful social guardian, the 'new political economy' of neoliberalism tried to demonstrate how politics is an inevitably corrupting force on the economy. The neoliberal political economists have argued that we need therefore to 'de-politicise' the economy by restricting the scope of the state and by reducing the room for policy discretion in those few areas where it is allowed to operate, for example, by strengthening the rules on bureaucratic conduct and by setting up 'politically independent' agencies bound by rigid rules (e.g., independent central banks, independent regulatory agencies).

There have been many powerful criticisms of neoliberal political economy, and we do not feel that this is a place to go into the details (e.g., see, in chronological order, Toye 1987; King 1987; Gamble 1988; Toye 1991; Chang 1994a; Evans 1995; Chang and Rowthorn, 1995a and 1995b, both of whose translations appear in Chang 1996). However, we want to point out some basic issues in order to highlight some fundamental problems in the neoliberal (and indeed old liberal) view of politics.

3.4.1 All Prices are 'Political'

First of all, the establishment and distribution of property rights and other entitlements that define the 'endowments' that neoclassical economics take as given is a highly political exercise. The most extreme example will be the various stories of 'original accumulation' such as the Great Plunder or the Enclosure in the early days of British capitalism or the 'shady' deals that dominate the privatisation process in many ex-Communist countries these days; however, the continuous political campaigns that established environmental and consumer rights as legitimate rights at least in the OECD countries are less dramatic but perhaps equally important examples.

Moreover, there are practically no prices in reality which do not have some 'political' element in them. To begin with, two critical 'prices' which affect almost every sector, namely, wages and interest rates, are politically determined to a very large degree. Wages are affected not only by minimum wage legislation, but also by various regulations regarding labour standards, welfare entitlements, and most importantly immigration control. Interest rates are also highly political prices, despite the guise of 'de-politicisation' that those who support central bank independence want to give to the process of interest rates determination. The recent debate in Europe on the relationship between political sovereignty and autonomy in monetary policy, which was prompted by the approaching European Monetary

Union, shows this very clearly. When we add to them those numerous regulations in the product markets regarding safety, pollution, import content, and so on, there is virtually no price which is 'free from politics'.[14]

Of course, all these are not to deny that a certain degree of de-politicisation of the resource allocation process may be necessary. For one thing, unless the resource allocation outcome is at least to a degree accepted as 'objective', the political legitimacy of the market-based system itself may be threatened. Moreover, an enormous amount of 'transaction costs' would be incurred on search and bargaining activities if every decision on allocation was regarded as negotiable, as it was in the case of the ex-Communist countries. However, this is not to say that no price under any circumstances should be subject to political negotiations, because in the final analysis, there is no price which is really free from politics.

3.4.2 De-politicisation: The Disguised Revival of Old Liberal Politics

If what appear to be 'objective' outcomes of 'impersonal' markets are in the end the results of certain (explicit and implicit) 'political' decisions about property rights, entitlements and prices, the neoliberal proposal for 'de-politicisation' of the economic policy-making process as a means to restore 'economic rationality' also cannot be taken at its face value.

One basic problem with the neoliberal proposal for de-politicisation is that the 'rationality' that such an exercise wants to 'rescue' from the corrupting influences of politics can only be mean-ingfully defined with reference to the existing institutional structure, which is itself a product of politics (see Vira 1998, for a further

---

14 We were reminded of this clearly in the British coal crisis in the early-1990s, in which the British coalminers were told to accept the logic of the 'world market' and face mine closures with grace. However, the world market prices, which the then British government argued to be beyond political negotiation, turned out to be determined by the 'political' decisions of the German government to give subsidies to their coal, of the French government to allow the export of their subsidised nuclear electricity, and of the many developing country governments to allow, at least *de facto*, child labour in their coal mines.

exposition of this point). So when the basic institutional parameters of the economy have been, and can only be, set through an 'irrational' political process, a call for de-politicisation of the economic process on 'rationality' grounds rings hollow.

Another problem with the neoliberal proposal for de-politicisation is that its politics is not what it pretends to be. The call for de-politicisation is often justified in populist rhetoric as an attempt to defend the 'silent majority' from greedy politicians and powerful interest groups. However, the diminution of the legitimate domain of politics that de-politicisation will bring only serves to further diminish what little political influence these underprivileged people have in modifying the market outcomes, which, we repeat, are heavily influenced by politically-determined institutional parameters. Thus seen, the neoliberal call for the de-politicisation of the economy aims to revive the old liberal politics in a disguised form (Bobbio 1990 provides an excellent anatomy of the old liberal politics). Like the neoliberals, the old liberals believed that allowing political power to those who 'do not have a stake' in the existing institutional arrangements would inevitably result in the modification either of such arrangements or of their outcomes mediated through the market. However, unlike the old liberals, who could openly oppose democracy, the neoliberals cannot do that, so they try to do it by arguing against 'politics' in general and making proposals which ostensibly seek to reduce the influence of those 'untrustworthy politicians' but ultimately aim to diminish democratic control itself (e.g., proposals for 'independent' central banks or regulatory agencies).

The last, but not least, problem with the call for de-politicisation is that it may not be a politically feasible recommendation. For good or bad reasons, all countries have accumulated politically organised groups and have developed certain (at least implicitly accepted) ways to modify 'politically' certain market outcomes.[15] Some of these, of course, could be easily eliminated, but others may be so entrenched that they may be eliminated only at very high political and economic costs. Hence the apparent paradox that radical economic liberalisation

---

15 We should also note that political activities are often ends in themselves and people may derive value from the activities *per se* as well as from the products of such activities (see Hirschman 1982b: pp.85-6).

frequently requires harsh authoritarian politics, in order to achieve the high degree of de-politicisation that is required for such policy, as graphically exemplified by the liberalisation attempt by the Pinochet regime in Chile (also see Gamble 1988). But the truth is that, however harsh the political regime which may have been pursued, de-politicisation has never been, nor can be, complete in practice, and may even backfire.

4.   CONCLUSION: TOWARDS AN INSTITUTIONALIST POLITICAL ECONOMY

After pointing out some internal fault lines and indeterminacy in the neoliberal intellectual agenda, we critically examined some of its basic concepts and assumptions from the institutionalist point of view. As we have repeatedly emphasised, the real point of our criticism is not that neoclassical theory is too little (or for that matter too much) interventionist. As we have pointed out repeatedly, a full-blooded neoclassical economist can legitimately endorse anything from a minimal state to socialist planning, depending on his/her assumptions about technological conditions (and implicitly property rights). What we are really trying to argue is that the way in which the relations between the state and the market (and other institutions on those rare occasions when they feature) are envisaged in neoclassical economics prevents an adequate understanding of some fundamental issues surrounding the role of the state. We propose that an approach which may be called 'institutionalist political economy' should be the way forward, and suggest some elements of this theory.[16]

Our starting point should be to reject the assumption of market primacy that underlies neoclassical economics. As we pointed out earlier, neoclassical economics sees the market as a 'natural' institution (if it is ever acknowledged that it is an institution) which spontaneously emerges, but sees other institutional arrangements, be they state institutions or firms (or 'hierarchies'), as emerging only when the market 'fails'. However, saying that the market emerged as a result of

---

16 I have attempted to develop this theory in a number of my previous works. See Chang (1994b, 1995), Chang and Rowthorn (1995b), and Chang (1997).

the failure of 'planning' (not necessarily by the state, but also by other organisations) or 'hierarchy' is probably closer to the historical truth, which of course is much more complex. We should see the market as an institution which, both logically and historically, has no primacy over other institutions; it is therefore as 'natural' (or, for that matter, as 'artificial') as other institutions. Only when we do that will we be able to see the relations between market, state, and other institutions in a balanced and historically more accurate way.

Secondly, we should remember that there is more than one view of what the 'ideal' market can do, and that the neoclassical view is only one of many plausible views – and not a particularly good one at that. Accordingly, it becomes possible that the same market may be seen as failing by some with one 'theory of the market' and as succeeding by others with another theory. Only when an economist makes his/her own theory of the market explicit will we be able to judge the merit of his/her view that the market is 'failing' (or not) and thus to accept or reject the 'solution' to the problem, whether it is some kind of state intervention or the establishment of some non-market institutions and/ or organisations.

Thirdly, we need to realise that the neoclassical theory is essentially a theory of the market (and a very schematic and misleading one at that). However, capitalism, as a socio-economic system, is more than a collection of markets, and is made up of many institutions. These include, among others, firms as institutions of production, markets as institutions of exchange, the state as an institution for addressing collective interests politically, and various producer and consumer groupings (e.g., conglomerations of firms, producer associations, trade unions, purchasing cooperatives, and subcontracting networks). Thus seen, market failure becomes, somewhat paradoxically, less of a problem in the institutionalist framework than in the neoclassical framework, because in the former framework even widespread and severe market failures would not necessarily suggest that the whole 'economy' is failing, whereas the latter framework would see it as just that.

Fourthly, we need to understand that the market is a fundamentally political construction. A market cannot be defined except with reference to the specific rights/obligations structure that underpins it. And since these rights and obligations are determined through a political process, and not by any 'scientific' or 'natural' law as neoclassical (and other neoliberal) commentators want us to believe, all markets have a fundamentally 'political' origin. Therefore, it is impossible to decide whether a market is 'free' or not, without specifying the position of the person(s) making that statement regarding the legitimacy of the current rights/obligations structure. Added to this is the more explicit control of prices found in many markets through price caps, price ceilings, state setting of certain prices, and quantity controls. While some prices may be more politically administered than others in a given context, ultimately no price is free from politics.

This brings us to our fifth element in the institutionalist theory on the role of the state, namely, the need to build a theory of politics which takes a much more broad, balanced, and sophisticated view of politics than what is offered by neoliberalism. Neoliberal thinkers see politics as a market-like process, where material benefits are exchanged for political support, but as a process that ultimately corrupts the 'rationality' of the market, because of the discretionary powers that it confers upon those who can make and/or influence political decisions. However, this is a fundamentally jaundiced view of politics. The main problem with this view is that the 'rationality' that it wants to preserve through 'de-politicisation of the economy', which is in fact a euphemism for emasculating democracy, makes sense only in relation to the underlying rights/obligations structure, which is a fundamentally political construction. Thus, we need a theory of politics which is not merely an extension of market logic.

Lastly, we need to pay attention to the institutional diversity of capitalism (Albert 1991; Berger and Dore (eds.) 1996; Chang 1997).[17] Unfortunately, neoclassical economics has little to say about the issue of institutional diversity, because it is a theory of an abstract market economy, or rather of an 'exchange economy' based on barter, as we

---

17 The issue has been discussed in various areas, including: the organisation of finance (capital market-based vs. bank-led vs. state-dominated); corporate governance (U-form vs. M-form; H-firm or A-firm vs. J-firm); wage bargaining structure (centralised vs. decentralised); union organisation (centralised vs. industrial vs. company vs. craft); mode of state intervention (Anglo-American, East Asian, Scandinavian, etc.); industrial policy (general vs. selective). For more details, see Chang (1997).

have pointed out earlier. Partly for this reason, the neoliberal economists have found it difficult to admit that there are many ways for the
state to intervene other than through taxes/subsidies and public ownership, thus misrepresenting, although for somewhat different reasons, certain countries as being much less interventionist than they
actually are (e.g., Japan, Korea, the US; see Section 3.1.2). In discussing this issue of institutional diversity, understanding the role of the
state is critical, not simply because the international differences in the
mode of state intervention are a major source of this diversity, but also
because the exact institutional forms of, say, corporate governance or
labour representation will have to be legitimised in the eyes of the
(current and prospective) market participants, either through formal
legislation by the state or through informal support from the state.

Constructing an institutionalist political economy which satis-
fies all the above criteria (and I am sure that there are more important
criteria that I have not thought of) is surely a tall order. However,
without a radical restructuring of the ways in which we conceptualise
the market, the state, and politics, and the ways in which we analyse
the relationships between them, we will not be able to overcome the
neoliberal world view, which has dominated the political and intellectual agenda of our time, in my view with many negative consequences.

BIBLIOGRAPHY

Albert, M. (1991). *Capitalism vs. Capitalism.* New York: Four Walls Eight Windows.

Arrow, K. (1974). *The Limits of Organisation.* New York and London: W. W. Norton and Company.

Baumol, W. (1965). *Welfare Economics and the Theory of the State,* 2nd edn. London: London School of Economics.

Berger, S. and Dore, R. (eds.) (1996). *National Diversity and Global Capitalism.* Ithaca and London: Cornell University Press.

Bobbio, N. (1990). *Liberalism and Democracy.* London: Verso.

Buchanan, J. (1986). 'Contractarianism and Democracy', in *Liberty, Market and State.* Brighton: Wheatsheaf Books Ltd.

Chang, H.-J. (1994a). *The Political Economy of Industrial Policy.* London and Basingstoke: Macmillan.

Chang, H.-J. (1994b). 'State, Institutions, and Structural Change', *Structural Change and Economic Dynamics,* vol.5, no.2, pp.293-323.

Chang, H.-J. (1995). 'Explaining "Flexible Rigidities" in East Asia', in T. Killick (ed.), *The Flexible Economy.* London: Routledge.

Chang, H.-J. (1996). *El Papel del Estado en el Cambio Economico.* Mexico City: Editorial Planeta Mexicana.

Chang, H.-J. (1997). 'Markets, Madness, and Many Middle Ways: Some Reflections on the Institutional Diversity of Capitalism', in P. Arestis, G. Palma and M. Sawyer (eds.), *Essays in Honour of Geoff Harcourt – Volume 2: Markets, Unemployment, and Economic Policy.* London: Routledge.

Chang, H.-J. and Nolan, P. (1995). 'Europe versus Asia - Contrasting Paths to the Reform of Centrally Planned Systems of Political Economy', in H.-J. Chang and Nolan, P. (eds.), *The Transformation of the Communist Economies – Against the Mainstream.* London: Macmillan.

Chang, H.-J. and Nolan, P. (1996). 'La Transición en Europea Oriental y en Asia: Caminos Contrapuestos, Politicas Económicas Diferentes', *Revista de Estudios Asiaticos,* (3), pp.11-34.

Chang, H.-J. and Rowthorn, R. (1995a). 'Introduction', in H.-J. Chang and R. Rowthorn (eds.), *Role of the State in Economic Change.* Oxford: Oxford University Press.

Chang, H.-J. and Rowthorn, R. (1995b). 'Role of the State in Economic Change – Entrepreneurship and Conflict Management', in H.-J. Chang and R. Rowthorn (eds.), *Role of the State in Economic Change.* Oxford: Oxford University Press.

Coase, R. (1992). 'The Institutional Structure of Production', *American Economic Review,* vol.82., no.4, pp.713-719.

Deane, P. (1989). *The State and the Economic System.* Oxford: Oxford University Press.

Elster, J. (1983). *Sour Grapes.* Cambridge: Cambridge University Press.

Evans, P. (1995). *Embedded Autonomy – States and Industrial Transformation.* Princeton: Princeton University Press.

Evans, P., Rueschemeyer, D. and Skocpol, T. (eds.) (1985). *Bringing the State Back In.* Cambridge: Cambridge University Press.

Freeman, C. (1989). 'New Technology and Catching-up', *European Journal of Development Research*, vol.1, no.1, pp.85-99.

Friedman, M. (1962). *Capitalism and Freedom.* Chicago and London: The University of Chicago Press.

Gamble, A. (1988). *The Free Economy and the Strong State: The Politics of Thatcherism.* London and Basingstoke: Macmillan.

Hall, P. (ed.) (1989). *The Political Power of Economic Ideas: Keynesianism Across Nations.* Princeton: Princeton University Press.

Hayek, F. (1949). *Individualism and Economic Outlook.* London: Routledge & Kegan Paul.

Hirschman, A. (1958). *The Strategy of Economic Development.* New Haven: Yale University Press.

Hirschman, A. (1982a). 'Rival Views of Market Society', *Journal of Economic Literature*, vol.48, no.4, pp.1463-1484.

Hirschman, A. (1982b). *Shifting Involvements.* Princeton: Princeton University Press.

Johnson, C. (1982). *MITI and the Japanese Miracle.* Stanford: Stanford University Press.

King, D. (1987). *The New Right: Politics, Markets and Citizenship.* London and Basingstoke: Macmillan.

Kozul-Wright, R. (1995). 'The Myth of Anglo-Saxon Capitalism: Reconstructing the History of the American State', in H.-J.Chang and R. Rowthorn (eds.), *Role of the State in Economic Change.* Oxford: Oxford University Press.

Krueger, A. (1990). 'Government Failure in Economic Development', *Journal of Economic Perspective,* vol.4, no.3, pp.9-23.

Lavoie, D. (1985). *Rivalry and Central Planning.* Cambridge: Cambridge University Press.

Lazonick, W. (1991). *Business Organisations and the Myth of the Market Economy.* New York: Cambridge University Press.

Lucas, R. (1990). 'Review of *Trade Policy and Market Structure* by E. Helpman and P. Krugman (1989, Cambridge, Massachusetts, MIT Press)', *Journal of Political Economy*, vol.98, no.3, pp.664-667.

Marglin, S. and Schor, J. (eds.) (1990). *The Golden Age of Capitalism.* Oxford: Clarendon Press.

North, D. (1994). 'Economic Performance Through Time', *American Economic Review*, 84 (3), pp.359-368.

Nozick, R. (1974). *Anarchy, Utopia and the State.* Oxford: Basil Blackwell.

Pagano, U. (1985). *Work and Welfare in Economic Theory.* Oxford: Basil Blackwell.

Polanyi, K. (1957). *The Great Transformation.* Boston: Beacon Press.

Schotter, A. (1985). *Free Market Economics – A Critical Appraisal.* New York: Saint Martin's Press.

Schumpeter, J. (1987). *Capitalism, Socialism and Democracy,* 6th edn.. London: Unwin Paperbacks.

Scitovsky, T. (1954). 'Two Concepts of External Economies', *Journal of Political Economy,* vol.62, no.2, pp.143-151.

Shonfield, A. (1965). *Modern Capitalism.* Oxford: Oxford University Press.

Short, R. (1984). 'The Role of Public Enterprises: An International Statistical Comparison', in R. Floyd, C. Gary and R. Short (eds.), *Public Enterprises in Mixed Economies: Some Macroeconomic Aspects.* Washington, D.C.: International Monetary Fund.

Simon, H. (1991). 'Organisations and Markets', *Journal of Economic Perspectives,* vol.5, no.2, pp.25-44.

Stiglitz, J. (1992). 'Alternative Tactics and Strategies in Economic Development', in A.K. Dutt and K. Jameson (eds.), *New Directions in Development Economics.* Aldershot: Edward Elgar.

Toye, J. (1987). *Dilemmas of Development.* Oxford: Blackwell.

Toye, J. (1991). 'Is there a New Political Economy of Development?', in C. Colclough and J. Manor (eds.), *States or Markets?: Neo-liberalism and the Development of Policy Debate.* Oxford: Oxford University Press.

Vira, B. (1998). 'The Political Coase Theorem: Identifying Differences Between Neoclassical and Critical Institutionalism', *Journal of Economic Issues*, vol.31, no.3, pp.761-779.

Williamson, O. (1975). *Markets and Hierarchies.* New York: The Free Press.

World Bank (1991). *World Development Report 1991.* New York: Oxford University Press.

World Bank (1995). *Bureaucrats in Business.* New York: Oxford University Press.

World Bank (1997). *World Development Report 1997.* New York: Oxford University Press.

Chapter 4

The Political Economy of Industrial Policy

1. INTRODUCTION

UNTIL recently there existed a moderate consensus on the agenda of the debate on the role of the state, although there were intense debates concerning how best to achieve the individual items on the agenda. The items on the agenda included an improvement in income distribution, the achievement of macroeconomic stability, the provision of public goods (e.g., infrastructure, education and environmental protection) and, more controversially, anti-trust activities. State intervention in industry was, except anti-trust activities, looked at with suspicion as opening the window of opportunity for business interests to loot the state exchequer. This suspicion seemed more than natural when state intervention in industry – or industrial policy – did not make theoretical sense according to the conventional framework. Nevertheless, the rise of East Asian economies where the state has implemented strong industrial policy measures with great success has aroused interest in industrial policy, as manifested in the ongoing debate on the applicability of industrial policy in other, notably Anglo-Saxon, countries.

In this chapter we argue that industrial policy not only makes sense but can sometimes provide a better alternative both to the unregulated market and to other forms of state intervention (for example, central planning). After reviewing the industrial policy debates, we introduce some recent theoretical developments in the studies of economic institutions and technical change and spell out the logic of industrial policy, both from the static and the dynamic points of view. Regarding the former, we discuss why the market mechanism may lead to coordination failures and why such failures can be costly. Then we discuss the role of industrial policy in overcoming such failures. Regarding the latter, we discuss the nature of economic change and see what role industrial policy can play to promote it. We then move on to discuss possible problems of industrial policy, where problems of information, rent-seeking, politics and institutions are examined.

1.1 The Industrial Policy Debates

Despite the fact that industrial policy, far from being a novelty of East Asia, has been an integral part of economic policies of many advanced capitalist countries during the postwar period, it has become an important issue only since the late-1970s. In the English-speaking world the OECD has been the pioneer in this area (see the series of country studies published by the OECD in the early-1970s). In the UK, industrial policy became a controversial issue with the (not hugely successful) introduction of industrial policy programmes by the Labour government in the late-1970s.[1] The famous UK deindustrialisation debate also, to a degree, discussed industrial policy as a possible way to halt deindustrialisation and revive the economy.[2] During the 1980s, studies of various European countries' policy responses to the industrial crisis of the late-1970s also emerged.[3] The issue of industrial policy, however, has probably been most hotly debated in the USA, especially in the early-1980s, with the *Harvard Business Review* as the major forum.[4] The recent rise in strategic-trade-policy literature has also been heavily influenced by (and has influenced) the industrial-policy debates.[5]

---

1 See NEDO (1978), Stout (1979), and Cairncross *et al.* (1983).
2 See Singh (1977), Blackaby (ed.) (1979), and Rowthorn and Wells (1987).
3 See Pinder (ed.) (1982), Jacquemin (ed.) (1984), Cox (ed.) (1986), and Duchêne and Shepherd (eds.) (1987).
4 For some interesting reviews of the debate, see Norton (1986) and Thompson (1989).
5 See essays in Kirzkowski (ed.) (1984) and Krugman (ed.) (1988).

1.1.1 Does Manufacturing Matter?

One of the central points made by the proponents of industrial policy is that manufacturing does matter, although a pro-manufacturing attitude does not necessarily imply an endorsement of industrial policy.[6] The proponents of industrial policy argue that the UK and the US economies are deindustrialising (the shrinking share of industrial output and employment in the national economy) due to neglect of the manufacturing industries, and that, given the vital importance of the manufacturing sector for a prosperous economy, this is a dangerous sign (Cohen and Zysman 1987). They think that macroeconomic measures, while important, are not sufficient for a vigorous development of manufacturing since allocation of capital is more important than aggregate capital formation for productivity growth (Reich 1982: p.75). The conclusion, then, is that the state should intervene to promote industrial development, if necessary, using industrial targeting (Reich 1982; Johnson (ed.) 1984).

Many opponents of industrial policy argue that the advanced capitalist economies are moving towards becoming post-industrial economies, where service activities become the centre of economic life (for example, Bhagwati 1988: pp.110-14). Given that the tendency to move towards service activities is dictated by market forces (that is, demand for services increases as income rises), the argument goes, favouring manufacturing is not only unnecessary but also harmful. That is, favouring manufacturing would block the natural-selection mechanism of the market by hampering the necessary reallocation of resources towards service activities, and therefore damage the long-term viability of the economy (e.g., Burton 1983). Therefore, it is argued that we need not, and indeed should not, have policies that favour manufacturing, not to mention industrial policies geared to the needs of specific sectors (for the most sophisticated version of this argument, see Bhagwati 1989).

---

6 For example, Dornbusch *et al.* (1988) take a pro-manufacturing position but recommend better macroeconomic management rather than industrial policy as the major solution to the current industrial decline of the USA.

Confusion about the very concept of deindustrialisation and lack of understanding of the logic of long-term structural change (away from manufacturing towards services) seem to have produced many ill-informed discussions on the deindustrialisation issue. Fortunately some recent studies have spotted the source of confusion and clarified some of the major theoretical issues (Rowthorn and Wells 1987; Baumol *et al.* 1989). The conclusions emerging out of the 'manufacturing matters' debate are the following.

First of all, the long-term structural shift towards a service economy does not happen solely because people want more services as they grow richer, as was believed by some proponents of the theory of post-industrial economy. The major reason for such a structural shift in employment towards services seems to be the (relative) cost-inflation of services due to their lagging productivity growth (compared with that of manufacturing), rather than a real shift in demand towards services as incomes rise.[7]

Secondly, deindustrialisation, defined as the decrease in the share of manufacturing employment in total employment (and the decrease in the share of manufacturing output in total output in current prices), is an inevitable long-term result of differential productivity growth rates between manufacturing and services, and is not necessarily related to the declining competitiveness of the economy's manufacturing sector. Even successful exporters of manufactures, such as Japan and West Germany, have experienced deindustrialisation in this sense. This implies that, contrary to what was believed by those who condemned deindustrialisation as a sign of industrial decline, deindustrialisation and industrial decline are not one and the same thing, although industrial decline can affect the timing and scale of deindustrialisation (see Rowthorn and Wells 1987: Chapter 1). Therefore it is wrong to argue that an economy's manufacturing sector is in

---

7 Of course, this is not to argue that a change in the employment structure has no impact on our socio-economic life. Growing importance of service activities may have significant impacts on people's lifestyles, on their relationships with other human beings, their perceptions of the world, etc., especially by providing people with different work experiences from those in the manufacturing sector (on the 'constitutive' nature of labour processes, see Bowles and Gintis 1990). I thank Michael Landesmann for raising this important point.

trouble solely on the ground that it is deindustrialising in terms of the above definition.

Thirdly, the fact that deindustrialisation is an inevitable long-term trend does not necessarily mean that a country can ignore manufacturing completely and rely fully on services. This is largely because many services are either basically non-tradable (e.g., governmental services, legal services, child care, elementary and secondary education) or have a large non-tradable component (for example, transportation, distribution), although there are other services that have become, or are rapidly becoming, tradable (e.g, financial services, management consultancy, higher education). With a growing share of services in national income, compensating productivity growth in manufacturing is needed – on the reasonable assumption that no dramatic increases in productivity in agriculture and services are likely in the foreseeable future – if a country wants to maintain its income level without running into balance-of-payments problems.

1.1.2 What is Industrial Policy?

A major problem with industrial policy issues is that the very concept of industrial policy is not clearly defined, resulting in heated but often fruitless debates. A good example of this is the discussion on the postwar Japanese experience, which inspired many of the industrial-policy debates. Opponents of industrial policy point out that subsidies and governmental loans to industries in Japan are small (in relative terms), even smaller than in many European countries, and on this ground claim, as the title of one article goes (Trezise 1983), that 'industrial policy is not the major reason for Japan's success'. Proponents of industrial policy argue that the non-quantifiability of the famous Japanese 'administrative guidance' system makes people underestimate the success of Japanese industrial policy (Boltho 1985). Unless we define what we mean by industrial policy, we cannot judge who is correct and who is not.

Reich (1982), the most prominent proponent of industrial policy in the USA, includes the following policy measures in his definition of industrial policy: favouring promising industries; creating skilled workforces; developing infrastructure; regional policy (p.75). Pinder

(1982), a British proponent of industrial policy, goes a step further and regards all of the following as components of industrial policy: general industrial support policies such as manpower policy; fiscal and financial incentives for investment; public investment programmes; public procurement policies; fiscal incentives for R&D; firm-level policies such as specific R&D support; anti-trust policy; merger policies to create 'national champions'; support for small firms; regional policies such as the development of physical and social infrastructure and the establishment of industrial complexes; generalised trade protection; sectoral policies such as the organisation of recession cartels in depressed industries; product upgrading in labour-intensive industries (pp.44-52).

The tendency to adopt an encompassing definition exists even among those who oppose industrial policy. Donges (1980), an ardent European critic of industrial policy, categorically states that industrial policy 'embraces all government actions which affect industry' (p.189). Corden (1980) also implicitly adopts this definition when he states that 'the best industrial policy may be to provide an adequate infrastructure, some limits on the powers of monopolies and cartels, an education system that helps to generate the human capital for industrial success, indicative guidance about industrial prospects (without compulsion or subsidies), stability and simplicity in the system of taxation, a free and flexible capital market and a steady movement towards zero sectional protection, whether direct or indirect' (pp.182-3).

Despite the fact that all the above policies would have implications for industrial development, we do not think that classifying every policy that affects industrial development as industrial policy is a useful way to proceed. In the above examples, industrial policy is used as a catch-all term for policies affecting industrial performance, that is, effectively, every economic policy. Such a practice overloads the concept of industrial policy, rendering the concept meaningless.

Johnson (1984) provides a more focused definition of industrial policy by defining it as 'a summary term for the activities of governments that are intended to develop or retrench various industries in a national economy in order to maintain global competitiveness' (p.7), but falls into the same trap of overloading the concept when he includes not only what he calls 'micro' policy of 'industrial targeting', but also such policies as 'governmental incentives for private saving, investment, research and development, cost-cutting, quality control, maintenance of competition, and improvements in labour-management relations' (p.9) into the category of industrial policy.

As Johnson (1984) rightly points out (p.9), targeting or micro-industrial policy cannot succeed without favourable macroeconomic conditions. However, why should all policies that constitute preconditions for the success of another policy be treated as components of the latter? If one adopts this logic, one can argue that targeting should be a component of macroeconomic policy because, under certain conditions, it is possible for targeting to have an impact on such macroeconomic variables as savings and investments. For example, targeting some big projects and financing them through inflationary means may increase *ex post* savings. However, does this make such industrial targeting a macroeconomic policy? We think not. In our opinion the best way of defending industrial policy is not to include in it everything that is good for industrial development, but to narrow its definition and demonstrate that its benefits are bigger than its costs.

Landesmann (1992) makes an important contribution by emphasising the particularistic, or discriminatory, nature of industrial policy. According to him, industrial policy is 'designed to be specific, i.e., directed towards particular industries, firms, regions, groups in the labour market, etc., rather than general ... Implicit in industrial policy formulation and execution are therefore always trade-offs between different groups, regions, industries, etc.' (p.245). According to this definition, we may exclude such general policies as creating skilled workforces or improvements in labour-management relations from the realm of industrial policy, making the concept more focused.

However, Landesmann's concept of industrial policy is still somewhat overloaded, because it includes policies designed to affect both particular regions and particular groups in the labour market. True, industrial policy affects different regions and different groups differently, but its effects on particular regions and groups are better viewed as by-products than as aims of the policy. Likewise regional and group-oriented policies may affect particular industries (e.g., setting up an industrial park for the garment industry in a high-unemployment region), but this does not make them industrial policies.[8]

The existing definitions of industrial policy, then, tend to be too overloaded to be useful in practice. We propose to define industrial policy as a policy aimed at *particular industries* (and firms as their components) to achieve the outcomes that are *perceived by the state* to be *efficient* for *the economy as a whole*. This definition is close to what is usually called 'selective industrial policy' (e.g., by Lindbeck 1981).[9]

In our definition, first of all, we emphasise the words *particular industries*, and therefore implicitly exclude policies designed to affect industry in general (e.g., educational investment, infrastructural development) and policies aimed principally at categories other than industry (for example, regional policy, group-oriented policy) from the domain of industrial policy. Secondly, we emphasise the word *efficient* to stress that the guiding principle of industrial policy in its purest form is efficiency, and not other aims (e.g., equity). Efficiency is defined more broadly than in conventional economics and includes transaction-cost economising as an important dimension. Thirdly, we emphasise the phrase *the economy as a whole* to stress that, although it is directed at specific industries, industrial policy ultimately aims to improve the efficiency of the economy as a whole and not just that of particular industries. Therefore, in an industrial-policy regime, whenever the efficiency objective of an individual industry and that of the whole economy clash with each other, the latter is permitted to dominate.[10] Lastly, we emphasise the phrase *perceived by the state*, to

---

8   Lawrence (1984) argues against using industrial policy as a surrogate regional or group-oriented policy on the grounds that 'particular objectives – such as meeting national defense needs, redistributing incomes, and promoting regional development – can all be achieved by more precise policies' (p.115).

9   Our definition of industrial policy is based on a stylised version of industrial policy conducted in the 'industrial policy states' like Japan, France, and Korea. On Japanese industrial policy, see Magaziner and Hout (1980), Johnson (1982), Dore (1986), and Okimoto (1989). On Korean industrial policy, see Jones and Sakong (1980), Luedde-Neurath (1986), Amsden (1989), and Chang (1993). On French industrial policy, see Cohen (1977), Hayward (1986), and Hall (1987).

10   For example, in their study of Japanese industrial policy, Magaziner and Hout (1980) document that MITI often 'will suggest that a company participate in an unappealing foreign investment project or delay a capacity addition *to accomplish a broader end*' (italics added) (p. 34).

stress that the perception of the state may not necessarily be correct or justifiable to everyone.[11]

2.   THE LOGIC OF INDUSTRIAL POLICY (I): THE STATIC DIMENSION

We defined industrial policy as a policy intended to affect particular industries to achieve outcomes that are perceived by the state to be efficient for the economy as a whole. More concretely, it means that there is a case for the state 'selectively monitoring entry, establishing mechanisms to make possible more *ex ante* coordination than is possible through market mechanisms alone, and for governmental regulation or overview to constrain or supplement profit incentives' (Nelson 1981: p.109). However, what is the logic behind opting for *ex ante* coordination by the state instead of *ex post*, or 'spontaneous' (in Hayek's words), coordination by the market? Broadly we can say that this is because markets fail, but this seems hardly enough. To answer this question we need to look more closely at the nature of the coordination problem the market mechanism is supposed to solve, but often fails to do.

2.1   The Nature of the Coordination Problem

In the model of perfect competition, upon which mainstream industrial economics is based, there is no need for *ex ante* coordination of the plans of different agents regarding production and pricing decisions (Pagano 1985: Chapter 8). In this 'perfect decentralisation

---

11 This part of the definition helps us deal with those who downgrade the importance of industrial policy, say in Japan, by saying that Japan would have grown fast and become rich anyway given factors like the 'catching-up effect' and high savings ratios (e.g., Krugman 1984). From our perspective, however, the important point is not whether Japan would have become rich or not without industrial policy but whether the structure of the present Japanese economy is in line with what the Japanese state intended when it implemented industrial policy measures (by choosing what technology to deploy, where to channel the savings, etc.). And in this respect, there is no doubt that the Japanese industrial policy has played a crucial role.

model', as Demsetz (1982) aptly calls it, there is no need for *ex ante* coordination because assumptions are made to ensure that the actions of individual agents are negligible – infinitesimally small in the limiting case – in the sense that a unilateral action of a single agent is unable to change the aggregate outcome (Khan 1987: pp.831-4). When individual agents are negligible, there is no interdependence among individual agents and hence no need to coordinate their activities *ex ante*.

One crucial assumption to guarantee the total absence of interdependence supposed in the neoclassical model of perfect competition is that production technology is characterised by decreasing returns to scale (DRS) – at an infinitesimally small output level in the limiting case. Even under the widely-used assumption of constant returns to scale (CRS) – not to mention the disturbing case of increasing returns to scale (IRS) – the perfect-competition model does not guarantee a solution to the coordination problem, as was pointed out long ago by Richardson (1960: pp.31-2). When CRS technology prevails in a large-number setting, *ex ante*, firms may behave as if the demand curve is horizontal (that is, as if they are individually negligible), but *ex post* there is no guarantee that the market will clear, since an individual firm, not being bound by production technology, can produce as much as it wants. In other words there is no way to determine the number of the firms and their respective outputs in an industry characterised by a CRS production technology, as is recognised even by standard neoclassical textbooks (e.g., Varian 1984: p.88). Therefore even with CRS technology there may be so few firms in a market as to give rise to interdependence and consequently to the need for *ex ante* coordination.[12]

Of course the coordination problem will not exist except in the case of IRS technology if all the firms can correctly predict how much the other firms will produce, as implicitly assumed in textbooks. However, as Hayek (1949a) remarks, '[t]he statement that, if people know everything, they are in equilibrium is true simply because that is

---

12 Moreover, as Williamson (1988) states, 'it does not suffice to demonstrate that a condition of large numbers competition obtains at the outset. It is also necessary to examine whether this continues or if, by reason of transaction specific investments and incomplete contracting, a condition of bilateral trading *evolves* thereafter' (italics original) (p.71).

how we define equilibrium' (p.46). If everybody knows everybody else's plan, then why do we need a price system or any other coordination mechanism? In other words, equilibrium in the perfect-competition model is attained only because the coordination problem is assumed away from the beginning!

As Hayek (1978) somewhat derogatorily says, 'a state of affairs which economic theory curiously calls "perfect competition"', that is, 'a situation in which all the facts are supposed to be known', leaves 'no room whatever for the activity called competition' (p.182).[13] He argues that '[t]he peculiar nature of the assumptions from which the theory of competitive equilibrium starts stands out very clearly if we ask which of the activities that are commonly designated by the verb "to compete" would still be possible if those conditions were all satisfied... Advertising, undercutting, and improving ('differentia-tion') the goods or services produced are all excluded by definition – "perfect" competition means indeed the absence of all competitive activities' (Hayek 1949b: p.96).

Models of oligopoly in the neoclassical tradition recognise the coordination problem arising from the indeterminacy of the market outcome in a small-number setting. However their solutions to the coordination problem are not entirely satisfactory. The usual solution to the problem is to employ the concept of the mixed (or randomised) strategy (e.g., patent race in Rasmusen 1989: pp.295-8). However a mixed strategy does not guarantee an optimal solution except in the probabilistic sense that, if the situation occurred an infinite number of times, randomising one's actions would yield the highest average payoff. When the situation is not recurrent, employing the concept of probability is less than meaningful (for a classic discussion, see Knight 1921, Part III), and it is therefore dubious to describe the mixed strategy equilibrium as optimal. For example, how can firm A's strategy regarding its investment in production capacity for a 4Mb

---

13 What Hayek calls the 'competition as a state of affairs' view is still dominant in the field of industrial economics (on different notions of competition, see Hayek 1949b, 1978; McNulty 1968; O'Driscoll 1986). For example, even the most updated industrial economics textbook, Tirole (1988), argues that replacement of one monopolist by another through a patent race 'does not mean competition, as one monopolist replaces another' (p. 396, no.12). However, Hayek would have argued that the replacement was a result of 'the activity called competition'.

memory chip be 'randomised' in any meaningful sense, when, given the speed of technical progress, it is clear that the next round of investment will be in a 16Mb memory-chip capacity?

One way of avoiding the difficulty of employing probabilistic behaviour by individual agents in non-recurrent situations is to interpret the mixed strategy as an 'evolutionarily stable strategy' (ESS), whereby individual agents do not randomise their actions but there are sufficiently different types of agents in the population for the aggregate outcome to be the same as when individual agents randomise (for the concept of ESS, see Maynard Smith 1982). However, even in the biological world where the concept originated, the ESS equilibrium holds only approximately, because '[genetic] heterogeneity and changing conditions must mean that often populations are not perched at adaptive peaks. *Even when the conditions are constant*, selection becomes progressively weaker towards the peak of a continuous fitness function; *infinite time and infinite populations would be needed to achieve the peak itself*' (emphasis added) (Parker and Maynard Smith 1990, p.31). And the intuitive meaning of ESS becomes even less clear in many industrial markets where the conditions change so rapidly that the selection mechanism does not have time to work to its full extent and where the agents (being humans) learn and change not only their 'genes' (behavioural characteristics) but also the selection mechanism (the environment) and consequently the ESS itself (see Section 3.1 below).

The deficiency of the unregulated market as a coordination device was already recognised by Marx, who saw firms as islands of planned economy in the capitalist sea of anarchy. According to him, '[t]he same bourgeois consciousness which celebrates the division of labour in the workshop, the lifelong annexation of the worker to a partial operation, and his complete subjection to capital, as an organisation of labour that increases its productive power, denounces with equal vigour every conscious attempt to control and regulate the process of production socially, as an inroad upon such sacred things as the rights of property, freedom, and the self-determining "genius" of the individual capitalist.... [I]n the society where the capitalist mode of production prevails, anarchy in the social division of labour and despotism in the manufacturing division of labour mutually condition each other ...' (Marx 1976: p. 477).[14] Marx saw an enormous waste of resources in the failure of the market as a coordination device (what he called the anarchy of the social division of labour) and hoped to extend the *ex ante* coordination that already existed in the firm to the economy-wide level – what he called the despotism in the manufacturing division of labour or what Williamson (1975) calls the 'hierarchy' – through central planning or at least some form of central coordination of individual activities (Pagano 1985: Chapter 3).[15]

Why are coordination failures 'wasteful'? There are coordination failures, the counterargument may run, but are not such failures corrected via the competitive process whereby firms perish unless they correct their mistakes? If so, why should any *ex ante* coordination be necessary? For example, it may be argued that even when an industry is characterised by IRS technology, it would still not require *ex ante* coordination, because if more than the optimal number of firms enter the industry, some would inevitably go bankrupt through competition, thereby finally achieving the optimal outcome.

The above reasoning assumes that resources invested in the bankrupt firms can be instantaneously and without costs shifted to other activities. Nevertheless it is only in the financiers' world (or the economists' world?), where every asset is 'general' and 'liquid' (as in Keynes' concept of liquidity preference), that any investment, if found unprofitable, can be instantly withdrawn at no, or at most little, cost.[16] However, in modern industrial economies, assets are often specific to investments and therefore cannot be redeployed without a loss in their value (for the concept of 'asset specificity', see Williamson 1975 and 1985). In a world with asset specificity, *ex post* coordination through

---

14 Dobb (1925: Ch. 23) expresses a similar concern. He describes the capitalist economy as an 'economic anarchy', which gives fluidity to the economy but at the cost of instability due to coordination failure. In particular, he points out that miscalculations by competing firms might not cancel out because expectations tend to move in the same direction.

15 It should, however, be noted that Marx had another vision of socialist society organised on the basis of more democratic and less specialised division of labour, which Pagano (1985) aptly calls 'anti-firm communism' (p. 60).

16 Amadeo and Banuri (1991) argue that there is a correlation between the liquidity of the assets owned by different groups (e.g., financiers, industrialists, workers) and their degrees of support for unregulated competition in the market.

the market can be wasteful, as Marx argued, because a coordination failure that involves specific assets means a net reduction in the amount of resources available to the economy.[17]

If the market fails to solve the coordination problem and if such failure can produce waste, there is a case for non-market, or *ex ante*, coordination (Pagano 1985: Chapter 8). As new institutional economics demonstrates, the firm (or the hierarchy, in Williamson's words) is the most representative form of non-market coordination, but other diverse forms of non-market coordination mechanisms exist. As Winter (1988) puts it, '[m]arkets appear and disappear; firms expand in scope and then turn back toward specialisation; quasi-firms and quasi-markets proliferate' (p.168).[18] Central planning is also an institutional device to solve the coordination problem (Richardson 1971), and industrial policy is another such device.

2.2 Industrial Policy as a Device of Coordination

One characteristic of modern industrial economies is the use of production technologies that require large fixed investments, mainly in the form of machinery.[19] Large fixed costs mean a decreasing average cost curve, or scale economies. Moreover, a large part of these fixed assets are specific or 'sunk' in the sense that their costs cannot be fully recovered when sold elsewhere. Scale economies often force firms to produce at a scale that will allow no more than a few firms in an industry, because, by producing at the most efficient scale, a firm can undercut its competitors and force them out of the industry. Out of fear of extinction, other firms have to adopt the same (or more

---

17 Some recent developments in mainstream theory attempt to incorporate these observations through modelling 'wasteful R&D' and the like. However, this type of model is not generally extended to the theory of competition in general.

18 The very diversity of coordination devices in a capitalist economy is a testimony to the diversity of coordination problems to be solved. And this is one reason why we emphasise the particularistic nature of industrial policy, since, to be successful, it has to be custom-designed to fit the nature of the coordination problem involved in a particular instance.

19 Marx's concept of 'constant capital' (which was absent in the Ricardian system) and the Austrian concept of 'roundabout methods of production' are two important ways of theorising such a characteristic.

efficient) technology or perish. The outcome is an oligopolistic industry in which strategic interdependence among the decisions of the firms exist.

Under certain likely conditions, strategic interdependence may lead to inefficiency (see below; also Telser 1987 and Yamamura 1988), providing a case for state intervention. The intervention needed here is not necessarily an antitrust-type policy, because the benefits from breaking up the oligopolistic firms (that is, reduction in the deadweight loss) may be more than offset by higher production costs due to sub-optimal scales of production. Below, we show the role of industrial policy in this context.

2.2.1 Investment Coordination

An industry whose cost structure is characterised by significant scale economies is likely to experience a price war – firms selling at long-term losses (or at prices that do not cover fixed costs) to undercut competitors. Under adverse demand conditions, which might occur due to factors like external shocks (for example, a rise in energy prices) and a slower demand growth than was expected at the time of the investment decision, firms in the industry might prefer to engage in a price war rather than forego sales, and hence incur heavier losses due to their inability to recover fixed costs. This makes an industry with scale economies subject to the dangers of under-investment or over-investment, which may not be easily resolved through the market mechanism.

In a new industry (or an expanding industry) with scale economies, if many of the potential entrants expect that enough others would enter the industry to start a price war, there may be insufficient entry, resulting in a sub-optimal level of output – a case of under-investment. On the other hand, if they expect that not many competitors would enter, too much investment may be undertaken, because then they have an incentive to install as much capacity as possible to reduce their unit costs (which would provide a distinct advantage in future competition) – a case of over-investment. However, in Richardson's words, 'over-investment, by causing a collapse of prices, will penalise all suppliers' (Richardson 1971: p.441). And if some firms go bankrupt in this process, the resources put into their investments will have been wasted, insofar as they involve specific assets.

Since under- and over-investment are essentially problems of strategic uncertainty (each potential entrant not knowing the intentions of others), the state can intervene in this industry to assure optimal entry by guaranteeing potential entrants that there will not be more than optimal entry. It can do this through arbitrating private bargaining among potential entrants, but also by superseding private dealing and thus reducing the transaction costs involved in such bargaining. Licensing entry and regulating capacity expansion are the most common forms of state-imposed investment coordination. The negotiated industry-wide investment plans (the so-called 'investment cartels') in Japan during the 1960s for industries like steel, vinyl chloride, synthetic fibres, pulp, paper, cement, petroleum, petrochemicals, cars, machine tools and some branches of electronics are classic examples of investment coordination achieved through state-led private negotiation (Dore 1986; Magaziner and Hout 1980). An interesting variety of investment coordination is 'conditional entry' whereby the state links the number of entrants (or the scale of new capacity) to changes in demand conditions. An example of conditional entry is the Korean passenger-car industry, where, faced with a lagging demand growth, the state forced one of the three existing firms to exit on the condition that it would be allowed back when demand expanded.

2.2.2 Recession Cartel

Even industries with optimal capacity may experience price wars if there are unforeseen fluctuations in demand due to, say, downturns in the business cycle, a sudden import penetration, changes in raw-material prices or world recession (in the case of export-oriented industries). If the fall in demand is temporary, it may be desirable to organise a 'recession cartel', whereby individual firms limit their production for a limited period of time, rather than allow a price war.

In the conventional wisdom, cartel arrangements are strongly opposed because they are seen as creating allocative inefficiency (that is, deadweight loss) in the process of transferring consumer surplus to producers (that is, the process of creating monopoly profit). However the costs of cartels (that is, the deadweight loss) should be weighed against their possible benefits. First of all, as we have already discussed, when there are specific assets involved, price wars can lead to bankruptcy and therefore social waste. Recession cartels may allow such waste to be avoided. Moreover, even assuming that there is no waste involved in bankruptcy, prohibiting recession cartels may increase allocative inefficiency in the longer run. As Okimoto (1989) points out, without a recession cartel stronger firms will survive at the cost of weaker ones, eventually extracting more monopoly profit after the recovery. Thirdly, and most importantly, letting firms engage in a price war may have disastrous consequences for long-term productivity growth if firms have to reduce their investment levels in order to make up their losses from the price war.

As was common in the interwar period in many advanced capitalist countries, recession cartels may be organised through private initiatives. Nevertheless such cartel arrangements may be costly to organise, for example, when a large number of firms are involved, due to the cost of overcoming the collective-action problem. For another example, if the sellers do not publicly quote prices and make separate deals with separate buyers (say, because the number of the buyers is small), it will be difficult to detect breaches of the cartel agreement (Tirole 1988: p.241). In this case the cartel may have to spend a lot of resources on monitoring. Or if the history of the industry is such that firms do not trust each other, working out an arrangement may incur a large bargaining cost. If, for whatever reason, it is costly to make a recession cartel work on private initiatives, the state may intervene and organise a more credible arrangement, thus cutting down the transaction costs involved (e.g., on state-led recession cartels in Japan, see Magaziner and Hout 1980, and Dore 1986).

2.2.3 Negotiated Exit/Capacity Scrapping

If the demand downturn turns out to be of a long-term nature, the cumulative costs of a recession cartel may exceed its benefits. In this case, apparently, there is a need for market forces to weed out the weak. However leaving the adjustment to the new long-term demand situation to market forces can also be costly. A permanent fall in demand requires some firms to exit, but this may cause a war of attrition, whereby no firm wants to exit first because it will benefit by staying if others exit first (Ghemawat and Nalebuff 1985; Fudenberg and Tirole 1986).[20] A war of attrition can lead to a protracted price war, leaving everybody worse off than they would have been with timely exits (Tirole 1988: p.313).

Of course, if there is no specific asset involved, the form of adjustment in this situation may not matter because exit (and the consequent redeployment of physical and human capital) does not cost anyone anything. However, when the assets involved are specific there is a case for orderly exit or capacity scrapping. Obviously, if there are no transaction costs, the parties involved may work out a contract with side-payment schemes. However the existence of transaction costs hinder such contracts, and there is a case for state intervention. Orderly exit or capacity-scrapping arrangements organised or assisted by the state can take the following forms.

First of all, some firms can exit altogether in return for some side-payments. Side-payment may take the form of direct compensation by the remaining firms, as seen in the Japanese textile industry in the early-1980s (Dore 1986).[21] State subsidies may quicken the process, especially when negotiations over side-payments prove difficult. Mergers can also make it easier to devise side-payment schemes, as seen in the reorganisation of the French chemical industry (Hall 1987: pp.208-9). Side-payment can also take the form of an increase in a firm's share in other markets in return for exit from one market. This option may be feasible if the firms concerned belong to larger entities

---

20 Of course, there are other options open for firms. One is to find a hitherto unexploited market, say, through exporting. Another is to diversify into other related industries, as shown in the examples of some Japanese firms in declining industries like textile, brewing, and food-processing, which have successfully diversified into biotechnology (see Okimoto 1989: p.128).

21 However, devising a side-payments scheme is not easy because the estimate of future costs and benefits from exit may differ among the agents concerned. For example, in some branches of the Japanese textile industry dominated by many small-scale firms which were hard-pressed by imports from the NICs in the early-1980s, the government put the view that exit compensation should be financed by the remaining firms who benefit from such exit, while the remaining firms argued that the exiters' share of the total market was minute (and hence benefit negligible) and that any room left in the market by the exit of home producers was likely to be taken up by imports (see Dore 1986: p.236).

simultaneously operating in multiple markets (for example, conglomerates) – the 1980 industrial reorganisation programme in Korea is a good example of this.

Secondly, all firms can scrap some of their capacities according to some established criterion, for example according to each firm's share in total industrial capacity or according to its market share. The best examples are seen in the capacity-scrapping arrangements in the Japanese aluminium, shipbuilding, textile, petrochemical and steel industries in the 1970s and the 1980s (Dore 1986: p.142; Okimoto 1989: p.110).[22] The advantage of capacity scrapping based on an exit arrangement is that it can improve the vintage structure of capital, thus raising overall productivity (on the vintage effect, see Salter 1960). A capacity-scrapping arrangement may need state intervention more than an exit arrangement does because it is more difficult to monitor the compliance of the parties involved. It is fairly obvious whether a firm is in operation or not, but it is difficult to observe whether a firm really has scrapped its capacity. The presence of government inspectors in capacity-scrapping processes, as in some Japanese capacity-scrapping arrangements, may help to solve this problem (see Dore 1986).

Thirdly, there is the interesting practice of 'mothballing', defined as stripping equipment down and concreting in the mountings so that it requires a good deal of time and effort to rehabilitate it, as practised in Japan (Dore 1986: p.142). This mitigates the problem of credibility that is inherent in recession cartels by making cheating costly. However it keeps open the option of returning to the former levels of production if necessary (although at a cost) and therefore avoids the risk of scrapping too much capacity due to an unduly pessimistic forecast of future demand. As a hybrid between recession cartels and capacity-scrapping arrangements, mothballing may be appropriate when it is uncertain whether the demand downturn is permanent, while recession cartels (capacity-scrapping arrangements)

---

22 In this case, side-payments will mainly involve compensations for workers who are laid off. For example, in the case of the Japanese shipbuilding industry, additional unemployment benefits and special placement services for workers, provided by the state, were important in arranging a speedy capacity-scrapping arrangement (see Renshaw 1986: p.145; Dore 1986: p.143).

are appropriate when the demand downturn is certain to be temporary (permanent).[23]

Fourthly, with state arbitration or even decree, firms can divide a market into segments and exit from some segments in return for the exit of others from the segments where they are given permission to stay. Such a segmentation arrangement may be a good idea when the industry can easily be divided into segments (e.g., ships over or under a certain tonnage). One example of such market-segmenting or specialisation arrangement is given by the reorganisation of the Korean electronic telephone-switching-system industry in 1980, when, faced with serious overcapacity, each of the four incumbent firms was forced by the state to specialise in a different product. The market-segmentation arrangement in the Japanese industrial machinery industry in the late-1960s is another such example (Dore 1986: pp.137-8).

2.3 Concluding Remarks: Credibility, Fairness and Flexibility

In the first part of this section we discussed why the market mechanism may fail to solve the coordination problem, and why coordination failures can be costly. In the second part we discussed how state intervention can prevent and/or redress coordination failures. Investment coordination, recession cartels and negotiated exit/ capacity-scrapping arrangements were examined.

Common to all these forms of industrial policy is the problem of strategic uncertainty. Of course the existence of strategic uncertainty does not necessarily mean that state intervention is the optimal solution. After all many non-market institutions enable long-range planning by reducing strategic uncertainty (Schumpeter 1987: pp.102-3; Eatwell 1982: p.210).[24] Long-term supply contracts, technological cooperation and vertical integration between firms all fall into this category (Richardson 1972). In a situation of strategic uncertainty,

---

23 In the case of the Japanese textile industry, some equipment was mothballed in 1978, but eventually scrapped in 1981 since the demand downturn proved to be permanent (Dore 1986: pp.235-6).

24 More generally, given the limited human capacity to process information, the introduction of rigidity in behaviour through such long-term binding contracts may well be essential to achieve rational decisions (Simon 1983; Heiner 1983).

making one's commitment credible is vital in working out a coordinated outcome. And, as we argued, state intervention can help overcome the problem of credibility in such situations. Investment coordination by the state is a way of avoiding over-investment and underinvestment due to the difficulty of making credible commitments concerning one's investment decision. A state-led recession cartel is a way of overcoming mistrust inherent in a private recession-cartel arrangement. The presence of government inspectors in capacity-scrapping or mothballing arrangements can also help to make the commitments credible.

Another problem common in all the arrangements we discussed is that of devising a scheme that is considered fair among the participants. Decisions regarding the quota of each firm in recession cartels, which firms should exit, which firm should cut how much capacity, and so on, all involve the question of fairness. The capacity or the market share of each firm may provide focal points for such fairness, but they need not do so necessarily, especially when the firms involved are heterogeneous. For example, in the case of the Japanese shipbuilding industry, '[t]he large companies and efficiency-oriented civil servants wanted to see the big companies cut capacity, and many of the small companies to close down. The small companies wanted the large ones to take all the cuts. Companies which had newly invested in up-to-date berths...wanted special exemptions' (Dore 1986: p.l45).[25] Although the state may not necessarily be better situated to work out a 'fair' norm, it can help this process by representing the national interest, which may serve as a focal point in negotiations.

The third problem is the question of flexibility. The limits of human cognition (or bounded rationality) mean that the demand (and other) forecasts on which investment decisions are based can prove wrong.[26] For example, even if demand has fallen substantially, we do

---

25 In this particular case, no exit was negotiated, and the cut was graduated to the size of the firm, ranging from 40% for the seven biggest firms to 15% for the 21 smallest (Dore 1986: p.145).

26 And this is why '[c]onsumers do not wish to contract for their future purchases because they cannot foretell what their future needs and opportunities will be; and producers do not generally wish to commit themselves to forward purchases of inputs because they cannot predict the productive possibilities that will be open to them' (Richardson 1971: p.437).

not know whether this situation will last long enough to justify exit or capacity scrapping. And if it is not implausible that demand might improve in the future, it may be wise to bear certain short-term costs, say through a recession cartel, in order to keep open the option of exploiting improved demand in the future.[27] Conditional entry is one device to maintain flexibility in an expanding industry. Mothballing is a device to maintain flexibility in declining industries where demand is unlikely to improve.

3.   THE LOGIC OF INDUSTRIAL POLICY (II): THE DYNAMIC DIMENSION

In the previous section we paid little heed to endogenous technical change, considering mainly changes in demand. However we cannot possibly ignore this issue, as the very strength of the capitalist system is its ability to generate endogenous technical change. By its nature, technical change is an unpredictable process, and no one, including the state, can claim superior knowledge of its future course. Moreover, it is often argued, technical change is an evolutionary process, whereby only those who develop better technology survive. Therefore some opponents of industrial policy argue (e.g., Burton 1983) that, however well industrial policy may solve the 'static' problem of coordination, it will do more harm than good in the long run because it hampers the workings of the natural-selection mechanism of the market economy.

   After all, does not the failure of central planning prove that the coordination problem (which it solved at least to a degree) may be far less important than the attainment of dynamic efficiency? Indeed the advocacy of central planning is usually based on the proposition that a centrally-planned economy can solve the coordination problem as well as, if not better than, a market economy, and not that it generates more dynamism (see essays by Lange and Taylor in Lippincott (ed.)

---

27 In the case of the Japanese aluminium smelting industry, one reason put forward for not cutting capacity to the level dictated by current relative prices (mainly due to the oil price hike and the consequent rise in electricity prices) was the need to maintain a sizeable industry to support an R&D capacity, which is an important precondition for regaining international competitiveness if the cost situation improves in the future (Dore 1986: p.143).

1938; see also Lavoie 1985: Chapter 4).[28] As Rosenberg and Birdzell (1986) argue, '[t]he failure of planning can be attributed in part to its conception of an economy system as a lifeless machine, without the internal capacity to change, adapt, grow, renew, reproduce itself and shape its own future. Plans ... do not ordinarily provide for creating extensive classes of people with capacity to engage in independent economic activities not envisioned by the plan. But a growth system is like a living organism with impulses of its own. The result of planning for growth is to produce an economy that is, if not a wholly lifeless statute of the real thing, at best a tame zoo-bred shadow of the natural animal' (p.331). How then can industrial policy cope with the problem of change? Before we answer this question we need to look more closely at the nature of economic change.

3.1 Knowledge, Change and Evolution

According to Hayek and the Austrian school, the essence of our economic problem is that those variables treated as data by orthodox (that is neoclassical) economics keep changing (Hayek 1949b: pp.93-4). The market, far from already embodying all the information necessary for coordination, can only gradually reveal them through a competitive process (Kirzner 1973: Chapter 1). Hayek (1949c) argues that '[t]he various ways in which the knowledge on which people base their plans is communicated to them is the crucial problem for any theory explaining the economic process, and the problem of what is the best way of utilising knowledge initially dispersed among all the people is at least one of the main problems of economic policy – or of designing an efficient economic system' (pp.78-9).

According to Hayek, human knowledge can never be fully codified, and therefore the crucial question in economics becomes: '[h]ow can the combination of fragments of knowledge existing in different minds bring about results which, if they were to be brought

---

28 While arguing that the coordination failure of the market entails enormous waste and therefore needs to be replaced by less wasteful *ex ante* coordination through central planning, Marx was also a precursor of the Schumpeterian, and to some extent the Austrian, 'process' view of competition which emphasises the role of market competition in developing the 'forces of production' (see e.g., Marx 1981: pp.373-4).

about deliberately, would require a knowledge on the part of the directing mind which no single person can possess' (Hayek 1949a: p.54).[29] In particular, as Svennilson puts it, when the knowledge involved is technical knowledge, 'only a part, and mainly the broad lines, of [such] knowledge is codified by non-personal means of intellectual communication or communicated by teaching outside the production process itself' (quoted in Rosenberg 1976: p.155).[30]

The virtue of the market mechanism, according to this argument, is that it acts as the most economical mechanism through which dispersed agents exchange information without explicit coordination. If this is the case, the market mechanism may need to be preserved to promote economic change, because it is 'highly conducive to the achievement of many different individual purposes not known as a whole to any single person, or relatively small group of persons' (Hayek 1978: p.183).

If we recognise the importance of competition in generating change, should we not understand the market process as an evolutionary process, whereby natural selection operates to pick the winners? And does this not mean that industrial policy is harmful because it attempts to tinker with the natural-selection mechanism, which is beyond any human comprehension? We think likening economic process to an evolutionary process is a helpful analogy.[31] However an analogy is an analogy, and therefore should not be taken too literally.

First of all, biological evolution is characterised by the lack of conscious planning (Gould 1983; Dawkins 1986), whereas economic evolution is characterised by the human ability to learn consciously (from one's own and others' experience) and accordingly change one's behaviour. That is, mutation at the genetic level is essentially a random process, whereas economic mutation – or 'industrial muta-

---

29 In contrast, in the neoclassical framework, every piece of 'information' (or knowledge) is seen as obtainable, albeit at a cost (e.g., search cost) (for similar views, see Heiner 1988, p.148, and Pelikan 1988, p.385).

30 The importance of the migration of skilled technicians in transmitting technical knowledge from one to another part of the then industrialised world during the 19th century (i.e., Europe and the US) documented by Rosenberg (1976: pp.154-5) shows the difficulty of codifying technical knowledge.

31 For evolutionary arguments in economics, see Alchian (1950) and Nelson and Winter (1982).

tion' in Schumpeter's language (Schumpeter 1987: p.83) – is often subject to intentional changes.[32] That this is the case is potently demonstrated by the examples of some late-developing nations which forged ahead by overcoming initial disadvantages through conscious learning, despite the existence of 'cumulative causation' – where the initial (dis)advantage leads to further (dis)advantages – in modern industrial economies (Abramovitz 1986; Nelson 1991).[33]

Secondly, biological evolution is essentially a Darwinian process in which only hereditary characteristics can be transmitted, whereas economic evolution is essentially a Lamarckian process in which acquired characteristics can also be transmitted (Hodgson 1988: p.143). This is because human beings have the ability to codify knowledge (for example, languages and signs), and, more importantly, store it (for example, books, computer memories), however limited such ability may be. And that acquired characteristics, and not just hereditary characteristics, can be transmitted means that learning plays an important role in the process of economic evolution.

Thirdly, natural selection in the biological world, while systematic, is independent of the actions of the units of selection, that is, the individual organisms. However the selection mechanism in economic life is not 'natural' in the sense that it is totally out of reach of the conscious attempts by the objects of selection (in this case, firms) to change it to their advantage. The participants in economic life enhance their ability to survive not only by changing themselves (the genes) but also by changing the environment (the selection mechanism). For example, a firm operating in an industry with network externalities (for example, typewriters, computers, telecommunications) can change its chance of survival by spreading its own technology – for example by encouraging other smaller firms to produce clones of its products or by providing loans to its customers. Advertising is another example whereby firms change their possibility of survival by changing the selection mechanism – that is, consumer preference.

---

32 The same view of economic evolution lies in the French state's claim that it was involved in rescue operations of the declining sectors not 'to save endangered species but to provide funds for their *mutation*' (italics added) (*Fortune*, 9 April, 1978; quoted in Hall 1987: p.190).
33 On the notion of cumulative causation, see Young (1928), Kaldor (1985), and Stigler (1951).

3.2   Industrial Policy as a Device to Promote Change

In the previous section we examined the nature of change in the capitalist economy. In particular we examined the evolutionary argument, which likens the process of change in the capitalist economy to biological evolution. We argued that the fundamental difference between biological and economic evolution is that, in the latter, the units of selection have the capacity to intentionally 'mutate' and change the selection mechanism itself, at least to a degree. This is essentially due to the human ability to learn, especially from others, and to the ability to pass on (at least part of) the knowledge acquired through codification (e.g., by writing a book on Japanese business management) and institutionalisation (for example, by introducing some elements of Japanese business management). How then can industrial policy be used as a means to promote economic change and learning?

3.2.1 Economic Change, Coordination and Industrial Policy

One important point not addressed by the opponents of industrial policy who employ the (misunderstood) evolutionary argument is that economic changes may require coordination to be successful. In a world of interdependence, the existence of a better alternative does not necessarily mean the advent of a change. For example, there exist more efficient alternatives to the QWERTY typewriter (and computer) keyboard, but an agent (or even a group of agents) who unilaterally shifts to an alternative keyboard will be penalised unless others also opt for it (David 1985). More generally, when interdependence prevails between economic agents, changes would not automatically be made without the guarantee that complementing changes would also be made (Richardson 1960: Chapter 2).

For example, if a successful computer industry depends on a strong semiconductor industry, people will be reluctant to invest in the computer industry unless there is a credible commitment for adequate investment by the potential investors in the semiconductor industry, and vice versa.[34] As Abramovitz (1986) argues, 'if the capital stock of a country consists of an intricate web of interlocking elements', then 'it is difficult to replace one part of the complex with more modern and efficient elements *without a costly rebuilding of other components*' (emphasis added) (pp.401-2). Now, '[t]his may be handled efficiently if all the costs and benefits are internal to a firm', but when the capital stock is *interdependent in use but divided in ownership*, and thus the accompanying costs and benefits of change are divided among different firms and industries, 'the adaptation of old capital structures to new technologies may be a difficult and halting process' (emphasis added) (p.402).[35]

Although it is possible that potential investors in complementary projects may devise a contract between themselves, such a contract may be costly to draw up, particularly when there is asymmetry in asset specificity of investments between different investors (the failure of the complementary investments to materialise can be more damaging to the investor with greater asset specificity). State intervention in this case may cut sharply the transaction costs involved in such contracts. Such intervention need not involve financial resources such as subsidies. As we discussed earlier, governmental announcements (for example, the French and East Asian 'indicative-planning' exercise) may suffice if they can provide obvious focal points for coordination between complementary investments.[36] Financial incentives provided by the state, say, for cooperative research in new industries, although not necessary, may make the state's commitment to its announcement more credible by serving as a signalling device (Porter 1990: Chapter

---

34 Of course, computer firms may decide on in-house production of semiconductors, but there is no guarantee that scale economies in computer production and semiconductor production will be of the same magnitude. If the semiconductor industry is subject to a larger scale economy (as is the case), the in-house production option will be costly compared to the option of production by independent semiconductor producers.

35 Porter (1990) reports that '[i]n the United States and often in Europe, the process of reaching technical standards is frequently protracted as firms jockey for their individual positions. In Japan, MITI has frequently applied significant pressure on firms to set basic standards, pushing them to move on to the next stage in the innovation cycle' (p.653). Also see the examples of the Japanese computer and machine tools industries in Dore (1986: pp.134-6).

36 It may not matter whether a country goes for superconductivity or biotechnology, but it matters whether enough complementary investments are made in either of these industries.

12). Thus seen, industrial policy that coordinates complementary investment decisions may be essential for economic change in a world of interdependence, rather than be an obstacle to it.[37]

3.2.2 Codifiability of Knowledge, Product Cycle and Industrial Policy

The limited codifiability of technical knowledge requires that we have to incorporate the problem of knowledge generation into our industrial-policy framework. The problem of knowledge generation is captured in more practical terms by the theory of the 'product cycle' (see Vernon 1987), which is known to be incorporated into Japanese industrial-policy practice (Okimoto 1989: Chapter 1; Magaziner and Hout 1980: Chapter 4).[38]

According to this theory, a young market is characterised by a phase of experimentation in which different ways of doing the same thing vie with each other. As the market matures, most technical knowledge becomes codified and easily transmittable. When a few technologies emerge as the best-practice ones, they are adopted across the industry, as firms learn from the experiences of others. As a market matures and finally becomes senile, the discovery potential in that market gradually diminishes (as knowledge becomes more codified) and the role of 'competition as a discovery procedure' (Hayek 1978) is accordingly reduced.[39] Let us examine how the idea of the product cycle can be incorporated into the practice of industrial policy.

---

37 For a classic discussion of the problem of coordinating complementary investments, see Richardson (1960). Also related are concepts like Hirschman's 'linkages' (Hirschman 1958) and Dahmén's 'development blocks' (Dahmén 1988).

38 Magaziner and Hout (1980) argue that 'MITI's greatest strength appears to be its understanding of the competitive stages through which an industry moves and its ability to fashion appropriate policy' (p.38). They document that '[f]or businesses in the early, rapid growth phases of development . . . policy calls for protection from foreign competition, concentration among producers, government support of the industry's cash flow, and stimulation of new technology . . . . For businesses which are already internationally competitive . . . government assistance recedes [with the significant exception of occasional officially sanctioned recession and export cartels co-ordinated by the industry associations] as it is no longer necessary. Finally, for businesses in competitive decline, MITI becomes active again, this time trying to bring about capacity reduction and rationalisation' (pp.38-9).

In the infant stage of an industry, where experimentation is necessary to generate new knowledge, industrial policy should encourage it. More aggressive experimentation and learning can be encouraged by providing firms with a more stable environment (through, say, patent systems, subsidies, tariffs or other types of entry barrier), as the familiar infant-industry argument goes. At this stage it would also be necessary for the state to set up institutional arrangements that can cope with the new externalities generated by this new industry (Nelson and Soete 1988: pp.633-4). Moreover industrial policy has a valuable coordinatory role to play at this stage. Introducing national product and, if necessary, process standards, coordinating competing investment decisions to prevent under-investment and over-investment, and ensuring that complementary investments are made will all be useful at this stage.

As the industry matures, experimentation becomes less important. According to Hayek, when 'we have a highly organised market of a fully standardised commodity produced by many producers, there is little need or scope for competitive activities because the situation is such that the conditions which these activities might bring about are already satisfied to begin with. The best ways of producing the commodity, its character and uses, are most of the time known to nearly the same degree to all members of the market' (Hayek 1949b: p.103). When the technology has been stabilised and codified, on the one hand, and the institutional arrangements necessary to cope with new configurations of asset specificity and the resulting uncertainty have been set up, on the other hand, the 'static' dimension of industrial policy, which we discussed earlier, becomes more important.[40]

---

39 Of course, we should not forget the possibility of 'rejuvenation', whereby a new series of exogenous technical changes turn a mature industry into a young one again, although we may not go as far as Pierre Dreyfus, a former French Minister of Industry, who argued that '[t]here are no condemned sectors; there are only outmoded technologies' (quoted in Hall 1987: p. 210). I thank Nathan Rosenberg for reminding me of this important point.

40 A good example of the shift in policy emphasis according to product cycle is the production cartel among six Japanese computer peripheral equipment producers organised by MITI in the late-1970s. 'The products handled through the cartel included [mainly] standard peripherals whose design had stabilised and where further innovation was remote' (Magaziner and Hout 1980: pp. 83-4).

As an industry enters its senile stage, production shrinks, labour is shed and capacity is scrapped. The material and human resources employed in an industry may be highly specific to that industry so their redeployment may be extremely difficult, or even impossible. In the face of a possible loss in value of specific assets, the owners of the assets will resist change, and this may result in a considerable waste of resources if a war of attrition among the firms concerned or protracted labour disputes take place. The role of industrial policy in this phase will be to encourage private negotiations regarding exit and capacity scrapping between the relevant agents, or even to impose a centralised solution when negotiations reach a stalemate. Retraining and reloca- tion programmes organised by the state will also greatly assist the process of negotiation by reducing the would-be displaced workers' resistance to the firm's decision to exit or scrap the capacity.

3.2.3 Diversity of Innovatory Sources and Industrial Polity

Nelson (1981), in discussing the innovation mechanism of the capitalist economy, argues that the waste that is bound to be generated by competitive innovative attempts (say, due to duplication) may be a price worth paying to avoid the dangers of relying on a single mind for innovation (that is, monopoly). Or as Abramovitz (1986) puts it, 'in the uncertainty that obscures early efforts to explore new fields, it would be quite unwise to concentrate all efforts on a single approach to a still cloudy goal' (p.41). This is because innovation is basically a chase after a moving target, a job in which nobody can claim absolute superiority. That is, 'were man omniscient and omnipotent, he would not choose to organise his R&D activities through private enterprise [given the wasteful nature of competitive R&D activities]. The case for private enterprise as an engine of progress must be posed in recogni- tion of bounded rationality' (Nelson 1981: pp.108-9).

This is a powerful argument. Unless human rationality is un- bounded, there will be a pressing need to preserve a diversity of the sources of knowledge in an ever-changing world – although this statement should not necessarily be interpreted as an advice against all 'collusive' behaviours amongst firms (Jorde and Teece 1990: pp. 81-

2).[41] However, does the state have any role to play, if this is the case? Should it not just leave things to evolve on their own?

One point against the apparent *laissez-faire* implication of this 'diversity' argument is that imperfections in the capital market put a follower firm in a disadvantaged position if there is a high fixed-investment requirement.[42] In this situation the state can act as a surrogate capital market and subsidise a potential entrant that is deemed to be at least equally capable as the incumbent firm except in its financial ability. State-organised venture-capital schemes conducted in countries such as Korea, France and the United Kingdom are good examples of this.

The state can contribute to increasing the diversity of innovatory sources in a more direct manner. For example, it may expand the pool of potential entrants into an industry with high R&D components by subsidising related R&D activities by firms which operate in similar lines. Or, alternatively, it may encourage related basic research in universities or public laboratories, which will publicise the results of their research. This of course carries some possibility of duplication, but it may be a price worth paying to preserve and develop diversity.

3.3 Concluding Remarks: The Socialisation of Risk

In the first half of this section we discussed the nature of change in the capitalist economy. We argued that the process of change in the capitalist economy is best characterised as a quasi-biological evolutionary process whereby the agents can and do change both their own 'genes' (behavioural characteristics) and the selection mechanism (or environment). Drawing on this argument, we discussed the dynamic dimension of industrial policy in the second half of the section. It was pointed out that coordinating changes, encouraging experimentation and preserving diversity are the most important roles industrial policy can play.

---

41 On the role of diversity in the economic system, see Johnson and Lundvall (1989: pp.103-4). On the role of genetic diversity in the biological world, see Axelrod (1984: p.170).

42 See the 'long purse story' (pp. 337-9) and the case of high fixed R&D costs (p. 414) in Tirole (1988) for the implications of an imperfect capital market for R&D activities.

The crucial theme emerging from our discussion in this section is that of the 'socialisation of risk', whereby risks involved in economic changes are borne by society rather than by individuals. In the models in the orthodox tradition, where individuals make decisions in an atomised fashion, risks involved in changes are necessarily borne by the individuals. To those who subscribe to this view, the socialisation of risk opens doors to the moral hazard of excessive risk-taking by those individuals whose risks are borne by society (see Section 4.1 below). However in the real world many changes involve interdependent decisions. If the risks involved in these situations have to be solely borne by the individuals, necessary changes may not come about. The socialisation of risk through state intervention is a means of promoting changes that involve interdependence.

Contrary to what is implicitly assumed in mainstream economics, the capitalist economy has developed on the basis of the growing socialisation of risk. As Rosenberg and Birdzell (1986) argue, '[t]he West has grown rich, by comparison to other economies, by allowing its economic sector the autonomy to experiment in true development of new and diverse products, methods of manufacture, modes of enterprise organisation, market relations, methods of transportation and communication, and relation between capital and labour' (p. 333). And in such a process, institutional arrangements that, by 'internalising benefits and externalising costs of private investment' (North 1981: p.62), allow experimentation and risk-taking beyond a scale whose risk can personally be borne by the experimenter (for example, systems of limited liability) have played an important role. The socialisation of risk through state intervention, then, may be seen as but one extension of these already existing institutional arrangements.

4.   POSSIBLE PROBLEMS OF INDUSTRIAL POLICY

4.1 Problems of Information

One common objection to industrial policy is based on problems of information (e.g., Burton 1983; Grossman 1988). There are two major elements in this argument. First of all, it is argued that the state does not possess enough information to decide correctly on the future industrial structure of the economy. This is the problem of 'insufficient information'. Secondly, it is argued that the state is at an informational disadvantage *vis-à-vis* the firms that are subject to industrial policy. The firms, the argument goes, may use their informational advantage to extract more than they deserve on social grounds (a moral hazard problem). This is the problem of 'asymmetric information'.

With the exception of some staunch free-marketeers (e.g., Burton 1983), those who employ informational arguments (e.g., Cairncross *et al.*1983; Grossman 1988; OECD 1989) support a generalised industrial policy targeted at certain types of activities rather than at particular industries (e.g., investment, R&D), against selective industrial policy – the type of policy we defined as industrial policy proper at the beginning of the chapter. If the state has all the relevant information, the argument goes, particularistic interventions may work, but since this is unlikely to be the case, the state should support productive behaviour in general rather than pick the winners on the basis of incomplete information (Price 1980; Lindbeck 1981).

4.1.1 Insufficient Information

Concerning the insufficient-information argument, note first that insufficient information does not prevent us from planning our future economic life. Actually the uncertainty of the future is exactly the reason why we plan for the future. Overcoming uncertainty is one of the most important functions of business management, especially in large modern corporations (Richardson 1960; Williamson 1975; Stinchcombe 1990). A firm chooses its production technology, capacity, liquidity position, inventory level and so on, to minimise the potential loss in case of abrupt changes in environmental factors such as market demand, macroeconomic conditions and the state of technological development – in other words, to overcome parametric uncertainty. A firm goes into long-term binding contracts concerning its purchases of raw materials, labour power, parts and equipment, on the one hand, and its sales of products, on the other, to minimise a potential loss in the event of opportunistic behaviour by its business partners – in other words, to overcome strategic uncertainty. It is inadequate to argue that the state should not attempt to plan the future of the national economy because of insufficient information, when firms can and do plan their own future despite – or rather, precisely because of – insufficient information.

Secondly, the informational requirement for intelligent state intervention is not always so great as to disallow state intervention altogether. Entrepreneurs themselves often operate on the basis of informed guesses or of 'animal spirits' in making investment decisions. Frequently much of the information used by the firm to make investment decisions – for example, estimates of present and future demand, the availability of best-practice technology, the financial situation of the firm, the distribution network of the firm – are readily available to anybody, and not just to the firm itself. Moreover, a large part of the information used by the firm is acquired from external sources such as consultants, research institutes and state agencies (e.g., a central statistical bureau). Thus seen, it is not necessarily true that the state suffers from insufficient information whereas the firms do not. In fact one of MITI's resources in dealing with the private sector has been its 'superior information' (Okimoto 1989: p.145), thanks to the more extensive informational network in the hands of the state.[43]

Thirdly, in the context of late development (on the concept of late development, see Gerschenkron 1966), the problem of identifying desirable industrial structures is far less serious. This is because late-developers can have the 'second-mover advantage', by which they can watch the countries on the frontier of economic development and learn from their experiences.[44] Even in a country like Japan, which was pretty close to the frontier of industrial development, it is recognised that '[s]etting priorities, picking the next likely winners, has not been difficult throughout the postwar period when the objectives of policy were primarily "catching up" objectives' (Dore 1986: p.135). The insufficient-information argument loses most of its force in the case of late-developers (that is, almost all countries) where the scope for 'conscious mutation' is great (also see Dore 1989).

---

43 Needless to say, due to the limited human ability to process information, the greater availability of information does not guarantee a better decision (see Chang 1994: Chapter 2, Section 2.1.2). See also the Korean case discussed in Chang (1993).
44 Of course, it has to be recognised that there exists 'second-mover disadvantage', because the first-movers would reap more rents from innovation. I owe this point to Sandeep Kapur. Also see Landes (1990) and Amsden and Hikino (1993).

4.1.2 Asymmetric Information

Concerning the asymmetric-information argument, note first that asymmetric information is not confined to the relationship between the state and firms, but is a ubiquitous problem in economic life, as we have repeatedly pointed out. Informational asymmetries exist between firms and lending institutions and between managers and shareholders. It exists, moreover, within the firm itself, that is, between headquarters and subsidiaries (or other component parts of the firm). If the asymmetry of information is always so severe as to disallow state intervention, neither financing somebody else's investment projects nor managerial planning can be justified. After all, large modern corporations came into being despite the dangers of the principal-agent problem, because there are ways of controlling managerial excesses (see Chandler 1962). And likewise there are ways and means to reduce informational asymmetry between the state and firms.

Secondly, the problem of asymmetric information is not unique to industrial policy as defined by us, but it applies to other policies too. Moreover, general industrial policy, which its supporters assume to have no moral-hazard problem due to asymmetric information (for example, Corden 1980: pp.182-3; Balassa 1985: p.319), may suffer even more acutely from such a problem. As contracts become more and more general, the contingencies to be considered become more and more numerous, resulting in prohibitive transaction costs in drawing up effective contracts. This means that general industrial policy can be compromised by unforeseen contingencies. An interesting example is the US 1981 tax-code provisions, which were originally intended to boost industrial R&D but ended up subsidising advertising firms (Lawrence 1984: p.140, no.45). Industrial policy, as defined by us, being particularistic in its nature, tends to involve contracts that are more custom-designed and hence allow fewer unforeseen contingencies and less moral hazard. The use of plan contracts with specified targets between the state and individual firms in France is the best example of preventing moral hazard through the use of custom-designed policy (see Hall 1987: p.207).

Thirdly, the asymmetric-information argument assumes that local information is always better than global information because it is more finely-meshed.[45] However, people with localised information may make a substantively less rational decision due to the sub-goal-identification problem. If the aim of industrial policy is to improve the efficiency of the economy as a whole, it may actually be better, under certain circumstances, not to be affected by the localised information possessed by the firm. Especially when the decision involves externalities that are not borne by the firm, the state can make a better decision solely due to the more global nature of its information, and not because it is a superior being.

4.2 Problems of Rent-Seeking and Entrepreneurship

The ever-changing nature of the capitalist economy – or Schumpeter's 'gales of creative destruction' (Schumpeter 1987) – and the consequent pervasiveness of uncertainty give entrepreneurship a vital role to play in the capitalist development process as the generator and/or finder of new knowledge (Schumpeter 1987; Dobb 1925; Kirzner 1973; Nelson 1986). However, as Baumol (1990) argues, depending on the incentive structure in the economy, the existing stock of entrepreneurial talents may be diverted away from productive purposes into unproductive or even destructive ones. According to him, entrepreneurial talents can be used for destructive purposes when rents are granted to those who are best at destroying existing assets (for example, warmongering in Europe in the Middle Ages). They can be used for unproductive purposes when rents are granted to those who are best at transferring existing assets, as in rent-seeking (also see North 1990b: Chapter 8).

The state has a major role to play in preventing the diversion of entrepreneurial talents into unproductive venues by reducing profit-

---

45 Interestingly, some Marxist denunciation of the 'revisionist' strategies of 'co-opted' trade union leaderships in favour of rank-and-file militancy (e.g., Panitch 1981) is based on the same view of information. As Tomlinson (1982) argues, this position ultimately depends on 'a belief that the experience of the ordinary employee, his/her experience of the oppressive and exploitative relations of capitalist wage labour will guarantee the appropriate socialist direction in the struggle. The experience gives a privileged access to the appropriate means to change the capitalist enterprise whereas the experience of the trade union official may lead him or her to a different *and wrong assessment*' (italics added) (pp.44-5).

able opportunities in those areas. The nature of unproductive activities is that they are transaction-cost-generating activities, and many such activities exist because of strategic uncertainty. Thus seen, for example, the reduction in macroeconomic instability through appropriate macroeconomic management would reduce the need for activities that are specifically designed to deal with it (e.g., financial hedging), and therefore limit the diversion of entrepreneurial talents into these activities. The same applies to activities intended to deal with more specific coordination problems. Investment coordination through indicative planning and the establishment of national product standards are areas where the state can intervene to reduce strategic uncertainty inherent in the coordination problem and therefore the scope for unproductive entrepreneurship.

Another crucial condition for entrepreneurship to be a productive activity is that the rent accruing to the entrepreneur should be durable but not permanent, as already pointed out by Marx (1981) and Schumpeter (1987). In general, people pursue rents primarily because they value the quiet life that follows from the acquisition of a monopoly position, and not because they are devoted to the cause of productivity growth (although this may be the case in certain contexts). Therefore, if the monopoly position (and the accompanying rent) is too quickly eroded, there will be little incentive to innovate (Schumpeter 1987: pp.104-5). However, if the monopoly position lasts too long, the cumulative deadweight loss due to its existence will ultimately cancel out the initial productivity gains made in the process through which such a monopoly position was established. Thus the important question is: how can it be ensured that the rent lasts long enough to motivate people to capture it but short enough to force people to keep improving productivity (Richardson 1960: Chapter 3)? In employing industrial policy measures, which are bound to create rents, this question becomes particularly relevant. Then how can the state ensure that the rents are durable but do not become permanent?

One obvious way is to use the patent system. The patent system, by guaranteeing a monopoly position, frees the innovator from the fear of being caught up with, but at the same time, by limiting the length of such a guarantee, ensures that the cumulative deadweight loss will not ultimately cancel out the initial productivity gains. However, when it is not just a particular product or process that enhances social productivity but a whole investment project (say, through spillover effects), the patent system may not be used. And in this case, the necessary incentive, the rent, needs to be created in other ways such as subsidies, import protection and industrial licensing.

If the rents are created by means other than the patent system, the crucial question becomes whether the state is able to withdraw the rent whenever necessary. This means, first of all, that when it is contemplating an industrial policy, the state should set strict performance criteria so that the rents would not go on regardless of the performance of their recipients. For example, in France the provision of state aid to ailing industries dependent on their performance is not unrelated to the relative effectiveness of those aids (Hall 1987: p.210). Secondly, the state has to ensure that it has the power to punish the firms if they resist the elimination of the rents. It is not a coincidence that industrial policy exercises were more successful in France, whose state has control over the banking sector, than in, say, the UK, whose state has had only a limited control over the flow of financial resources in the economy.[46]

In addition, some industrial policy measures that may be used as means to preserve diversity – for example, venture-capital schemes and subsidisation of related commercial R&D and basic research – can also be used as means of keeping rents from becoming permanent. Even when new entry does not add to diversity (that is, when the entrants have the same technology and organisational structure), prohibiting the incumbent firm from expanding its capacity beyond what is justified by scale-economy considerations and allowing new entrants can prevent permanency of the rent.

4.3 Political Problems: Legitimacy and Democratic Control

An industrial-policy regime is not merely a technical means to achieve efficiency, but is fundamentally a regime of political economy. This means that a discussion of industrial policy cannot be satisfactory without discussion of the political problems associated with it. There

---

46 For discussions of the different relationships between the state and finance in different OECD countries and their implications for industrial adjustment, see Zysman (1983) and Cox (eds.) (1986). On the same issue in the French context, see Hall (1987). For the Korean case, see Chang (1993).

are several political problems related to industrial policy, but we shall discuss only the two which are the most relevant in this context – legitimacy and democratic control.

4.3.1 Legitimacy

Some may argue that industrial policy should not be used because it undermines the legitimacy of the state. First of all, by opening the door for special interests, industrial-policy practice can erode the image of the state as a social guardian and therefore make people question its intentions.[47] Secondly, industrial policy gives bureaucrats the power to allocate property rights and hence creates scope for bureaucratic corruption. In addition to its efficiency conse-quences (e.g., an industrial licence may go to an inefficient producer), corruption may have consequences for the legitimacy of the political system (Krueger 1990: p.18). If industrial policy may endanger the legitimacy of the political system, should we not refrain from it, whatever its efficiency gains may be?

First of all, it should be pointed out that legitimacy is concerned with the socio-economic system as a whole, of which the political system is only a part. People may be generally disenchanted with the outcome of the socio-economic system – for example, high income inequality – even if the state is impartial and honest. For example, Dobb (1925) argues that monopoly 'may give occasion for a psycho-logical tendency to antagonism and distrust on the part of dependent groups and classes towards those in a position of advantage.... If this happens ... the society may cease to have the "general will" which is supposed to exist in a harmonious democratic community; its sections may not respond to the same idealistic appeals, and their latent antagonism may prevent them from subordinating their own sectional interests to the success of the whole' (pp.157-8).[48] The problem of

---

47 For a discussion of this problem in the French context, see Hall (1987: pp.176-80).

48 And he continues: As a consequence, 'harmony can only be obtained by coercion or by a series of compromises . . . and purely strategic considerations may tend more and more to override any considerations of maximum welfare and efficiency.' It 'may also produce class struggle', and, '[i]n conflicts of this kind, *a considerable part of the economic resources of a community may be consumed, either in their conduct or in their prevention'* (italics added) (p.158).

legitimacy is much more fundamental than whether or not a particular government, or a specific type of policy, is open to corruption.

Moreover, although the erosion of legitimacy is a serious danger when conducting industrial policy, it is by no means a possibility confined to industrial policy. Other, more general, policies may also suffer from the problem of legitimacy. For example, monetary policy may *prima facie* appear to be immune to interest-group activities, but it is well known that industrialists often lobby for expansionary monetary policies whereas financiers usually lobby for tight monetary policies. And there is no guarantee that such lobbying would not involve corruption and therefore endanger the legitimacy of the state.

4.3.2 Democratic Control

The fact that an industrial-policy regime apparently requires an elite bureaucracy has often raised concerns about democratic control. Especially among those who believe in parliamentary democracy of the Anglo-Saxon variety, the weakness of legislature in 'industrial-policy states' such as Japan and France (not to mention Korea, which has been non-democratic for the major chunk of its modern history) has been a great concern. To them the fact that bureaucrats, who are not subject to popular mandate, are powerful means that the whole political process is rigged to ensure that efficiency dominates democratic values.[49] They believe that industrial policy is less subject to democratic control because it is open to bureaucratic discretion, in contrast with other 'even-handed' or general policies.

Against this view, it should firstly be pointed out that some degree of bureaucratic control is necessary for any society of reasonable sophistication, because 'many decisions have to be taken in response to rapidly changing situations and cannot, except at the cost of total stasis and chaos, be "left" until a highly democratic decision-making process has been completed. Almost immediately then, in any

---

49 It has to be pointed out, however, that parliamentary representation (the representation of individuals *qua* individuals) is not the only legitimate form of representation. Representation along class lines (as in Scandinavian neo-corporatism) or even 'issues' (as in some American lobbying organisations) are all too pervasive to be dismissed as illegitimate (see Maier 1987, on different forms of representation).

real situation it becomes necessary to delegate powers from larger, more democratic bodies... to smaller, more "efficient" bodies. However, once such delegation has occurred, a great deal of the real day-to-day decision-making power is taken out of democratic channels and placed in the hands of small minorities which may then be beyond the effective control of the larger bodies' (Kitching 1983: p.39). That is, there may be a certain trade-off between democratic control and efficiency in decision-making. However no *a priori* criterion can tell us which mix of democratic control and efficiency – including the one existing in an industrial-policy regime – is the most desirable.

Secondly, it is not just industrial policy that suffers from the problem of democratic control. For example, those who criticise industrial policy usually support an independent central bank, but it is not clear to us why the democratic credentials of an official in the Japanese MITI or the British DTI should be viewed with suspicion whereas those of a German Bundesbank official should be accepted without question. No policy is free from the personal discretion of the policy-maker. Moreover other policies may be even less subject to democratic control than industrial policy due to their less transparent nature (Dore 1987: pp.199-201). Industrial policy usually clearly reveals the beneficiaries of the policy, whereas other policies (e.g., monetary policy) often do not clearly reveal who is benefiting from them. Such transparency may make it easier to exercise democratic control over industrial policy than in the case of other policies, if there is a will to do so.

4.4   The Problem of Supporting Institutions

Opponents of industrial policy often point out that 'industrial-policy states' have a particular set of institutional arrangements, especially an elite bureaucracy with a wide discretionary range and a cooperative government-business relationship.[50] They argue that it is

---

50 Interestingly, American authors like Badaracco and Yoffie (1983), Schultze (1983: pp. 9-10), and Lawrence (1984: pp.112-5) usually emphasise the absence of an elite bureaucracy and British authors like Hare (1985: pp.112-3) emphasise the hostility between the state and the capitalists as the major obstacle to an effective industrial policy, reflecting the institutional characteristics in their respective countries.

difficult to change institutions and therefore that industrial policy cannot be a realistic option for other countries that lack such institutional arrangements, no matter what merits it may have.

Although an effective industrial-policy regime does require an appropriate set of supporting institutions, the difficulty of building it should not be exaggerated. Countries learn from their own past experience and from other countries and engage in institutional innovations. For example, in Japan many of the institutions that are often said to have arisen because of Japan's unique culture are actually products of conscious institution building. The fact that Japanese labour, product and financial markets were vastly more volatile in the early-1950s than they have been since shows that the renowned 'collectivist' characteristics of the Japanese are 'not just a "hangover" of ancient (feudal) cultural traditions' (Dore 1986: p.250) but also products of conscious institutional innovation (see also Magaziner and Hout 1980: p.2). Moreover, institutional innovation does not necessarily take a long time. The famous Japanese lifetime employment is basically a postwar creation (Johnson 1982: p.14). The French state, which is renowned for its interventionist and 'modernising' attitude, was famous for its *laissez-faire* and 'anti-modern' attitude before the Second World War (Cohen 1977; Kuisel 1981). The well-known Swedish labour-capital consensus emerged in a relatively short period of time out of one of the most contested industrial relations in Europe of the 1920s (Korpi 1983). Moreover learning from other countries with different institutions does not necessarily mean that a country has to exactly copy their institutions. It is often possible to create functional equivalents of foreign institutions. For example, the Swedish 'active labour-market policy' and Japanese lifetime employment are very different institutional arrangements, but they are functionally equivalent in creating a positive attitude among workers toward technological change by guaranteeing them jobs. In this regard, the following quotation from Dore (1986) is well worth consideration:

'[Learning from the Japanese experience] need not mean that we [the British] have to become Japanese, absorb the Confucian ethic, or raise our sense of national identity to the Japanese levels. What it does mean is that we should ask ourselves whether there are not other ways in which some of the things which Japanese institutions and traditions achieve for the Japanese might be obtained by other methods, other institutional arrangements, more consonant with our own tradition. If close cooperation and consultation between managers and workers seems to be a precondition for rapid innovation in manufacturing firms, and if it is difficult to achieve this, given our adversarial traditions, what forms of industrial democracy or workplace decision-sharing might substitute for the easy acceptance of bureaucratic hierarchy which facilitates cooperation in Japanese firms? If we cannot have, and do not want, lifetime employment to be the norm, if we want to preserve a more mobile system with the greater personal freedom which that provides, can we at the same time devise schemes which would give British employers the same incentive to invest in training their employees as the lifetime employment expectation gives Japanese employers? If the crucial aspect of the Japanese system of financing industry seems to be the way in which it facilitates long-term planning and investment, and reduces preoccupations with next year's bottom line, is there any way in which our own financial institutions could be mended to achieve the same effect, without necessarily modeling our stock exchange on Japan's? If inflation control in Japan crucially depends on institutionalised wage leadership and a nationally simultaneous pay settlement date, does that not suggest the wisdom of re-examining the many suggestions that have been made for introducing synchro-pay in Britain?' (p.252).

5. CONCLUSION

The common reaction to the argument for industrial policy has been one of suspicion and incredulity. The opponents of it regard industrial policy either as a bureaucratic meddling that is at best irrelevant – for example, 'Industrial policy is not the major reason for Japan's success' (Trezise 1983, title) – or as a peculiar form of state intervention that works only in countries with a particular culture – for example, 'Industrial policy: It can't happen here' (Badaracco and Yoffie 1983, title). Such reactions are more than understandable when thinking that orthodox economic theory hardly recognises any form of coordination other than the idealised perfect market and ignores the role of endogenous technical change and learning.

However, as we have tried to show, industrial policy is a policy practice that can be firmly anchored in economic theory if we incorporate recent developments in economic theory that take seriously the issues of institutional diversity and technical change. As a coordination mechanism, industrial policy can be most efficient in a context where interdependence and asset specificity are important. In this context, coordination through the market would incur high bargaining costs and coordination through central planning, high information costs; while industrial policy is likely to incur little of both types of cost. When we take the issue of technical change into account, industrial policy also emerges as a superior way to promote it. Industrial policy does not kill off the profit motive – which is the most important, if not the only, driving force behind technical progress – as central planning would and, through the socialisation of risk, it can promote changes that are additional to what the market can produce on its own.

Industrial policy, needless to say, is no panacea. Like any other policy, or any other form of economic coordination, it has its own costs and benefits. Its benefits seem to have more than offset its costs in success stories like those of Japan and Korea, but we have plenty of other examples that show that its costs may overwhelm its benefits. The real question is not whether industrial policy can work or not (because it does), but how it can be made to work. In this chapter we have tried to provide some theoretical grounds for identifying the economic, political and institutional conditions under which industrial policy would work and have suggested some ways and means to achieve them.

BIBLIOGRAPHY

Abramovitz, M. (1986). 'Catching Up, Forging Ahead, and Falling Behind', *Journal of Economic History,* vol.46, no.2.

Alchian, A. (1950). 'Uncertainty, Evolution and Economic Theory', *Journal of Political Economy,* vol.58, no.3.

Amadeo, E. and Banuri, T. (1991). 'Policy, Governance, and the Management of Conflict', in T. Banuri (ed.), *Economic Liberalisation: No Panacea.* Oxford: Clarendon Press.

Amsden, A. (1989). *Asia's Next Giant.* New York: Oxford University Press.

Amsden, A. and Hikino, T. (1993). 'Borrowing Technology or Innovating: An Exploration of Paths of Industrial Development', in R. Thomson (ed.), *Learning and Technological Change.* London and Basingstoke: Macmillan.

Axelrod, R. (1984). *The Evolution of Co-operation.* New York: Basic Books Inc..

Badaracco, J. and Yoffie, D. (1983). '"Industrial Policy": It Can't Happen Here', *Harvard Business Review,* Nov./Dec. 1983.

Baumol, W. (1990). 'Entrepreneurship: Productive, Unproductive, and Destructive', *Journal of Political Economy,* vol.98, no.5.

Baumol, W., Blackman, S., and Wolff, E. (1989). *Productivity and American Leadership.* Cambridge, MA: The MIT Press.

Bhagwati, J. (1988). *Protectionism.* Cambridge, MA: The MIT Press.

Bhagwati, J. (1989). 'U.S. Trade Policy at Crossroads', *The World Economy,* vol.12, no.4.

Blackaby, F. (ed.) (1979). *De-Industrialisation.* London: Gower.

Boltho, A. (1985). 'Was Japan's Industrial Policy Successful?', *Cambridge Journal of Economics,* vol.9, no.2.

Bowles, S. and Gintis, H. (1990). 'Contested Exchange: New Microfoundations for the Political Economy of Capitalism', *Politics and Society,* vol.18, no.2.

Burton, J. (1983). *Picking Losers . . . ?: The Political Economy of Industrial Policy.* London: Institute of Economic Affairs.

Cairncross, A., Kay, J. and Silberston, Z. (1983). 'Problems of Industrial Recovery', in R. Matthews and J. Sargent (eds.), *Contemporary Problems of Economic Policy.* London: Methuen.

Chandler, A. (1962). *Strategy and Structure.* Cambridge, MA: The MIT Press.

Chang, H.-J. (1993). 'The Political Economy of Industrial Policy in Korea', *Cambridge Journal of Economics,* vol.17, no.2.

Chang, H.-J. (1994). *The Political Economy of Industrial Policy.* London and Basingstoke: Macmillan.

Cohen, S. (1977). *Modern Capitalist Planning: The French Model,* 2nd edn.. Berkeley: University of California Press.

Cohen, S. and Zysman, J. (1987). *Manufacturing Matters.* New York: Basic Books.

Corden, W. (1980). 'Relationships between Macro-economic and Industrial Policies', *The World Economy,* vol.3, no.2.

Cox, A. (ed.) (1986). *State, Finance, and Industry in Comparative Perspective.* Brighton: Wheatsheaf Books.

Dahmén, E. (1988). '"Development Blocks" in Industrial Economics', *Scandinavian Economic History Review,* vol.36, no.1.

David, P. (1985). 'Clio and the Economics of QWERTY', *American Economic Review,* vol.75, no.2.

Dawkins, R. (1986). *The Blind Watchmaker.* Harmondsworth: Penguin Books.

Demsetz, H. (1982). *Economic, Legal, and Political Dimensions of Competition.* Amsterdam: North-Holland.

Dobb, M. (1925). *Capitalist Enterprise and Social Progress.* London: Routledge & Sons Ltd..

Donges, J. (1980). 'Industrial Policies in West Germany's Not so Market-oriented Economy', *The World Economy,* vol.3, no.2.

Dore, R. (1986). *Flexible Rigidities: Industrial Policy and Structural Adjustment in the Japanese Economy 1970-80.* London: The Athlone Press.

Dore, R. (1987). *Taking Japan Seriously.* London: The Athlone Press.

Dore, R. (1989). 'Latecomers' Problems', *European Journal of Development Research,* vol.1, no.1.

Dornbusch, R., Poterba, J. and Summers, L. (1998). 'Macroeconomic Policy Should Make Manufacturing More Competitive', *Harvard Business Review,* Nov./Dec. 1988.

Duchêne, F. and Shepherd, G. (eds.) (1987). *Managing Industrial Change in Western Europe.* London: Frances Pinter.

Eatwell, J. (1982). 'Competition', in I. Bradley & M. Howard (eds.), *Classical and Marxian Political Economy.* London: Macmillan.

Fudenberg, D. and Tirole, J. (1986). 'A Theory of Exit in Duopoly', *Econometrica,* vol.54, no.4.

Gerschenkron, A. (1966). *Economic Backwardness in Historical Perspective.* Cambridge, MA: Belknap Press.

Ghemawat, P. and Nalebuff, B. (1985). 'Exit', *The Rand Journal of Economics,* vol.16, no.2.

Gould, S. (1983). *The Panda's Thumb,* Pelikan Books edn. Harmondsworth: Penguin Books.

Grossman, G. (1988). 'Strategic Export Promotion: A Critique', in P. Krugman (ed.), *Strategic Trade Policy and the New International Economics.* Cambridge, MA: The MIT Press.

Hall, P. (1987). *Governing the Economy.* Cambridge: Polity Press.

Hare, P. (1985). *Planning the British Economy.* London and Basingstoke: Macmillan.

Hayek, F. (1949a). 'Economics and Knowledge', in F. Hayek, *Individualism and Economic Order*. London: Routledge & Kegan Paul.

Hayek, F. (1949b). 'The Meaning of Competition', in F. Hayek, *Individualism and Economic Order*. London: Routledge & Kegan Paul.

Hayek, F. (1949c). 'The Use of Knowledge in Society', in F. Hayek, *Individualism and Economic Order*. London: Routledge & Kegan Paul.

Hayek, F. (1978). 'Competition as a Discovery Procedure', in F. Hayek, *New Studies in Philosophy, Politics, Economics and the History of Ideas*. London: Routledge & Kegan Paul.

Hayward, J. (1986). *The State and the Market Economy*. Brighton: Wheatsheaf Books.

Heiner, R. (1983). 'The Origin of Predictable Behaviour', *American Economic Review*, vol.73, no.4.

Heiner, R. (1988). 'Imperfect Decisions and Routinised Production: Implications for Evolutionary Modeling and Inertial Technical Change', in G. Dosi, C. Freeman, R. Nelson, G. Silverberg and L. Soete (eds.), *Technical Change and Economic Theory*. London: Pinter Publishers.

Hirschman, A. (1958). *The Strategy of Economic Development*. New Haven and London: Yale University Press.

Hodgson, G. (1988). *Economics and Institutions*. Cambridge: Polity Press.

Jacquemin, A. (ed.) (1984). *European Industry: Public Policy and Corporate Strategy*. Oxford: Clarendon Press.

Johnson, B. and Lundvall, B. (1989). 'Limits of the Pure Market Economy', in *Samhällsventenskap, Ekonomi och Historia – Festskrift till Lars Harlitz*. Göteborg: Daidalos.

Johnson, C. (1982). *MITI and the Japanese Miracle*. Stanford: Stanford University Press.

Johnson, C. (1984). 'Introduction: The Idea of Industrial Policy', in C. Johnson (ed.), *The Industrial Policy Debate*. San Francisco: Institute for Contemporary Studies.

Johnson, C. (ed.) (1984). *The Industrial Policy Debate*. San Francisco: Institute for Contemporary Studies.

Jones, L. and Sakong, I. (1980). *Government, Business and Entrepreneurship in Economic Development: The Korean Case*. Cambridge, MA: Harvard University Press.

Jorde, T. and Teece, D. (1990). 'Innovation and Cooperation: Implications for Competition and Antitrust', *Journal of Economic Perspectives*, vol.4, no.3.

Kaldor, N. (1985). *Economics without Equilibrium*. Cardiff: University College of Cardiff Press.

Khan, M. A. (1987). 'Perfect Competition', in *The Palgrave Dictionary of Economics*, vol.3. London: Macmillan.

Kirzkowski, H. (ed.) (1984). *Monopolistic Competition and International Trade*. Oxford: Oxford University Press.

Kirzner, I. (1973). *Competition and Entrepreneurship.* Chicago: The University of Chicago Press.

Kitching, G. (1983). *Rethinking Socialism: A Theory for a Better Practice.* London: Methuen.

Knight, F. (1921). *Risk, Uncertainty, and Profit.* Chicago: The University of Chicago Press.

Korpi, W. (1983). *The Democratic Class Struggle.* London: Routledge & Kegan Paul.

Krueger, A. (1990). 'Government Failure in Economic Development', *Journal of Economic Perspective,* 1990, no.3.

Krugman, P. (1984). 'The U.S. Response to Foreign Industrial Targeting', *Brookings Papers on Economic Activity,* 1984, no.1.

Krugman, P. (ed.) (1988). *Strategic Trade Policy and the New International Economics.* Cambridge, MA: The MIT Press.

Kuisel, R. (1981). *Capitalism and the State in Modern France: Renovation and Economic Management in the Twentieth Century.* Cambridge: Cambridge University Press.

Landes, D. (1990). 'Why Are We So Rich and They So Poor?', *American Economic Review,* vol.80, no.2.

Landesmann, M. (1992). 'Industrial Policies and Social Corporatism', in J. Pekkarinen, M. Pohjola and B. Rowthorn (eds.), *Social Corporatism.* Oxford: Clarendon Press.

Lavoie, D. (1985). *Rivalry and Central Planning.* Cambridge: Cambridge University Press.

Lawrence, R. (1984). *Can America Compete?.* Washington D.C.: Brookings Institution.

Lindbeck, A. (1981). 'Industrial Policy as an Issue in the Economic Environment', *The World Economy,* vol.4, no.4.

Lippincott, B. (ed.) (1938). *On the Economic Theory of Socialism.* Minneapolis: The University of Minnesota Press.

Luedde-Neurath, R. (1986). *Import Controls and Export-Oriented: A Reassessment of the South Korean Case.* Boulder and London: Westview Press.

Magaziner, I. and Hout, T. (1980). *Japanese Industrial Policy.* London: Policy Studies Institute.

Maier, C. (1987). *In Search of Stability.* Cambridge: Cambridge University Press.

Marx, K. (1976). *Capital,* vol.1. Harmondsworth: Penguin Books.

Marx, K. (1981). *Capital,* vol.3. Harmondsworth: Penguin Books.

Maynard Smith, J. (1982). *Evolution and the Theory of Games.* Cambridge: Cambridge University Press.

McNulty, P. (1968). 'Economic Theory and the Meaning of Competition', *Quarterly Journal of Economics,* vol.82, November.

NEDO (National Economic Development Office). (1978). *Competition Policy.* London: Her Majesty's Stationery Office.

Nelson, R. (1981). 'Assessing Private Enterprise: An Exegesis of Tangled Doctrine', *The Bell Journal of Economics,* vol.12, no.1.

Nelson, R. (1986). 'Incentives for Entrepreneurship and Supporting Institutions', in B. Balassa and H. Giersch (eds.), *Economic Incentives.* London and Basingstoke: Macmillan.

Nelson, R. (1991). 'Diffusion of Development: Post-World War II Convergence Among Advanced Industrial Nations', *American Economic Review,* vol.81, no.2.

Nelson, R. and Soete, L. (1988). 'Policy Conclusions', in G. Dosi, C. Freeman, R. Nelson, G. Silverberg and L. Soete (eds.), *Technical Change and Economic Theory.* London: Pinter Publishers.

Nelson, R. and Winter, S. (1982). *An Evolutionary Theory of Economic Change.* Cambridge, MA: Belknap Press.

North, D. (1981). *Structure and Change in Economic History.* New York: W. W. Norton & Co..

North, D. (1990). *Institutions, Institutional Change and Economic Performance.* Cambridge: Cambridge University Press.

Norton, R. (1986). Industrial Policy and American Renewal, *Journal of Economic Literature,* vol.24, no.1.

O'Driscoll, G. (1986). 'Competition as a Process: a Law and Economics Perspective', in R. Langlois (ed.), *Economics as a Process.* Cambridge: Cambridge University Press.

OECD (Organisation for Economic Cooperation and Development) (1989). *Industrial Policy in OECD Countries; Annual Review 1989.* Paris: OECD.

Okimoto, D. (1989). *Between MITI and the Market: Japanese Industrial Policy for High Technology.* Stanford: Stanford University Press.

Pagano, U. (1985). *Work and Welfare in Economic Theory.* Oxford: Basil Blackwell.

Panitch, L. (1981). 'Trade Unions and the Capitalist State', *New Left Review,* no.125.

Parker, G. and Maynard Smith, J. (1990). 'Optimality Theory in Evolutionary Biology', *Nature,* vol. 348, no.1.

Pelikan, P. (1988). 'Can the Innovative System of Capitalism be Outperformed?', in G. Dosi, C. Freeman, R. Nelson, G. Silverberg and L. Soete (eds.), *Technical Change and Economic Theory.* London: Pinter Publishers.

Pinder, J. (1982). 'Causes and Kinds of Industrial Policy', in J. Pinder (ed.), *National Industrial Strategies and the World Economy.* London: Croom Helm.

Pinder, J. (ed.) (1982). *National Industrial Strategies and the World Economy.* London: Croom Helm.

Porter, M. (1990). *Competitive Advantage of the Nations:* London and Basingstoke: Macmillan.

Price, V. (1980). 'Alternatives to Delayed Structural Adjustment in "Workshop Europe"', *The World Economy,* vol.3, no.2.

Rasmusen, E. (1989). *Games and Information.* Oxford: Basil Blackwell.

Reich, R. (1982). 'Why the U.S. Needs an Industrial Policy', *Harvard Business Review,* Jan./Feb. 1982.

Renshaw, J. (1986). *Adjustment and Economic Performance in Industrialised Countries.* Geneva: ILO.

Richardson, G. B. (1960). *Information and Investment.* Oxford: Oxford University Press.

Richardson, G. B. (1971). 'Planning versus Competition', *Soviet Studies,* vol.22, no.3.

Richardson, G. B. (1972). 'The Organisation of Industry', *Economic Journal,* vol. 82, no.3.

Rosenberg, N. (1976). *Perspectives on Technology.* Cambridge: Cambridge University Press.

Rosenberg, N. and Birdzell, L. (1986). *How the West Grew Rich.* London: I. B. Tauris & Co. Ltd.

Rowthorn, B. and Wells, J. (1987). *Foreign Trade and De-Industrialisation.* Cambridge: Cambridge University Press.

Salter, W. (1960). *Productivity and Technical Change.* Cambridge: Cambridge University Press.

Schultze, C. (1983). 'Industrial Policy: A Dissent', *The Brookings Review,* Fall, 1983.

Schumpeter, J. (1987). *Capitalism, Socialism and Democracy,* 6th edn.. London: Unwin Paperbacks.

Simon, H. (1983). *Reason in Human Affairs.* Oxford: Basil Blackwell.

Singh, A. (1977). 'UK Industrialisation and the World Economy: A Case of De-Industrialisation', *Cambridge Journal of Economics,* vol.1, no.2.

Stigler, G. (1951). 'The Division of Labour is Limited by the Extent of the Market', *Journal of Political Economy,* vol.59, no.3.

Stinchcombe, A. (1990). *Information and Organisation.* Berkeley and Los Angeles: University of California Press.

Stout, D. (1979). 'De-industrialisation and Industrial Policy', in F. Blackaby (ed.), *De-industrialisation.* London: Gower.

Telser, L. (1987). *A Theory of Efficient Cooperation and Competition.* Cambridge: Cambridge University Press.

Thompson, G. (1989). 'The American Industrial Policy Debate: Any Lessons for the UK?', in G. Thompson (ed.), *Industrial Policy: USA and UK Debates.* London: Routledge.

Tirole, J. (1988). *The Theory of Industrial Organisation.* Cambridge, MA: The MIT Press.

Tomlinson, J. (1982). *The Unequal Struggle?: British Socialism and the Capitalist Enterprise.* London: Methuen.

Trezise, P. (1983). 'Industrial Policy is not the Major Reason for Japan's Success', *The Brookings Review,* vol.1, spring.

Varian, H. (1984). *Microeconomic Analysis.* New York: W. W. Norton.

Vernon, R. (1987). 'Product Cycle', in *The Palgrave Dictionary of Economics,* vol.3. London: Macmillan.

Williamson, O. (1975). *Markets and Hierarchies; Analysis and Antitrust Implications.* New York: The Free Press.

Williamson, O. (1985). *The Economic Institutions of Capitalism.* New York: The Free Press.

Williamson, O. (1988). 'The Logic of Economic Organisation', *Journal of Law, Economics and Organisation,* vol.4, no.1.

Winter, S. (1988). 'On Coase, Competence, and the Corporation', *Journal of Law, Economics and Organisation,* vol.4, no.1.

Yamamura, K. (1988). 'Caveat Emptor: The Industrial Policy of Japan', in P. Krugman (ed.), *Strategic Trade Policy and the New International Economics.* Cambridge, MA: The MIT Press.

Young, A. (1928). 'Increasing Returns and Economic Progress', *Economic Journal,* vol.38, no.4.

Zysman, J. (1983). *Governments, Markets and Growth: Financial Systems and the Politics of Industrial Change.* Oxford: Martin Robertson.

Chapter 5

The Economics and Politics of Regulation

1. INTRODUCTION

DURING the last two decades, in the context of a broader disillusionment with the efficacy and desirability of state intervention, many countries have embarked on a path of extensive regulatory reform, mostly (if not exclusively) in the form of deregulation. This was in stark contrast to the mood of the first couple of decades after the end of the Second World War, when state involvement in the economy increased dramatically in most countries. Why was there such a sea change? What were the consequences of such change? And how can we improve our understanding and policy practices in this area? In this chapter, we shall try to answer these questions by tracing the evolution of the perspectives on regulation (and deregulation) in the postwar era. In doing so, we shall also provide an overview of the economic and political developments in the real world, which affect and are affected by the evolution of ideas. Before doing that, however, some conceptual clarifications are in order.

Regulation is usually defined as the government (or the state)[1] directly prescribing and proscribing what private sector agents can and cannot do, so that their actions do not contradict the 'public interest'. Defined in this way, regulation is distinguished from the government provision of public goods out of tax revenues and from the provision of commercial goods and services through public enterprises. It is also distinguished from activities that are intended to affect the behaviours

---

1   We shall use the two terms interchangeably. Although there are many good reasons to draw a distinction between them, such a distinction is not crucial for the purpose of this survey.

of private sector agents indirectly by modifying price signals such as the administration of taxes and subsidies.

Of course, in reality, the picture is not so straightforward. To begin with, it is not easy to define the 'public interest'. What is called the public interest in conventional economic literature is defined in relation to the particular notion of social welfare derived from neoclassical economics, which is by no means universally accepted. Moreover, even within the neoclassical framework, there is an ongoing debate as to the exact definition of social welfare (Stiglitz 1988: Chapter 4; Cullis and Jones 1992: Chapter 1). Lastly, even if economists (or other social scientists) can theoretically define the public interest in an unambiguous way, what the government perceives as the public interest may not coincide with that definition – and this is even before we question whether the government actually intends and is able to promote the public interest, an important theme to which we shall return later.

Moreover, the distinction between regulation and other types of government intervention drawn in the above definition is quite often blurred in practice. For example, taxes and subsidies, if they are significant enough, in practice can amount to outright proscriptions or prescriptions (Gray 1995: p.6). Also, the distinction between the public provision of goods and services, on the one hand, and regulation, on the other, is not clear-cut in practice, because there are some agents whose status is neither entirely 'public' nor entirely 'private'. For example, is a government which affects the decision of a public-private joint venture 'regulating' it or not, according to the definition used above? There are also countries where public enterprises have a high degree of autonomy and operate on the basis of a formal contract with the government (e.g., the French 'plan contract'). The real, as opposed to nominal, distinction between them and, say, publicly regulated utilities in the US, is not entirely clear.

Let us sum up our discussion in this section. The conventional definition of regulation is government activity that is intended to affect directly the behaviours of private sector agents in order to align them with the 'public interest'. This excludes the provision of public goods through budget disbursement or the operation of public enterprise, as well as tax/subsidy measures, from the realm of regulation. Although we acknowledge that it has a number of ambiguities, this is the definition we adopt. Let us now begin our main discussion by looking at the historical evolution of perspectives on regulation.

2.   HISTORICAL EVOLUTION

2.1   The Age of Regulation (1945-70)

The quarter-century after the end of the Second World War, which for the purpose of our survey we call the 'age of regulation', witnessed a general rise in the level of government involvement across the world (for an overview of these developments, see Chapter 1).[2] For various reasons that we shall discuss below, during this period governments of many countries began to practise more activist macroeconomic policies, nationalised many enterprises (or established new public enterprises), increased spending (as a share of national income) and, most importantly for the purpose of our survey, increased the range and the depth of regulatory activities.

In the developed countries, with the emergence of new reform-minded 'corporatist' political coalitions, there was a marked swing of political opinion against *laissez-faire* economic policies, which were associated with the spectacular failures of capitalism during the interwar period. Full employment and the prevention of violent macroeconomic fluctuations were put at the top of the policy agenda, and were regarded as achievable through the use of activist macroeconomic policies based on Keynesian economics. Many countries in Western Europe nationalised a large number of enterprises in 'strategic' industries, in order to provide the government with a 'commanding height'. Many countries also used various regulatory measures in order to control the 'excesses' of capitalist institutions, and, more importantly for countries other than the US and the UK, to modernise their economies.

The US, despite its reputation as the quintessential free market economy, was in fact ahead of other developed countries in many areas

---

2   In this chapter, we exclude the discussion of the (now mostly vanished) socialist countries, where the notion of 'regulation' as we define it had very little meaning, as most of them did not have a private sector, outside agriculture (in some countries) and some services.

of regulation. In contrast to most other developed countries which adhered to *laissez-faire* policies during the interwar period, the reformist forces in the US had already succeeded by the late-1930s in establishing an extensive regime of natural monopoly regulation in various 'utilities' (telecommunications, water, electricity, gas, oil), transport (trucking, airlines, railways), wholesale and retail distribution, and finance (Vietor 1994: Chapter 1). These regulations were aimed at improving efficiency in allocation in the face of significant scale economies, to improve productive efficiency (or x-efficiency – the term comes from Leibenstein 1966) in the absence of competitive pressure, to prevent 'excessive' competition that often led to destabilising price wars, and to make services universally available.[3] In addition, the enforcement of anti-trust regulation was significantly strengthened during the period.

In the other developed countries, i.e., the Western European countries and Japan, regulatory regimes took different forms from that in the US, although these differences may be diminishing now (Majone (ed.) 1990: Introduction). There were three notable differences.

The first difference was that in most of these countries natural monopolies were usually dealt with 'through public enterprises', which, technically, were not 'regulated', whereas, in the US, they were the primary targets for regulation. This difference is, of course, in many ways more nominal than substantive, because the government ministries and agencies supervising the public enterprises in these countries had to deal with the same kinds of problems as those the US regulators faced.

Secondly, they did not put as much emphasis on anti-trust regulation as the US did. The anti-trust law in Japan, for example, was implemented in a notoriously lax way until recently. The French government, especially in the 1960s, explicitly encouraged mergers, in the belief that French firms needed to become bigger in order to survive international competition. The anti-trust laws in the UK and

---

3   What is interesting to note is that not all industries which were put under regulation were subject to large scale economies (the best example being trucking), and that not all industries with large scale economies were put under regulation. This partially reflects the fact that the American regulatory system was significantly determined by court cases rather than designed by a centralised bureaucracy, which made the system rather 'haphazard' (Sherman 1989: p.15).

West Germany had many provisions to absolve restrictive practices on the ground of 'mitigating circumstances' (Swann 1988: p.16). This was not simply, or even mainly, because the government-business relationship in these countries was much less adversarial than that in the US. It was more due to the fact that the view of competition held by their governments was closer to what may be called the 'Continental' view (represented by people like Marx, Schumpeter, and Hayek), which regards the existence of market power as an inevitable consequence of the competitive struggle through technological and organisational innovation, than to the neoclassical view (that was behind the American-style anti-trust legislation), which views the existence of market power as an anathema to competition (on different notions of competition, see Hayek 1949; McNulty 1968).

The most important difference between the US and other developed countries, however, was in their objectives of regulation. In Western Europe and Japan, which were in 'catching-up' positions *vis-à-vis* the US, the regulatory regime was often shaped by 'developmental' objectives, which put emphasis on 'dynamic' considerations (such as improving productivity, upgrading technology, and achieving efficient structural change), whereas the US regulatory regime was mainly shaped by the concern for 'static' productive and allocative efficiencies, and some concern for equity.[4]

In tandem with such developments in the real world, there was a series of new theoretical developments during this period in the area of welfare economics (Pigou 1920 is the seminal work), which provided systematic justifications for state intervention. The most significant developments included the following (for some textbook presentations, see Musgrave and Musgrave 1984; Stiglitz 1988).

Samuelson (1954) systematised the theory of public goods, where the difficulty of exclusion of the non-payers (the 'non-excludability' condition) and the absence of adverse effect from the addition of extra consumers (the 'non-rivalry in consumption' condition) lead to a situation where people have incentives to free ride on others for the provision of goods, thus justifying government provision, or regula-

---

4   This distinction roughly corresponds to Johnson's famous distinction between the 'regulatory state' (exemplified by the postwar American state) and the 'developmental state' (represented by the postwar Japanese or French states) (Johnson 1982: Ch.1).

tion of the private sector providers, of goods and services like defence, law and order, and physical infrastructure.

A direct extension of Pigou's work during this period was the analysis of externalities through the works of Scitovsky (1954) and others. It was argued that when externalities exist, individual costs and benefits diverge from social costs and benefits, and therefore unconstrained individual actions will result in too many actions with negative externalities (e.g., pollution) and too few actions with positive externalities (e.g., basic R&D). Although it is generally agreed that taxes and subsidies are theoretically better measures for dealing with externalities than regulation, the latter is often used for this purpose, owing to the administrative and political difficulties associated with tax/subsidy schemes (e.g., emission control on cars).

The area of welfare economics which had most direct link with regulation (as defined in this chapter) is that of natural monopoly. It was argued that in some industries with significant sunk costs, the lowest costs of production will be achieved by a single firm producing for the entire market (or a small number of firms, in the case of 'natural oligopoly'), but that this will result in all those vices associated with non-competitive markets – 'deadweight welfare loss' due to allocative inefficiency, productive inefficiency (or x-inefficiency) due to lack of competitive pressures, increased possibility of collusion among firms, increased possibility of 'predatory pricing' or 'pre-emptive investments' and other 'wasteful' behaviour, increased possibility of exploitation of consumers and of input suppliers by the dominant firms. And, naturally, it was deemed necessary that the government regulate the behaviour of the monopoly firms (or even break them up) to minimise these vices.

All these theories suggested that the government should engage in direct provision (or at least funding) of public goods, use taxes and subsidies in order to encourage certain activities (those with positive externalities) and discourage certain others (those with negative externalities), and put restrictions on what the firms in natural monopoly (or natural oligopoly) industries can do in terms of pricing, investment, and so on. With these developments, many existing regulatory practices gained a firmer grounding, and some new practices could be provided with secure theoretical justification when they were introduced later (e.g., environmental regulation).

In the developing countries, developmental objectives played a much more important role in shaping the regulatory framework than in the developed countries during this period, given their desire to gain economic as well as political independence from their former colonial masters. Deliberate attempts were made to promote industrial development through a wide range of regulatory and other policy measures. A large proportion of investment decisions were either taken or regulated by the government through its controls over public enterprises, public sector investment programmes, and sometimes the financial sector. Regulations on imports and foreign direct investments were imposed in order to shelter 'infant' industries from foreign competition, control the pace and form of technology imports, and promote the development of indigenous technological capabilities. Domestically, industrial licensing and other forms of entry regulations were used in order to induce manufacturing investments by guaranteeing profit to investors who would otherwise invest in less risky non-manufacturing activities, to coordinate complementary investment decisions, and to influence the amounts and types of investments in accordance with the overall industrialisation strategy.

In the formation of this regulatory regime, the rise of the sub-discipline of economics dubbed 'development economics' provided some useful ammunition, although it would be wrong to believe that such theories were entirely, or even mainly, responsible for the regulatory practices that actually existed. The so-called 'big push' or 'balanced growth' theory argued that, in the face of scale economies and demand complementarities, entrepreneurs in developing countries with a small industrial base would not have the incentive to invest in modern industries, unless there were some extra-market guarantee of complementary investments through investment planning by the government (Rosenstein-Rodan 1943; Nurkse 1952; Scitovsky 1954). While pointing out the uncertainties inherent in the developmental process and the lack of managerial resources that together make the balanced growth approach impracticable, Hirschman's 'unbalanced growth' approach also focused on the idea of complementarities between industries, and argued that the government should target and stimulate those industries with most 'linkages' with other sectors, which would then stimulate spontaneous growth in the related sectors (Hirschman 1958).

The 'age of regulation' was a period when most countries, developed and developing, experienced rapid growth and unprecedented material prosperity. While it is impossible to make a general statement about the efficacy of the regulatory regimes across countries during this period, it is clear that in many countries the regulatory framework that came into existence at the beginning of this period (and for some ex-colonial countries, by the early-1960s, after independence) worked reasonably well. Many developed countries of Western Europe and Japan achieved spectacular successes with economic modernisation. It is also considered that the regulatory regime in the US largely accomplished its own objectives of providing '[h]igh quality, widely available services, secure contractual arrangements, and stable (often cross-subsidised) pricing' during this period (Vietor 1994: p.9). The picture in the developing world was more mixed, but in most countries, the postwar regulatory regimes worked reasonably well during the period, and were indeed very successful in quite a few countries. Although there were some lone voices who attacked government regulation, and government intervention in general (Hayek 1944; Friedman 1962; Buchanan and Tullock 1962), there emerged a firm consensus by the end of this period that an activist regulatory regime was necessary in order to improve efficiency, promote growth, and spread the fruits of economic progress more evenly.

To summarise this section: for various political and economic reasons, there was a general shift towards more activist policy regimes across the world after the Second World War. However, there were significant differences between the regulatory regimes in the most developed countries such as the US, and to a lesser extent the UK, and those adopted by the rest. The regulatory regimes in the former put more emphasis on the correction of 'market failures' in the neoclassical sense, while those in the latter put more emphasis on 'developmental' objectives. During this period, there emerged a range of economic theories which provided justification for a more activist role for government. In addition to the development of Keynesian macroeconomics, the development of welfare economics and of development economics led to the increasing sophistication of interventionist arguments, which hitherto had not had the strong intellectual backing that *laissez-faire* policies enjoyed. At least partly, and in some cases largely, thanks to the postwar regulatory regimes, the capitalist countries achieved unprecedented economic progress, and the 'interventionist' regimes and the theories backing them seemed to have become firmly established.

2.2   The Transition Period (1970-80)

The 1970s was clearly a period of transition in many ways. The world economy witnessed the end of its 'Golden Age', and plunged into a new period of less robust economic performances, spiked with a few massive shocks such as the two oil crises and the debt crisis. Politically, in many countries, there were noticeable shifts to the Right, which advocated a substantial reduction in state intervention and a wider application of market principles. Intellectually, also, this period witnessed an upsurge in pro-market theories which challenged the postwar orthodoxy of 'regulated capitalism'.

During the 1970s, many, although not all, of the developed countries went through a period of industrial crisis, as their firms lost out to the new competitors emerging from Japan and the East Asian NICs. When combined with the strengthening of the workers' bargaining power as a result of near full employment, this deterioration in economic performance often meant an intensification of distributional struggle (usually manifested in accelerating inflation), and led to a collapse in the corporatist political settlements of the early postwar period. The changing political climate of the time was exemplified by the end of more than 40 years of unbroken social democratic rule in Sweden in 1976, the large-scale deregulatory drive initiated by the Carter administration in the US in the late-1970s, and the election of the Thatcher government in the UK in 1979. (Hirschman 1982 provides a fascinating account of the changing political climate around this time.)

Although many studies of the Golden Age provide explanations for its collapse in which increased or excessive government regulation plays at best a secondary role (Marglin and Schor (eds.) 1990; Armstrong *et al.* 1991; Cairncross and Cairncross (eds.) 1992), the existing regulatory frameworks did not survive these changes unscathed. Partly because of the failings in the existing regulatory regimes, which became more apparent during the period of crisis, but mainly because of the changing political climate, there was a growing opinion that the existing regulatory regimes were not working well and were even impairing the effective functioning of the economy.

One observation that has to be added here is that not everything during this period was pointing to a shrinkage in the regulatory remit of the government. In many developed countries, with the rise in affluence, there was a serious re-assessment of the (human and environmental) costs of rapid industrialisation, and a resulting rise in political movements which demanded a reduction in such costs. As a result, an increasingly wide range of 'social' issues (e.g., consumer protection, labour standards, environmental protection) have been brought into the realm of regulation, which was previously mostly occupied by 'economic' issues. So, during this period, there was a broadening of the regulatory mandate of the government in social areas, while there started a process of shrinkage in such a mandate in economic areas.

In the developing countries, the 1970s also witnessed growing disillusionment with the existing models of state-led industrialisation, often (somewhat misleadingly) dubbed 'import substitution industrialisation' models. While, as we pointed out before, the state-led industrialisation experiences had been on the whole successful in some countries, these experiences had not been without their problems, and were downright unsuccessful in many other countries. Moreover, even in countries where the earlier state-led industrialisation was quite successful, the regulatory regime did not necessarily adapt effectively to the changes in domestic economic conditions (which were caused in part by the success of the state-led industrialisation itself) and to the changing state of the world economy. However, in the case of developing countries, major deregulation drives came later than in the developed countries, that is, in the 1980s – although Chile was already embarking on a path of 'neoliberal revolution' under the brutal rule of General Pinochet by the mid-1970s. Until the debt crisis, many developing countries could continue to finance their development through the international capital market, and therefore could sustain their early postwar policy regimes. Nevertheless, the 1970s saw the gradual evaporation of the consensus in many developing countries on their existing models of state-led industrialisation.

Partly reflecting these real world experiences, and partly affecting the way real world policy-making evolved, a series of economic theories, which can be broadly called 'government failure' arguments, were developed during the 1970s (see Mueller 1979; Cullis and Jones 1987). The gist of the government failure argument is that the government is not the benevolent, all-knowing, and all-powerful agent that it is assumed to be in welfare economics, or in other pro-interventionist economic theories. First, it was argued that the government is an organisation which is run by groups of self-seeking individuals (politicians seeking re-election and bureaucrats seeking higher salaries and more power) and is influenced by interest groups, with the result that it implements policies that serve these groups rather than the public interest. Second, it was contended that, even if we can assume that the government has the intention of promoting the public interest, it does not have the ability to achieve this, because policy design and implementation are costly and because it may create harmful unintended consequences such as the diversion of resources into 'wasteful' lobbying activities (the so-called 'rent-seeking' theory).

Although few economists who used the (often implicit) characterisation of the government as an all-knowing, all-powerful social guardian in their theories regarded it as a realistic description of actual existing governments (e.g., Toye 1991), it cannot be denied that the earlier interventionist theories had relatively little to say about how, in reality, policies are formulated and implemented, as opposed to what the 'right' policies should be. By attacking this crucial weakness, the government failure approach played an important role in turning the intellectual tide against interventionist theories. Two arguments are notable for the purpose of this chapter (see Chang 1994: Chapters 1-2 for a more detailed discussion).

First, the so-called 'regulatory capture' argument, first proposed by Stigler (1971) and Posner (1974) and developed by Peltzman (1976), proposed that the regulatory agencies, once they are set up, become the objects of 'capture' by interest groups, including producers, consumers, and 'public interest' groups such as the environmental lobby. Although no group may be successful in capturing the regulatory agency completely, it is argued that the producer groups are most likely to be effective in such a capture because they, being small in number and well-endowed with resources, are better at organising 'collective actions' (the term comes from Olson 1965). Thus, the theory of regulatory capture predicts that regulatory agencies will end up promoting producer groups' interests rather than the public interest, by, say, implementing regulations which effectively set up entry barriers that deter new entrants with little positive effect on social welfare.

Second, this period also witnessed the rise of the theory of rent-seeking developed by Tullock (1967), Krueger (1974) and Buchanan *et al.* (eds.) (1980). According to this argument, monopolies (and the associated 'rents') are mostly, if not exclusively, created by the imposition of government regulations. Given this, it is argued, it pays for people to spend resources on influencing the government's decisions. The theory argues that such 'influence costs' (the term comes from Milgrom and Roberts 1990), which are called 'rent-seeking costs', may be a worthwhile price to pay for those who acquire the rents, but will be a net reduction to the social output (and therefore a 'waste' from the social point of view). Thus, the theory argues that the social costs of monopolies are not just those allocative inefficiencies usually associated with them, but also the costs of 'creating monopolies', that is, the rent-seeking costs.

Another relevant development during this period was the idea that 'franchise auctioning' could be better than direct regulation. The idea, which was developed following the seminal article by Demsetz (1968), was that government regulation of natural monopolies, which tries to simulate the competitive outcome, can be replaced by 'competition for the monopoly position'– that is, the competitive bidding process for a monopoly franchise granted to the highest bidder, usually for a specified period of time. This idea was later applied, for example, to the franchising of regional TV channels in the UK, and is deemed to have provided an interesting alternative to the direct regulation of natural monopolies.

With regard to developing countries during this period, there was a growing theoretical attack, based on 'efficiency' concerns, on the existing regulatory regimes (see e.g., Balassa *et al.* 1982; Little 1982; Lal 1983; for a critical review of the literature, see Toye 1987). This attack, sometimes called the 'get the prices right' argument, contends that attempts to go against the market logic and 'force' industrialisation in developing countries have resulted in a host of inefficiencies. The policies, it was argued, that made capital 'artificially' cheap with a view to promoting investments, especially when combined with policies such as minimum wage laws which make labour 'artificially' expensive, meant that the production techniques used in many developing countries were often of the 'wrong' (i.e., 'excessively' capital-intensive) kind, resulting in an inefficient use of resources. It was argued that these industries could survive only with the help of tariff protection and quantitative restrictions on imports, which created price distortions and further added to economic inefficiencies. This 'artificial' industrialisation, it was argued, also resulted in the atrophy of agriculture, and, when combined with other policies that discouraged cash crop exports (e.g., overvalued exchange rates), also limited the ability of these countries to earn foreign exchange, leading to further balance-of-payments difficulties.

In addition to the above 'efficiency' arguments, many 'political economy' arguments, which try to explain the emergence and continuance of particular policies in terms of political forces, were also put forward in relation to developing countries. During this period, a seminal rent-seeking model was developed by Krueger (1974) with specific reference to trade policies in developing countries (India and Turkey), but the more powerful political economy critiques came from a group of radical economists working in the tradition of the so-called 'dependency theory' (for a review, see Palma 1978). They argued that the reason 'inefficient' regulatory regimes persist in many developing countries is that they serve the interests of imperialist countries and the indigenous 'compradore' interests. Another radical economist, Lipton (1977), proposed a model of political economy called the 'urban bias' argument, which was later utilised by many right-wing political economists (see Section 2.3). The argument was that government policies in developing countries have an 'urban' (or 'anti-agriculture') bias that creates inefficiencies and inequalities, because urban groups such as industrialists and organised labour have disproportionate political influence when compared to the geographically dispersed and politically ill-organised farmers (for a critique, see Byres 1979). One interesting point to note is that many of these radical arguments have a logic that is essentially the same as that behind Stigler's capture theory (on this point, see Chang 1994: pp.18-22; see also Toye 1991).

The 1970s was a decade of transition. Although the postwar consensus on economic policy held through this decade in most developed countries other than the US and the UK, it was coming under increasing strain. Most developing countries had less difficulty in maintaining their earlier policy regimes during the 1970s, but even there this period witnessed a growing dissatisfaction with the existing state-led industrialisation programmes. There began to emerge a series of powerful arguments which questioned the (often implicit) assumption in many pro-interventionist theories that the government could be treated as an omniscient and omnipotent social guardian – the theory of regulatory capture and rent-seeking theory are notable examples. Similar arguments which question the 'intention' behind government intervention were put forward in relation to developing countries, mostly by radical economists, such as dependency theory and the urban bias argument. Regulatory practices in the developing countries also began to be criticised for their inefficiencies, by the so-called 'get the prices right' argument.

2.3   The Age of Deregulation (1980-the Present)

The political and intellectual tidal wave against regulation and government intervention in general, which started to surge during the 1970s, began to sweep the whole world from the early-1980s. During this period, following various external and internal pressures, many countries embarked on the path of extensive restructuring of the relation between state and economy, including regulatory reforms, budget cuts, and privatisation. There also arose numerous economic theories that built on the insights provided by the government failure arguments of the 1970s.

The continued lagging economic performance in the developed countries since the mid-1970s discredited, rightly or wrongly, their former models of economic management that relied on Keynesian aggregate demand management and extensive government regulation. In addition to the fall from grace of Keynesian macroeconomic policy and the attempts to reduce significantly the tax burdens imposed by the welfare state, there was a growing concern that excessive regulation was holding back many developed countries, especially in Western Europe, against the competition from countries like Japan and the East Asian NICs – the most famous of these arguments being the institutional ossification thesis of Olson (1982) and the so-called

'Eurosclerosis' argument (Giersch 1986).[5] By the early-1980s, the US and the UK were in the middle of a significant drive for deregulation (and privatisation in the case of the UK) (see Swann 1988; on the US, see Winston 1993, Vietor 1994; on the UK, see Vickers 1991). Although very significant deregulation (and privatisation) have been, at least until now, confined to the US and the UK, other developed countries also moved, in varying degrees and speeds, towards deregulation and a general reduction in government involvement in the economy, through spending cuts, sales of state assets (if not wholesale privatisation), introduction of more 'commercial' criteria into the operations of public enterprises and welfare provision, and the introduction of more 'market-oriented' methods of regulation such as franchise bidding (see Section 2.2) and 'yardstick competition'.[6] Simultaneously, there was a significant reduction in the 'developmental' activities of the government in many developed countries, best exemplified by the slow demise of the French *dirigiste* industrial policy – although this period also saw, somewhat ironically, the emergence of a lively debate on 'developmentalist' industrial policy in the US, prompted by the success of such policies in its main competitor economy, Japan (for reviews of this debate, see Chapter 4; also see Johnson (ed.) 1984).

We have already mentioned that many developing countries could sustain their early postwar policy regimes during the 1970s thanks to the availability of cheap finance recycled by the oil-exporting countries. However, this option became increasingly expensive with the introduction of restrictive macroeconomic policies (espe-

---

5 One problem with this argument is that most of the regulations which are accused of holding back the Western European countries already existed during the Golden Age. Another important point to note is that many of the regulations condemned by the 'Eurosclerosis' argument exist in the supposedly 'flexible' economies of Japan and East Asia (see Chang 1995). Thus seen, while it may be true that in certain areas regulations became excessive in Western European countries, it is difficult to believe that excessive regulation was the main reason, at least in the direct sense in which the proponents of the Eurosclerosis argument put it, for the recent difficulties experienced by these countries.

6 Yardstick competition refers to the practice where the market is divided up between sub-monopolies (e.g., regional monopolies) and the regulator explicitly uses their comparative performances to set general performance targets (see Vickers and Yarrow 1988: Ch.4).

cially high-interest policies) in the developed countries from the end of the 1970s, and finally became unsustainable with the Mexican default of 1982. With the sudden drying up of international capital, except for the most creditworthy (e.g., Korea), many developing countries, mainly from Latin America and Africa, plunged into a period of prolonged recession and economic decline during this 'lost decade of development' (the term comes from Singh 1990).

Although it is still debated how exactly the 'responsibilities' for their economic troubles during this period should be allocated between poor internal management and adverse external macroeconomic shocks (e.g., compare Sachs (ed.) 1989 and Hughes and Singh 1991), it was clear that these countries could not go on as they had been doing. When combined with the spreading domestic dissatisfaction with the earlier models of state-led industrialisation, the external pressures from the international lending agencies led most developing countries to embark on serious reform of their regulatory regimes, and more generally of the way government relates to the private sector. Needless to say, not all countries embraced the reform policies with an equal degree of enthusiasm. Some countries simply refused to reform, often ending up having to do more later because of their economic collapse. Some did accept the need for reform, but did it in a very gradual fashion (notable examples include Korea, Taiwan, and China). And some did it more thoroughly than others (notable examples include Chile, Mexico, and Ghana).

The age of deregulation witnessed a marked development in the anti-interventionist theoretical literature, although the latter part of this period also saw the rise in new theories that provided further justification for government intervention, albeit in a more nuanced way than their predecessors, such as the 'strategic trade' theory (e.g., Krugman (ed.) 1988), the 'new growth' theory (e.g., the special symposium in *Journal of Economic Perspectives* 1994), and the economics of technological change (e.g., Dosi *et al.* (eds.) 1988; Nelson (ed.) 1993).

The government failure literature which emerged during the 1970s was further developed during this period, and provided more justification for the drive towards deregulation and other state disengagement, although there was no new contribution that was comparable in originality to those made in the 1970s (see Section 2.2). This period also witnessed a rise in the so-called 'new economics of regulation', which puts emphasis on informational and incentive problems in the regulatory process. The models in this vein analyse how the existence of informational asymmetry between the regulator and the regulated firms results in extra monitoring costs, 'slacks' (or x-inefficiency) in production, the use of 'wrong' combinations of factors of production, and other inefficiencies (see Tirole and Laffont 1993 for a comprehensive treatment; Caillaud *et al.* 1988 provide a technical review). One interesting recent extension of this literature concerns the issue of 'credible commitment' in regulatory reform (for some recent examples, see Levy and Spiller 1994; Willig 1994). A government, it is argued, that suffers from a credibility problem (e.g., due to a past record of policy volatility) should deliberately take actions that limit its policy flexibility in order to make its commitment to reform credible – possible actions include things like binding itself to some simple and rigid rules, setting up politically independent regulatory agencies, or even 'borrowing' the credibility of some external authorities (e.g., international financial institutions)[7].

This period also witnessed the emergence of the theory of the 'contestable market' (Baumol *et al.* 1982), which argued that government regulation of a natural monopoly may not be necessary, if there is no need for significant 'sunk' investments to enter the industry. The intuition behind this argument is that, with low entry barriers, the market becomes 'contestable', if not 'competitive', in the sense that new entry can happen easily and that the threat of new entry will keep the incumbent monopolist on its toes. If this were the case, it was argued, what appears to be a natural monopoly may in fact be approximating the competitive market outcome, making regulation unnecessary. Although its applicability is limited by the fact that natural monopoly situations usually happen because of the need for sunk investment, this argument led to a re-examination of some conventional wisdoms in the theory of regulation.

Another interesting theoretical development of this period is the extension of the literature on property rights, originating with Coase

---

7 However, such policy inflexibility can be costly in the long run, as it means that the country may not be adequately able to adjust its regulatory regime to changing conditions (see also Section 3.4).

(1960), to issues pertaining to regulation (Barzel 1989 provides a good exposition of this literature). According to this view, externality problems are in a sense problems of the absence of certain property rights, and therefore can be solved by redefining property rights and creating relevant markets – of course with the important proviso, which was emphasised by Coase himself but often ignored by many of his followers, that the transaction costs of doing so are not too great. For example, it was argued (and put into practice in some areas) that a more efficient way of pollution control is through the establishment of a market for tradable pollution permits rather than by government directly regulating, say, the choice of production technologies by individual firms.

In relation to the developing countries, the new political economy models that have emerged since the 1980s have tended to emphasise the capture of the government apparatus by sectional interests (for a critical review, see Colclough 1991). Bates (1981) applied Lipton's urban bias model (see Section 2.2) and criticised the policies of many African governments as serving the interests of the industrialists, organised workers and powerful farmers, at the cost of unorganised workers in the urban area and the small farmers. Bardhan (1984) argued that the inability of the Indian state to impose order over the dominant proprietary groups of industrialists, rich farmers, and urban professional classes results in the limited tax base of the government (mainly thanks to its inability to tax agriculture) and in the frittering away of government resources, which could be invested in socially productive infrastructure, in the forms of subsidies and tax concessions. The so-called 'macroeconomics of populism' literature argued that the political power of organised working-class movements in some Latin American countries leads to the election of 'populist' governments which engage in unsustainable macroeconomic policies, including increased public spending and wage hikes, in the belief that this will lead to a continued expansion of the economy (which in their view is suffering from demand deficiency due to skewed income distribution) – with the often disastrous results of hyperinflation and soaring budget deficits (see Dornbusch and Edwards (eds.) 1991). Many (though not all) of these theories specifically recommended deregulation as a solution to the 'capture' problem, in the belief that the best way to prevent the capture of government is to make it pointless by taking away its power to change market outcomes.

It is not easy to make a general statement about the success or otherwise of the deregulatory moves in different countries during the 'age of deregulation', as the patterns of such reforms and their results vary across countries. The fact that in many countries deregulation was implemented together with a host of other policy measures – privatisation, macroeconomic stabilisation, etc. – also makes it difficult to isolate the effects of deregulation.

In certain areas, the deregulation moves were quite successful – especially when it concerned industries where there were few economic justifications for regulation in the first place, such as the US trucking industry,[8] or where technological changes made the old regulatory regime obsolete, such as long-distance telecommunications industries in many countries. In other areas, especially in the financial sector, there are many cases of disastrous outcomes, especially when deregulation was mistakenly equated with a complete withdrawal of the government, such as the financial deregulation disaster in Chile in the early-1980s (Diaz-Alejandro 1985), the US Savings & Loans fiasco (White 1993), and the 1995 Mexican debacle. There were also many areas where the results were mixed.

At the level of the overall economy, the impact of deregulation seems much less positive. Despite some sectoral success stories, the two leading countries in deregulation, namely the US and the UK, have not succeeded in markedly improving their economic performances after their deregulation drives. The deregulation moves in other developed countries have not been as substantial as the Anglo-Saxon ones, but whatever their magnitudes, their impact is not very visible, at least as yet. In Latin America, countries which went for the most radical forms of deregulation (e.g., Argentina, Bolivia, and Mexico) failed to raise their trend rates of growth, while the move is believed to have contributed to a significant fall in their investments, making their long-term growth prospects weak (Solimano 1992; UNCTAD 1995). In the case of the African economies, those which went for radical deregulation (e.g., Ghana) did initially improve their economic

---

8 Many commentators (e.g., Vietor 1994: Ch.1) point out that the most important motivation for the regulation of the trucking industry was to minimise its corroding effects on the regulatory regime of the rail industry.

performances quite substantially. However, this was mainly due to increased capacity utilisation and the improvement in the availability of imported inputs, and rather quickly seemed to run out of steam (Haque *et al.* 1996: Chapter 5). More positive effects of deregulation on the overall economic performance may be found in many Asian countries, where a more gradual approach was adopted and where an already strong investment performance was strengthened, partly through deliberate policy measures.

One apparent puzzle in interpreting this evidence is that, while there are many sectoral success stories of deregulation, there seem to be many fewer positive stories about its impact on the national economy. Two things must be considered here. One is that most of the sectoral studies come from the US, and to a lesser extent the UK, and therefore do not give an adequate picture of what has been happening in the rest of the world – more sectoral studies from other countries are needed. The second, more important, consideration is that sectoral assessments and economy-wide assessments are often talking about different things. Most sectoral studies, having been authored by neoclassical economists, assess the deregulation exercise in terms of static productive and allocative efficiencies, while the economy-wide assessments are often made in terms of 'dynamic' efficiency – that is, growth and productivity performances (see Section 3.4). So it is perfectly possible that deregulation has led to significant improvements in static efficiency in certain sectors, but that such gains were essentially of a once-and-for-all nature and did not have much long-term impact, or even that they adversely affected the growth dynamic at the national level. As a result, many countries which went into a deregulation drive with the expectation that it would 'revitalise' the economy by freeing entrepreneurs from government restrictions and thus promoting innovation and productivity growth, rather than just hoping for static efficiency gains, were often bitterly disappointed.

Let us summarise the discussion in this section. Since the 1980s, most countries, developed and developing alike, deregulated their economies, at least to a degree. Deteriorating economic performances during the 1970s were often attributed to excessive government involvement in the economy, and consequently attempts were made to cut government spending, privatise public enterprises, and deregulate the economy. In the theoretical world, there was an impressive growth in the number of models developing the insights of the government failure approach that originated in the 1970s. It is difficult to make a general statement about the impact of deregulation during this period, but it seems fair to say that, while there are some notable sectoral success stories, at least when seen from a static efficiency point of view, the often-expected dynamic benefits of deregulation at the economy-wide level do not seem to have materialised in any great quantity in most countries.

3. GOING BEYOND: SOME NEGLECTED THEMES

Whatever the merits and demerits of the individual theories discussed in the previous section, it seems fair to say that we now have a better understanding of many regulatory issues than we had in the immediate postwar years. We have a better understanding of the causes and the mechanisms of market failures that call for regulation, or some other intervention by government. We are also wiser about the political processes around the operation of regulatory regimes, and around state intervention in general. However, we are still some way from a satisfactory understanding of this multi-faceted and complex issue called regulation. In this section, we shall suggest some ways to improve our understanding of the economics and the politics of regulation, by dealing with some important themes that have been either neglected in the existing discussions or dealt with in an inadequate way.

3.1 The Need for Regulation

Given the current anti-government mood, there is a popular belief that the fewer regulations there are, the better. However, it should be remembered that well-functioning markets need effective regulation regarding certain basic aspects of their operation, and therefore that less regulation is not necessarily better. Any market requires regulations not only on fraudulent activities but also, more generally, on what constitutes 'fair' trading (however defined), in order to maintain its integrity. In some markets where the buyer cannot know the value of the goods or services exactly even after the purchase (e.g., markets for professional services or technical consultancy), certain regulations on who can supply them may be necessary. Ronald Coase, the 1992 Nobel prize-winner and a leading institutionalist economist, has pointed out that even the stock market and the commodity exchange, which are thought to proximate the ideal market described in textbooks most closely, can function well only when they have strict regulations on what can be traded, who can trade, how much prices can vary in a given period of time, and so on (Coase 1988).

At a more theoretical level, recent developments in institutional economics have shown that complex modern economies require a certain degree of 'rigidity' imparted by things like intra-organisational rules, long-term relational contracting, and government regulations (see especially Simon 1991; for some representative contributions, see Langlois (ed.) 1986). This perspective emphasises that human beings have only limited computational and decision-making capabilities and therefore cannot deal with complex problems, unless they use certain rigid behavioural rules which allow and encourage them to ignore certain possible courses of action – otherwise, they will not be able to cope with the complexity (the so-called 'bounded rationality' argument: see Simon 1983; see also Arrow 1974; Hayek 1988: pp.11-28). Somewhat paradoxically, then, the totally 'flexible' economy, without any rules other than those necessary for exchange to occur at all (such as property rules), which provides the ideal benchmark for many proponents of deregulation, may not be able to sustain much more, to borrow Coase's analogy, than lone individuals exchanging nuts and berries on the edge of the forest (Coase 1992: p.718). Complex modern economies need an array of 'rules' (and the consequent binding commitments and behavioural rigidities) in order to function at all.

Of course, many of these rules can be, and often are, provided by the private sector itself. As Coase (1988) points out, the 'regulations' in the stock market are often provided by the stock exchange itself. Many professions in many countries impose 'self-regulation' on their members' qualifications and practices. In this sense, many markets which are apparently regulation-free are, in fact, heavily regulated – although not necessarily by the government. Choosing between government regulation and self-regulation is at one level a matter of relative efficiency – government regulation may have a cost advantage owing to scale economies in information processing, the possibility of moral hazard may make self-regulation less efficient, etc.. However, government regulation and self-regulation are not, in the final analysis, full substitutes, because self-regulation has ultimately to be backed by the government through legislation and other directives that draw boundaries around 'permissible' behaviour. In this sense, deregulation should not be equated with the abolition of all government regulations, although which are the strictly 'necessary' regulations is another, very difficult question.

It should also be pointed out that deregulation in certain areas may require increased government regulation in other areas. For example, deregulation of industry and finance may require increased regulation regarding protection of consumers and depositors, respectively (Swann 1988, p.1). The recent US Savings & Loans debacle or the Chilean banking crisis in the early-1980s show how freeing financial institutions from certain regulations (say, on interest rates setting) should have been complemented by increased regulations regarding things like capital base, the kind of assets certain types of financial institutions can hold, and so on. Similarly, the removal of entry restrictions in industries with sunk costs may only be effective when anti-trust-type regulation on predatory behaviour is strengthened (Vickers 1991). The recent tendency of many governments to apply more severe regulations to incumbent firms than to the new entrants in certain industries (e.g., telecommunications) also reflects a similar concern. It has also been argued, on the basis of the experiences of the UK and other countries, that privatisation often needs to be accompanied by fortified, rather than weakened, regulatory regimes, since it leads to 'a significant increase in the number, scope and complexity of contractual relations, as relations which were previously internal to publicly owned industries are now the subject of market contracts between private firms, or of "contracts" between regulator and provider' (Michie 1995: p.129).

3.2 The Need to Create Markets

An important issue that is hardly recognised in the existing literature on regulation is that government intervention may be necessary not just to regulate markets, but also to 'create' them.[9] This problem of 'creating markets' is not absent in the developed countries, but is much more serious in developing countries and especially the economies in transition, where property rights are not clearly and securely defined and where an effective legal framework for business conduct does not exist. Some believe that 'markets develop naturally' (Stiglitz 1992: p.75), but this plainly is not the case. As Polanyi (1957) and Coase (1988) argue, even in Britain, where many believe the market system to have emerged totally spontaneously, the government's role in establishing property rights and providing a basic regulatory framework for particular markets was essential. The problem is that creating markets is a much more complicated exercise than it first appears.

First of all, the government needs to decide, in light of society's 'preferences', whether or not to create markets for certain goods and services. This decision is not purely 'economic', because there are certain goods and services which that society may not want to be provided by the market (and want to be allocated according to merits and/or needs), even if it is more 'efficient' to do so. For example, some societies simply will not accept markets in blood or human organs. Some societies are not willing to allow private firms to provide police services or prison services, whatever the efficiency gains might be. Different countries use markets in different degrees in the provision of 'merit goods' like health or education. Many societies have made deliberate decisions that certain utilities are not going to operate fully according to market principles, and so on. Some of these decisions may have been costly in economic terms (and some of them are now therefore being reconsidered), but it is important to recognise that the boundaries of markets are determined not only by efficiency considerations but also by non-economic, or even 'moral', considerations – such as legitimacy (police services and prison services), fairness (health or utilities), merit (education or health), or even the belief that 'there are some things that money cannot buy' (markets in organs or

---

9   Moreover, government regulations create not only markets but also their main protagonists, namely firms, by setting the rules regarding the constitution and dissolution of 'legal persons' and regarding their rights and obligations. I thank one of the anonymous referees for raising this important point.

blood). Unfortunately, the current discussions on regulatory reform have little to say on this front.

Once it has been (at least implicitly) decided that some goods and services are going to be provided through the market, property rights have to be assigned and enforced. Assigning property rights is, again, not so simple as it seems. We usually think that owning something is a straightforward matter. However, even if one owns a resource the uses to which it can be put are limited by the property (and other) rights of others. For example, I may own a knife but I am not allowed to kill you with it, because society values your right to live more than my freedom to use my property freely. Or you may own a certain piece of machinery but you may not (or may) be allowed to operate it if it pollutes my private lake, if society values my right to keep my property from getting dirty more (or less) than your right to use your machine as you like. In other words, the delineation of property rights is not independent of what rights members of society accept as legitimate, and as a result most, if not all, property rights are 'truncated' in a most complex manner (Demsetz 1988; see also Barzel 1989).

That this is the case is best illustrated by the example of child labour. Most people living in 20th century OECD countries, including most of those who could potentially benefit from employing children, would not regard the prohibition of child labour as a regulation in the conventional sense, because they value the right of children not to work more than the right of employers to hire whomever they find most desirable. However, many 19th century European capitalists (and indeed many capitalists in current developing countries) did (and do) regard it as an unwarranted regulation that interferes with the 'free' workings of the labour market, because they did not (and do not) share the value judgement of 20th century OECD citizens. This shows that what a society regards as the legitimate system of rights differs across time and place, and therefore that an 'unregulated' (or 'free') market cannot be defined without explicit reference to the system of rights regarded as legitimate by the society in question. And as there are always disputes and struggles going on about defining the legitimate system of rights, creating a 'free' market is not as simple as some people think (for a fuller discussion, see You and Chang 1993).

3.3   Distributional Issues

Many real life regulations have been motivated by distributional considerations as well as by the concern for efficiency (Bryer 1990: p.36). Regulation of natural monopoly often involves limiting, directly and indirectly, the amount of monopoly rents that the firm can appropriate. Through franchise bidding, governments can extract at least a part of the rent element from producers, which may be redistributed in the form of tax cuts or subsidies to some other groups. Many countries force firms providing things like electricity, telephone services, postal service, and railway services to provide a 'universal service', on the ground that the fact that someone lives, say, on a remote island should not deprive him/her of, say, a postal service or electricity. This not only redistributes income from the producers to consumers, but also from other customers to the 'disadvantaged' customers. Regulations regarding the relationship between large assemblers and small subcontractors, which often limit the ability of large firms to increase their shares of joint surplus by exercising their superior bargaining power, are another example of distribution-oriented regulation. Regulations on labour standards, as another example, also have an element of redistribution from the employers (and consumers, if firms can pass on the cost to them) to the workers.[10] The examples could go on.

Recent deregulation moves, naturally, have also had significant distributional impacts. For example, many studies point out that often the biggest 'losers' in deregulation moves have been those 'disadvantaged' customers who were subsidised under the old regime but were now often denied access to the service or charged much higher prices, on the one hand, and the employees of the affected firms, who were sometimes made redundant or forced to work in worse conditions, on the other (see Joskow and Rose 1989; and Winston 1993, for a review of the empirical literature). While it is possible, and perfectly legitimate, to argue that the losses made by some groups are outweighed by

---

10 It should be noted that, if better labour standards elicit higher productivity, no one has to lose from it, although how much exactly employers, workers and consumers would gain respectively would depend on circumstances.

the overall gains (according to the so-called 'compensation principle'; for a classic discussion of this issue, see Dobb 1969: Chapter 6), the distributional consequences of such moves need to be made explicit and discussed, which is not very often done, as this will enable policy-makers to deal better with the political implications of such consequences.

For example, even if there is a net social gain from deregulation, it may be difficult to judge it as positive, when we consider that the losers from deregulation may lose in a big way – especially when they are the owners of 'firm-specific' or 'industry-specific' physical or human assets whose values diminish sharply outside their current employments (on the concept of asset specificity, see Williamson 1985: Chapter 1) – while most of the gainers may not gain that very much individually. For example, do we (society) really want to make 1,000 airline employees redundant in order to give an average $100 savings to 500,000 customers? Or do we think that it is acceptable if those 100,000 who live in remote areas are denied rail services in order to allow the average rail traveller $25 savings per year? Maybe we do, and there is no God-given reason why we should not, but these questions need to be highlighted, rather than buried under some estimated figures for net gains and losses. This will also help society to devise acceptable 'compensation schemes', if the gainers care to pay out part of their gains actually to compensate the losers.

Even among the gainers of regulatory reform, there is still a problem of dividing up the gains. For example, recently there has been an intense public debate about the massive increases (anything between 50% and 500%) in compensation among the top executives of the privatised British utility companies (gas, water, and electricity), which were put under relatively lenient regulatory regimes after privatisation. While many consumers gained from the increased cost-effectiveness and some also from the changes in tariff structure, many consumers who were gainers (not to speak of the employees made redundant or those 'disadvantaged' consumers who lost out) were not convinced that the company executives should get such a large share of the gain – although, again, there is no one 'just' way of dividing up those gains.

As Joskow and Rose (1989: p.1487) point out, the traditional literature on regulation has unfortunately neglected the distributional implications of regulation and deregulation, in favour of static efficiency issues. While some 'aggregate' judgement across different individuals and groups is inevitable, distributional issues should not be neglected. Especially given that the concern for 'fairness' (however defined) of the outcome is often a very important factor determining whether people accept or reject a particular policy change, the success of a regulatory reform depends at least partly on making people accept the fairness of its distributional consequences. Although the more recent work on the politics of regulation has given more attention to distributional issues, our understanding in this area is still inadequate (Joskow and Rose 1989; Noll 1989).

3.4 Dynamic Considerations

The existing literature on regulation does not give adequate attention to 'dynamic' issues, or what this chapter called 'developmental' issues, as opposed to the issue of static efficiency. Some authors conduct their analyses of regulation and deregulation purely in terms of static efficiency, and the impacts of regulatory reform on productivity and growth are not even considered.[11] This is a highly inadequate approach, given that the gains (or losses) from improved static efficiency are usually relatively small and of a once-and-for-all nature, whereas the dynamic gains (or losses) could be very large and long-lasting.[12] Thus, even if the regulatory reform in the form of, say,

---

11 In their review of the empirical literature on the impact of regulation (and thus by extension deregulation) in the US, Joskow and Rose (1989) argue: 'It is distressing that so little effort has been devoted to measuring the effects of regulation on innovation and productivity growth. Much of what we do know is now quite dated. The static gains and losses from regulation are probably small compared to the historical gains in welfare resulting from innovation and productivity growth. Further research on what, if any, effect regulation has on the dynamics of productivity growth and the development of new goods and services therefore seems essential' (p.1484). See also Winston (1993: p.1268).

12 The classic estimate by Harberger (1954) of the loss from allocative inefficiency due to monopoly in the US put the figure around 1% of GNP. Later estimates which took into account 'rent-seeking' costs put the figures around 4-5% of GNP. McCormick *et al.* (1984) argue that, as past 'rent-seeking' costs cannot be recouped through deregulation (as they already have been expended), '[t]he gain from deregulation is less than the Harberger costs, perhaps one-half percent of GNP' (p.1078).

increased 'anti-trust' activities reduces the productivity growth rate only moderately (which it may do; see below), the improved static efficiency gains from such a reform will quickly be more than offset by such losses in dynamic efficiency. Some authors do acknowledge the importance of dynamic efficiency, but believe that achieving higher static efficiency either by deregulation or by stricter anti-trust regulation (depending on the situation) will generally lead to higher dynamic efficiency. The well-known World Bank regression between price distortion indexes and growth rates across countries reflects such a view (e.g., World Bank 1983, 1991). However, as even one of the leading neoclassical economists points out (see Krueger 1980), there is no economic theory which tells us that achieving higher static efficiency will necessarily lead to higher dynamic efficiency (see also Taylor 1993) – and, of course, there is a 'prior' problem that, at the economy-wide level, removing 'distortions' in more, but not all, markets does not necessarily improve even the static allocative efficiency of the economy (the so-called 'second-best theorem' of Lipsey and Lancaster 1956).

Schumpeter (1987) argued that monopoly rents (or what he called entrepreneurial profits) provide the incentive to innovate and, in the modern age of large-scale R&D, the resources to innovate. If this is true, there may even be trade-offs between static and dynamic efficiencies. If the regulatory reform involves reductions in market power and the associated monopoly rents (e.g., by intensifying anti-trust regulation), the rate of innovation and productivity growth may be adversely affected. Of course, as recent researches on the economics of technological change show, the story is not so straightforward (see Dosi *et al.* (eds.) 1988; Nelson (ed.) 1993). Market power is only one of many determinants of innovation and productivity growth, which are also affected by many other institutional and technological factors. The point is not that a certain type of regulatory regime (e.g., lax anti-trust regulation) is necessarily good for dynamic efficiency or not, but that the current discussions on regulatory reform do not give adequate attention to considerations of dynamic efficiency.[13]

It also has to be noted that the relationship between regulatory regime and technological change (which is an important determinant of dynamic efficiency) is not unidirectional. In the above, we talked about the impact of changes in the regulatory regime on technological innovation and productivity growth, but changes in technologies can also affect the effectiveness of the existing regulatory regime. For example, if technical progress leads to larger (smaller) scale economy in a particular industry, the need for regulations to control the problems resulting from market power in that industry will increase (decrease).

Technological progress can also lead to the 'unbundling' of a natural monopoly industry, which makes deregulation of certain segments of the industry feasible and desirable – as seen in the recent developments in the electricity and the telecommunications industries (see Gray 1995: p.9). Technological progress may also blur the traditional boundaries between industries, calling for a 're-packaging' of existing regulatory measures – as seen in the recent inter-penetration of the computer and the telecommunications industries. Technological progress also leads to the emergence of entirely new industries, for whose future development a timely establishment of a stable regulatory regime, especially in relation to product and process standards, can be crucial (Chang 1994: pp.76-7). All these suggest that regulatory regimes should not be taken as given, but should be adapted to changing technological conditions in a dynamic way.[14]

---

13 One useful way of highlighting the dynamic efficiency issues may be to distinguish, as we did in Section 2, between regulations which are intended to take care of static welfare (let us call them 'welfarist' regulations) and regulations which are intended to facilitate long-term productivity growth (let us call them 'developmental' regulations). Both types of regulation can involve the same measures – entry restrictions, pricing control, technology standards, etc. – but the purposes they are intended to serve are often very different. Of course, at one level, both developmental regulations and welfarist regulations can be cast in the languages of 'market failure', as far as both talk about the failings of the market mechanism in achieving some supposed ideal. However, this interpretation is not very helpful, because it tries to lump together two very different bodies of theory, whose policy recommendations can even clash with one another, as we suggested above.

14 Even without technological progress, continuous adaptation of the regulatory regime may be inevitable. Given bounded human rationality, it is inevitable that regulatory rules, when they are first written, cannot foresee every possible contingency. With the passage of time, this exposes the rules to increasing danger of 'inventive' re-interpretation and 'legal' evasion, thus making additional regulations necessary. I thank one of the anonymous referees for raising this point.

Of course, all the above does not mean that the regulatory regime should constantly be changed. In fact, if it did, the notion of regulation would become meaningless, as regulation is supposed to provide stable rules defining the parameters that the private sector should take into account so that its activities do not contradict the public interest. If the regulatory regime changes too often, there may be excessive costs of adjustment.

However, it is crucial that policy makers accept the fact that regulatory regimes should change according to changing conditions and try to provide a policy environment in which such change can be promoted (e.g., by regular reviews).

3.5   The Politics of Regulation

The politics of regulation is hardly a neglected issue in the current literature on regulation. In fact, it was the focus of the government failure argument and the recent literature on the politics of regulation is an extension of that. However, the current state of our understanding in this area still leaves a great deal to be desired. As there is not the space to go into detail (Noll 1989 provides a very good review of this area), in this section we shall, without claiming to be comprehensive, take issue with some of the main underlying premises of the government failure approach (for more detailed criticisms, see Chang 1994: Chapters 1-2).

It would be wrong to deny the central proposition of the government failure school that the government is not an impartial guardian of the public interest with an unlimited capability to collect information and enforce decisions, but an organisation comprised of, and influenced by, self-seeking individuals and their groupings. However, this should not lead us to believe that self-interest is all that counts. Self-seeking, although very important, is not the only human motivation.

Even in the (largely) 'private' domain of the economy, where self-seeking is the dominant motivation, people often act according to certain moral values (e.g., rule-abiding attitudes, *esprit d' corps*, class solidarity, pride in workmanship, generalised altruism), which are not merely 'veils of disguise' for self-seeking (McPherson 1984) nor simply 'optical illusions' ultimately based on some hidden sanctioning mechanisms (e.g., social ostracism, reputation, psychological 'guilt' from breaking rules).[15] Indeed, as Simon, Arrow, and others have repeatedly pointed out, if human beings were totally selfish, all modern economies based on a complex division of labour would collapse under the weight of prohibitive bargaining and monitoring costs.[16] When it comes to activities in the 'public' domain, people tend to behave even more on the basis of moral values (e.g., public service ethic, concern for the integrity of the government, desire for social cohesion, nationalism – in addition to the above-mentioned).[17] Moreover, individual preferences are not unalterable data that people are born with, but are partly determined by the 'socialisation process', which goes on inside the family, schools, communities, places of work (including government organisations), and the media, which frequently inculcate (with substantial success) many non-selfish 'moral' codes.[18]

Now, if what we say above is true, it may be possible to limit the private usurpation of public power, otherwise than by reducing the scope of state intervention as the government failure school believes. For example, if people are capable of holding 'non-selfish' values and if their values can be changed through socialisation processes, we may be able to mitigate many problems of government failure through moral persuasion against exploiting public offices or looting govern-

---

15 The sanctioning mechanisms themselves, being 'public goods' in the sense that those who did not contribute to their supply cannot be excluded from their benefits, will not be supplied in adequate amount in a world inhabited by purely self-seeking agents – unless, of course, we assume the existence of an exogenously imposed impartial third party, such as the state, as in the pro-interventionist theories criticised by the government failure approach.

16 That this is the case is powerfully testified by the fact that one popular method of industrial action is to 'work to rule'. As formal rules can never specify the level of efforts by workers which are necessary for the production process to run smoothly, it is known that workers can easily reduce output by 30-50% by working exactly according to the rule book.

17 Indeed, Noll (1989) points out in his review of the literature on the politics of regulation in the US that there is robust evidence that the regulatory bureaucrats and politicians involved are motivated by many more things than pure self-interest – be they concern for the 'public interest' or their ideological beliefs (p.1281).

18 This, of course, does not mean that 'generalised' moral codes are enough to hold society together. Our morality is often embedded in the specific social relations in which we find ourselves (Granovetter 1985). I thank one of the anonymous referees for this point.

ment coffers for selfish purposes. Although many proponents of the government failure argument would denounce this view as 'naive', this is one important way in which 'good' governments, or for that matter any other well-managed organisation (including private corporations), control the misuse of corporate (including public) power by individuals inside and outside the organisation.[19] In fact, by preaching a 'cynical' view of political life (that everyone in politics is simply out to advance narrowly-defined self-interest), the government failure school may be encouraging our politicians and bureaucrats to discard what little morality they had. And if we actually end up with politicians and bureaucrats who are exactly as described in the government failure literature, the consequences could be truly disastrous.

This is not to deny the possibility, and the reality, of the appropriation and misuse of government by sectional interests (inside and outside government) or even influential individuals. Nor do we believe that moral persuasion alone is enough to constrain such abuses. We believe that designing good incentive systems within and around government is extremely important, as this allows the aligning of the interests of holders of public office and powerful interest groups with the public interest – however incomplete such alignment may be. And, indeed, this concern is behind the so-called new economics of regulation and, more broadly, other extensions of the 'principal-agent' literature (on the principal-agent literature, see Stiglitz 1987; Sappington 1991).

One critical problem with the current state of this literature, however, is that, as Arrow (1991) points out, its models are too simple, in the sense that they do not describe even approximately what is going on in and around large complex modern organisations (including the government), while the 'prescriptions' they produce as solutions to the principal-agent problem are often too complex to implement. In

---

19 For example, the world's most renowned bureaucracies (e.g., the Japanese, the French, or the British) are those which are able to imbue their members with a strong sense of public service, commitment to the national project, and *esprit d' corps*, etc.. Seen in this light, the high level of mistrust that the government failure models have of the state may reflect the fact that these models tend to originate from the USA, where such a bureaucratic tradition is missing. Even North, one of the founding fathers of this tradition (e.g., see North 1981), acknowledges in his later contribution the problem arising from the American origin of many government failure models (North 1994: p.366).

contrast, real life solutions to various principal-agent problems are usually very simple, which, according to Arrow (1991), is an inevitable consequence of our bounded rationality and transaction costs. As Arrow suggests, unless we understand why and how real life organisations are being run reasonably well on the basis of relatively simple incentive schemes, having complex models of incentive design is of little practical value in helping us construct better political, bureaucratic, and regulatory incentive systems. Such understanding is yet to come.

4.   CONCLUSION

In this chapter, after some brief discussion about conceptual difficulties involved in defining 'regulation', we reviewed the evolution of perspectives on regulation and deregulation during the last 50 years, trying to mesh this with economic and political developments in the real world which affected and were affected by this evolution. Categorising the developments of half a century in this particularly complex and intensely debated area is not without its problems, but we divided this 50-year period into three 'ages'. They were:

(i)   the age of regulation (1945-70), when most countries saw an increase in government intervention, in the forms of increased government expenditure, nationalisation, extension of regulation, with accompanying developments in interventionist economic theories;

(ii)   the transition period (1970-80), when the postwar regimes of intervention began to be exposed to significant political attack, helped by the rise of anti-interventionist economic theories;

(iii) the age of deregulation (1980-the present), when many countries attempted to reduce government intervention, by privatisation, budget cuts, and deregulation, often drawing justification from the theoretical extensions of the anti-interventionist theories that originated in the 1970s and were elaborated during the 1980s.

Following the historical review, we then suggested some major issues that need more attention if we are to improve our current understanding in the area.

First, we pointed out that deregulation should not be equated with a total withdrawal of the government, as there are some regulations which are essential for the very existence, not to speak of the effective functioning, of many markets. We also noted that deregulation in certain areas may require increased regulation in other areas.

Second, we argued that, especially in developing countries and economies in transition, government needs to create markets, and not just regulate them. The difficulty of drawing the boundary around the market sphere and the difficulty of assigning property (and other) rights in creating markets were emphasised.

Third, we discussed the need to introduce distributional considerations more explicitly into our design of regulatory reform. It was argued that, while some kind of aggregate judgement about the overall efficiency consequences of a particular regulatory reform is inevitable, its distributional consequences also have to be carefully considered, especially if we want to increase the chance of its success.

Fourth, we emphasised the need to give more attention to dynamic issues, as the impact of a regulatory reform on dynamic efficiency could easily overshadow its impact on static efficiency. We also discussed the need for the regulatory regime itself to adapt to 'dynamic' changes in technology and other conditions.

Finally, we discussed the problems with the current state of the theories on the politics of regulation. We argued that, while very important, self-seeking is not the only motivation that determines people's actions, especially when they operate in the public domain, and that the designers of regulatory reform ignore the importance of 'moral' motives at their peril. The importance of the 'incentive design' literature was acknowledged, but its current lack of practical applicability was noted.

After half a century of the rise, development, and fall of various theories of regulation (and of state intervention in general), on the one hand, and of the successes and failures of various real life regulatory regimes in different countries, on the other, we are perhaps much wiser than we were 50 years ago. But we still have a long way to go before we can pronounce, as many people have done before, that we have 'found the solution'. There are simply so many important issues that the existing theories have more or less ignored or have not explored in enough depth. The real world development towards regulatory reform in many countries may look torturously slow to those who believe that they have the solution, but given the imperfections in our understanding in this area, this may not necessarily be a bad thing. If there is one lesson that we can confidently draw from the experiences of the past 50 years, it is that the world is much more complex than many of us believe, or wish, it to be.

BIBLIOGRAPHY

Armstrong, P., Glyn, A. and Harrison, J. (1991). *Capitalism since 1945.* Oxford: Blackwell.

Arrow, K. (1974). *The Limit of Organisation.* New York and London: W. W. Norton.

Arrow, K. (1991). 'The Economics of Agency', in I. Pratt and R. Zeckhauser (eds.), *Principals and Agents: The Structure of Business.* Boston: Harvard Business School Press.

Balassa, B. *et al.* (1982). *Development Strategies in Semi-Industrial Economies.* Baltimore: The Johns Hopkins University Press.

Bardhan, P. (1984). *The Political Economy of Development in India.* Oxford: Basil Blackwell.

Barzel, Y. (1989). *Economic Analysis of Property Rights.* Cambridge: Cambridge University Press.

Bates, R. (1981). *Markets and States in Tropical Africa.* Berkeley and Los Angeles: University of California Press.

Baumol, W., Panzer, I. and Willig, D. (1982). *Contestable Markets and the Theory of Industrial Structure.* New York: Harcourt Brace Jovanovich.

Bryer, S. (1990). 'Regulation and Deregulation in the United States: Airlines, Telecommunications and Antitrust', in Majone (ed.), *Deregulation or Re-regulation? – Regulatory Reform in Europe and the United States.* London: Pinter.

Buchanan, J. and Tullock, G. (1962). *The Calculus of Consent.* Ann Arbor: University of Michigan Press.

Buchanan, J., Tollison, R. and Tullock, G. (eds.) (1980). *Toward a Theory of the Rent-Seeking Society.* College Station: Texas A&M University Press.

Byres, T. (1979). 'Of Neo-populist Pipe-dreams: Daedalus in the Third World and the Myth of Urban Bias', *Journal of Peasant Studies,* vol.6, no.2.

Caillaud, B., Guesnerie, R. and Rey, P. (1988). 'Government Intervention in Production and Incentives Theory: A Review of Recent Contributions', *RAND Journal of Economics,* vol.19, no.1.

Cairncross, F. and Cairncross, A. (eds.) (1992). *The Legacy of the Golden Age – The 1960s and Their Economic Consequences.* London: Routledge.

Chang, H.-J. (1994). *The Political Economy of Industrial Policy.* London and Basingstoke: Macmillan.

Chang, H.-J. (1995). 'Explaining "Flexible Rigidities" in East Asia', in T. Killick (ed.), *The Flexible Economy.* London: Routledge.

Chang, H.-J. and Rowthorn, R. (eds.) (1995). *The Role of the State in Economic Change.* Oxford: Oxford University Press.

Coase, R. (1960). 'The Problem of Social Cost', *Journal of Law and Economics,* vol.3.

Coase, R. (1988). 'The Firm, the Market, and the Law', in R. Coase, *The Firm, the Market, and the Law.* Chicago: University of Chicago Press.

Coase, R. (1992). 'The Institutional Structure of Production', *American Economic Review*, vol.82, no.4.

Colclough, C. (1991). 'Structuralism versus Neo-liberalism: An Introduction', in C. Colclough and J. Manor (eds.), *States or Markets?: Neoliberalism and the Development Policy Debate.* Oxford: Clarendon Press.

Colclough, C. and Manor, J. (eds.) (1991). *States or Markets? Neoliberalism and the Development Policy Debate.* Oxford: Clarendon Press.

Cullis, J. and Jones, P. (1987). *Microeconomics and the Public Economy: A Defence of Leviathan.* Oxford: Basil Blackwell.

Cullis, J. and Jones, P. (1992). *Public Finance and Public Choice.* London: McGraw-Hill.

Demsetz, H. (1968). 'Why Regulate Utilities?', *Journal of Law and Economics*, vol.11.

Demsetz, H. (1988). 'A Framework for the Study of Ownership', in H. Demsetz, *Ownership, Control, and the Firm.* Oxford: Basil Blackwell.

Diaz-Alejandro, C. (1985). 'Good-bye Financial Repression, Hello Financial Crash', *Journal of Development Economics*, vol.19, nos.1-2.

Dobb, M. (1969). *Welfare Economics and the Economics of Socialism.* Cambridge: Cambridge University Press.

Dornbusch, R. and Edwards, S. (eds.) (1991). *The Macroeconomics of Populism in Latin America.* Chicago: University of Chicago Press.

Dosi, G., Freeman, C., Nelson, R., Silverberg, G. and Soete, L. (eds.) (1988). *Technical Change and Economic Theory.* London: Pinter.

Friedman, M. (1962). *Capitalism and Freedom.* Chicago and London: University of Chicago Press.

Giersch, H. (1986). 'Liberalisation for Faster Economic Growth', Occasional Paper no. 74. London: Institute of Economic Affairs.

Granovetter, M. (1985). 'Economic Action and Social Structure: The Problem of Embeddedness', *American Journal of Sociology*, vol.91, no.3.

Gray, C. (1995). 'Options for State Intervention in a Market Economy – from Laissez-Faire to Command and Control', unpublished paper prepared for Economic Development Institute. Washington, D.C.: World Bank.

Haque, I., Bell, M., Dahlman, C., Lall, S. and Pavitt, K. (1996). *Trade, Technology and International Competitiveness.* Washington, D.C.: World Bank.

Harberger, A. (1954). 'Monopoly and Resource Allocation', *American Economic Review,* vol.44, no.2.

Hayek, F. (1944). *The Road to Serfdom.* London: Routledge and Kegan Paul.

Hayek, F. (1949). 'The Meaning of Competition', in F. Hayek, *Individualism and Economic Order.* London: Routledge and Kegan Paul.

Hayek, F. (1988). *The Fatal Conceit — The Errors of Socialism.* London: Routledge.

Hirschman, A. (1958). *The Strategy of Economic Development.* New Haven and London: Yale University Press.
Hirschman, A. (1982). *Shifting Involvement.* Princeton: Princeton University Press.
Hughes, A. and Singh, A. (1991). 'The World Economic Slowdown and the Asian and Latin American Economies: A Comparative Analysis of Economic Structure, Policy, and Performance', in T. Banuri (ed.), *Economic Liberalisation: No Panacea.* Oxford: Clarendon Press.
Johnson, C. (1982). *MITI and the Japanese Miracle.* Stanford: Stanford University Press.
Johnson, C. (ed.) (1984). *The Industrial Policy Debate.* San Francisco: Institute for Contemporary Studies.
Journal of Economic Perspectives, 1994, no.1, Symposium on 'New Growth Theory'.
Joskow, P. and Rose, N. (1989). 'The Effects of Economic Regulation', in R. Schmalensee and R. Willig (eds.), *Handbook of Industrial Organisation,* vol. 2. Amsterdam: Elsevier Science Publishers.
Krueger, A. (1974). 'The Political Economy of the Rent-seeking Society', *American Economic Review,* vol.64, no.3.
Krueger, A. (1980). 'Trade Policy as an Input to Development', *American Economic Review,* vol.70, no.2.
Krugman, P. (ed.) (1988). *Strategic Trade Policy and the New International Economics.* Cambridge, MA: MIT Press.
Lal, D. (1983). *The Poverty of Development Economics.* London: Institute of Economic Affairs.
Langlois, R. (ed.) (1986). *Economics as a Process.* Cambridge: Cambridge University Press.
Leibenstein, H. (1966). 'Allocative Efficiency vs X-efficiency', *American Economic Review,* vol.56, no.3.
Levy, B. and Spiller, P. (1994). 'Regulations, Institutions and Commitment in Telecommunications: A Comparative Analysis of Five Country Studies', in *Proceedings of the World Bank Annual Conference in Development Economics 1993.* Washington, D.C.: World Bank.
Lipsey, R. and Lancaster, K. (1956). 'General Theory of the Second Best', *Review of Economic Studies,* vol.24, no. 63.
Lipton, M. (1977). *Why Poor People Stay Poor — Urban Bias in World Development.* Cambridge, MA: Harvard University Press.
Little, I. (1982). *Economic Development.* New York: Basic Books.
Majone, G. (ed.) (1990). *Deregulation or Re-regulation? — Regulatory Reform in Europe and the United States.* London: Pinter.
Marglin, S. and Schor, J. (eds.) (1990). *The Golden Age of Capitalism.* Oxford: Clarendon Press.
McCormick, R., Shughart, W. and Tollison, R. (1984). 'The Disinterest in Deregulation', *American Economic Review,* vol.74, no.5.

McNulty, P. (1968). 'Economic Theory and the Meaning of Competition', *Quarterly Journal of Economics,* vol.82, no.4.

McPherson, M. (1984). 'Limits of Self-seeking: The Role of Morality in Economic Life', in D. Colander (ed.), *Neoclassical Political Economy.* Cambridge, MA: Ballinger Publishing Company.

Michie, J. (1995). 'Institutional Aspects of Regulating the Private Sector', in J. Groenewegen, C. Pitelis and S.-E. Sjostrand (eds.), *On Economic Institutions — Theory and Applications.* Aldershot: Edward Elgar.

Milgrom, P. and Roberts, J. (1990). 'Bargaining Costs, Influence Costs, and the Organisation of Economic Activity', in J. Alt and K. Shepsle (eds.), *Perspectives on Positive Political Economy.* Cambridge: Cambridge University Press.

Mueller, D. (1979). *Public Choice.* Cambridge: Cambridge University Press.

Musgrave, R. and Musgrave, P. (1984). *Public Finance in Theory and Practice,* 4th edn. New York: McGraw Hill.

Nelson, R. (ed.) (1993). *National Innovation Systems.* Oxford: Oxford University Press.

Noll, R. (1989). 'Economic Perspectives on the Politics of Regulation', in R. Schmalensee and R. Willig (eds.) *Handbook of Industrial Organisation,* vol.2. Amsterdam: Elsevier Science Publishers, B.V.

North, D. (1981). *Structure and Change in Economic History.* New York: W. W. Norton & Co.

North, D. (1994). 'Economic Performance Through Time', *American Economic Review,* vol.84, no.3.

Nurkse, R. (1952). 'Some International Aspects of the Problem of Economic Development', *American Economic Review,* vol.42, no.2.

Olson, M. (1965). *The Logic of Collective Action.* Cambridge, MA: Harvard University Press.

Olson, M. (1982). *The Rise and Decline of Nations.* New Haven: Yale University Press.

Palma, G. (1978). 'Dependency: A Formal Theory of Underdevelopment or a Methodology for the Analysis of Concrete Situations of Underdevelopment?', *World Development,* vol.6, nos.7-8.

Peltzman, S. (1976). 'Toward a More General Theory of Regulation', *Journal of Law and Economics,* vol.19.

Pigou, A. (1920). *The Economics of Welfare.* London: Macmillan.

Polanyi, K. (1957). *The Great Transformation.* Boston: Beacon Press.

Posner, R. (1974). 'Theories of Economic Regulation', *Bell Journal of Economic and Management Science,* vol.5.

Rosenstein-Rodan, P. (1943). 'Problems of Industrialisation of Eastern and South-Eastern Europe', *Economic Journal,* vol.53, no.3.

Sachs, J. (ed.) (1989). *Developing Country Debt and the World Economy.* Chicago and London: University of Chicago Press.

Samuelson, P. (1954). 'The Pure Theory of Public Expenditure', *Review of Economics and Statistics,* vol.36, no.4.

Sappington, D. (1991). 'Incentives in Principal-Agent Relationships', *Journal of Economic Perspectives*, vol.5, no.2.

Schumpeter, J. (1987). *Capitalism, Socialism and Democracy*, 6th edn.. London: Unwin Paperbacks.

Scitovsky, T. (1954). 'Two Concepts of External Economies', *Journal of Political Economy*, vol.62, no.2.

Sherman, R. (1989). *The Regulation of Monopoly*. Cambridge: Cambridge University Press.

Simon, H. (1983). *Reason in Human Affairs*. Oxford: Basil Blackwell.

Simon, H. (1991). 'Organisations and Markets', *Journal of Economic Perspectives*, vol.5, no.2.

Singh, A. (1990). 'The State of Industry in the Third World in the 1980s: Analytical and Policy Issues', Working Paper no.137, The Helen Kellogg Institute for International Studies. Indiana, USA: University of Notre Dame.

Solimano, A. (1992). 'After Socialism and Dirigism — Which Way?', Policy Research Working Paper, Country Economics Department. Washington, D.C.: World Bank.

Stigler, G. (1971). 'The Theory of Economic Regulation', *Bell Journal of Economic and Management Science*, vol.2.

Stiglitz, J. (1987). 'Principal-Agent Problem', *The Palgrave Dictionary of Economics*, vol. 3. London: Macmillan.

Stiglitz, J. (1988). *Economics of the Public Sector*, 2nd edn.. New York: W.W. Norton & Co.

Stiglitz, J. (1992). 'Alternative Tactics and Strategies in Economic Development', in A.K. Dutt and K. Jameson (eds.), *New Directions in Development Economics*. Aldershot: Edward Elgar.

Swann, D. (1988). *The Retreat of the State – Deregulation and Privatisation in the UK and US*. New York: Harvester Wheatsheaf.

Taylor, L. (1993). 'Review of *World Development Report 1991* by the World Bank', *Economic Development and Cultural Change*, vol.41, no.2.

Tirole, J. and Laffont, J.-J. (1993). *A Theory of Incentives in Procurement and Regulation*. Cambridge, MA: MIT Press.

Toye, J. (1987). *Dilemmas of Development*. Oxford: Blackwell.

Toye, J. (1991). 'Is There a New Political Economy of Development?', in C. Colclough and J. Manor (eds.), *States or Markets?: Neoliberalism and the Development Policy Debate*. Oxford: Clarendon Press.

Tullock, G. (1967). 'The Welfare Costs of Tariffs, Monopolies and Theft', *Western Economic Journal*, vol.5, no.3.

UNCTAD (United Nations Conference on Trade and Development) (1995). *Trade and Development Report 1995*. New York and Geneva: United Nations.

Vickers, J. (1991). 'Government Regulatory Policy', *Oxford Review of Economic Policy*, vol.7, no.3.

Vickers, J. and Yarrow, G. (1988). *Privatisation*. Cambridge, MA: MIT Press.

Vietor, R. (1994). *Contrived Competition — Regulation and Deregulation in America*. Cambridge, MA: Harvard University Press.

White, L. (1993). 'A Cautionary Tale of Deregulation Gone Awry: The S&L Debacle', *Southern Economic Journal*, vol.59, no.3.

Williamson, O. (1985). *The Economic Institutions of Capitalism*. New York: The Free Press.

Willig, R. (1994). 'Public Versus Regulated Private Enterprise', in *Proceedings of the World Bank Annual Conference on Development Economics 1993*. Washington, D.C.: World Bank.

Winston, C. (1993). 'Economic Deregulation — Days of Reckoning for Microeconomists', *Journal of Economic Literature*, vol.31, no.3.

World Bank (1983). *World Development Report 1983*. New York: Oxford University Press.

World Bank (1991). *World Development Report 1991*. New York: Oxford University Press.

You, J. and Chang, H.-J. (1993). 'The Myth of the Free Labour Market in Korea', *Contributions to Political Economy*, vol.12.

Chapter 6

Public Enterprises in Developing Countries and Economic Efficiency: A Critical Examination of Analytical, Empirical, and Policy Issues

1. INTRODUCTION

SINCE the late-1970s, a large number of developing economies, particularly in Africa and Latin America, have been subject to extremely stringent foreign exchange constraints. As a consequence, these countries have had to go to the international financial institutions – the IMF and the World Bank – for balance-of-payments support and economic assistance. Invariably such assistance has only been forthcoming from the Bretton Woods institutions, subject to overlapping and detailed conditionality involving both demand- and supply-side measures. The latter include, *inter alia*, as Avramovic (1988) notes, 'growth' conditionality which is 'focussed on giving free hand and incentives to the private sector of the economy, including "privatisation" of government-owned enterprises (the World Bank terminology for public enterprises) as much as possible, rationalisation of the rest, promotion of foreign direct investment'.

Unlike the US Agency for International Development which promotes privatisation for avowedly ideological reasons (see Aylen 1987), the IMF/World Bank deny any ideological motives for their endeavours. Instead they suggest that their main argument for privatisation is the poor economic performance and the manifest inefficiency of the state-owned enterprises and the over-extension of the role of the state. Thus the Berg Report on Sub-Saharan Africa (World Bank 1981) concluded that:

'It is now widely evident that the public sector is overextended, given the present scarcities of financial resources, skilled manpower, and organisational capacity. This has resulted in slower growth than might have been achieved with available resources, and accounts in part for the current crises. Without improved performance of public agencies, stepped-up growth will be difficult to achieve' (p.5).

In the same vein, the *World Development Report* for 1987 observed: 'The performance of SOEs (state-owned enterprises) varies widely between countries, but their record has frequently been poor, particularly in developing countries. They have clearly failed to play the strategical role in industrialisation that governments had hoped for. Financial rates of return have generally been lower for the SOEs than, for the private sector as recent comparative studies for Brazil, India, and Israel have indicated. Financial profitability has often been compromised by price controls, but the indications are that the SOEs have also had a generally poor record of social profitability. They have often put large burdens on public budget and external debt' (pp.66-7).

Such unfavourable assessments of public enterprises and the role of the state in the economic sphere have also been echoed by some influential mainstream economists. Thus Balassa *et al.* (1986) maintain that 'the essential factor that gave impetus... to the severity of the economic and social crisis of the 1980s was the pervasive and the rapidly expanding role of the state in most of Latin America'. Similarly, Vernon (1988: pp.18-9) suggests that privatisation today is being driven by a spirit of pragmatic reaction to at least three decades of failed experiments in public enterprise.

The present chapter first examines the analytical arguments and evidence which are available concerning the economic efficiency of public enterprises in the non-centrally-planned, mixed-economy, developing countries. And then it discusses some of the options that are open to governments which want to improve the performance of their public enterprises, including privatisation, organisational reform, increase in competition, and political reform.

2.   THE 'INEFFICIENCY' OF PUBLIC ENTERPRISES: PRELIMINARY CONSIDERATIONS

The allegation that public enterprises (henceforth PEs) are invariably 'inefficient' or that most of them perform badly cannot survive even an elementary examination of facts. Consider the following.

Public enterprises are ubiquitous in mixed economies throughout the world – they have not simply been confined to left-wing regimes or underdeveloped or poorly performing countries. In view of the differences in definitions of what constitutes a PE, and a variety of other statistical problems, it is difficult to obtain data on an internationally comparable basis of the relative size of PE sectors in different economies (for a discussion of this point, see Short 1984). Nevertheless, the best available information from the IMF suggests that excluding centrally-planned economies, in the mid-1970s, PEs in the developing countries accounted on average for 8.6% of GDP and 27% of total gross fixed capital formation. In the industrial market economies, the share of the PEs in GDP was slightly higher, 9.6%, although in gross fixed capital formation, it was considerably lower, being 11.1% (for more detailed information, see Short 1984: Table 1).[1]

Table 1 provides information on the size of the PE sector for a selection of developing countries. As the table indicates, PEs play a significant role in the economies of highly successful East Asian newly industrialising countries (henceforth NICs), that is, Taiwan and South Korea. In fact, the PE sector in these countries is at least as large, if not larger, than in other leading NICs like India, Argentina, Brazil, and Mexico, and clearly larger than that in countries like the Philippines or Peru, which are often dubbed as classic 'failure' cases. In Taiwan, hardly a 'socialist' regime, PEs have contributed a third of gross fixed capital formation throughout the years 1950 to 1975, a period which saw the most spectacular growth and industrialisation of that country. In Africa, the data in Table 1 show that PEs have played almost as large a role in the market-oriented (and often regarded as successful) economies of Ivory Coast and Kenya as they have done in 'socialist' Tanzania. Jones and Mason (1982) suggest that, although ideology does have an influence, there are very important structural factors which can account for the relative size of the PE sector in less developed countries (LDCs).

---

1   The share of PEs in fixed capital formation is greater in developing countries than in industrialised countries, while their shares in GDP are similar because, in relative terms, the capital-output ratio of PEs in developing countries is much higher than the economy-wide average while that of PEs in developed countries is not so.

Table 1: Output and Investment Shares of Public Enterprises in Selected Developing Countries

Country	Years	Percentage Share in GDP at Factor Cost	Percentage Share in Gross Fixed Capital Formation
India	1960-61	5.3	34.7
	1966-69	6.5	29.6
	1978	10.3	33.7
Pakistan	1961	4.5	n.a.
	1974-75	6.0	33.3
	1978-81	n.a.	44.6
Philippines[1]	1960	n.a.	2.0
	1965	n.a.	1.8
	1974-77	1.7	9.5
Taiwan	1951-53	11.9	31.4
	1966-69	13.6	28.0
	1978-80	13.5	32.4
South Korea[1]	1963-64	5.5	31.2
	1970-73	7.0	21.7
	1978-80	n.a.	22.8
Mexico[2]	1975-77	n.a. (6.1)	27.0 (21.8)
Brazil	1968	n.a.	14.0
	1980	n.a.	22.8
Argentina[3]	1968-69	n.a.	15.4
	1974-75	n.a.	18.2
	1978-80	4.6	19.6
Venezuela[4,5]	1968	n.a.	15.3
	1978-80	27.5 (3.0)	36.3 (25.7)
Peru	1960	n.a.	5.1
	1968-69	n.a.	11.2
	1978-79	n.a.	14.8
Tanzania	1966-69	9.3	22.7
	1974-77	12.3	30.3
	1978-79	n.a.	16.3
Kenya	1964-65	7.5	9.7
	1970-73	8.7	10.6
	1978-79	n.a.	17.3
Ivory Coast[4]	1965-69	n.a.	16.5
	1970-73	n.a.	27.9
	1979	10.5	39.5

Source: Short (1984): Table 1

Notes
1   Share in Gross Domestic Capital Formation (rather than GFCF)
2   Figures in parentheses exclude iron ore and petroleum enterprises nationalised in 1975
3   Major enterprises only
4   Share in GDP at market prices
5   Figures in parentheses include 22 major public enterprises only

Table 2: Relationship between Public Enterprise Sector, Income Level, and Growth	
	Rank Correlation Coefficient
Share of public enterprise output in GDP, and income per capita	0.22
Share of public enterprise investment in GFCF, and income per capita	-0.13
Share of public enterprise output in GDP, and growth in income per capita (1960-81)	-0.05

Source: Kirkpatrick (1986)

Kirkpatrick (1986) has examined the relationship between the size of the PE sector, per capita GDP and the rate of growth of GDP between 1961 and 1981 for a sample of 23 LDCs in Asia, Africa, and Latin America. He found the rank correlation coefficients between these variables reported in Table 2.

If PEs always performed poorly, other things being equal, one would expect a negative correlation between the size of the PE sector in a country and its economic performance. However, the observed correlation coefficients above are very small and statistically insignificant and do not always have the correct sign. Clearly at the very least the notion that the PE sector is inimical to economic growth fails to be confirmed by such aggregate analysis.[2]

Table 3 presents data on the size of the PE sector in advanced capitalist countries (henceforth ACCs). In these economies, the intercountry differences in the incidence of PEs are due to a rather different set of factors than for LDCs. Following the end of the Second World War, many firms were nationalised in Western Europe as a consequence of either the accession to power of left-wing governments (as,

---

2   There is a large literature on the relationship between the size of the public sector as a whole or of its various components (not just the PE sector) and economic growth (see e.g., Rubinson 1977; Marsden 1983; Gemmell 1983; Landau 1983, 1986; Singh and Sahni 1984; Ram 1986; Conte and Darrat 1988). On the whole, these studies show that the relationship is complex and ambiguous.

for example, in the UK), or as a result of the confiscation of assets of the 'collaborators' as in France and Italy (see Byé 1955: pp.74-81 on the 'punitive nationalisations' in postwar France).

Again we observe at the aggregate level that France and Austria, the two countries where the incidence of PEs was very high, had an extremely successful record of economic growth in the quarter-century 1950-1975. In this context, the case of Austria is particularly significant. As Kaldor (1980: p.3) reminds us, '[i]t is perhaps not generally known that next to Japan, Austria had the fastest rate of economic growth since the Second World War, and the fastest increase in real income per head – in sharp contrast to the inter-war period when her economy was stagnant throughout most of the period, with heavy unemployment'. Kaldor observes that 'the public sector of Austria, accounting for 16% of all employees, 20% of total output, and 25% of exports, is the largest (in relative terms) among the developed countries of the West.'

Take another example. As it happens, the most efficient steel company in the world is the giant Korean enterprise POSCO (Pohang Steel Company). POSCO is state-owned; it produced 467 tons of crude steel per person in 1986 compared with an average of 327 tons for Japan's five biggest steel producers. POSCO's efficiency advantage is passed on to its Korean customers. It charges its domestic steel consumers $320 per ton – far less than American or Japanese carmakers who (according to POSCO) pay $540 and $430 respectively (*The Economist,* 21 May 1988, p.16; also see Amsden 1989: pp.298-9). If PEs are thought to be inherently poor performers (whether this is actually true or not will be examined in the following sections), the Posco example does raise the important analytical question – why should that be so? If POSCO is an exception, the obvious issue is – what makes it so?

As we shall see below, although POSCO is not typical, it is not that much of an exception either. We shall also see that empirical evidence on the poor performance of PEs relative to private firms (henceforth PFs) in properly conducted comparisons – which control for the effects of industry, size, age, market power, etc. (more on this in Section 4) – is far from being either universal or conclusive. Suffice it to note here that even in countries where the PE sector is not thought to be generally successful in the mainstream accounts, there are

Table 3: Output and Investment Shares of Public Enterprises in Selected Developed Countries

Country	Years	Percentage Share in GDP at Factor Cost	Percentage Share in Gross Fixed Capital Formation
Austria[1]	1970-73	15.8	n.a.
	1978-79	14.5	19.2
France[4]	1959-61	12.7 (7.6)	23.0 (14.5)
	1966-69	12.8 (6.9)	19.0 (10.2)
	1974	11.9 (5.3)	14.0 (7.3)
	1982	n.a. (6.5)	n.a. (12.5)
Italy[1]	1967-69	7.0	14.2
	1974-77	7.7	17.2
	1979-80	n.a.	15.2
Japan[2]	1965	n.a.	13.6
	1970-73	n.a.	9.9
	1978-81	n.a.	11.2
Sweden[1,3]	1978-80	n.a (6.0)	15.3 (11.4)
United Kingdom	1938	n.a.	4.7
	1946-49	n.a.	11.0
	1950-53	n.a.	21.5
	1962-65	10.3	19.8
	1974-77	11.3	18.6
	1982	11.2	17.1

Source: Short (1984): Table 1

Notes
1   Share in GDP at market prices
2   Share in Gross Domestic Capital Formation (rather than GFCF)
3   Figures in parentheses exclude public enterprises at the regional or local level
4   Figures in parentheses are for large enterprises only

nevertheless acknowledged outstanding cases of efficient PEs (see Nellis and Kikeri 1989). For example, in Sub-Saharan Africa, notable examples of successful PEs include the following: the Kenyan Tea Development Authority, the Ethiopian Telecommunications Authority, the Tanzanian Electricity Supply Company Limited (see World Bank 1983: pp.78-85), and the Guma Valley Water Company of Sierra Leone (see Luke 1988).

In view of the above, it may seem strange that there is such widespread prejudice against PEs and that throughout the world there are calls for their privatisation (also see Commander and Killick 1988: pp.19-69). The change in people's attitude towards public ownership since the 1980s has been so dramatic that it appears to be difficult to understand the shift except in terms of what Hirschman (1982) calls 'the public-private cycle' due to the inevitability of 'disappointment' with different (that is, public and private) modes of preferences and actions in our socio-economic life.

3.   THE 'EFFICIENCY' OF PUBLIC ENTERPRISES: THEORETICAL PERSPECTIVES

Before we consider the empirical studies on the relative efficiency of PEs in the LDCs, it will be useful to examine the theoretical arguments for and against PEs.

3.1 Public Enterprises and Economic Development

The analytical reasons for the establishment and operation of PEs, particularly in LDCs, have a long standing in the literature and are well-known. They arise partly from 'market failure' and partly from other broader considerations. Very briefly, these reasons may be stated as follows:

(a)   In view of incomplete or underdeveloped capital markets, the government may have to step in to establish firms in many areas where the country may have a dynamic comparative advantage but where the scale of investments required is too large (e.g., steel, chemical, etc.) for the private sector to undertake. As the classic thesis of Gerschenkron (1962) goes, such need may be greater for countries which embark on industrialisation later due to the growing scale of efficient production.

(b)   Similar considerations apply even more strongly to large infrastructural investments in developing countries (electricity, transport, telecommunications, etc.). These industries, more-over, often tend to be natural monopolies which can provide in many circumstances an additional justification for either nationalisation or the establishment of public enterprises (more on this in Section 4.1.1).

(c) An important set of arguments for PEs to dominate the economy as a whole derive from macroeconomic considerations, and especially the nature of private investment in a mixed economy. Kaldor (1980) provides a classic statement on this point: 'when public investment is part of a national plan, it is possible to take into account all kinds of criss-cross effects (or indirect effects) into consideration which would not be possible with private investment. Keynes once said that in the face of complete uncertainty investors generally rely on a convention that the future will be just like the present, and for that reason "the effects of the existing situation enter, in a sense disproportionately, into the formation of long-term expectations". Hence capacity is only likely to be created in so far as its use appears to be profitable at the existing state of demand. Since the demand for commodities depends on the levels of incomes which are generated in production, the additional production generated in the future by the sum of the investment decisions of the present will itself increase the demand of commodities in comparison with the present level – a factor which private investors cannot take into account (or can do so only imperfectly) since they take their decisions independently of each other. Investment by public enterprises, on the other hand, can take the comprehensive effect of all investments into account in judging the social profitability of any particular investment project. It should be noted, however, that a state plan is capable of doing this even when the investment is undertaken by private enterprises, as the Japanese example shows. What is required is that there should be a fairly comprehensive state investment plan for industrial development, and the state should be capable of giving effect to this plan, through the "administrative guidance" of the privately-owned firms – provided that, as in Japan, these are native and not foreign-owned firms.'

(d) The domination of a developing economy by foreign enterprises may be regarded as being not conducive to long-term economic planning and growth if it hampers the accumulation of local technological capability. Given this, the establishment of public enterprises, or joint ventures between public and foreign firms, may in many cases be the only effective alternative.

(e)   Apart from the issue of overall economic efficiency, there are very respectable distributional and equity arguments for the establishment of public enterprises in many areas of the economy. Using public enterprise pricing policy to achieve distributional objectives may save the high information gathering and monitoring costs involved in running the equivalent tax/subsidy schemes.

These theoretical reasons for the establishment of public enterprises are important for assessing empirical evidence on the relative performance of public and private enterprises, as we shall see below. But they do not tell us anything about how efficiently the operations of the public enterprises will be conducted once they have been set up. On this important issue, there is another, much more recent, branch of theoretical literature from the fields of the theory of the firm and industrial organisation which is relevant. It is to that we now turn.

3.2   The Operation of Public Enterprises (I): The Principal-Agent Problem

3.2.1 The Argument

A PE is definitionally run by managers who do not own the firm. Since nobody, being a self-seeking agent, takes care of somebody else's business as seriously as one's own, the managers of a PE would not strive to improve the efficiency of the firm as an owner-manager would do with his own firm. Of course, this problem will be overcome if 'the public', who are the, at least *de jure*, owners of the PEs, can perfectly monitor the manager's efforts. However, since somebody who is actually doing the job knows more about the job better than anybody else, and since it is inherently difficult to fully differentiate the changes in performances that are due to the changes in managerial efforts from such changes that are due to other factors, it will be impossible to perfectly monitor the manager's effort level.

To put it in terms of the current concerns in the theory of the firm, there is a principal-agent problem, which results from the inability of the principals (the public in this case) to contain the consequences of self-seeking behaviour by the agents (the PE managers in this case) due to imperfect, and especially asymmetric, information (on the principal-agent problem, see the classic paper, Jensen and Meckling 1976; for a summary discussion, see Stiglitz 1987).

Needless to mention – although this point is not often mentioned by the opponents of PEs – the same problem exists for PFs as far as they are not run by the owner-manager (Baumol 1980 raises the same point). However, it is argued, there is another layer of principal-agent problem in the case of PEs (Yarrow 1989).[3] That is, since the direct responsibility of monitoring the performances of the PE managers falls on the government, which is made up of politicians and bureaucrats who are acting as the agents of the public and are as self-seeking as anybody, the public will find it difficult to monitor whether the government as an agent is putting in enough effort to monitor the PE managers (Yarrow 1989).[4]

Therefore, it is argued that privatisation, by eliminating the two-tier delegation structure (the public – ministers – PE managers) and constructing a direct link between the principal and the agent (shareholders – PF managers), would reduce the harmful inefficiency consequences of public ownership (Yarrow 1989).

3.2.2 Criticisms

a.   The Problem of 'Shareholder Collective Action'

Privatisation does not necessarily guarantee an effective monitoring of managerial behaviour, even if we ignore the problem of divergent and possibly incompatible objectives of individual shareholders (see Vickers and Yarrow 1988: p.11). This is because, unless

---

3   Yarrow emphasises the principal-agent problem much more in his 1989 article than he did in his 1986 article, which we refer to later.

4   Moreover, the principal-agent problem between the public and the government is aggravated by the limits of the electoral system. That is, since 'a typical member of the public . . . . will have an opportunity to vote once every four or five years and will face an almost zero probability of influencing the outcome of the election' and since 'the election will be concerned with a wide range of issues, not just with the question of the stewardship of any one publicly owned firm', 'the average voter has very little incentive to acquire costly information about the performance of elected representatives in monitoring particular firms' (Vickers and Yarrow 1988: p.31).

the share is sold to a very small number of individuals, there exists the problem of what we can call, adapting Olson (1965), 'shareholder collective action'. That is, when the shareholder group comprises a large number of individuals, no individual shareholder will have an incentive to collect relevant information and monitor the managers, because the individual cannot reap the full benefits from his/her action, as the improved performance is a public good from which every shareholder will benefit without paying for it (for similar arguments, see Stiglitz 1985; Vickers and Yarrow 1988: pp.12-3; also see Yarrow 1989: p.58).

In the case of public ownership, there will be a single or at most a few agencies (ministries, public enterprise agency, public holding companies) who are responsible for the performance of PEs, and therefore there may be less problems of collective action in relation to monitoring activities. In this sense, privatisation can actually worsen public enterprise performance by substituting more effective ministerial monitoring with less effective monitoring through 'shareholder collective action'.

Of course, it is perfectly possible that the ministries who are in charge of public enterprise monitoring, being the agents of the public as principals, may not faithfully do their duties, and the public, being numerous, would also have collective action problems in monitoring the supervisory agencies. However, given the existence of political parties and other political groups as institutionalised mechanisms of collective action, it may be that a collective action by the voting public is often easier than collective action by the shareholders, who lack an institutional device for collective action.

b.   One, Two, or Many Levels of Delegation?

As argued above, the fact that PEs have one more level of delegation does not necessarily mean that they will be less subject to monitoring pressures from the principals than PFs. Moreover, the distinction between public and private enterprises in terms of the levels of delegation is a bogus one. This is because any sizable enterprise, be it public or private, will have more than one layer in the managerial hierarchy. Any large firm is already fraught with the problems of the multiple layers of delegation within the firm. And, therefore, it is not clear whether adding one more level of delegation (ministers-managers) to the existing multiplicity of intra-enterprise delegations of authority would make so much difference to the performance of the enterprise.

Moreover, there is no clear way to determine what will be the overall number of delegations for a firm on the basis of ownership alone. For example, the levels of delegation (or the levels of managerial hierarchy) within a Japanese firm are usually less than those in an American firm within the same industry (see Dertouzos *et al.* 1987: p.97). For another example, in the case when a public enterprise is sold to a foreign firm, it will simply substitute one level of delegation (ministers-managers) with another one (headquarters-local managers), thus leaving the number of levels of delegation unchanged. In other words, it is not clear whether privatisation will reduce the levels of delegation involved in the management of the enterprise.

c.   Self-seeking Managers and Bureaucrats?

The assumption of self-seeking individuals, which is (together with imperfect information) necessary for the principal-agent problem to exist, is also suspect. For example, if the bureaucrats and PE managers are only interested in their own affairs, why are PEs run very efficiently in non-democratic countries, where the public has very little control over them, like Taiwan – which had been a one-party state for almost forty years until the late-1980s – and South Korea – which had had only very sporadic interludes of democratic politics between long stretches of highly authoritarian politics until the late-1980s?

In these countries, there had been no check whatsoever on the agents (bureaucrats and PE managers) by the principals (the public) through the 'political market' (voting) (see below). However, South Korea has a very efficient PE sector (World Bank 1983), some of which are among the most efficient firms in the world (e.g., POSCO, see above). The Taiwanese case is even more striking. In 1952, 57% of industrial production in Taiwan was accounted for by PEs and the share remained as high as 46% in 1962. During this period (1953-62), total industrial production in Taiwan grew by 11.7% per annum, a performance which does not fall short of the period 1973-80, when the share of PEs in total industrial production was much lower at below 20% (19% in 1975; 18% in 1980) (see Amsden 1985).

Although we are by no means suggesting that the Taiwanese or

Korean bureaucrats or PE managers are selfless saints, we think preferences are often endogenously formed so that bureaucrats and PE managers may put public interest first (to a large extent) if they operate in such an environment where they are required (say, through traditional cultural values like Confucianism) to regard themselves, rightly or wrongly, as 'the guardian of public interests'.[5]

3.3 The Operation of Public Enterprises (II): The Disciplinary Mechanism

3.3.1 The Argument

Even if there is no principal-agent problem, it could be argued that PEs are very likely to be inefficient because there is no effective way to punish their bad performance. In the case of PFs, dissatisfied customers 'exit' from a badly-performing firm (that is, they stop buying from the firm), which results in the falling profitability of the firm (for the concept of 'exit' as a disciplinary mechanism, see Hirschman 1970: p.4). Falling profitability, in turn, leads to the 'exit' of the shareholders (i.e., the shareholders selling their shares), resulting in a fall in the share price of the firm, which exposes the firm to the possibilities of takeover (see Singh 1971, 1975). Under the threat of the exercise of the 'exit' option by the customers, which can ultimately make the firm bankrupt, the argument goes, the managers are forced to manage the firm efficiently.

PEs are often monopolies, and therefore, dissatisfied customers do not have the exit option. Moreover, PEs are usually immune from the threat of takeover and are free from the threat of bankruptcy. Therefore, PE managers are not likely to be as motivated to improve the efficiency of the firm as their private counterparts who live under the threats of takeover and bankruptcy (Yarrow 1989). In other words, due to their exclusion from the capital market, or to the absence of the 'market for corporate control' for PEs (Yarrow 1986: p.330), PEs do

---

5   Of course, factors other than non-self-seeking preferences, for example, incentive mechanisms for the bureaucrats and the PE managers, may have been important, although this is not very likely, given the relatively poor pay for the bureaucrats and public enterprise managers in these countries.

not have the same pressure to remain efficient as PFs. Hence their inefficiencies.

3.3.2 Criticisms

a. Exit and Voice

The view that the capital market is the only disciplinary mechanism for the firm depends on the assumption that the 'exit' option is the only possible disciplinary measure for a badly-performing organisation (including the firm). Nevertheless, in addition to the 'exit' option (which ultimately results in takeover/bankruptcy of the firm), there exists the 'voice' option, where '[t]he firm's customers or the organisation's members express their dissatisfaction directly to management or to some other authority to which management is subordinate or through general protest addressed to anyone who cares to listen' (Hirschman 1970: p.4). Thus, even when a PE is not subject to the threats of takeover and bankruptcy, it may well be disciplined through the 'voice' option (for a similar argument, see Aharoni 1986: p.194). Moreover, private ownership *per se* does not guarantee an efficient functioning of the 'exit' option. Many private monopolies are protected by natural and man-made entry barriers and therefore customers may not in effect have the 'exit' option open.

And as a matter of fact, it is not true that PEs can never go bankrupt. Public enterprises can go, and have gone, bankrupt, in the form of 'liquidation'. There have been numerous cases of PE liquidation in such diverse countries as the UK, Italy, Israel, the Ivory Coast, Brazil, and Singapore (see Shirley 1983: p.55; Aharoni 1986: pp.63-4). The truth of the matter is that large firms (be they public or private) rather than public enterprises tend not to be allowed to go bankrupt, as is testified by the numerous cases of state rescue operations, including nationalisation, for large private firms on the verge of bankruptcy (e.g., Chrysler of the USA, Volkswagen of West Germany; also see Aharoni 1986: pp.63-4). The size factor is particularly important in LDCs where the employment situation is often extremely difficult. For example, the Indian government is being invariably obliged to bail out or take over so-called 'sick' large private sector enterprises due to the pressure to preserve employment (Ahluwalia 1987).

b.   The Efficiency of the Capital Market as a Disciplinary Mechanism

The supposed virtue of firm discipline through the market for corporate control (i.e., the capital market) has been the linchpin of the arguments for privatisation of nationalised firms in the UK (see e.g., Littlechild 1986). In brief, the suggestion is that even for privatised natural monopolies, where by definition the product market discipline is bound to be inadequate, forces of competition in the capital market, principally through the takeover mechanism, will ensure efficiency.

However, this line of reasoning is seriously flawed. First, there are important *a priori* reasons (the free-rider problem, transaction costs, etc.) which suggest that, even in theory, the market for corporate control may not work 'efficiently'. Secondly and more significantly, empirical research suggests that contrary to the folklore of capitalism, it is not just the 'inefficient' or 'unprofitable' firms which are eliminated by the takeover mechanism and the 'efficient' and the share-holder-wealth-maximising firms which survive. Empirical studies show that selection for survival in the market for corporate control takes place only to a limited extent on the basis of efficiency or the profitability but to a far greater extent on the basis of size. Moreover, on average, profitability of merging firms does not improve after merger. To the extent that monopoly power of the acquiring firm in the product market increases as a consequence of takeover, the evidence is compatible with reduced efficiency in resource utilisation following mergers. This is hardly the picture of the disciplinary role of the capital market conveyed by the proponents of privatisation.[6]

There are reasons to believe that the situation may in fact be much worse than that. The capital market discipline may not just be inadequate, but it may very well be perverse. On the basis of the above findings, Singh (1971, 1975) had suggested that instead of disciplining large firms whose managers seek growth for empire building or power motives, the market for corporate control may encourage them to seek a further increase in size precisely in order to avoid being taken over. Paradoxically such firms may be able to achieve that end through the

---

6   There is a large theoretical and empirical literature on these issues. For surveys, see Hughes and Singh (1987) and Hughes (1989). See also Singh (1971, 1975, 1990), Grossman and Hart (1980), and Stiglitz (1985).

takeover mechanism itself by acquiring smaller but relatively more profitable firms (see also Greer 1986, on this point).

Turning from the narrow issue of firm profitability and stock market discipline to the broader concept of 'overall economic efficiency', which must inevitably involve questions of investment and economic growth, Keynes's strictures on the role of the stock market continue to be pertinent and need to be seriously addressed. In Chapter 12 of *General Theory*, Keynes had observed: 'Speculators may do no harm as bubbles on a steady stream of enterprises. But the position is serious when enterprise becomes the bubble on a whirlpool of speculation. When the capital development of a country becomes a by-product of the activities of a casino, the job is likely to be ill-done. The measure of success attained by Wall Street, regarded as an institution of which social purpose is to direct new investment into the most profitable channels in terms of future yield, cannot be claimed as one of the outstanding triumphs of *laissez-faire* capitalism . . .' (Keynes 1936).

To add to these Keynesian worries which derive from the role of speculation, the volatility of stock market prices and the fact that such prices may not be efficient in the 'fundamental valuation' sense of Tobin (1984)[7], Cosh, Hughes and Singh (1990) suggest that the takeover mechanism may in a number of ways further encourage 'short-termist' outlook on the part of management to the detriment of long-term investment, economic growth, and international competitiveness (for a fuller analysis, see Cosh, Hughes and Singh 1990; also see Dertouzos *et.al.* (1988).

3.4 Concluding Remarks

In the above, we have considered the traditional theoretical case for public enterprises as well as the case against, which derives from certain developments in the theory of the firm and that of industrial organisation. We have found the latter unconvincing even in its own terms. As we have seen, it disregards the problems of 'shareholder collective action', organisational complexities of modern firms, the

---

7   On these issues, there is again a large literature. See e.g., Tobin (1984), Shiller (1981), Summers (1986), Camerer (1989), Nickell and Wadhwani (1989).

existence of non-selfish motivations of bureaucrats and managers, the manifold problems of reliance on the capital market for investment decisions, and the nature of the market for corporate control. Any argument which does not recognise the multiplicity of human motivation and the institutional complexity of modern economic life should be accepted with a grain of salt.

4.   ASSESSMENT OF EMPIRICAL EVIDENCE ON RELATIVE EFFICIENCY OF PUBLIC ENTERPRISES: CONCEPTUAL ISSUES

Before reviewing the existing empirical evidence on the relative efficiency of public and private enterprises, it is essential to examine some critical conceptual and practical issues concerning the measurement of the performance of PEs (for a good introduction to the problems involved, see Nove 1973: Chapter 1).

4.1   Profitability

The most conventional measure of the performance of an enterprise, both public and private, is its profitability. And despite the lack of consensus as to which of the many possible profitability measures (e.g., operating surplus, return on assets, return on equity) should actually be used, profitability is one of the most commonly used performance indicators in the studies of PE performances, not least because it can be derived from the most readily available data, that is, their balance sheets and profit and loss accounts (see, e.g., World Bank 1983: Chapter 8; Shirley 1983; Short 1984; Georgakopolous *et al.* 1987; Luke 1988).

4.1.1 Profitability as the Enterprise Performance Indicator

Despite its widespread use in studying enterprise performance, profitability is not a fully satisfactory performance indicator even for private enterprises for the following reasons.

First of all, profitability depends not only on enterprise performance but also on accounting procedure. The difficulty of profitability accounting in an inflationary period is especially well-known (see, for example, Likierman 1984: p.163). And more generally, 'calculations of profits over a short period may be substantially influenced by arbitrariness in accounting conventions, changes in accounting conventions, or actions taken to reconstruct company balance sheets' (Bishop and Kay 1988: p.5; for a detailed discussion, see Edwards, Kay and Mayer 1987).

Second, short-term profitability may not be a good indicator of long-term performance of an enterprise. For example, a company may have a favourable balance sheet at a certain point of time simply because it has stopped investing and is currently, so to speak, living off its past investments, with possibly detrimental consequences for its long-term viability. Judging a company's performance by its share price on the stock market does not overcome this problem. For all the reasons discussed at length earlier (see Section 3.3.2 b.), stock market prices do not in practice reflect long-term expected profitability of firms; rather, these prices are likely to be dominated by 'short-term' considerations. Therefore, despite their limitations, it is necessary to use long-term accounting rates of return, averaged over a number of years, to properly judge enterprise performance. This consideration is especially important for enterprises in capital-intensive industries (a likely condition for a PE), where lack of current investments can lead to a serious deterioration in its future performance. For an opposite kind of example, enterprises in infant industries (a likely condition for a PE in a developing country) may be performing poorly in terms of current profitability, but they may be expected to improve their performance in the near future, if they manage to reduce their operating costs through 'learning by doing'. Such learning effect will especially be important for PEs in developing countries.

4.1.2 Profitability as the Public Enterprise Performance Indicator

When it comes to the case of public enterprises, we have some additional problems in using profitability as the performance indicator. This is because, as seen earlier, PEs are often established for reasons other than making profits, and, even when they were initially established for pure profit reasons, they will be often, if not always, used for (justifiable or unjustifiable) non-profit reasons by the government (see Nove 1973; Millward 1982; Likierman 1984).

First of all, many PEs have been established out of distributional considerations. According to Vernon (1981), many PEs, especially in the ACCs after the Second World War, have been established for the aim of 'shifting economic power from the leaders of big business in the private sector to leaders elsewhere, such as leaders of government or leaders of labour' (p.14). Some PEs have been set up to improve the relative position of a certain region (the Italian PEs in the South) or a certain ethnic group (the Malaysian PEs; see Mallon 1982) (for a theoretical discussion of this problem, see Fernandes 1983).

Second, PEs are often used by the government to achieve some macroeconomic objectives, although the effectiveness of PEs in achieving such aims may be open to dispute (see Rees 1976: p.22; Jones and Mason 1982: pp.28-31; Floyd 1984). PE employment policy has often served as a means to create and preserve jobs in the face of unemployment. PE investment policy has also been used by the government as a counter-cyclical device (see Shepherd 1965 for the British case, where such an attempt was not very successful; Galán 1980, for the Spanish case, where such an attempt was very successful). In inflationary periods, PE pricing policies have often been used as an anti-inflationary device (see, e.g., Millward 1982: p.62).

Third, PEs are often used as a means to promote private industries. For example, PE procurement policies are employed in many instances to boost demand for infant or declining industries.[8] Lower prices for PE products can have a substantial impact on private profitability, especially when the products are basic inputs like electricity, fertilisers, and steel. Thus, 'if a subsidy given to farmers is granted directly, (a public enterprise) making fertilisers may be profitable; if the same subsidy is given as a reduced price of fertilisers, the firm would show losses that are not necessarily a reflection of its efficiency' (Aharoni 1986: p.188).

---

8   The procurement policy of the Japanese telecommunication public enterprise (NTT) has been very important in promoting high-tech industries in the country. See Okimoto (1989).

Therefore, if PEs have objectives other than making profit, it is not justifiable to use profitability alone to judge the performance of the PEs concerned. Indeed, ideally, 'the process of performance evaluation ought to follow a sequential procedure of identifying the objectives set for the public enterprise, constructing indicators to measure the degree of attainment, and then measuring performance', although in practice, 'objectives are seldom specified in a clear and unambiguous way, objectives may be mutually inconsistent, there are problems in devising satisfactory single- and multiple-good performance measures, and the necessary data are often not available' (Cook and Kirkpatrick 1988: p.11). Hence the dearth of studies which actually do this.[9]

4.1.3 Using Profitability in Empirical Studies

When it is actually employed in empirical studies, the inadequacy of profitability as the performance indicator is aggravated by the difficulty of conducting a study which controls for the effects of those factors other than ownership which may affect an enterprise's profitability performance. Let us discuss some of these 'intervening' factors.

a.   Country-specific Factors

The PE sector of a certain country may be inefficient due to country-specific reasons which are unrelated to ownership *per se*. For example, PEs in a country may be performing badly due to reasons which apply both to the public and the private firms. It has often been pointed out that the lack of managerial skills has affected the performances of PFs as well as those of PEs in many LDCs. Deficiencies of accounting systems in LDCs are also thought to have affected overall and not just public enterprise performances in those countries. According to a World Bank report (World Bank 1983), 'SOEs (state-owned

---

9 There are, however, a handful of studies which do use multiple criteria (e.g., Killick 1983 and Green 1985), which we will discuss later. But even these studies do not address the important issue of whether the objectives which the PEs are asked to pursue are the most appropriate ones. This major question will be discussed in Section 6.

enterprises; the Bank's terminology for PEs) (*as well as private companies* (italics added)) are not audited according to uniform standards; more than 70 developing countries have no accounting standards. Trained accountants are scarce, because in many developing countries (outside Latin America) accounting became part of the university curricula only after 1960. Even now there are often no uniform standards of training' (p.82).

Macroeconomic conditions also affect enterprise performance, public and private alike. Therefore, for example, the fact that the PE sector of some countries (e.g., Turkey and Senegal) which broke even or recorded surplus until the early-1970s began to make losses in the late-1970s and the early-1980s, which is taken by the World Bank as evidence of worsening PE performances (World Bank 1983), may be nothing but a reflection of the adverse macroeconomic conditions during the latter period.

Moreover, in a period of adverse macroeconomic conditions, often some large PFs which have virtually gone bankrupt are nationalised to be allowed to remain as a going concern, because they are thought to be too important (often, if not predominantly, for employment reasons) to be allowed to go under. The most well-known examples are the nationalisations of some Western European automobile manufacturers, for example, British Leyland (the UK) and Volkswagen (West Germany in the 1970s). When the macroeconomic conditions of a country are not favourable, the PE sector of the country will include many such enterprises, and therefore it will perform even worse in terms of profitability than it could without such enterprises. For example, in Greece, 43 virtually-bankrupt PFs were nationalised between 1983 and 1987, a period of economic difficulty for the country, which seriously affected the performance of the PE sector as a whole (see Georgakopolous *et al.* 1987).

b.   Industry-specific Factors

The PE sector may be performing badly in profitability terms simply because it has many enterprises operating in 'wrong' industries. The 'wrong' industries may include industries which are temporarily experiencing trouble, but more importantly declining industries (e.g., coal and ship-building in Western Europe) or infant industries (e.g., many capital-intensive industries in LDCs). If the PE sector includes many firms operating in these industries, which is all the more likely given the pressure on the government to nationalise bankrupt large PFs (see above), it is more than natural for the sector to perform badly in terms of profitability.

c.   Firm-specific Factors

PEs may perform badly due to firm-specific characteristics such as size, market power, and age, rather than due to their ownership characteristics. First, PEs tend to be large. And large size may affect PEs positively (if scale economy is significant) or adversely (if scale diseconomy is significant). This is especially true in developing countries where many PEs were established exactly in those sectors where a large-scale investment was necessary but no private investor could finance it due to the underdeveloped capital market (for evidence, see Short 1984: p.143). Secondly, the age of PEs may also affect their performances. Young firms may perform worse than older firms because of their lack of 'learning' (on this point, see Jenkins and Lahouel 1983: p.15), but they may perform better under certain circumstances because of their freedom from antiquated managerial and organisational habits or inertias. And vice versa for the older firms. Thirdly, PEs may be performing well in terms of profitability simply because they have greater market power, and not because they are inherently more efficient. On the other hand, the usually strict government control over the pricing policy of the PEs on the ground that they have significant market power may keep them from raising prices even when it is necessary, and this may appear in the balance sheet as a deterioration in their performances (see Cook and Kirkpatrick 1988: p.16). In developing countries where PEs are more likely to be monopolists or oligopolists due to the small size of the domestic market (relative to the enterprise size), it will be more important to take the market power possessed by PEs in evaluating their performance.

There is a large literature on microeconomic performance of the firms for the advanced economies which indicates that such performance (whether measured in terms of profitability or growth) is influenced by each of the factors mentioned above, i.e., age, firm size, industry the firm belongs to, and market power, among other things (see Singh and Whittington 1968, 1975; Meeks and Whittington 1976; Kumar 1984; Evans 1987a and 1987b). Although there are few empirical studies for the developing countries, in view of the results from the advanced country studies, and the sound theoretical reasons for the importance of these factors as independent causal influences on firm performance, they clearly must be fully considered in any appropriate assessment of microeconomic efficiency of enterprises, whether public or private, in the poor countries.

4.2 Other Measures of Enterprise Efficiency

In view of the problems discussed above with the use of profitability as a performance indicator for PEs, economists have tried to employ other measures of efficiency. There are basically two groups of such indicators, that is, technical efficiency measures and cost efficiency measures.

4.2.1 Technical Efficiency as Performance Indicator

The most preferred efficiency indicator used in empirical studies of PEs is technical efficiency. The idea here is that, by estimating how much inputs are required to produce a unit of output for different firms – of course, after controlling for factors other than ownership which may affect enterprise performances like country, industry, firm size – one can compare the production efficiency of a firm with those of others. The most desirable method in this line is estimating an appropriate production function. Another popular method is the total factor productivity measure, which is equivalent to the production function method, if the production function is homogeneous, or, on a more practical level, if it is of constant returns to scale – although the assumption of constant returns to scale is difficult to justify in practice (see Millward 1988: p.148).

However, this method may not be readily used because there is no unambiguous way to construct quantity data both for inputs and outputs in the case of multi-product, multi-factor firms, which practically means all modern firms of reasonable size. Constructing quantity indexes is necessary to do justice to the method, because the idea behind the method is to isolate production efficiency (or technical efficiency) from pricing efficiency (or allocative efficiency). When various market imperfections, such as monopoly, exist, value indexes can be misleading.

In the real world, many firms are multi-product firms, and, therefore, it is very difficult to aggregate their outputs. In some cases, products are relatively homogeneous (e.g., cooking oil) so that straight volume measures can be used. For some outputs, it may be possible to convert them into common measures (e.g., different grades of coal into caloric units). However, there is no obvious method of constructing a quantity index for different types of, say, furniture. Although this problem may be overcome to an extent by comparing firms with identical or at least broadly similar product mix, again, there is a problem of quality differences between products of different firms (Parris *et al.* 1987: pp.148-9). Even for such seemingly homogeneous products as electricity, it has been pointed out that 'Californian private electric utilities have conceded that their costs are higher than publicly owned electric companies but argue that their territories are more difficult to serve' (Millward 1982: p.63).[10]

4.2.2 Cost Efficiency Measures

To overcome the problems due to the lack of quantity data, various studies use cost efficiency indicators by measuring cost per unit of output. However, cost efficiency measures have the following drawbacks. First, input prices are not the same for all the firms. Public and private firms may face different factor prices, for example, subsidised capital and inputs for PEs or lower wage rates for PFs (see Short 1984: pp.142-3; Cook and Kirkpatrick 1988: p.16; MacAvoy and McIsaac 1989: Appendix 1). Even within the private sector, firms may face different input prices for various reasons. Different firms may face different input prices because they have different long-term raw material supply contracts. Firms may face different costs for capital equipment with identical physical characteristics because they have respectively purchased them at different points of time (with different interest rates) and in different terms of, say, instalments. Firms operating in different regions may face different wage rates if

---

10 The comparative study of PEs and PFs in West German life and automobile insurance industries conducted by Fisinger (1984) is one of the rare attempts to incorporate the quality dimension, by considering factors like customer complaints.

labour mobility is not perfect. Second, unless the production technology is such that there exist constant returns to scale, comparisons based on unit cost measures do not do justice to firms of different size. This admittedly is a lesser problem than the case of different factor prices, because it may be overcome by comparing firms of similar size, whereas the latter problem requires full information about different input prices which different firms are facing.

4.2.3 General Limitations of Technical and Cost Efficiency Measures

In addition to their respective problems we have pointed out above, the two efficiency measures have the following common drawbacks.

First, as we argued when discussing the validity of using profitability as the performance indicator, PEs may generate externalities in the forms of more jobs, higher aggregate demand, lower inflation rate, higher demand for infant industries, lower input costs for PFs, and so on. If this is the case, even when the unit cost of a PE is higher than that of a comparable PF, or when various productivities of a PE are lower than those of a comparable PF, it is not clear whether the PE is using its production resources in a less efficient way from the social point of view.

Second, technical or cost efficiency indicators at one point in time measure static efficiency only. Although there can be no agreement as to which of the many possible time horizons should be adopted in evaluating the performance of an enterprise (be it public or private), it seems reasonable to suggest that it is necessary to observe the efficiency performance of a PE over a period of time, by using, say, the shift in the cost function or the trend in productivity changes. Studies using cost functions tend not to observe the changes in such cost functions, but some of the studies using productivity measures give some attention to changes in productivity (e.g., Dholakia 1978; Pryke 1980; Krueger and Tuncer 1982; Manasan *et al.* 1988).[11]

---

11 Productivity growth measures will presumably be more important for LDCs, given the fact that the LDCs are likely to have more infant industries, where the learning effect will be more pronounced.

4.3   Concluding Remarks

As seen above, all the performance indicators used in empirical studies of enterprise performance suffer from various measurement problems. Moreover, the fact that PEs tend to generate positive externalities means that it becomes very difficult to estimate their social contribution. This suggests that there is no single fully satisfactory indicator of PE performance. Therefore, a fairer judgement of PE performance may be based on multiple criteria, and not just one or two, especially when PEs are usually expected to serve multiple objectives. This will inevitably make any conclusions from comparisons of PE and PF performances much fuzzier than a lot of people want them to be, but that is the only sensible approach to the problem. The choice of criteria to be employed should be decided upon after considering the specific conditions faced by the industry and by the country concerned. This is because the objectives of individual PEs are not all identical, and because similar PEs ·in different countries may serve different purposes.

5.   EMPIRICAL EVIDENCE ON PUBLIC ENTERPRISE PERFORMANCE IN THE LDCs

5.1   Profitability or Accounting Surplus/Deficit Studies

Even from the studies using profitability, a measure of performance which is inherently disadvantageous to PEs, it is difficult to conclude that PEs in LDCs are invariably inefficient. Even when the profitability of the PE sector is low, it may be performing better than the private sector (the Philippines case during 1981-3; see Manasan *et al.* 1988). At a more disaggregated level, many PEs run at a profit even in an economically-depressed area like Africa, and some do better than comparable PFs in profitability terms (the Singaporean shipbuilding case; see Sikorski 1989). Of course, this is not to argue that financial performance indicators should be ignored or that there is nothing to be desired for the PEs in LDCs in terms of their financial performance.[12]

---

12 An extremely important point to bear in mind here is that the financial surplus of PEs can be improved simply by putting up prices without necessarily improving their 'economic efficiency'.

Bad financial performances of PEs in LDCs are disappointing, especially when considering that, in many LDCs, PEs were set up as the major means to generate investible surplus in the face of the difficulty of raising substantial tax revenue from the rural area.

5.2 Efficiency Studies

The existing efficiency studies suffer from several drawbacks. First, many of these are static and therefore not particularly appropriate for developing economies, where 'learning' plays an important role. Second, the available studies are biased in the sense that very few studies exist for countries where PEs are deemed to be efficient. Such as they are, these studies do tend to indicate inferior 'static' efficiency performances of PEs. However, the problem is whether these studies compare like with like. Some studies pool and compare vastly different enterprises from different countries or in different lines of activities. Others control for these things by comparing firms with similar technology and similar product mixes, but do not properly consider the effect of firm size. In general, firm size seems to be more important than ownership in determining enterprise performances. In short, as Millward (1988) notes in his review, '[t]here is no evidence of a statistically satisfactory kind to suggest that public enterprises in LDCs have a lower level of technical efficiency than private firms operating *at the same scale of operation* (italics added)' (p.157). Moreover, various studies show that PEs range from the best practice to the worst, and that PEs often perform far better in terms of the more appropriate dynamic measures of efficiency such as productivity growth.

5.3 Multiple Criteria Studies

We have suggested earlier that there is no single satisfactory performance indicator for PEs, and therefore that it may be desirable to use multiple criteria, not least because PEs are more often than not expected to serve multiple objectives. There are very few studies of this type, mainly due to the lack of reliable data concerning the performance criteria other than financial variables. Notable examples include Killick (1983) and Green (1985). These studies suggest that the evidence is consistent with the possibility that the unimpressive performances of PEs studied are more due to adverse general economic situations in these countries than public ownership.

5.4 Conclusion on Empirical Studies

The most widely-used performance indicator, profitability, was shown to be seriously deficient for assessing PE performance, especially in the developing country context. Given that other widely-used performance measures, e.g., unit cost, productivity, are also not fully satisfactory and in light of the fact that PEs are usually supposed to serve multiple objectives, we have argued in favour of using multiple performance indicators, including, for example, employment creation (or preservation), balance-of-payments contribution, and income redistribution. We also suggested that the choice of performance criteria should depend on the specific characteristics of the individual industry and of the country which the enterprises studied belong to. Concerning the PE performance in the LDCs, there are relatively few satisfactory empirical studies. The studies using profitability measures, by providing highly aggregated data, conceal the fact that there are many individual PEs performing as well as, or even better than, PFs. Moreover, whatever the level of aggregation, there are times and places when PEs as a whole do as well as, or even better than, PFs, even in terms of profitability, which is an indicator inherently biased against PEs. When we look at the studies using efficiency measures, we find that many of them compare firms which are, strictly speaking, incomparable, and that, even when similar firms are compared, when firm size is taken into account, there is no statistically significant evidence that PEs are less efficient than PFs. Again, PEs range from the best practice to the worst in terms of efficiency.

6.   HOW CAN PUBLIC ENTERPRISE PERFORMANCE BE IMPROVED?

Although there is no rigorous empirical evidence showing the general inferiority of public enterprises, this does not mean that everything is fine with PEs or that there is no room for improvement. The important policy question in many LDCs is how PE performance can be improved. The most popular and simplistic answer to this question has been privatisation. However, as is suggested by many authors, and as will be argued below, privatisation may not be the only, let alone the best, or even an acceptable solution to the problems of bad PE performance (for more extensive analyses on the issue of privatisation, see Aharoni 1986, Vickers and Yarrow 1988, Vernon-Wortzel and Wortzel 1989, Rowthorn 1990a; for developing countries, see Aylen 1987, Cook and Kirkpatrick 1988, Commander and Killick 1988, Bienen and Waterbury 1989, Basu 1990; for socialist countries, see Singh 1990, Newbery 1990, Rowthorn 1990b).

6.1 Privatisation

If one agrees with the critique of public enterprises that their bad performance owes mainly, if not entirely, to public ownership, privatisation appears to be the most obvious solution to the (real and alleged) problems associated with PE performance. Literally, and most relevantly to our discussion, privatisation means the transfer of ownership of a going concern from the state or semi-independent public organisations like a public holding company (e.g., ÖIAG in Austria, ENI in Italy) to private investors, although many people would not hesitate to extend its meaning to include such things as franchise bidding or contracting-out.

Since, as pointed out earlier, there are numerous factors other than ownership which affect the efficiency of the firm, privatisation clearly cannot be the only solution to the problems of PE performances. The degree of competition in the market, size and age of the firm, the state of the industry (e.g., whether it is an infant, mature, or declining industry) are all factors which are important in this respect (see Section 4). Therefore, unless these non-ownership factors which influence enterprise performances are rectified at the same time, privatisation is unlikely to improve their performances. The case studies of the privatisation attempts in the UK (Bishop and Kay 1989; Rowthorn 1990b), Chile (Yotopolous 1989), and in other developing countries (for a summary of the results, see Vernon-Wortzel and Wortzel 1989) indicate that increased competition and organisational reforms (which often happened under public ownership) have been much more important in improving the performances of public enterprises than mere transfer of ownership (see Newbery 1990; Rowthorn and Chang 1993). Moreover, there are practical problems involved in privatising public enterprises. We can classify these problems into two categories, that is, the ones applying to privatisation in general and the ones applying to privatisation in the LDCs.

6.1.1 Problems of Privatisation in General

Many PEs operate in industries with low profitability for various reasons. As we have pointed out, PEs are often those private firms which have been nationalised due to their bad performance. Moreover, some such (ex-private) PEs operate in declining industries, where the profitability is likely to be low without massive restructuring. When the PE put for sale is unprofitable, it is doubtful whether there will be many buyers. In other words, the government wants to sell the least profitable PEs, which private investors are the least willing to buy (World Bank 1987: p.68, Box 4.3).

The most obvious solution to this problem is to improve the performances of such enterprises before privatisation (like the Thatcher government did with the privatised PEs like British Steel and British Airways; see Daring 1989 and Rowthorn 1990b), in order to make them attractive to the potential buyers (see Bienen and Waterbury 1989; Heller and Schiller 1989). However, if the performances of PEs can be improved under public ownership, there is no efficiency reason to sell them, although the government may still want to sell them for other reasons, for example, ideological reasons like in the UK under Thatcher or Chile under Pinochet.

Moreover, it should be remembered that privatisation is not a costless business. First of all, there is the problem of valuation of the PEs put on sale. Often, the assets of PEs have been purchased at subsidised prices, whose value when sold to the private sector is hard to estimate.[13] This problem is often aggravated in the LDCs, where there exists no reliable accounting system and there is an acute

---

13 The obvious solution to this problem is to use a comparable PF as the benchmark for such valuation, but the problem here is that often there exists no such PF due to the simple fact that many PEs are monopolists.

shortage of qualified accountants. Thus, valuing many PEs for an extensive privatisation programme may take up substantial valuable time and resources of the government (see Bienen and Waterbury 1989). Second, there are costs involved in flotation and underwriting for the shares of the PEs which are sold. And in developing countries which are attempting privatisation mainly out of budgetary reasons, this can constitute an obstacle to actual privatisation.

More importantly, it should be pointed out that selling off PEs carries an opportunity cost in the sense that the future income streams from those enterprises are foregone by the government. In the cases of those PEs which were mainly serving a revenue-raising function (e.g., alcohol and tobacco monopolies), this is obvious. Even when the PEs concerned were making losses, it is not obvious that selling them off will actually improve the budgetary situation. If such enterprises have been used as a means to subsidise consumers (e.g., subsidised public transport) or private producers (e.g., subsidised electricity or fertiliser), even if they are sold, these subsidies may still have to be provided. This means that taxes have to be raised to finance the subsidies. And there is no guarantee that running the tax/subsidy scheme is going to be less costly than doing it through a PE, because such a scheme would impose costs of information collection, tax collection, and monitoring for tax evasion or false reporting from the recipients of subsidies. It should be remembered that one important reason for setting up PEs is to save the often prohibitive costs involved in running tax/subsidy schemes.

Of course, it may still be argued that privatisation is necessary because non-commercial objectives like subsidies to particular groups are better served through other policy measures than through PEs. Although we do not have the space to do justice to this complex issue, let us take the case of employment creation (or preservation) through PEs. It is often argued that creation of employment *per se* is not a suitable objective for the PEs to pursue, and that employment is best promoted through other governmental measures, e.g., macroeconomic policy. Stated in this way, the argument seems unexceptional. However, in practice, the typical situation, whether in an advanced or a poor economy, is much more complicated. For example, in a period of rapid structural change within the context of an economic crisis like the 1970s and the 1980s, macroeconomic policies on their own would be insufficient to maintain the employment level, if only because it takes time to train and retrain workers for the new industries. And in this situation, 'over-manning' some PEs for a period of time may be the most 'efficient' alternative available to the government.

Most importantly, privatisation does not necessarily mean that the government can simply pull out of responsibility. Except for the PEs set up for pure revenue reasons (e.g., tourist hotel, tobacco monopoly), most of the now-privatised PEs will have to be put under regulation, since they either possess market power (e.g., monopoly or oligopoly) or generate (positive and negative) externalities. Again, it should not be forgotten that the difficulty of effective regulation has traditionally been one major reason behind the establishment of PEs or the nationalisation of PFs.

6.1.2 Problems of Privatisation in the LDCs

a.   Stock Market Flotation

Privatisation requires the sale of the shares of a going concern. The most common measure suggested to achieve this is floating the shares of a public enterprise in the stock market. However, in the LDCs, the sale of shares through the capital market is often impossible due to the underdevelopment of the stock market (World Bank 1987: p.86, Box 4.3). Actually, many developing countries do not have capital markets of any sort. For example, in Sub-Saharan Africa, as of the late-1980s there existed only four stock markets, that is, Lagos, Harare, Nairobi and Abidjan (Commander and Killick 1988: p.112). Even in countries where there are stock markets, they are often so small that they cannot raise enough funds to purchase any substantial numbers of PEs, which tend to be the largest firms in many LDCs. In this context, it should also be remembered that the underdevelopment of capital markets will mean that, even when it can be sold, a large ex-PE may not become fully subject to the discipline of the capital market, because the threat of takeover bids will be minimal, given the difficulty of raising large funds (on this issue, see Singh 1990).

Moreover, even when it is achievable, diffused sale of shares may create more problems than it solves. The large number of shareholders created by the diffused sales militates against the effective monitoring of managerial behaviour by the shareholders, because the individual costs of a tighter monitoring (the costs involved in collecting information, etc.) may outweigh the individual benefits from it (increased share price and dividends due to improved performance). This apparently makes selling the public enterprise to a small number of individuals, or even to a single individual, a better option.

b.   Sales to Small Number of Individuals

It is not often a feasible option for a developing country to attempt to sell many PEs to a small number of individuals, as there may not be enough rich individuals who are able to buy them all. Actually, the widespread public ownership in the LDCs, and especially in Sub-Saharan Africa, has been partly due to the lack of private capital big enough to start up modern industries. Moreover, this method may raise serious political opposition in the LDCs, because the sale of PEs, which often are the biggest enterprises in these countries, to a small number of individuals can easily be seen as aggravating the already serious inequality in the distribution of income and wealth. Also, there is the danger that privatisation by a sale to a small number of individuals may be used as a means to promote 'crony capitalism' by selling PEs at undervalued prices to individuals who are politically well-connected (Commander and Killick 1988).

c.   Sales to Foreign Interests

The underdevelopment of capital markets and the lack of individuals who are able to buy the often-large PEs have led to the suggestion that the PEs be sold to foreign interests. Although purchases by foreign interests may help the troubled PEs to acquire advanced managerial techniques and production skills more easily (as far as they happen to be the firms within the same or similar industry), or enable them to make major new investments necessary for an improvement in their efficiencies, they may also create several problems. First of all, as pointed out earlier, sale to a foreign interest does not solve the acute principal-agent problem that public enterprises are all alleged to have (of one more layer of delegation – the public-ministers-managers – compared with private enterprises). That is, the sale of a PE to a foreign firm will simply substitute one level of delegation (ministers-managers) with another one (headquarters-local managers), thus leaving the number of levels of delegation concerning the now-foreign-owned ex-PE unchanged. Moreover, in developing countries where economic and political situations are often volatile, foreign capital may just leave the country in the face of short-term adversity in economic and political conditions with detrimental long-term consequences. Actually, the fear of footloose multinational capital was one of the most important reasons for nationalisation in many developing countries. In other words, sales of major enterprises to foreign interests will carry a big cost by making it difficult for the state to control them in a way that fits the national economic developmental needs.

6.2   Other Measures

In view of the many problems associated with privatisation as a means of improving PE performance, what are the alternatives? We briefly consider below some of these measures without claiming to be comprehensive.

6.2.1 Organisational Reforms

a.   Clarifying the Objectives
PEs are usually required to serve multiple objectives. Of course, serving multiple objectives is not necessarily bad, because these activities may generate beneficial externalities (for the discussion, see Sections 3 and 4). However, more often than not, it is not clear what exactly the objectives of a PE are or what the priority between the potentially conflicting objectives is. And such confusion often seriously compromises the performance of PEs. The following changes can be made in this regard (see Vernon-Wortzel and Wortzel 1989 for a theoretical discussion; for some examples see Trivedi 1988, Arcirio 1988, and Song 1986). First, it should be made clear which objectives the PE concerned is supposed to serve. Second, it may be necessary to reduce the number of objectives served by the PE concerned, because pursuing too many objectives may stretch the managerial resources, which tend to be scarce in the LDCs, and hence damage the performance of the firm. Third, in cases when multiple objectives are to be served, it will be necessary to assign priorities amongst the objectives, given that some of these objectives may be achieved only at the cost

of others (e.g., a counter-cyclical investment strategy may not be compatible with high profitability).

b.   Improving Information Collection

As we mentioned in our previous discussion, some countries have lacked even the most basic information as to the basic positions and behaviours of their PEs. For example, before its public enterprise control reform in 1979, the Brazilian government did not even have consolidated information on the earnings, spending or debt of its public enterprises (World Bank 1983: p.80, Box 8.4). The Senegalese case before the introduction of a French-style contract system in 1980 was even more dismal.   Many PEs lack serious information on their own operations, not to speak of basic corporate planning (Trivedi 1988). Given the lack of information owned by the regulating agencies, it seems surprising that some of the public enterprises in such countries have performed well at all. Given that the acquisition of information on the operations and the behaviour of PEs is the first step to exercise control over them, it seems to be an urgent task for the LDCs to establish some informational base both at the individual PE level and at the governmental level.

c.   Incentive Reforms

One of the common criticisms of PEs is that their managers and the workers do not have adequate incentives (rewards and punishments) to perform well.

On the reward side, linking remuneration to performance is possible and to a degree practical for both managers and workers, although the following two points should be noted. First, it is not possible to establish a strict link between effort and outcome. For the managers, it is difficult to know whether the improved (or otherwise) performance of the firm is due to better management or to factors beyond their control. For the workers, when they work as 'teams', it is not easy to isolate the efficiency consequences of an individual worker's increased effort. Second, remuneration need not be pecuniary, as is often supposed. For example, the high status provided by the fact that they work in a PE, which is often among the largest firms in the country, may compensate for their lower pay.

On the managerial punishment side, it will be necessary to

eliminate 'soft budget constraints'. Of course, in hardening the budget constraints, the positive externalities generated by the PE in question should be taken into account. On the workers' punishment side, the 'iron rice bowl' enjoyed by some PE sector workers in some LDCs should be broken. This is not to argue that workers should get no protection from the dangers of unemployment and the consequent deprivation, but to argue that nobody should be allowed to have a quasi-property right in a particular job, which can obstruct the shift in the employment pattern necessary for an efficient structural transformation of the economy.

d.   Lessening the Monitoring Burdens on the Government

Another important way to improve PE efficiency is lessening the burden on the agencies which are supervising the public enterprises, which are already laden with a multitude of tasks. Although it is often suggested that actually the bureaucrats may choose to be in an apparently 'overburdened' position – because the motives of the bureaucrats are such that they want to expand their seignorage (according to Niskanen's theory of self-seeking bureaucrats) – it is clear that such situations can be detrimental to the monitoring activities of the ministries.

The creation of a special agency totally devoted to the monitoring of PEs is one frequently recommended solution. The creation of a Special Secretariat for Control of the State Enterprise in Brazil is a good example (World Bank 1983: p.80, Box 8.4). Concentration of the monitoring responsibility in one agency is another way of dealing with this problem – the concentration of such power in the Board of Audit and Inspection in Korea being an example in this case (see Song 1986). Reducing the number of agents to be monitored through means like the mergers of PEs in similar lines or the creation of public holding companies, as is actually practised in many advanced and developing countries, can also be helpful.

6.2.2 Increased Competition

In the discussions concerning privatisation, it has been frequently pointed out that 'privatising monopolies which face little competition . . . has relatively little impact on efficiency, compared to liberalising industries which are potentially competitive' (Newbery 1990: p. 9). And in practice, in many developing countries with large public sectors, often the lack of product market competition leads to the abuse of trade union power or managerial slack and inefficiency, which are not only economically undesirable but also socially unfair to the public at large and to the vast majority of workers in the unprotected informal sector.[14] In such circumstances, the promotion of competition is often more important than changing ownership title for the improvement of PE performances.

There are several possible avenues for such competition. First, competition can come from other public enterprises. The improvement of rail service in Britain following the introduction of competition from the government-owned bus company is a good example (Rowthorn 1990b: pp.7-8).[15] Secondly, the competition can mainly come from domestic private firms. The good performance of the Italian publicly-owned steel-maker Finsider and the French auto-producer Renault for the last few decades can at least partly be explained by the rather fierce competition from domestic private firms (Ayub and Hegstad 1986: p.18). Thirdly, the competition can also come from competitors in the export market. The examples here include CVRD of Brazil (iron ore), OCP of Morocco (phosphates), ICL of Israel (chemicals), HMT of India (machine tools) (Ayub and Hegstad 1986: p.18). POSCO, which we discussed above, is another good example where competition in the export market was important in increasing productivity. Lastly, import liberalisation may be a possible way of increasing competition, although the applicability of

---

14 It is important to emphasise that such monopolistic abuses are not the monopoly of the public sector. They are as ubiquitous in the private monopolistic industries.

15 'Following the de-regulation of long-distance road passenger transport in 1980, there arose fierce competition for long-distance transport between the government-owned bus company NBC and the government-owned railways BR. This competition forced the railways to improve their service in a variety of ways and led to a far more flexible pricing structure (off-peak tickets, etc.). These competition-induced improvements, it must be noted, occurred against the background of extreme capital starvation for the railways. If competition had been accompanied by an adequate level of investment in the railways, the benefits of competition would have been considerably greater' (Rowthorn 1990b: pp.7-8).

the strategy will be limited by the fact that many PEs in developing countries, still being at an 'infant' stage, will not be able to withstand foreign competition. More importantly, at the macroeconomic level, there may be adverse balance-of-payments implications of such competition. Therefore, other things being equal, domestic competition should in general be preferred to foreign import competition (see, further, Singh and Ghosh 1988 on this point).

6.2.3 Political Reform

In many LDCs, public enterprises constitute the major source of manufacturing employment, which tend to provide higher remuneration than alternative employment sources do. Oftentimes, they also constitute the major source of subcontracting for private sector firms. Given the number of jobs and the size of the funds involved in the operation of the PEs, it is no wonder that public enterprises in many LDCs have been used by the rulers as a means to redistribute income to politically favoured groups, for example, through managerial appointment policies, employment policies, politically-decided contracts.

Such 'clientelist' use of PEs has been more acute in developing countries with a weak state, which does not have other sources of legitimisation other than outright purchase of political support (Khan 1989). In these countries, the operations of PEs become subject to short-term political pressure and lobbying, resulting in poor management and monitoring. The examples include the abuse of PEs as tools for patrimonial politics in some African countries (Sandbrook 1985 and 1988; Bienen & Waterbury 1989) and the establishment of some Malaysian PEs for the purpose of redistributing income from the economically-dominant Chinese community to the politically-dominant but economically-disadvantaged Malay community (Mallon 1982).

If the establishment and the operation of PEs, for whatever reason, constitutes an integral part of clientelist politics, it becomes difficult to expect the improvement of PE performance through 'policy' solutions, be it privatisation, organisational reform, or macroeconomic remedy. Economic problems, in other words, are never completely technical in the sense that they are 'politics-free', and are the question of political economy (on this point, see Rowthorn and Chang 1993). Thus seen, in many LDCs, an improvement in PE performance would not be forthcoming simply through technical formulae but would require a political reform with a view to nation-building, a process through which the now-developed capitalist countries had grown out of their politics of patronage in the mercantilist period.

7.   CONCLUDING REMARKS

In this chapter, we have examined three main questions, that is, whether there are reasons why public enterprises should be less efficient than private enterprises; whether public enterprises, especially in developing countries, are really inefficient; and what are possible remedies for such inefficiencies, if they exist at all. What we ended up with in the process of answering these questions is a very complex picture, which involves various technological, behavioural, organisational, institutional, and political factors. The sources of bad (or good) public enterprise performance are extremely diverse and therefore the remedies are also diverse. And engineering those changes which are supposed to deliver improvements in the performance of public enterprises is not simply a question of pure economics, but fundamentally one of organisation, institution-building, and political economy.

BIBLIOGRAPHY

Aharoni, Y. (1986). *The Evolution and Management of State-Owned Enterprises.* Cambridge, MA: Ballinger Publishing Company.

Ahluwalia, I. (1987). 'The Role of Policy in Industrial Development', paper presented at the Orstom Conference on Economies Industrielles et Stratégies d'Industrialisation dans Le Tiers Monde, Paris.

Amsden, A. (1985). 'The State and Taiwan's Economic Development', in P. Evans, D. Rueschemeyer and T. Skocpol (eds.), *Bringing the State Back In.* Cambridge: Cambridge University Press.

Amsden, A. (1989). *Asia's Next Giant.* New York: Oxford University Press.

Arcirio, R. (1988). 'The Brazilian Public Enterprise Performance Evaluation System', *Public Enterprise*, vol.8, no.1.

Avramovic, D. (1988). 'Conditionality: Facts, Theory and Policy – Contribution to the Reconstruction of the International Financial System'. Helsinki: WIDER.

Aylen, J. (1987). 'Privatisation in Developing Countries', *Lloyds Bank Review,* January 1987.

Ayub, M. and Hegstad, S. (1986). 'Public Industrial Enterprises', *World Bank Industry and Finance Series*, vol.17. Washington, D.C.: The World Bank.

Balassa, B. *et al.* (1986). *Toward Renewed Economic Growth in Latin America.* Washington D.C.: Institute for International Economics/Mexico City: Colegio de Mexico.

Basu, P. (1990). 'Some Strategic Issues in the Management of India's Central Public Enterprises: Does "Government's Failure" Overshadow "Managerial Failure"', Management Studies Research Paper, no.9/90, Engineering Department, University of Cambridge.

Baumol, W. (1980). 'On the Implications of the Conference Discussions', in W. Baumol (ed.), *Public and Private Enterprises in a Mixed Economy.* London and Basingstoke: Macmillan.

Baumol, W. (ed.) (1980). *Public and Private Enterprises in a Mixed Economy.* London and Basingstoke: Macmillan.

Bienen, H. and Waterbury, J. (1989). 'The Political Economy of Privatisation in Developing Countries', *World Development,* vol.17, no.5.

Bishop, M. and Kay, J. (1988). 'The Impact of Privatisation on the Performance of the UK Public Sector', paper presented to the Fifteenth Annual Conference of EARIE, Erasmus University, Rotterdam.

Bishop, M. and Kay, J. (1989). 'Privatisation in the United Kingdom: Lessons from Experience', *World Development,* vol.17, no.5.

Byé, M. (1955). 'Nationalisation in France', in M. Einaudi, M. Byé and E. Rossi, *Nationalisation in France and Italy.* Ithaca: Cornell University Press.

Camerer, C. (1989). 'Bubbles and Fads in Asset Prices', *Journal of Economic Surveys,* vol.3, no.1.

Commander, S. and Killick, T. (1988). 'Privatisation in Developing Countries: A Survey of the Issues', in P. Cook and C. Kirkpatrick (eds.), *Privatisation in Less Developed Countries.* New York: Harvester Wheatsheaf.

Conte, M. and Darrat, A. (1988). 'Economic Growth and the Expanding Public Sector: A Re-examination', *Review of Economics and Statistics.*

Cook, P. and Kirkpatrick, C. (1988). 'Privatisation in Less Developed Countries: An Overview', in P. Cook and C. Kirkpatrick (eds.), *Privatisation in Less Developed Countries.* New York: Harvester Wheatsheaf.

Cosh, A., Hughes, A. and Singh, A. (1989). *Openness, Financial Innovation, Changing Patterns of Ownership and the Structure of Financial Markets,* Discussion Paper, Helsinki, World Institute for Development Economics Research.

Cosh, A., Hughes, A. and Singh, A. (1990). *Takeovers, Short-termism and Finance-Industry Relations in the U.K. Economy,* Department of Applied Economics, University of Cambridge.

Daring, R. (1989). *Successful PE: The Code of the Double Paradox,* the 1989 Hatfield Lecture, Hatfield Polytechnic.

Dertouzos, M., Lester, R. and Solow, R. (1989). *Made in America.* Cambridge, MA: The MIT Press.

Dholakia, B. (1978). 'Relative Performance of Public and Private Manufacturing Enterprises in India: Total Factor Productivity Approach', *Economic and Political Weekly*, no.1.

Edwards, J., Kay, J. and Mayer, C. (1987). *The Economic Analysis of Accounting Profitability.* Oxford: Clarendon Press.

Evans, D. (1987a). 'Tests of Alternative Theories of Firm Growth', *Journal of Political Economy,* vol.95, no.4.

Evans, D. (1987b). 'The Relationship between Firm Growth, Size, and Age: Estimates for 100 Manufacturing Industries', *Journal of Industrial Economics,* vol.35, no.4.

Fernandes, P. (1983). 'An Approach to Evaluating the Performance of Public Industrial Enterprises', *Industry and Development,* no.7.

Fisinger, J. (1984). 'The Performance of Public Enterprises in Insurance Markets', in M. Marchan, P. Pestieau and H. Tulken (eds.), *The Performance of Public Enterprises: Concepts and Measurement.* Amsterdam: North Holland.

Floyd, R. (1984). 'Some Topical Issues Concerning Public Enterprises', in R. Floyd, C. Gary and R. Short (eds.), *Public Enterprises in Mixed Economies: Some Macroeconomic Aspects.* Washington, D.C.: International Monetary Fund.

Funkhouser, R. and MacAvoy, P. (1979). 'A Sample of Observations on Comparative Prices in Public and Private Enterprises', *Journal of Public Economics,* vol.11, no.3.

Galán, T. (1980). 'Thoughts on the Role of Public Holdings in Developing Economies: INI's Experience in Spain', in W. Baumol (ed.), *Public and*

Private Enterprises in a Mixed Economy. London and Basingstoke: Macmillan.

Gemmell, N. (1983). 'International Comparison of the Effects of Non-Market Sector Growth', *Journal of Comparative Economics,* vol.7.

Georgakopolous, T., Prodromidis, K. and Loizides, J. (1987). 'Public Enterprises in Greece', *Annals of Public and Cooperative Economics,* vol.58, no.4.

Gerschenkron, A. (1962).' Economic Backwardness in Historical Perspective', in *Economic Backwardness in Historical Perspective.* Cambridge, MA: The Belknap Press.

Green, R. H. (1985). 'Malaise to Recovery: An Overview', *Journal of Development Planning,* no.15.

Greer, D. (1986). 'Acquiring in Order to Avoid Acquisition', *Antitrust Bulletin,* vol.31, Spring.

Grossman, S. and Hart, O. (1980). 'Takeover Bids, the Free-rider Problem, and the Theory of the Corporation', *The Bell Journal of Economics,* Spring, 1980.

Heller, P. and Schiller, C. (1989). 'The Fiscal Impact of Privatisation, with Some Examples from Arab Countries', *World Development,* vol.17, no.5.

Hirschman, A. (1970). *Exit, Voice and Loyalty – Responses to Decline in Firms, Organisations, and States.* Cambridge, MA: Harvard University Press.

Hirschman, A. (1982). *Shifting Involvements – Private Interest and Public Action.* Oxford: Basil Blackwell.

Hughes, A. (1989). 'The Impact of Merger: A Survey of Empirical Evidence for the U.K.', in J. Fairburn and J. Kay (eds.), *Mergers and Merger Policy.* Oxford: Oxford University Press.

Hughes, A. and Singh, A. (1987). 'Takeovers and the Stock Market', *Contributions to Political Economy,* vol.6.

Jenkins, G. and Lahouel, M. (1983). 'Evaluation of Performance of Industrial Public Enterprises: Criteria and Policies', *Industry and Development,* no.7.

Jensen, M. and Meckling, W. (1976). 'Theory of the Firm: Managerial Behaviour, Agency Costs and Ownership Structure', *Journal of Financial Economics,* vol.3.

Jones, L. and Mason, E. (1982). 'Role of Economic Factors in Determining the Size and Structure of the Public Enterprise Sector in Less-developed Countries with Mixed Economies', in L. Jones (ed.), *Public Enterprise in Less-developed Countries.* Cambridge: Cambridge University Press.

Kaldor, N. (1980). 'Public or Private Enterprise – the Issues to be Considered', in W. Baumol (ed.), *Public and Private Enterprises in a Mixed Economy.* London and Basingstoke: Macmillan.

Keynes, J. M. (1936). *The General Theory of Employment, Interest, and Money.* London and Basingstoke: Macmillan.

Khan, M. H. (1989). 'Clientelism, Corruption, and Capitalist Development: An Analysis of State Intervention with Special Reference to Bangladesh', unpublished Ph.D. thesis, Faculty of Economics and Politics, University of Cambridge.

Killick, T. (1983). 'The Role of Public Sector in the Industrialisation of African Developing Countries', *Industry and Development*, no.7.

Kirkpatrick, C. (1986). 'The World Bank's View on State Owned Enterprises in Less Developed Countries: A Critical Comment', *Rivista Internazionale di Scienze Economiche e Commerciali*, vol.33, nos.6-7.

Krueger, A. and Tuncer, B. (1982). 'Growth of Factor Productivity in Turkish Manufacturing Industries', *Journal of Development Economics*, vol.11, no.3.

Kumar, M. (1984). *Growth, Acquisition and Investment.* Cambridge: Cambridge University Press.

Landau, D. (1983). 'Government Expenditure and Economic Growth: A Cross-Country Study', *Southern Economic Journal*, vol.49.

Landau, D. (1986). 'Government and Economic Growth in the Less Developed Countries: An Empirical Study for 1960-80', *Economic Development and Cultural Change*, vol.35.

Likierman, A. (1984). 'The Use of Profitability in Assessing the Performance of Public Enterprises', in V. Ramanadham (ed.), *Public Enterprise and the Developing World.* London: Croom Helm.

Littlechild, S. (1986). *Economic Regulation of Privatised Water Authorities.* London: HMSO.

Luke, D. (1988). 'The Economic and Financial Crisis Facing African Public Enterprise', *Public Enterprise*, vol.8, no.2.

MacAvoy, P. and McIsaac, G. (1989). 'The Performance and Management of United States Federal Government Corporations', in P. MacAvoy, W. Stanbury, G. Yarrow and R. Zeckhauser (eds.), *Privatisation and State-Owned Enterprises: Lessons from the United States, Great Britain and Canada.* Boston: Kluwer Academic Publishers.

Mallon, R. (1982). 'Public Enterprise versus Other Methods of State Intervention as Instruments of Redistribution Policy: the Malaysian Experience', in L. Jones (ed.), *Public Enterprise in Less-developed Countries.* Cambridge: Cambridge University Press.

Manasan, R., Amatong, J. and Beltran, G. (1988). 'The Public Enterprise Sector in the Philippines: Economic Contribution and Performance, 1975-1984', *Public Enterprise*, vol.8, no.4.

Marsden, K. (1983). 'Links between Taxes and Economic Growth: Some Empirical Evidence', World Bank Staff Working Paper, no.605.

Marshall, J. and Montt, F. (1988). 'Privatisation in Chile', in P. Cook and C. Kirkpatrick (eds.), *Privatisation in Less Developed Countries.* New York: Harvester Wheatsheaf.

Meeks, G. and Whittington, G. (1976). 'The Financing of Quoted Companies in the United Kingdom', Background Paper no.1, Royal Commission on the Distribution of Income and Wealth. London: HMSO.

Millward, R. (1982). 'The Comparative Performance of Public and Private Ownership', in E. Roll (ed.), *The Mixed Economy*. London and Basingstoke: Macmillan.

Millward, R. (1988). 'Measured Sources of Inefficiency in the Performance of Private and Public Enterprises in LDCs', in P. Cook and C. Kirkpatrick (eds.), *Privatisation in Less Developed Countries*. New York: Harvester Wheatsheaf.

Nellis, J. and Kikeri, S. (1989). 'Public Enterprise Reform: Privatisation and the World Bank', *World Development*, vol.17, no.5.

Newbery, D. (1990). 'Reform in Hungary: Sequencing and Privatisation', paper to be presented at the Fifth Annual Congress of the European Economic Association, Lisbon, September, 1990.

Nickell, S. and Wadhwani, S. (1989). 'The Effects of the Stock Market on Investment: A Comparative Study', *The European Economic Review*, vol.33.

Nove, A. (1973). *Efficiency Criteria for Nationalised Industries*. London: George Allen and Unwin.

ÖIAG (Österreichische Industrieholding Aktiengesellschaft) (1990). *Austrian Industries: The New Economic Power of Austria*. Vienna: ÖIAG.

Okimoto, D. (1989). *Between MITI and the Market: Japanese Industrial Policy for High Technology*. Stanford: Stanford University Press.

Olson, M. (1965). *The Logic of Collective Action*. Cambridge, MA: Harvard University Press.

Parris, H., Pestieau, R. and Sayner, P. (1987). *Public Enterprises in Western Europe*. London: Croom Helm.

Pryke, R. (1980). 'Public Enterprise in Practice: The British Experience of Nationalisation during the Past Decade', in W. Baumol (ed.), *Public and Private Enterprises in a Mixed Economy*. London and Basingstoke: Macmillan.

Ram, R. (1986). 'Government Size and Economic Growth: A New Framework and Some Evidence from Cross-Section and Time-Series Data', *American Economic Review*, vol.76.

Rees, R. (1976). *Public Enterprise Economics*, 2nd edn. Oxford: Philip Allan.

Rowthorn, B. (1990a). 'Notes on Competition and Public Ownership', mimeo., Faculty of Economics and Politics, University of Cambridge.

Rowthorn, B. (1990b). 'Privatisation in the UK', mimeo., Faculty of Economics and Politics, University of Cambridge.

Rowthorn, B. and Chang, H.-J. (1993). 'Public Ownership and the Theory of the State', in T. Clarke and C. Pitelis (eds.), *The Political Economy of Privatisation*. London: Routledge.

Rubinson, R.m (1977). 'Dependency, Government Revenue, and Economic Growth, 1955-70', *Studies in Comparative International Development*, vol.12.

Sandbrook, R. (1985). *The Politics of Africa's Economic Stagnation*. Cambridge: Cambridge University Press.

Sandbrook, R. (1988). 'Patrimonialism and the Failing of Parastatals: Africa in Comparative Perspective' in P. Cook and C. Kirkpatrick (eds.), *Privatisation in Less Developed Countries*. New York: Harvester Wheatsheaf.

Shepherd, W. (1965). *Economic Performance under Public Ownership: British Fuel and Power*. New Haven and London: Yale University Press.

Shiller, R. (1981). 'Do Stock Prices Move Too Much to be Justified by Subsequent Changes in Dividends?', *American Economic Review*, vol.71, June.

Shirley, M. (1983). 'Managing State-Owned Enterprises', World Bank Staff Working Papers, no.577. Washington D.C.: World Bank.

Short, R. (1984). 'The Role of Public Enterprises: An International Statistical Comparison', in R. Floyd, C. Gary and R. Short (eds.), *Public Enterprises in Mixed Economies: Some Macroeconomic Aspects*. Washington, D.C.: International Monetary Fund.

Sikorski, D. (1986). 'Public Enterprise (PE): How is it Different from the Private Sector – A Review of Literature', *Annals of Public and Cooperative Economics*, vol.57, no.4.

Sikorski, D. (1989). 'Competitive Advantages of State-Owned Enterprises - Comparative Case Studies of National and Private Companies in Singapore', *Public Enterprise*, vol.9, no.1.

Singh, A. (1971). *Takeovers: Their Reference to the Stock Market and the Theory of the Firm*. Cambridge: Cambridge University Press.

Singh, A. (1975). 'Takeovers, Economic Natural Selection and the Theory of the Firm: Evidence from the Post-war U.K. Experience', *Economic Journal*, vol.85, Sept.

Singh, A. (1990). 'The Stock Market in a Socialist Economy', in P. Nolan and F. Deng (eds.), *The Chinese Economy and Its Future*. Cambridge: Polity Press.

Singh, A. and Ghosh, J. (1988). 'Import Liberalisation and New Industrial Strategy in India', *Economic and Political Weekly, 1988*.

Singh, A. and Whittington, G. (1968). *Growth, Profitability and Valuation*. Cambridge: Cambridge University Press.

Singh, A. and Whittington, G. (1975). 'The Size and Growth of Firms', *Review of Economic Studies*.

Singh, B. and Sahni, B. (1984). 'Causality between Public Expenditure and National Income', *Review of Economics and Statistics*, vol.66.

Song, D. (1986). 'The Role of the Public Enterprises in the Korean Economy', in K. Lee (ed.), *Industrial Development Policies and Issues*. Seoul: Korea Development Institute.

Stiglitz, J. (1985). 'Credit Markets and the Control of Capital', *Journal of Money, Credit and Banking*, vol.17, no.2.

Stiglitz, J. (1987). 'Principal-Agent Problem', in J. Eatwell, M. Milgate and P. Newman (eds.), *The Palgrave Dictionary of Economics*. London and Basingstoke: Macmillan.

Summers, L. (1986). 'Does the Stock Market Rationally Reflect Fundamental Values?', *Journal of Finance*, July.

Tobin, J. (1984). 'A Mean-Variance Approach to Fundamental Valuations', *Journal of Portfolio Management*.

Trivedi, P. (1988). 'Theory and Practice of the French System of Contracts for Improving Public Enterprise Performance: Some Lessons for LDCs', *Public Enterprise*, vol.8, no.1.

Vernon, R. (1981). 'Introduction', in R. Vernon and Y. Aharoni (eds.), *State-Owned Enterprise in the Western Economies*. London: Croom Helm.

Vernon, R. (1988). *The Promise of Privatisation: A Challenge for U.S. Policy*. New York: Council on Foreign Relations.

Vernon, R. and Aharoni, Y. (eds.) (1981). *State-Owned Enterprise in the Western Economies*. London: Croom Helm.

Vernon-Wortzel, H. and Wortzel, L. (1989). 'Privatisation: Not the Only Answer', *World Development*, vol.17, no.5.

Vickers, J. and Yarrow, G. (1988). *Privatisation: An Economic Analysis*. Cambridge, MA: The MIT Press.

Vickers, J. and Yarrow, G. (1989). 'Privatisation in Britain', in P. MacAvoy, W. Stanbury, G. Yarrow and R. Zeckhauser (eds.), *Privatisation and State-Owned Enterprises: Lessons from the United States, Great Britain and Canada*. Boston: Kluwer Academic Publishers.

World Bank (1981). *Accelerated Development in Sub-Saharan Africa*. Washington, D.C.: World Bank

World Bank (1983). *World Development Report 1983*. New York: Oxford University Press.

World Bank (1987). *World Development Report 1987*. New York: Oxford University Press.

Yarrow, G. (1986). 'Privatisation in Theory and Practice', *Economic Policy*, 1986.

Yarrow, G. (1989). 'Does Ownership Matter?', in C. Valjanovski (ed.), *Privatisation and Competition*. London: IEA.

Yotopoulos, P. (1989). 'The (Rip)Tide of Privatisation: Lessons from Chile', *World Development*, vol.17, no.5.

Chapter 7

Globalisation, Transnational Corporations, and Economic Development: Can the Developing Countries Pursue Strategic Industrial Policy in a Globalising World Economy?*

1. INTRODUCTION

DURING the last quarter of a century, we witnessed a sea change in the prevailing view on the role of the state. The earlier interventionist orthodoxy that ruled the 'Golden Age of Capitalism' (1950-73) has been subjected to some severe, and in some areas fatal, criticisms, and currently the neoliberal vision, which draws its inspirations from the old liberal world order of the 1870-1913 period, dominates. On the domestic front, the current orthodoxy seeks to restore entrepreneurial dynamism and social discipline by rolling back the boundaries of the state through budget cuts, privatisation, and deregulation. At the international level, it seeks to accelerate global integration and convergence (a trend that orthodox economists believe started around 1870 but was reversed after the First World War) by reducing restrictions on the international flows of trade, direct and portfolio investments, and technology.[1]

---

* Parts of this chapter draw heavily from the paper, 'Transnational Corporations and Strategic Industrial Policy', presented at the World Institute for Development Economics Research (WIDER) conference, 'Transnational Corporations in the Developed, Developing, and Transitional Economies: Changing Strategies and Policy', September 1995, King's College, Cambridge, UK. The research support from WIDER is duly acknowledged. I benefited greatly from discussions with William Milberg and Richard Kozul-Wright in writing the earlier paper.

1 It is interesting to note that most neoliberal authors hardly mention the issue of international flow of labour, much less the possibility of liberalising international migration. Cable (1995) is one of the few neoliberal writers who directly confront the issue of international labour mobility. For a discussion of this issue from a 'progressive' perspective, see Hirst and Thompson (1996: Ch.8). For a critical economics, see Chang and Rowthorn (1995: Introduction).

Yet even when considering the shift in the overall intellectual and policy atmosphere, the debate on developing country governments' policies regarding transnational corporations (TNCs) has arguably experienced the most dramatic about-turn. (For some recent critical reviews of the literature, see Helleiner 1989 and Lall (ed.) 1993: Introduction.) Once regarded by many commentators as agents distorting, if not actually hampering, the development of poorer nations, TNCs are now regarded by many, including some of their earlier critics, as indispensable agents of development, promoting the integration of developing countries into the emerging network of globalised production and thus enhancing their efficiency and growth (e.g., see Julius 1990, 1994; UNCTC 1992; Michalet 1994; Brittan 1995). Even some of those who do not agree with this rose-tinted picture of TNCs accept the fact that increasing international economic interdependence, or 'globalisation', and especially the growth in the importance of TNCs in the process, is now unstoppable. Therefore, they argue, countries should adopt a more accommodating attitude toward TNCs whether they like it or not (e.g., see Stopford 1994).

This chapter critically examines the currently popular view that TNCs are the essential agents of economic development in the globalising economy, and it discusses whether the rise of TNCs would prevent the pursuit of 'strategic' or 'selective' industrial policy by developing countries, as is often alleged.

The structure of this chapter is as follows. After examining some basic facts about globalisation and the rise of TNCs in that process, we discuss the role of TNCs in economic development, drawing on some recent theoretical literature and on the experiences of certain East Asian countries, especially South Korea and Taiwan. We then discuss how much the recent (alleged) rise of TNCs has diminished the ability of developing country governments to conduct strategic industrial policy and examine the policy options open to developing countries on this front. The final section presents our conclusions.

2. GLOBALISATION AND THE RISE OF TNCs: MYTHS, FACTS AND NEGLECTED DETAILS

Discussions of recent trends in the rise of TNCs are often strewn with impressive facts and figures testifying to the increasing importance of foreign direct investment (FDI) and other activities by TNCs, even when compared to other international economic activities such as international trade.

First, for example, there are many statistics showing that FDI is playing an increasingly important and possibly leading role in the process of globalisation (all the following figures are from Stopford 1994, unless indicated otherwise). FDI has been growing four times faster than international trade since 1982. Since the 1970s, the combined output of TNCs has exceeded the volume of international trade. FDI in developing countries has increased as dramatically in recent years (for example, from $36.9 billion to $56.3 billion between 1991 and 1993; see Hutton 1995), suggesting that more and more countries are being drawn into the process of globalisation. TNCs manage about 75% of world trade in manufactured goods, over a third of which is intra-affiliate trade. They account for 75% of all industrial research and development in economies of the OECD (Organisation for Economic Cooperation and Development) (Archibugi and Michie 1995: p.130), and they dominate the international trade in technology payments. The examples could go on.

Secondly, it is argued, albeit anecdotally (partially, but not solely, because of an understandable difficulty in collecting the relevant data), that TNCs are becoming more and more 'transnational' and thus 'stateless'. This process, it is argued, occurs not simply because of the sheer increase in the share of TNC activities that are located outside the home countries, but more importantly, through the relocation of 'core' activities such as R&D, and sometimes even of the corporate headquarters, out of the home countries (this process is described as 'complex integration' by UNCTAD 1993: Chapter 5). The emergence of the concept of 'world car' or 'global car' in the automobile industry or the establishment of R&D centres in the US or Europe by the Japanese and Korean computer TNCs are some of the most frequently cited cases in support of this argument.

Thirdly, the fact that some countries that ostensibly have had 'liberal' policies toward FDI (or at least toward some form of active TNC involvement) have performed well is often used as a 'proof' that liberal FDI policies benefit the host countries (e.g., see UNCTAD 1995: Chapter 5, and Ozawa 1995). The East Asian countries (except Japan, whose illiberal policies toward TNCs are well known) and certain post-reform Latin American countries, especially Mexico (until the 1994-95 crisis), are often cited as examples of countries whose open attitudes toward TNCs led to industrial development and export success. It is argued that open trade and FDI policies have given them access not only to needed capital but also to advanced technologies, sophisticated managerial practices and distribution networks in the export markets, thus contributing to their spectacular growth and trade performance.

For many neoliberal commentators, such facts and figures seem to offer incontrovertible evidence that the world economy is becoming increasingly borderless and globalised, that in this process TNCs are playing an increasingly important (and now arguably leading) role, and that countries with open FDI policies have performed better than those with more restrictive policies. However, such a picture, as we shall see below, not only is inaccurate in many respects but, even where it is broadly correct, conceals an important degree of unevenness of the globalisation process across regions, countries, and industries. In the rest of this section, we offer an alternative picture to that painted by the supporters of globalisation, and try to show how many of their claims are exaggerated and overly generalised. Although some of the facts cited below are well known and are discussed in much further depth and in a much broader context elsewhere (for some recent examples, see Bairoch and Kozul-Wright 1996; Hirst and Thompson 1996; Milberg 1998), it will be useful to state them in summary form here in order to put our later policy discussions into perspective.

First, the bulk of FDI occurs among the developed countries; only a handful of developing countries take part in the transnational investment story (Dicken 1992: Chapter 4). For example, in 1989, the Group of Five (G5) economies alone received 75% of world FDI (Hirst and Thompson 1992: p.366). By comparison, between 1983 and 1989, only 19.7% of world FDI went to developing countries (see Table 4). Although this share has increased (to 29.2% during 1990-94), it is still not of the size it is often made out to be. Consider, for example, the assertion by Sir Leon Brittan, former vice president of the European Commission, that '[o]ver half of world FDI now goes to developing countries' (Brittan 1995: p.3). Especially when we exclude the flows

Table 4: The Share of Developing Countries in World's Total Foreign Direct Investment Inflows, Including and Excluding China, 1983-94
(Millions of dollars)

	1983-89 (annual average)	1990	1991	1992	1993	1994*	1990-1994 (annual average)
World total	106,827	211,072	162,662	164,399	206,320	231,125	195,116
Developing countries	21,024 (19.7%)	34,687 (16.4%)	40,878 (25.1%)	54,634 (33.2%)	72,642 (35.2%)	82,131 (35.5%)	56,994 (29.2%)
China	2,047 (1.9%)	3,487 (1.6%)	4,366 (2.7%)	11,156 (6.8%)	27,515 (13.3%)	33,800 (14.6%)	16,065 (8.2%)
Developing countries excluding China	18,977 (17.8%)	31,200 (14.8%)	36,512 (22.4%)	43,478 (26.4%)	45,127 (21.9%)	48,331 (20.9%)	40,929 (21.0%)

Note: Figures in parentheses are shares in world total
Source: Calculated from UNCTAD, *World Investment Report 1995*, Annex Table 1.
*Estimates

to China, the increase in the share for developing countries is even smaller (from 17.8% to 21.0% between 1983-89 and 1990-94).[2]

Moreover, even within the developing world, FDI is highly concentrated among a few countries. Between 1981 and 1992, the 10 largest developing countries receiving FDI accounted for 72% of the developing country total (UNCTAD 1994: p.14, Table 1.5).[3] These concentrations of FDI occurred despite the liberal FDI policies that many developing countries introduced during this period on the

---

2   Some commentators also suspect that a large portion of FDI into China is in fact domestic investment rerouted through overseas Chinese communities in order to exploit the privileges extended to foreign investors (see e.g., Hutton 1995).
3   Part of this concentration is obviously due to the fact that many of the largest recipients of FDI are also large economies (in terms of GDP). However, even after adjusting for the size of the economy, the concentration of FDI within the developing world still remains high. During the 1980s (1980-89), the 10 largest developing country recipients of FDI received 16.5% of the world's total FDI, even though these countries accounted for only about 7.3% of the world's total GDP (for 1980-89). The figures are extracted from Hirst and Thompson (1996: Tables 3.2 and 3.4).

recommendation of neoliberal economists.

Secondly, while increasing 'globalisation' of TNCs is occurring, it is happening at a much slower pace and in a more uneven pattern than the proponents of the globalisation thesis believe. Most TNCs remain international firms with a strong base, in terms of assets and production activities, in their 'home' countries, and the alleged recent reduction in the importance of the home countries has been neither marked nor uniform across countries and industries (Hirst and Thompson 1996: pp.95-7). In addition, at most TNCs, the top decision makers are home country nationals (Kozul-Wright 1995: p.160). And when 'core' activities are relocated, they are moved primarily to other developed countries, usually in North America, Europe, and Japan (Hirst and Thompson 1992: p.368). As a survey by *The Economist* puts it, generally speaking, 'what [TNCs] have done is to extend their home bases into neighbouring countries' (*The Economist*, March 27, 1993, pp.15-6). Archibugi and Michie (1995) corroborate this statement by showing that the globalisation of R&D, which is often regarded as the primary indicator of increasing globalisation of TNCs through complex integration, is basically a 'regional' phenomenon – specifically US and Japanese TNCs do not do much R&D outside their home bases (except in Canada in the case of the US firms), while European TNCs do substantial amounts of R&D outside their home bases but mostly in other European economies.[4]

Thirdly, the attempt to support pro-TNC policies by using the examples of East Asian developing countries needs to be critically scrutinised. Many countries in East Asia, while not against hosting TNCs in certain areas, have had rather restrictive policies overall toward FDI. Only Malaysia and Hong Kong had largely (and even then not entirely) liberal attitudes toward TNCs. Singapore heavily relied on TNCs, but deliberately directed FDI toward government-designated priority sectors. Only in these three economies among the seven East Asian developing countries has the contribution of FDI as a

---

4   Also note the parallel phenomenon that, despite its allegedly growing importance, intra-industry trade also remains basically a 'regional' phenomenon – that is, there is little intra-industry trade between the three regional 'blocs' (Rowthorn 1995). Taken together, these two phenomena seem to suggest that there is a minimal efficient scale of the economy of which all European economies fall short. Of course, this does not imply that the size of the economy is the only factor involved in the determination of trade and TNC activities.

source of capital accumulation been exceptionally high by international standards (see Table 5).

Table 5: Ratio of FDI Inflows to Gross Domestic Capital Formation for Various Regions and Selected Countries
(Annual average)

	1971-75	1976-80	1981-85	1986-90	1991-93
All Countries	n.a.	n.a	2.3%	4.1%	3.8%
Developed	n.a.	n.a.	2.2%	4.6%	3.3%
European Union	n.a.	n.a.	2.6%	5.9%	5.6%
Austria	1.8%	0.9%	1.3%	1.5%	1.5%
France	1.8%	1.9%	2.0%	4.1%	7.7%
Germany	2.1%	0.8%	1.2%	2.0%	1.4%
Netherlands	6.1%	4.5%	6.1%	13.3%	10.6%
Sweden	0.6%	0.5%	1.6%	4.0%	9.5%
UK	7.3%	8.4%	5.6%	4.6%	10.0%
Switzerland	n.a.	n.a.	2.3%	5.3%	3.1%
US	0.9%	2.0%	2.9%	6.9%	3.2%
Canada	3.6%	1.7%	1.0%	5.8%	4.3%
Japan	0.1%	0.1%	0.1%	0.0%	0.1%
Developing	n.a.	n.a.	3.3%	3.2%	5.7%
Africa	n.a.	n.a.	2.3%	3.5%	4.6%
Latin America	n.a.	n.a.	4.1%	4.2%	6.5%
Argentina	0.1%	2.1%	5.0%	11.1%	37.6%
Brazil	4.2%	3.9%	4.3%	1.7%	1.5%
Chile	-7.3%	4.2%	6.7%	20.6%	8.5%
Mexico	3.5%	3.6%	5.0%	7.5%	6.8%
Asia	n.a.	n.a.	3.1%	2.8%	5.5%
Bangladesh	n.a.	n.a.	0.0%	0.1%	0.2%
China	0.0%	0.1%	0.9%	2.1%	10.4%
Hong Kong	5.9%	4.2%	6.9%	12.9%	5.7%
India	0.3%	0.1%	0.1%	0.3%	0.4%
Indonesia	4.6%	2.4%	0.9%	2.1%	4.5%
Korea	1.9%	0.4%	0.5%	1.2%	0.6%
Malaysia	15.2%	11.9%	10.8%	11.7%	24.6%
Pakistan	0.5%	0.9%	1.3%	2.3%	3.4%
Philippines	1.0%	0.9%	0.8%	6.7%	4.6%
Singapore	15.0%	16.6%	17.4%	35.0%	37.4%
Taiwan	1.4%	1.2%	1.5%	3.7%	2.6%
Thailand	3.0%	1.5%	3.0%	6.5%	1.7%
Turkey	n.a.	n.a.	0.8%	2.1%	3.2%
Eastern Europe	n.a.	n.a.	0.0%	0.1%	12.2%

Source: UNCTAD, *World Investment Report 1993,* Annex Table 3 (for the 1971-80 data) and *World Investment Report 1995,* Annex Table 5 (for the rest).

It should also be noted that, even in the case of these economies, it is general economic conditions and not exceptional FDI-specific incentives that mainly explain the large FDI inflows (World Bank 1985: p.130); this phenomenon is observed all over the world, not just in East Asia (Helleiner 1989: p.1467). In Korea, Taiwan, and Indonesia, the contribution of FDI to capital accumulation was in fact below the developing country average, with Korea distinguishing itself as having one of the lowest such ratios in the world (if not quite approaching the Japanese level, which is arguably the lowest in the world; see Table 5). In Thailand, which is usually regarded as a model 'FDI-driven' economy, the ratio of FDI to gross fixed capital formation was not much above the developing country average, and the ratio has actually slipped below the average in the early-1990s. Thus, the alleged importance of TNCs in East Asian development largely depends on one country's experience, namely Malaysia, if we exclude the very exceptional cases of the two city-states of Hong Kong and Singapore.[5]

The above discussions show that, while TNCs are increasing in importance, the phenomenon is by no means a truly 'global' and even process. Most TNCs are still 'national' firms with peripheral operations abroad than truly 'stateless' bodies globally rearranging their activities in search of higher profits. Although there are signs that the picture is slowly changing, it is not clear at all how far this process will or can go (see Milberg 1998). Many developing countries and former Communist countries are still excluded from international FDI flows, and their ability to attract FDI has changed little (with some notable exceptions such as China and Vietnam), despite policy changes they have adopted during the last decade or so at the urging of (their own and foreign) neoliberal economists.

The alleged importance of TNCs in the developmental process of East Asia also turns out to be highly exaggerated. Many East Asian economies were not particularly reliant on FDI by international

---

5   Some commentators, while agreeing with our assessment of the past contribution of FDI to East Asian development, argue that the picture is changing, as shown in the rising importance of FDI within the East Asian region. However, this increase is mainly due to the recent rush of investment out of Japan and the first-tier newly industrialising countries (NICs) to the second-tier NICs and China. A lot of this investment is of a once-and-for-all nature, and therefore unlikely to be sustained.

standards, and most of their governments have taken 'strategic', rather than *laissez-faire*, attitudes toward TNCs to one degree or another and tried to influence the direction and the terms of engagement of incoming FDI. This is the broad empirical background against which we place our discussion.

3.   TNCs AND ECONOMIC DEVELOPMENT

Those who argue for the liberalisation of policies toward TNCs have a strong belief that what is good for TNCs is good for the host country, and that the recent trend in globalisation is eliminating whatever minor conflicts of interests may have once existed between the two. So, for example, Julius (1994: p.278) argues that '[I]t is no longer appropriate to assume that government and corporate objectives conflict'. They regard the restrictive TNC policies that were popular in the 1960s and 1970s in many developing countries as ideologically motivated, and argue that 'fortunately' now 'investment' is recognised for what it is: a source of extra capital, a contribution to a healthy external balance, a basis for increased productivity, additional employment, effective competition, rational production, technology transfer and a source of managerial know-how (Brittan 1995: p.2).

However, the fact that there are few justifications for the extreme anti-TNC view that was once popular in some developing countries should by no means suggest that TNCs are unambiguously beneficial for economic development. (For some recent literature reviews, see Helleiner 1989; Lall (ed.) 1993; and Chudnovsky (ed.) 1993). While some earlier concerns about the 'inappropriateness' of the production technology or the product mix of TNCs were often misconceived and exaggerated, the problem itself is real and can be important in certain circumstances. Earlier criticisms of 'surplus extraction' through transfer pricing or excessive royalty payments, again, may at times have been out of proportion but the practices exist and can be significant and damaging. Predatory behaviour or manipulation of consumer preference by TNCs may not necessarily be more severe than that carried out by their local equivalents, but these are still practices to be reckoned with. Restrictions imposed by TNC headquarters on the exporting or R&D activities of subsidiaries may not be as widespread or important as once thought but they nevertheless have to be minimised, especially if the host country government is keen on technological spillovers from the TNCs. The fears about manipulation of the overall national policy regime by TNCs through political influence may have been overplayed in the past, but these fears cannot simply be dismissed as unfounded.

More recently, careful analyses of empirical cases as well as developments in the economics of technology have shown the importance of domestic technological capabilities in sustaining long-term growth, and thus have raised further doubts as to whether inviting TNCs into a country is the best way to promote industrialisation (Fransman and King (eds.) 1984; Fransman 1986; Haq *et al.* 1996). There is a growing consensus that accepting a 'package' of finance, technology, managerial skills, and other capabilities offered by TNCs may not be as good for long-term industrial development as encouraging national firms to construct their own packages using their own managerial skills – with some necessary outsourcing. As Lall (ed.) (1993) points out, while having more FDI may, on the margin, bring in net benefits to the host country, there still is a question of choosing between different strategies regarding the role of FDI in long-term development.

This critique of TNCs does not mean to imply that countries cannot develop if they rely extensively on TNCs. Singapore, as one obvious example, has managed to thrive. However, it should be noted that the Singapore government, while welcoming and actively courting TNCs, did not take a *laissez-faire* attitude to TNCs; rather, it deliberately directed FDI into strategic sectors. If Singapore, given its city-state status and unique political economy, looks like too much of an exception (which it is), one can always cite the example of Malaysia, where FDI indeed has played a crucial role in development. However, these cases still do not prove the desirability of a pro-TNC developmental strategy or the feasibility of its widespread adoption. First of all, given its relative lack of experienced indigenous managers, qualified engineers, and skilled workers – a situation which is at least partly due to its reliance on TNCs – Malaysia is likely to find it difficult to move into the more sophisticated industries that will help it sustain long-term growth (e.g., see Lall 1995). Moreover, as Rowthorn (1996)

argues, those who recommend the 'Malaysian road' to other developing countries do not realise that an implausibly large amount of
additional FDI will have to be generated if the experience is to be
replicated on a large scale.[6]

The experiences of the two 'star performers' of East Asia,
namely, Korea and Taiwan, especially during their earlier days of
industrialisation, also provide interesting insights into the role of
TNCs in economic development. (For more details, refer to Koo 1993
on Korea and Schive 1993 on Taiwan).[7] While these countries have not
been hostile to foreign technology or capital *per se*, they have clearly
preferred, if the situation allowed, to use such technology and capital
under 'national' management, rather than relying on TNCs.[8] This
preference was necessarily somewhat more tempered in Taiwan than
in Korea due to the relative absence of large private sector firms in
Taiwan, but both their governments have possessed a clear and
sophisticated notion of the costs and benefits of inviting in TNCs, and
they approved FDI only when they thought there were potential net
benefits (the Korean government's 1981 *White Paper on Foreign*

---

6 Rowthorn (1996) calculates that if the share of FDI in GDP for the average
developing country (excluding the first-tier NICs of Korea, Taiwan, Hong Kong,
and Singapore) were to reach the same level as that of Malaysia between 1991 and
1993, namely, 10% of GDP, the total world level of FDI, which was already near its
historical peak during this period, would have to increase by seven times, reaching
a level equivalent to 1.7 times the total manufacturing investment of the OECD
countries – a spectacularly unrealistic scenario. Rowthorn, however, does not take
account of the fact that the 10% figure was exceptional even by Malaysia's own
historical standard, and therefore his calculation may exaggerate the situation.
However, even if we use the 5% benchmark, which is closer to the historical
average of Malaysia's ratio of FDI to GDP, the power of his argument is not
diminished, as the developing-worldwide replication of the Malaysian strategy
will still call for a 3.5-fold increase in world FDI.

7 At the time of final revision to this chapter (December 1997), it was announced
that FDI policy is to be greatly liberalised in Korea following the conditionalities
of the IMF bailout. However, the details of such changes are as yet not known, and
how much change this liberalisation will eventually bring to the role of FDI in the
Korean economy is not now clear.

8 This tendency was more pronounced in Korea. According to Amsden (1989),
only 5% of total foreign capital inflow into Korea between 1963 and 1982 (excluding foreign aid, which was important only until the early-1960s) was in the form
of FDI (p.92, Table 5).

Investment provides a fine specimen of such policy vision; see EPB 1981).[9]

The most important policies toward TNCs employed by Korea and Taiwan were the restrictions on entry and ownership. In entry, for example, FDI in industries supplying critical intermediate inputs using sophisticated technology (e.g., petroleum refinery, synthetic fibres) or labour-intensive export industries generating foreign exchange and jobs (e.g., textile, electronics assembly) was encouraged when compared, say, to domestic market-oriented consumer durable goods industries. In Korea as late as the early-1980s, around 50% of all industries and around 20% of manufacturing industries were still 'off-limits' to FDI (EPB 1981: pp.70-1). Even when entry was allowed, the governments of these countries tried to encourage joint ventures, preferably under local majority ownership, in an attempt to facilitate the transfer of core technologies and managerial skills. Again, in the case of Korea, even in sectors where FDI was allowed, foreign ownership above 50% was prohibited except in areas where FDI was deemed to be of 'strategic' importance, which covered only about 13% of all manufacturing industries (EPB 1981: p.70).[10] As a result, as of the mid-1980s only 5% of TNC subsidiaries in Korea were wholly

---

9 The Korean government's 1981 *White Paper on Foreign Investment* lists various benefits of FDI, such as investment augmentation, employment creation, industrial 'upgrading' effect, balance-of-payments contribution, and technology transfer, but it is also clearly aware of its costs from such factors as transfer pricing, restrictions on imports and exports of the subsidiaries, 'crowding out' of domestic investors in the domestic credit market, allocative inefficiencies due to 'non-competitive' market structure, retardation of technological development, 'distortion' of industrial structure due to the introduction of 'inappropriate' products, and even the exercise of political influence by the TNCs on the formation of policies (EPB 1981: pp.50-64). It is interesting to note that this list includes more or less all the issues identified by the more recent academic debate that we discussed above.
10 These included industries where access to proprietary technology was deemed essential for further development of the industry, and industries where the capital requirement and/or the risks involved in the investment were very large. The ownership ceiling was also relaxed if (1) the investments were made in the free trade zones; (2) the investments were made by overseas Koreans; or (3) the investments would 'diversify' the origins of FDI into the country – namely, investments from countries other than the US and Japan, which had previously dominated the Korean FDI scene. For details, see EPB (1981: pp.70-1).

owned, compared to 50% in Mexico and 60% in Brazil – countries that are often believed to have had much more 'anti-foreign' policy orientations than Korea (Evans 1987: p.208). Due to the scarcity of huge domestic firms that could become plausible joint venture partners, the Taiwanese government was more flexible on the ownership question, and thus in terms of ownership structure of TNC subsidiaries Taiwan was somewhere in between Korea and Latin America, with 33.5% of TNC subsidiaries (excluding the ones owned by overseas Chinese) being wholly owned as of 1985 (Schive 1993: p.319).

Policy measures other than the ones concerning entry and ownership were also used to control the activities of TNCs in accordance with national developmental goals. First, there were measures to ensure that the 'right' kinds of technologies were acquired in the 'right' terms. The technology that was to be brought in by the investing TNCs was carefully screened to ensure that it was not overly obsolete and that local subsidiaries were not subject to excessive royalties. Second, there were measures to maximise technology spillovers. Investors who were more willing to transfer technologies were selected over those who were not, unless the willing investors were too far behind in terms of technology. (For an interesting recent example, refer to the case of the Korean fast train project, described in the next section.) Third, local-content requirements were strictly imposed in order to maximise technological spillovers from the TNC presence. Targets for localisation were set realistically, however, so that the requirements would not seriously hurt the export competitiveness of the host country. It was in fact the case that in some industries they were more strictly applied to the products destined for the domestic market.

In this section, we have argued that the belief of some neoliberal commentators that what is good for TNCs is also good for the host economy is unwarranted. While some of the earlier criticisms of TNCs may have been misconceived, over-generalised, and exaggerated, there are many important areas where there exists an obvious conflict of interest between the TNCs and the host country. These include the issues of 'appropriateness' of technology, transfer pricing, monopolistic practices, restrictions imposed on the subsidiaries, particularly regarding exports and R&D, and even their ability to manipulate the overall national policy regime. Most importantly, recent theoretical developments and empirical studies suggest that long-term productivity enhancement may be better achieved by an industrialisation strategy that puts emphasis on building local managerial and technological capabilities and uses TNCs in a selective, strategic manner to accelerate that process. We further illustrated this point with the examples of Taiwan and Korea, briefly commenting on their policies on TNC entry, ownership, contractual terms, technological spillovers, and local-content requirements. The policies employed in Korea and Taiwan suggest that, while TNCs can and should be used, their role needs to be clearly defined in relation to the overall industrialisation strategy and with reference to the specific needs of the particular industries concerned.

4. DOES THE RISE OF TRANSNATIONAL CORPORATIONS MAKE STRATEGIC INDUSTRIAL POLICY BY DEVELOPING COUNTRIES IMPOSSIBLE?

The proponents of the globalisation thesis have emphasised the constraints that the high degree of globalisation has placed on the policy autonomy of national governments (e.g., Julius 1994; Michalet 1994). While sensible commentators are careful to dismiss the talk of the 'demise of the nation-state' as too simplistic and premature (e.g., Ostry 1990; Cable 1995), there seems to be a feeling among the majority of the writers on globalisation that a serious erosion, if not a total elimination, of national policy autonomy is only a matter of time, if it has not already happened. Together with the increased international financial capital flows that restrict the effectiveness of national macroeconomic policy, the role of TNCs in eroding such autonomy is often emphasised (Julius 1994; Michalet 1994).

These commentators argue that, in such an environment, it is not possible anymore for developing country governments to employ 'strategic' (or 'selective') industrial policy.[11] They believe that, whatever the benefits of this policy in the past (which they think were nonexistent or even negative anyway), it is not viable anymore, given the increasing importance of TNCs, which can relocate any or all of their activities in search of a better 'investment climate'. Thus, by 'voting with their feet', it is argued, TNCs force the governments to stick close to the industrial policy regimes of their competitors, and indeed to move toward a more liberal policy regime in their competitive bids to attract the FDI that, in their view, is becoming increasingly important for wealth creation.

At one level, it seems difficult to deny such a claim. As firms become less bound by national constraints, it seems only natural that the effectiveness of 'strategic' industrial policy at the national level is bound to be reduced. And if this is the case, it also seems only natural that putting restrictions on TNCs when competitor economies do not would lead to the exodus of TNCs. However, this kind of reasoning is based on a number of explicit and implicit assumptions that do not have sound empirical justification or are products of unwarranted extrapolation from a limited number of cases. Let us examine them one by one.

First, the argument that TNCs will migrate to the country offering the best deal is based on the assumption that TNCs always have an upper hand in bargaining. (For further discussion of the bargaining issue, see Helleiner 1989.) However, the relative bargaining strengths of TNCs and national governments depend on which industry and which country we are talking about and when the bargaining is taking place (relative advantages change over time).

---

11 Unlike some other terms used in economics, the term 'industrial policy', also known as 'strategic' or 'selective' industrial policy, suffers from a serious definitional ambiguity. While many authors have tried to define it as encompassing all policies that affect industrial performance, we reject such a broad definition, which almost entirely takes away the analytical edge that the term has, and adopt a narrow definition, namely a policy that attempts to affect the evolution of specific industries (and even specific firms when they are large enough) through state intervention in order to effect 'national' efficiency and growth. See Chang (1994: pp.58-61) for a more systematic discussion of this problem. Also, it should be noted that, in the context of the present chapter, aiming for 'national' efficiency and growth does not rule out the use of 'foreign' firms, as far as these firms do not seriously undermine national policy autonomy.

While there are some industries for which many countries qualify as feasible investment sites, there are certain other industries for which feasible investment sites are limited for a number of reasons; many mineral-related industries require investments near the depositories; some industries require particular types of skilled labour at reasonable prices, which many countries may not be able to supply; some countries have locational advantages, say, as an entry point into a big market; some countries have exceptionally large and/or fast-growing markets; and so on.

So, it is not just that governments compete for FDI, but also that TNCs compete for attractive host countries. The clearest example of the latter is the recent bargaining between the Chinese government and various automobile TNCs regarding the selection of a partner to produce the 'people's car'. Lured by the prospect of being the first mover (or at least one of the first movers) in what may soon become one of the biggest passenger car markets in the world, many TNCs (including the German luxury car makers Benz, BMW, and Porsche, which emphasised that its founder, Dr. Porsche, was the original designer of the proverbial 'people's car', Volkswagen) were putting forth fiercely competitive bids (*Financial Times*, November 23, 1994).

While few countries can expect to have China's level of bargaining power, they can still extract substantial concessions from TNCs. The recent granting by the Korean government of its fast train project to the Anglo-French joint venture GEC Alsthom, organised around the producer of French TGV (which offered more in terms of technology transfer than the Japanese or German firms that offered superior products), is one such example (*Financial Times*, August 23, 1993). Another instructive example comes from the upstaging of GM's talks with the Polish government regarding the takeover and restructuring of the ailing state-owned automobile company FSO by the South Korean automobile maker Daewoo (which, ironically, was a 50-50 joint venture with GM until 1992) in 1995. Daewoo's offer to inject a large amount of capital ($1.1 billion) in order to transform FSO as its major platform for exports of passenger cars and car parts (engine and gear boxes) to the European Union suddenly gave the Polish government enormous bargaining power. GM upped its offer, but eventually

Daewoo clinched the deal (*Financial Times,* various issues between August and October, 1995).[12]

These examples show how even governments from countries that do not have the Chinese government's kind of unique bargaining power can play one TNC against another in order to extract greater concessions. Needless to say, many developing countries have few attractive productive assets or locational advantages for which TNCs will compete, and as a result they may not be able to follow the Chinese lead. However, a few will have at least some 'bargaining chips'. And once TNCs are interested in a country, their political vulnerability as 'foreign' firms can make them even more responsive than their domestic equivalents to the demands of the government. It is also worth noting that newly-emerging TNCs from East Asia are pursuing an aggressive strategy of expansion in order to challenge the established TNCs from North America and Europe, thus offering valuable additional room for manoeuvre for host country governments – as was so dramatically illustrated by the Polish automobile industry example cited above.

Second, regarding the freedom of TNCs to seek the best deal, there are certainly some industries with low sunk costs involved in investments and which are therefore 'footloose' (e.g., garments, shoes, toys). But many other industries have high sunk costs, not only in terms of dedicated physical equipment (e.g., chemicals, pharmaceuticals) but also in terms of subcontracting networks and other relationship-specific activities that firms have taken time to build (e.g., advanced electronics, automobiles). In such industries, TNCs are not entirely footloose, and they cannot pull out at the slightest adverse change in host country policies.

Of course, this does not mean that in such industries governments can do anything they want once TNCs have made the investments, since what the government does now will affect future investment

---

12 It was reported that the granting of the deal for FSO to Daewoo could result in the injection of an extra $1 billion through the establishment of another joint venture to produce vans at FS Lublin, where Daewoo had entered into a separate joint venture to assemble small passenger cars. If that deal were to occur, the total investment from Daewoo could amount to $2.1 billion, which will be just under half the total FDI that has flowed into Poland since its economic reform (*Financial Times*, August 28, 1995).

decisions by TNCs. However, as Ostry 1990: p.98) suggests, the larger TNCs are able and often willing to accommodate a lot of 'restrictive' policy measures, as long as they are stable and the changes predictable. Thus, although we have surprisingly little systematic evidence in this regard, it seems reasonable to say that '[t]he real question to ask of [TNCs] is not why they are always threatening to up and leave a country if things seem to go bad for them there, but why the vast majority of them fail to leave and continue to stay put in their home base and major centres of investment' (Hirst and Thompson 1992: p.368).

Third, those who criticise 'restrictive' policies toward TNCs, assume that FDI decisions are mainly affected by the amount of business freedom granted to them (e.g., Julius 1994: pp.278-9). However, FDI decisions are much more strongly affected by the overall performance of the economy, especially the prospect for growth. Even the World Bank, which is often associated with liberal policies toward TNCs, argues that '[t]he specific incentives and regulation governing direct investment have less effect on how much investment a country receives than has its general economic and political climate, and its financial and exchange rate policies' (World Bank 1985: p.130). In other words, the evidence suggests that growth leads to FDI rather than the other way round (see Milberg 1998). If so, it is questionable whether adopting a more liberal FDI policy will lead to any substantial increase in FDI flows, since there is no evidence that such a policy leads to an improvement in the country's growth performance – which is by far the most effective way to attract FDI.

This argument is also supported by the fact that, as we also have seen above (Table 4), the share of developing countries (not counting China) in the world's total FDI has increased only marginally over the last decade, despite the extensive liberalisation of FDI policies. Thus, it may be argued that as far as they do not involve asset appropriation and other measures that threaten basic capitalist property relations, FDI policies seem to be much less important than other factors, such as the growth prospect of the country's domestic market or the country's political stability, in determining investment decisions by TNCs. Such an observation leads us to conclude that the current argument for liberal policies for TNCs in developing countries based on the 'globalisation' thesis is at best distracting our attention from more important issues, or at worst is being used, if unconsciously, as a stooge in the scare tactic to drive more developing countries onto a neoliberal 'reform' path.

This section discussed how the claims of the impossibility of strategic industrial policy in an era of growing TNC importance have been exaggerated and are based on questionable assumptions. It should be emphasised that, perhaps except for the poorest countries with meagre natural resource endowments, small domestic markets, and no locational advantage, potential host countries are not merely passive victims: they have, and often exercise with substantial success, considerable bargaining power in their dealings with TNCs. Claims about the footloose nature of TNCs are also often exaggerated. There are many industries where investments involve a large amount of sunk costs (both in terms of physical capital and production networks) that restrict the mobility of the firms involved. It is also the case that the largest TNCs are able and often willing to live with restrictive policies as long as they are stable and predictable. Overall, the regulatory regime for TNCs is, as far as it is not impossibly restrictive, only a minor consideration in TNCs' choice of investment sites when compared to things like the market growth prospect. Given that promoting growth is the most effective way to attract FDI, having a well-conducted selective industrial policy may, contrary to the conventional wisdom, help the country attract more FDI.

5.   POLICY OPTIONS FOR DEVELOPING COUNTRIES

All the skepticism expressed in the preceding sections regarding the conventional wisdom about the role of TNCs in developing countries is not meant to imply that therefore the rise of TNCs can be comfortably ignored. While the current claims about the end, or at least a serious weakening, of the nation-state are often exaggerated, it is true that the growth in the number and scope of TNCs (and globalisation in general) has resulted in restrictions on the scope of strategic industrial policy and other national policies as well (see Panic (1998)). Such restrictions result not only from the greater bargaining power that firms will have against national governments due to their ability to shop around for investment sites, but also from the concern by the government that, if it provides TNCs with some help as a part of its industrial policy, the benefits will spill over the national border and thereby reduce the cost effectiveness of the policy (Chang and Rowthorn 1995: pp.44-5).

Despite such problems, intelligent governments should try, and have tried (as seen in some East Asian countries), to use TNCs in a strategic way in order to acquire necessary capital, technology, marketing networks, and so on. What exactly the 'strategic way' means will depend on various factors, such as the country's relative bargaining position, the technological nature of the industry, the role of the particular industry concerned in the bigger scheme of industrial development, and so on, but we illustrate our point with a few examples. (See also Stopford and Strange 1991: Chapter 4.)

In those industries where what is needed is a simple injection of capital to create jobs and foreign exchange earning capability, it may be acceptable, or even important, that the country have an open policy toward FDI. 'Cash cow' industries like garments, shoes, and toys are examples of such industries. In industries where the capital and technological requirements are high and where the government expects the major return to be the 'rent' element – such as oil, mineral, and other natural resource extraction industries – having an open attitude toward FDI may be crucial. However, in such cases, the bargaining skills to extract the largest possible shares of the rent element and, more importantly, the plans to effectively use the rent from such industries for the development of other industries will be crucial to the success of overall industrial policy.

When the industries concerned are the ones in which a country hopes to become internationally competitive in the long run but that require a major injection of new technology and capital, TNC participation may be desirable. However, in such industries a tough bargaining position on issues like technology transfer or export and R&D restrictions imposed on the subsidiary will be crucial (as seen in the examples of the Chinese car industry and the Korean fast train project cited above). In other industries, where a country is reasonably close to achieving international competitiveness, keeping the TNCs out may be necessary in order to allow local firms maximum learning opportunities, especially if the domestic market is small. Even in high-tech industries, where the ability to keep up with the technological developments of the most advanced TNCs is (allegedly) becoming crucial, it is possible to devise effective 'national' technology policies based on selective interactions with foreign TNCs (see Fransman 1994 for the example of Japan; see Evans 1998 for examples from developing countries).

This list can be further elaborated, but the point here is that an intelligent government pursuing a strategic industrial policy will not have a 'uniform' policy toward TNCs across industries, as many neoliberal economists recommend. Each industry serves different functions in the greater scheme of industrial development, and it would be foolish to have either uniformly restrictive or uniformly liberal policies toward TNCs across different industries. This also means that the same industry may, and indeed should, become more or less open to FDI over time, depending on the changes in the various internal and external conditions that affect it. For example, the government could initially have a liberal FDI policy for a new industry in order to establish it, but subsequently impose tougher restrictions on TNC subsidiaries when it is deemed that the industry has developed enough local technological capability so that with continued, if diminishing, government support, it can operate competitively within the domestic economy and internationally. Alternatively, when there is a major technological change in a certain industry that makes the country's present technological capability inadequate for international competition, the government may relax rules concerning TNC participation in the industry in order to gain access to the new technology.

It is one thing to say that countries should use TNCs in a strategic manner and another to say that they can actually afford to play such a strategic game. The poorest developing countries, for example, will have weak bargaining power *vis-à-vis* TNCs in most industries, as the industries for which they are attractive investment sites are usually the ones in which TNCs are the most mobile. On the other hand, many developing countries have some 'bargaining chips', at least in relation to some industries. Some can offer the prospect of a large and/or rapidly growing domestic market, especially in industries where transportation costs are relatively high or where proximity to consumers is important for marketing (e.g., China, India, Brazil, and the rapidly growing East Asian countries). Some countries, somewhat paradoxically due to their anti-capitalist past, possess workforces that are relatively well educated and well trained for what they cost (e.g., Eastern Europe, Vietnam, and China). Some other countries possess the locational (and legal) advantage of having easier access to large markets (for example, Mexico, the Central European countries, and the Southern European countries). Even some very poor economies have mineral and other natural resources to offer.

Needless to say, having such potential bargaining power does not directly translate into the right amount and composition of FDI, unless general economic conditions are right. Achieving the right balance of FDI will require an internally coherent government that is politically willing and administratively capable of actually exercising such bargaining power.[13] However, adopting liberal FDI policies across all sectors and industries will mean giving up one's potential bargaining power in those sectors before even exercising it, and that does not seem to be particularly wise. Even if many developing countries have relatively little bargaining power *vis-à-vis* TNCs, and even if such power is diminishing with globalisation, they need not give up what little bargaining power they still have, since what national governments do still matters greatly for the determination of the costs and benefits of FDI.

6.   CONCLUSION

In this chapter, we tried to question some myths about globalisation, and more specifically myths about the growing importance of TNCs, by presenting some basic but often neglected facts. While the interdependence between different parts of the world may be increasing, and while the role of TNCs in that process is growing, it is still too early to say that we now live in a totally new world in which national policies are at best ineffective and at worst obstacles to the achievement of 'world efficiency', as some proponents of the globalisation thesis

---

13 Many governments suffer from interdepartmental rivalry in the design and execution of policies toward FDI. Moreover, a large country with a *de jure* and *de facto* decentralised power structure (e.g., the US, China) may see its national bargaining powers weakened due to competition among the local governments. The author thanks William Milberg for raising this point.

seem to believe.

We also argued that, while some of the early fears about TNCs were clearly unwarranted, there are good reasons to believe that an industrialisation strategy based on a *laissez-faire* attitude toward TNCs may not be as successful in the long run as a more selective, strategic approach, as seen in the examples of countries like Korea and Taiwan. Moreover, as we pointed out, despite the recent increases in their importance, TNCs do not have unambiguously superior bargaining power in all industries in relation to all countries. Their bargaining power ranges from almost absolute (e.g., Nike looking for an investment site for shoe production) to close to zero (e.g., automobile TNCs trying to curry the favour of the Chinese government for the people's car), depending on the industry and the country. This observation actually strengthens, and not weakens, the case for strategic industrial policy, because it means that governments should design their policies toward TNCs according to the particular sector concerned, rather than taking a uniform approach across sectors.

Although the constraint imposed by TNCs on national industrial policy may be growing, it is nowhere near the point where a strategic industrial policy is impossible. The current literature tends to regard the process of globalisation and the rise of TNCs as an unstoppable process that no one can control and in which nations, especially developing nations, are passive agents that will have to fully embrace this process or perish. However, such a view is misleading, since there is a lot of room for manoeuvre for national governments and since such room may even be increasing for some countries in some industries, especially with the recent aggressive expansion of some TNCs from East Asia (also see Milberg 1998 and Evans 1998). It would be a big mistake for a developing country to voluntarily give up all such room for manoeuvre by adopting a universally liberal FDI policy across all sectors. What is needed is a more differentiated and strategic approach to TNCs, which will allow host countries to intelligently 'use' TNCs for their long-term developmental purposes.

BIBLIOGRAPHY

Amsden, A. (1989). *Asia's Next Giant*. New York: Oxford University Press.

Archibugi, D. and Michie, J. (1995). 'The Globalisation of Technology: A New Taxonomy', *Cambridge Journal of Economics*, vol.19, no.2.

Bairoch, P. and Kozul-Wright, R. (1996). 'Globalisation Myths and Realities: Some Historical Reflections on Integration, Industrialisation and Growth in the World Economy', UNCTAD Discussion Paper, no. 113. Geneva: United Nations Conference on Trade and Development (UNCTAD).

Brittan, L. (1995). 'Investment Liberalisation: The Next Great Boost to the World Economy', *Transnational Corporations*, vol.4, no.1.

Cable, V. (1995). 'The Diminished Nation-State: A Study in the Loss of Economic Power', *Daedalus*, vol.124, no.2.

Chang, H.-J. (1994). *The Political Economy of Industrial Policy*. London and Basingstoke: Macmillan.

Chang, H.-J. and Rowthorn, B. (eds.) (1995). *Role of the State in Economic Change*. Oxford: Oxford University Press.

Chang, H.-J. and Rowthorn, B. (1995). 'The Role of the State in Economic Change – Entrepreneurship and Conflict Management' in H.-J. Chang & B. Rowthorn (eds.), *Role of the State in Economic Change*. Oxford: Oxford University Press.

Chudnovsky, D. (ed.) (1993). *Transnational Corporations and Industrialisation*. London: Routledge.

Dicken, P. (1992). *The Global Shift*. New York and London: Guilford Press.

EPB (Economic Planning Board) (1981). *Oegoogin Tooja Baeksuh* (White Paper on Foreign Investment) (in Korean). Seoul: The Government of Korea.

Evans, P. (1987). 'Class, State, and Dependence in East Asia: Lessons for Latin Americanists', in F. Deyo (ed.), *The Political Economy of the New Asian Industrialism*. Ithaca: Cornell University Press.

Evans, P. (1998). 'TNCs and Third World States: From the Old Internationalisation to the New', in R. Kozul-Wright and R. Rowthorn (eds.), *Transnational Corporations and the World Economy*. London and Basingstoke: Macmillan Press.

Fransman, M. (1986). *Technology and Economic Development*. London: Frank Cass.

Fransman, M. (1994). 'Is National Technology Policy Obsolete in a Globalised World?: The Japanese Response', mimeo., Institute for Japanese-European Technology Studies (JETS), University of Edinburgh.

Fransman, M. and King, K. (eds.) (1984). *Technological Capability in the Third World*. London and Basingstoke: Macmillan.

Financial Times, various issues.

Haque, I., Bell, Dahlman, C., Lall, S. and Pavitt, K. (1996). *Trade, Technology and International Competitiveness*. Washington, D.C.: World Bank.

Helleiner, G. (1989). 'Transnational Corporations and Direct Foreign Invest-
ment', in H. Chenery and T.N. Srinivasan (eds.), *Handbook of Develop-
ment Economics,* vol.2. Amsterdam: Elsevier Science Publishers, B.V.
Hirst, P. and Thompson, G. (1992). 'The Problem of "Globalisation":
International Economic Relations, National Economic Management and
the Formation of Trading Blocs', *Economy and Society,* vol.21, no.4.
Hirst, P. and Thompson, G. (1996). *Globalisation in Question.* Cambridge:
Polity Press.
Hutton, W. (1995). 'Myth that Sets the World to Right', *The Guardian,* 12
June 1995.
Julius, D. (1990). *Global Companies and Public Policy.* London: Pinter
Publishers.
Julius, D. (1994). 'International Direct Investment: Strengthening the Policy
Regime', in G. Kenen (ed.), *Managing the World Economy.* Washington,
D.C.: Institute for International Economics.
Koo, B. (1993). 'Foreign Investment and Economic Performance in Korea',
in S. Lall (ed.), *Transnational Corporations and Economic Develop-
ment.* London: Routledge.
Kozul-Wright, R. (1995). 'Transnational Corporations and the Nation State',
in J. Michie and J. Grieve Smith (eds.), *Managing the Global Economy.*
Oxford: Oxford University Press.
Lall, S. (ed.) (1993). *Transnational Corporations and Economic Develop-
ment.* London: Routledge.
Lall, S. (1995). 'Malaysia: Industrial Success and the Role of the Govern-
ment', *Journal of International Development.*
Michalet, C.-A. (1994). 'Transnational Corporations and the Changing
International Economic System', *Transnational Corporations,* vol.3,
no.1.
Milberg, W. (1998). 'Globalisation', in R. Kozul-Wright and R. Rowthorn
(eds.), *Transnational Corporations and the World Economy.* London
and Basingstoke: Macmillan Press.
Ostry, S. (1990). *Governments and Corporations in a Shrinking World.* New
York and London: Council on Foreign Relations Press.
Ozawa, T. (1995). 'The "Flying-geese" Paradigm of FDI, Economic Devel-
opment and Shifts in Competitiveness', mimeo. Fort Collins, Co.:
Colorado State University.
Panic, M. (1998). 'Transnationals, International Interdependence and Na-
tional Economic Policy', in R. Kozul-Wright and R. Rowthorn (eds.),
Transnational Corporations and the World Economy. London and
Basingstoke: Macmillan Press.
Rowthorn, R. (1995). 'Manufacturing in the National Economy and Related
Policy Issues', a paper presented at the 'Future of Manufacturing
Forum', organised by the Australian Manufacturing Council, April,
1995.

Rowthorn, R. (1996). 'Replicating the Experience of the NIEs on a Large Scale', mimeo., Faculty of Economics and Politics. Cambridge, UK: University of Cambridge.

Schive, C. (1993). 'Foreign Investment and Technology Transfer in Taiwan', in S. Lall (ed.), *Transnational Corporations and Economic Development*. London: Routledge.

Stopford, J. (1994). 'The Growing Interdependence between Transnational Corporations and Governments', *Transnational Corporations*, vol.3, no.1.

Stopford, J. and Strange, S. (1991). *Rival States, Rival Firms*. Cambridge: Cambridge University Press.

The Economist (1993). 'A Survey of Multinationals', 27 March 1993.

UNCTAD (United Nations Conference on Trade and Development) (various years). *World Investment Report*. New York and Geneva: United Nations.

UNCTC (United Nations Centre for Transnational Corporations) (1992). *World Investment Report*. New York: United Nations.

World Bank (1985). *World Development Report 1985*. New York: Oxford University Press.

Chapter 8

Intellectual Property Rights and Economic Development: Historical Lessons and Emerging Issues*

1. INTRODUCTION

AS will become clearer later in this chapter, the role of intellectual property rights (henceforth IPRs) in economic development has always been a controversial issue. However, the debate surrounding it has become even more heated after the Trade-Related Intellectual Property Rights (TRIPS) Agreement. Initially, TRIPS was not even a central issue in the Uruguay Round of the GATT talks that led to the birth of the World Trade Organisation (WTO) (Siebeck 1990a), and therefore did not get much attention. A number of recent events, however, have come together to make people realise that this could become the biggest point of contention in the running of the WTO in the coming years.

The first thing that drew public attention to TRIPS was the fact that the 'transition' period allowed for the developing countries to 'upgrade' their IPRs regimes in accordance with the TRIPS Agreement was coming to an end, thereby exposing them to greater dangers of trade sanctions by the advanced countries (end of 2000, except for the least developed countries, which were given until 2006). Second,

---

* The author thanks Sakiko Fukuda-Parr, Selim Jahan, and especially Kate Raworth for their helpful suggestions in this chapter. Bente Molenaar provided most efficient and creative research assistance. Erik Reinert provided illuminating discussions and commented on an early version of this chapter. The author also thanks Andrea Cornia, Ron Herring, Penny Janeway, Richard Kozul-Wright, Deepak Nayyar, Omar Noman, and Han-Kyun Rho for their comments on the earlier drafts.

many people were recently enraged by attempts by advanced country individuals and firms to patent products embodying knowledge that is commonly known in some developing countries, on the back of the TRIPS provision (e.g., the notorious turmeric case; see UNDP 1999: pp.70-1). Third, the recent controversy surrounding the attempts by pharmaceutical companies based in advanced countries to block the exports of cheap HIV/AIDS drugs by some developing countries (such as Argentina, India, Thailand, and Brazil) using TRIPS, has highlighted the potential conflict between TRIPS and greater human well-being.

TRIPS, like other WTO agreements, is an agreement on a legal framework, so its detailed *modus operandi* needs to be worked out through the accumulation of cases. For this reason, the exact future shape of the TRIPS regime cannot be predicted with certainty at this point. However, as the above examples show, the system seems to be evolving in a way that favours the advanced country producers over everyone else (e.g., consumers in the advanced and the developing countries, developing country producers). Therefore it is opportune for a rethink on the implications of TRIPS to see whether and how it should be changed in a way that increases the welfare of all.

This chapter seeks to contribute to the debate by rethinking the role of IPRs in economic development, and drawing some implications for a reform of the TRIPS agreement. A novel feature of this chapter is that it tries to do this from a historical perspective as well as from the point of view of contemporary developing countries. The first section will discuss the role that IPRs played in the development of the now-developed countries when they were industrialising, and draw some implications for the developing countries of today and for the world economy as a whole. The second section provides a discussion on the role of IPRs in economic development in the contemporary context, with a special emphasis on the patent system. This is followed by a third section critically examining the implications of TRIPS in light of the preceding discussion. The final section summarises and concludes the chapter.

2. TECHNOLOGY TRANSFER, IPRs, AND ECONOMIC DEVELOPMENT IN A HISTORICAL PERSPECTIVE

In the history of industrialisation, technology transfer has always played a key role. Technology transfer during the 16th and the 17th centuries from the then more advanced economies of Continental Europe (especially Venice and the Low Countries) was critical in Britain's transition from a backward raw material producer to a leading manufacturing nation (Reinert 1995; Cipolla 1993).[1] After the British Industrial Revolution, the effectiveness of technology transfer from Britain (and to a lesser extent from the Low Countries) became the key determinant of a country's prosperity (Landes 1969 is the definitive work on the transfer of British technology to the Continental European countries; see Jeremy 1981 on the transfer to the US).

Some of these transfers were obviously arranged through 'legitimate' means. Especially in the early days of industrialisation when the technologies employed were relatively simple to understand, a guided tour of a factory by an expert could be enough to capture the essence of technology. Even early on, however, some advanced producers refused to grant such tours or at least concealed what they considered crucial parts from the visitors. Apprenticeship was another common means to absorb advanced foreign technologies. However, until the mid-19th century, when machinery became the key embodiment of technological knowledge, the most important means of technological transfer was the transfer of skilled workers, in whom most technological knowledge was then embodied. As a result, countries tried to recruit skilled workers from the more advanced countries and also bring back nationals who were employed in advanced country establishments – sometimes through a concerted effort orchestrated and endorsed by the government (more on this later).

---

1 The policies of Henry VII were particularly important in this respect. He not only made efforts to secure skilled wool-manufacturing workers from the more advanced countries, but once some manufacturing base was established in the woollen industry, he imposed a ban on raw wool export, thus creating a powerful incentive to further import substitution (Reinert 1995).

Needless to say, these efforts were most effective when backed by policies intended to enhance what modern economics of technology calls 'technological capabilities' (see Fransman and King (eds.) 1984). Many governments set up institutions of teaching (e.g., technical schools) and research (e.g., various non-teaching academies). They also took measures to raise 'awareness' of advanced technology in a number of ways. They established museums, organised international expositions ('expos'), bestowed new machinery to private firms, and set up 'model factories' using advanced technologies. These governments also provided firms with financial incentives to use more advanced technology, especially through rebates and exemptions of duties on imports of industrial equipment (see Landes 1969: pp.150-1 for further details).[2]

Very often, it should be noted, acquisition of advanced technology was organised through 'illegitimate' means.[3] Firms naturally wanted to shroud their technologies in secrecy and therefore limited the access of foreigners to their factories.[4] Moreover, the governments of the more advanced countries played the critical role in limiting the outflow of key technologies (although exactly how effective they were is debatable). In the early days of industrialisation, the governments of the more advanced countries mainly concentrated on controlling the migration of the skilled workers, in whom most technologies then were embodied. In 1719, prompted mainly by the French attempt (organised by the legendary Scottish-born financier John Law of the Mississippi-Company fame) to recruit hundreds of skilled workers and to a lesser extent by a similar Russian attempt, Britain introduced a ban on the migration of skilled workers, and especially on attempts to recruit such workers for jobs abroad ('suborning').

According to this law, anyone suborning was punishable by a fine or even imprisonment. Emigrant workers who did not return home in six months after being warned to do so by an accredited British

---

2 It is interesting to note that this was one of the staple tools of East Asian industrial policy until recently.

3 We put quotation marks around the term, 'illegitimate', because what is illegitimate from one point of view may not always be so from other points of view.

4 However, the Dutch firms are known to have been extremely open about this until their technological superiority was visibly threatened from about the middle of the 18th century (Davids 1995).

official (usually diplomats stationed abroad) would in effect lose their right to lands and goods in Britain, and have their citizenship taken away. Specifically mentioned in the law were industries such as wool, steel, iron, brass or any other metal, and watch-making, but in practice the law covered all industries (see Jeremy 1977, and Harris 1998: Chapter 18 for further details). The ban on emigration of skilled labour and suborning lasted until 1825 (Landes 1969: p.148).

Subsequently, as increasing amounts of technologies got embodied in machines, machine exports came under control. Britain introduced a new Act in 1750 banning the export of 'tools and utensils' in wool and silk industries, while strengthening the punishments for suborning. The ban was widened and strengthened in subsequent legislations. In 1774, another Act was introduced to control machine exports in cotton and linen industries. In 1781, the 1774 Act was revised and the wording 'tools and utensils' changed to 'any machine, engine, tool, press, paper, utensil or implement whatsoever', indicating the increasing mechanisation of the industries. In 1785, the Tools Act was introduced to ban exports of many different types of machinery, which also included a ban on suborning (Harris 1998: pp.457-62; also see Jeremy 1977). This ban lasted until 1842 (Landes 1969: p.148).[5]

In response to these measures to prevent technology outflows by the advanced countries, the less advanced countries deployed all sorts of 'illegitimate' means to gain access to advanced technologies. The entrepreneurs and the technicians of these countries, often with explicit state consent or even active encouragement (including offers of bounty for securing specific technologies), were routinely engaged in industrial espionage.[6] Landes (1969), Harris (1991 and 1992), and Bruland (ed.) (1991), among others, document an extensive range of industrial espionage *vis-à-vis* Britain by countries such as France, Russia, Sweden, Norway, Denmark, the Netherlands, and Belgium.

---

5 Berg (1980: Ch.9) provides an informative discussion on the political and academic debates surrounding the abolition of the ban on export of machinery.
6 For example, in the 1750s, a former Manchester textile finisher and Jacobite officer, John Holker, was appointed as Inspector-General of Foreign Manufactures in the French government. While also advising French producers on technological problems, his main activity under this euphemistic job title consisted of industrial espionage and suborning of British skilled workers (Harris 1998: p.21).

Despite all these 'legitimate' and 'illegitimate' efforts, technological catching-up was not an easy task. As the recent literature on
technology transfer shows, technology contains a lot of tacit knowledge, which cannot be easily transferred. This problem was not easily
solved even by the importation of skilled workers even in the days
when they embodied most of the key technologies. These people had
language and cultural problems, and more importantly did not have
access to the same technological infrastructure that they had at home.
Landes (1969) documents how it took decades for the Continental
European countries to assimilate British technologies, even in the days
when technologies were relatively simple such that importing some
skilled workers and perhaps a key machine could in theory enable a
technological follower to replicate what the leader was doing.

By the late-19th century, the observation (or not) of patents and
other intellectual property rights became a key issue in technology
transfer (and knowledge transfer in general). The bans on skilled
worker migration and machinery exports by Britain were abolished by
the mid-19th century thanks to their increasing ineffectiveness. By the
middle of the 19th century, the key technologies became so complex
that importing skilled workers and machinery was not enough to
achieve command over a technology. In many areas, an active transfer
by the owner of technological knowledge through licensing of patents
emerged as a key channel of technology transfer.

Most now-developed countries established their patent laws
between 1790 and 1850 and established other elements of their IPRs
regimes, such as copyright laws (first introduced in Britain in 1709)
and trademark laws (first introduced in Britain in 1862), in the second
half of the 19th century.[7] All of these IPRs regimes were highly

---

7   The first patent system was invented in Venice in 1474 (it granted 10 years'
privileges to inventors of new arts and machines). In the 16th century, some
German states, notably Saxony, used patents, although not totally systematically.
The British patent law came into being in 1623 with the Statute of Monopolies,
although some argue that it did not really deserve the name of a 'patent law' until
its reform in 1852 (McLeod 1988). France adopted its patent law in 1791, the USA
in 1793, and Austria in 1794. Many of the other European countries established
their patent laws in the first half of the 19th century – Russia (1812), Prussia (1815),
Belgium and the Netherlands (1817), Spain (1820), Bavaria (1825), Sardinia (1826),
The Vatican state (1833), Sweden (1834), Wuerttemberg (1836), Portugal (1837),
Saxony (1843) (Penrose 1951: p.13).

'deficient' by the standards of our time. Patent systems in many countries lacked disclosure requirements, incurred very high costs in filing and processing patent applications, and afforded inadequate protection to the patentees. Few of them allowed patents on chemical and pharmaceutical substances (as opposed to the processes) – a practice that has continued well into the last decades of the 20th century in many countries.[8]

Of great relevance to this discussion is the fact that these laws accorded only very inadequate protection of the IPRs of foreign citizens (for further details, see Williams 1896; Penrose 1951; Schiff 1971; McLeod 1988; Crafts 2000; and Sokoloff and Khan 2000). For example, many of the patent laws were very lax on checking the originality of the invention. More importantly, in most countries, including Britain (before the 1852 reform), the Netherlands, Austria, and France, patenting of imported inventions by their nationals was often explicitly allowed.

In the USA, before the 1836 overhaul of the patent law, patents were granted without any proof of originality. This not only led to the patenting of imported technologies but encouraged racketeers to engage in 'rent-seeking' by patenting devices already in use ('phony patents') and by demanding money from their users under threat of suit for infringement (Cochran and Miller 1942: p.14).[9] The cases of Switzerland and the Netherlands in relation to their patent laws deserve even greater attention (see Schiff 1971 for further details).

The Netherlands, which originally introduced a patent law in 1817, abolished it in 1869, partly due to the rather deficient nature of

---

8 Chemical substances remained unpatentable until 1967 in West Germany, 1968 in the Nordic countries, 1976 in Japan, 1978 in Switzerland, and 1992 in Spain. Pharmaceutical products remained unpatentable until 1967 in West Germany and France, 1979 in Italy, and 1992 in Spain. Pharmaceutical products were also unpatentable in Canada until the early 1990s. For details, see Patel (1989: p.980).
9 According to Cochran and Miller (1942), therefore, the fact that between 1820 and 1830 the US produced 535 patents per year against 145 for Great Britain was mainly due to the difference in 'scruples' (p. 14). Contrast this to the argument by Sokoloff and Khan (2000) that it was thanks to a 'good' patent system that the US far exceeded Britain in patenting per capita by 1810 (p.5).

the law (even by the standards of the time)[10] but also having been influenced by the widespread anti-patent movement in Europe at the time. This movement condemned patents as being no different from other monopolistic practices (Schiff 1971; Machlup and Penrose 1950, document the anti-patent movement of the time in detail).

Switzerland did not provide any protection of intellectual property until 1888, when a patent law protecting only mechanical inventions ('inventions that can be represented by mechanical models'; Schiff 1971: p.85) was introduced. Only in 1907, partly prompted by the threat of trade sanction from Germany in retaliation to the Swiss use of its chemical and pharmaceutical inventions, did a patent law worth its name come into being. However, even this had many exclusions, especially the refusal to grant patents to chemical substances (as opposed to chemical processes). It was only in 1954 that the Swiss patent law became comparable to those of other advanced countries (Schiff 1971), although chemical substances remained unpatentable until 1978 (Patel 1989: p.980).

With the introduction of IPRs laws in an increasing number of countries, the pressures for an international IPRs regime naturally started growing from the late-19th century (the following details are from Penrose 1951: Chapter 3). The first attempt to create an international IPRs regime was the 1873 Vienna Congress. Especially controversial at this Congress was the 'compulsory working' requirement that Austria and some other countries had (in the Austrian case, a patented article had to be manufactured in Austria within a year from the issue of the patent or the patent would be revoked). The Congress concluded with a resolution that recommended 'compulsory licensing' instead of 'compulsory working', despite objections from some countries, notably the USA.

Another conference was held in Paris in 1878. Like the Vienna Congress, it was another 'unofficial' affair with no official government delegates. Unlike the Vienna Congress, however, it was a very

---

10 The 1817 Dutch patent law did not require a disclosure of the details of patents. It allowed the patenting of imported inventions. It nullified national patents of inventions that acquired foreign patents. And there was no penalty on others using patented products without permission as far as it was for their own business (Schiff 1971: pp.19-20).

pro-patentee gathering. However, its resolution still showed some recognition of 'public interest' arguments and accepted the principle of compulsory working (but, reflecting its pro-patentee bias, rejected 'compulsory licensing', on the ground that no one other than the patentee should be able to benefit from an invention, should the patentee prove unable to work it).

The 1878 Paris Congress set up a commission, which eventually produced a draft convention that was discussed in the first 'official' meeting on the international IPRs regime (with representatives from 19 governments) in Paris in 1880. This draft convention eventually got ratified by 11 countries in Paris in 1883 in the form of the Paris Convention of the International Union for the Protection of Industrial Property (the original signatories were Belgium, Portugal, France, Guatemala, Italy, the Netherlands, San Salvador, Serbia, Spain, Switzerland, and the UK). It covered not just patents but also trademark laws (which enabled patentless Switzerland and Netherlands to sign up to the Convention despite not having a patent law). In 1886, the Berne Convention on copyrights was signed. The Paris Convention was subsequently revised a number of times (notably 1911, 1925, 1934, 1958, and 1967) in the direction of strengthening patentee rights and, together with the Berne Convention, had formed the basis of the international IPRs regime until the TRIPS agreement (Shell 1998; see Section 4.1).

The Paris Convention had a number of characteristics (Penrose 1951: Chapter 4). First of all, despite strong US objection, it adopted a firm 'non-reciprocity' approach, where foreign citizens received national treatment but countries were not required to accord foreign citizens the same IPRs that they enjoyed in their home countries. Second, it accepted the 'right of priority', which meant that the filing of an application for a patent in one country gave the applicant the right to obtain recognition of his/her claim in all other countries in which his/ her invention was patentable. Most importantly, it adopted both compulsory working and compulsory licensing. The compulsory working agreement was subsequently revised in 1925 to be acceptable only when compulsory licensing proved ineffective.

However, despite the emergence of an international IPRs regime, even the most advanced countries were still routinely violating the IPRs of other countries' citizens well into the 20th century. We

already mentioned that, until this time, Switzerland and the Netherlands did not have a patent law. It is also interesting to note that the
USA, a strong advocate of patentee rights even then, did not acknowledge copyrights of foreigners until 1891.[11] And as late as in the late-
19th century, when Germany was about to technologically overtake
Britain, there was a great concern in Britain with German violation of
its trademarks (Williams 1896 provides many interesting details; also
see Landes 1969: p.328).[12]

Although Britain did not have a trademark law until 1862,
Kindleberger (1978) notes that 'as early as the 1830s a number of
British manufacturers were continuously engaged in litigation to
protect trademarks' (p.216). In 1862, it introduced a trademark law
(the Merchandise Mark Act), which banned 'commercial thievery',
such as the forging of trademarks and the labelling of false quantities
(Williams 1896: p.137). In the 1887 revision of the Act, mindful of
German (and other foreign) infringement of the British trademark law,
the British Parliament specifically added the place or the country of
manufacture as a part of the necessary 'trade description'. This
revision banned not only patently false descriptions but also misleading descriptions – such as the then widespread German practice of
selling counterfeit Sheffield cutlery with fake logos. According to this
Act, 'it [was] a penal offence to sell an article made abroad which has
upon it any word or mark leading the purchaser to believe that it is
made in England, in the absence of other words denoting the real place
of origin' (Williams 1896: p.137).

---

11 The US did not fully conform to the Berne Convention on international
copyright (1886) until 1988, when the country finally abolished the requirement
that copyrighted books had to be printed in the US or typeset with US plates
(Sokoloff and Khan 2000: p.9).

12 It is interesting to note that at that time, the British were criticising Germany not
only for using industrial espionage and the violation of trademark law but also for
exporting goods made with convict labour (recall the recent US dispute with China
on this account). On the other hand, exactly at the same time, the Germans were
complaining about the absence of a patent law in Switzerland and the consequent
'theft' of German intellectual property by Swiss firms, especially in the chemical
industry.

However, the Germans employed a range of measures to get around this Act (Williams 1896: p.138). They placed the stamp for the country of origin on the packaging instead of the individual articles, so that once the packaging was removed customers could not tell the country of origin of the product (said to be common amongst the imports of watches and files). They also sent some articles over in pieces and had them assembled in England (a method said to be common in pianos and cycles). They would also place the stamp for the country of origin where it was practically invisible.[13]

All the above discussions show how ill-informed many defenders of the TRIPS agreement are in relation to the historical importance of IPRs in promoting economic development. For example, the US-based National Law Center for Inter-American Free Trade (1997) claims that '[t]he historical record in the industrialised countries, which began as developing countries, demonstrates that intellectual property protection has been one of the most powerful instruments for economic development, export growth, and the diffusion of new technologies, art and culture' (p.1).

Historical evidence shows that, contrary to this kind of claim, in the early days of industrial development in the now-advanced countries, IPRs, especially other countries' IPRs, were not well respected. Compared to the developing countries of yesteryear, the contemporary developing countries seem to be behaving much better in many ways. And if that is the case, it seems unfair to ask the modern-day developing countries to behave to a standard that was not even remotely observed when the now-advanced countries were at similar, or even more advanced, stages of development.

With this historical background in mind, let us move to the next section and discuss the role of IPRs in economic development in the contemporary context.

---

13 'One German firm, which exports to England large numbers of sewing-machines, conspicuously labelled "Singers" and "North-British Sewing Machines", places the Made in Germany stamp in small letters underneath the treadle. Half a dozen seamstresses might combine their strength to turn the machine bottom-upwards, and read the legend: otherwise it would go unread' (Williams 1896: p.138).

3.   INTELLECTUAL PROPERTY RIGHTS AND ECONOMIC DEVELOPMENT

People who advocate TRIPS argue that a stronger protection of intellectual property rights is essential for knowledge generation and therefore economic development. However, when they talk about IPRs, they do not make a distinction between different forms of IPRs and assume that all IPRs are, and should be, 'private' IPRs. This is, however, wrong.

Those who do not distinguish between different forms of IPRs implicitly assume that the only alternative to private intellectual property rights (PIPRs) is a free-for-all open access regime. However, in fact many pieces of knowledge are publicly or communally owned and are therefore subject to certain rules of use and disposal. For example, the private-sector participants in a publicly-financed research consortium may be obliged to make all their findings public and/or be forced to share the resulting patents with other participants in the project.[14]

Even in a situation that looks like a pure 'open access' one, there may be certain laws and social norms concerning the use of particular types of knowledge for particular purposes. For example, even if the copyright of a book has expired, we do not allow other people to plagiarise from it. Another example is when many web-based software that adopt the 'open access' approach demand that the resulting (improved) products cannot be appropriated by individuals (UNDP 1999: p.73, Box 2.9). So instead of talking about IPRs in general, we should distinguish different forms of IPRs from one another. This also means that when they talk of the necessity of IPRs for the generation of new knowledge, the proponents of 'stronger' IPRs are in fact calling for stronger PIPRs. But is it true that we need strongly protected PIPRs in order to provide incentives to generate new knowledge? A further question is whether we need patents and other forms of 'monopoly' to do so. Let us examine these questions one by one.

---

14 For some such examples in the information technology industries, see Fransman (1990) on Japan and Evans (1995) on Korea.

3.1 The Case For and Against Private IPRs

Although the mainstream view these days is that PIPRs are an essential part of a market system, this view was not necessarily the dominant one at all times and in all countries. In other words, there are the historical and locational specificities of the prevailing view on what can be owned and not (for a theoretical exposition of this point, see Chang 2002). This point can be most clearly seen from the example of the third President of the USA, Thomas Jefferson, who argued that ideas by their nature cannot be confined or exclusively appropriated and therefore that '[i]nventions ... cannot, in nature, be a subject of property' (cited in Penrose 1951: p.23).[15]

Given that he was a slave-owner, Jefferson obviously saw no problem in owning human beings, but he was against ownership of ideas, which is exactly the opposite of what many people believe these days. Others, especially those associated with the mid-19th century anti-patent movement in Europe, objected to the idea of giving people PIPRs because they believed that any form of monopoly is bad (Machlup and Penrose 1950: pp.18-9). As we mentioned in Section 2, the Netherlands had once abolished its patent law on this ground.

However, eventually, the argument prevailed that, although PIPRs certainly create inefficiencies, they are a price that society has to pay, firstly, to motivate people to put energy into generating new ideas, and, secondly, to motivate people who have new ideas to make

---

15 The full quotation is: 'That ideas should freely spread from one to another over the globe, for the moral and mutual instruction of man, and improvement of his conditions, seem to have been peculiarly and benevolently designed by nature, when she made them, like fire, expansible over all space, without lessening their density in any point, and like the air in which we breathe, move, and have our physical being, incapable of confinement or exclusive appropriation. Inventions then cannot, in nature, be a subject of property,' Thomas Jefferson, Letter to Issac McPherson, August 13, 1813, in *The Complete Jefferson* edited by Saul Padover (New York, Duell, Sloan, Pearce Inc., 1943). Cited in Penrose (1951), pp.22-3. This may seem a curious remark from a man who, as the Secretary of State, chaired the first Patent Board of the country (the other members being the Secretary of War and the Attorney General), but during his tenure at the office he made strenuous efforts to grant patents only to truly original inventions. Knowing this, there were few patent applications and fewer still granted (Peterson 1970: p.450).

them public. However, these arguments are not as robust as they appear.

3.1.1 PIPRs as an Incentive to Generate New Knowledge

Against the argument that PIPRs are necessary as incentives for innovative activities, it should first of all be pointed out that people often pursue knowledge for its own sake, so they do not always need monetary incentives conferred by PIPRs. The UNDP (1999) cites some examples where open access has encouraged, rather than prevented, the generation of new knowledge in certain areas, such as Internet-based computer software (pp.72-3).

More importantly, even without patents, the innovator can enjoy many 'natural' protective mechanisms and therefore will be able to reap substantial financial gains.[16] These natural protective mechanisms include 'imitation lag' (due to the costs of absorbing new knowledge),[17] 'reputational advantage' (of being the first producer), and the head start in racing down learning curves (Scherer and Ross 1990: p.627). This was a popular argument against patents in the 19th century (Machlup and Penrose 1950: p.18) and the idea behind Schumpeter's vision of 'creative destruction' (Schumpeter 1987).

Indeed, a study by Levin *et al.* (1987) based on a survey of 650 high-level R&D managers of listed companies in the US found that patents are considered much less important than 'natural advantages' such as imitation lag and the ability to move down the learning curve more quickly as well as other 'efforts' such as sales or service effort in preserving an innovator's advantage. The survey also found that when it came to process innovation, even secrecy was regarded as more important than patents in preserving the advantage.

In another interesting survey, Mansfield (1986) asked the chief R&D executives of 100 US firms what proportion of the inventions they developed between 1981 and 1983 would not have been devel-

---

16 Scherer (1984) argues that '[n]atural inertia, secrecy, and the need to do some RD (his term for R&D) on one's own before mastering a new process all contribute to imitation lags' (pp.138-9).
17 Scherer and Ross (1990) argue that 'free riding on an innovator's technical contribution is often far from free. An appreciable but varying fraction of the original R&D may have to be replicated' (p.626).

oped had they been unable to obtain patent protection. Among the 12 industry groups surveyed, there were only three industries where the answer was 'high' (60% for pharmaceutical and 38% for other chemicals, and 25% for petroleum).[18] And there were six others where the answer was basically 'none' (0% for office equipment, motor vehicles, rubber products, and textiles or 1% for primary metals and instruments). Including three other industries where the answer can be interpreted as 'low' (17% for machinery, 12% for fabricated metal products, and 11% for electrical equipment), the overall ratio worked out to be around 14%, according to Mansfield's calculation – a rather low proportion. The result of this study is confirmed by a number of other studies conducted in the UK and Germany as well (Scherer and Ross 1990: p.629, footnote 46).

The relatively insignificant effect of the patent system on innovative activities is also confirmed by the historical experiences of Switzerland and the Netherlands that we mentioned above (Section 2). In a highly illuminating study of the two countries during their patentless periods, Schiff (1971) concludes that there is no evidence that the absence of a patent system held these two countries back in terms of technological development (Evenson 1990 also concurs with this verdict).

The case of Switzerland deserves a closer look in this context. After examining international patent statistics (patents acquired by different countries in the major industrial economies) and other case-based studies, Schiff (1971) concludes that in the late-19th century, despite their country not having a patent law, the Swiss were one of the most innovative people in the world. During this period, the Swiss made world-famous inventions in areas like textile machinery (the famous Honneger silk loom), steam engine, and food processing (milk chocolate, instant soup, stock [bouillon] cubes, baby food) (see pp.108-112 for some details).

He also points out that there is no evidence that the absence of a patent system worked as a deterrent to FDI and even cites some important cases, especially in the food processing industry, where its

---

18 This tallies with the fact that industries such as chemical, pharmaceutical, and computer software were the strongest advocates of TRIPS in the Uruguay Round.

absence was definitely a major reason behind FDI (pp.102-3). He also shows that, on the other hand, the introduction of patent law in 1907 did not lead to a noticeable increase in inventive activities.[19] He concludes that in the Swiss case, the absence of a patent law, on balance, actually helped the country's industrial development (especially in industries like dye, chemical, and electro-technical; p.104).

3.1.2 PIPRs as an Incentive to Disclose New Knowledge

The idea that PIPRs are necessary for us to make the inventors of new ideas disclose their new knowledge has been criticised on the following grounds (Machlup and Penrose 1950: pp.25-8). First, even if an inventor does not disclose his new knowledge, society will not suffer because 'usually the same or similar ideas are developed simultaneously and independently in several quarters' (p.26) – as we see in the proverbial anecdote of Bell and Wallace applying for a patent for the telephone on the same day. Second, it is impractical to keep any invention secret for a long time – the new ideas are worked out through reverse engineering, especially by people who were close to finding the same solution – although there is an inevitable imitation lag here. Third, '[w]here an inventor thinks he can succeed in guarding his secret, he will not take out a patent; hence, patent protection does not cause disclosure of concealable inventions but serves only to restrict the use of inventions that could not have been kept secret anyway' (p.26). Fourth, '[s]ince patents are granted only on inventions developed to a stage at which they can be reduced to practical use, the patent system encourages secrecy in the developmental stage of inventions' (p.26).

---

19 Of course, during its patentless period, the Swiss still could take out patents abroad, and this must have acted as an incentive to invent. However, on the basis of a careful analysis of 1901-1913 international patent statistics, Schiff (1971) argues that this alone cannot explain the high level of inventive activities by the Swiss during this period. His point is that the proportion of the Swiss inventors taking out patents only at home remained largely unchanged even after the introduction of the 1907 patent law (recall here that patenting did exist in Switzerland since 1888, although only in mechanical industries). This suggests that even for a small country, the exploitation of the home market remains the primary concern for many inventors and therefore that the possibility of acquiring patents abroad does not fully compensate for the absence of patent protection at home (p.114).

3.1.3 Problems with the Currently-Dominant IPRs System

More specifically, there are a number of problems with the currently-dominant IPRs regime that is built around the patent system.

First of all, as we suggested above, it is not clear whether we need patents in order to generate new ideas. Furthermore, there are many long-standing criticisms of the patent system for its potential 'wastefulness'. Many have argued that its 'winner-takes-all' nature encourages an all-out competition that often results in duplication of efforts and investments. Other critics have pointed out that resources may also be wasted in efforts to 'get around' existing patents, rather than to generate 'genuine' new knowledge. Also, given the cumulative and interactive nature of technological progress, 'strong protection of a key innovation may preclude the competitors making socially useful innovation' (Levin *et al.* 1987: p.788). Many people also ask why all inventions should get equal length of protection despite the differences in their social usefulness and also why the length of that protection should be as long as 17 or 20 years.

The above criticisms are all rather well-known, and we do not need to repeat them at length. Increasingly, however, there is concern about the granting of patents and other PIPRs to certain inventions that were created by using the ideas generated by publicly-funded research activities. This is a serious problem, when even according to the information provided by the US pharmaceutical industry association itself, only 43% of pharmaceutical R&D is funded by the industry itself, while 29% is funded by the US government's National Institutes of Health (NIH) (see http:// www. pharma. org/ publications/ profile00 /chap2.phtm#growth).[20]

For a more specific example, the anti-AIDS drug, AZT, was first invented in 1964 by a US researcher working with a grant from the NIH. The drug was then bought by the UK pharmaceutical company, Glaxo, for use on pet cats. When the AIDS epidemic broke out, the NIH later did all the work proving that AZT works on the HIV virus (because Glaxo refused to do the work). Despite the efforts of the NIH, it is Glaxo, which on learning about the effect of AZT on HIV lost no

---

20 The rest is funded by private charities and universities.

time in taking a patent out on it for use on HIV, that is reaping huge profits from the drug (Palast 2000).

For another (even more extreme) example, we can cite the case of the cancer drug, Taxol. There is no patent on Taxol, because it was discovered by the US government. However, the pharmaceutical company Bristol-Myers Squibb has an absolute control on the price of the drug in Britain, because the minor (but crucial in clinical situations) work on dosage calculation it conducted is protected by Britain's data protection law for 10 years (Palast 2000).

Another emerging problem is that, as increasingly minute pieces of knowledge (say, down to the gene level) become patentable, the risk of patents hindering rather than promoting progress is becoming greater. The case of the technology for the so-called 'golden rice' (with extra beta carotene), which can bring huge nutritional benefits to millions of people, is quite illustrative of this point. When selling the technology to the multinational company, Syngenta (formerly AstraZeneca), Ingo Potrykus (Swiss) and Peter Beyer (German), who pioneered the technology, cited the difficulties involved in negotiating for the estimated 70-105 patents as the primary reason for doing so. While critics point out that only about a dozen patents among the six to nine dozen cited by Potrykus and Beyer are in fact relevant for countries where the golden rice would have large benefits (see RAFI 2000), the case illustrates how the recent changes in technology have increased the hindering potential of patents.[21]

3.2 Alternatives to the Currently-Dominant IPRs System

Given all the problems associated with the currently-dominant IPRs system, what are the possible alternatives?

Needless to say, it is possible to do away with PIPRs altogether. Note that this is not to argue that there should be no IPRs at all ('open access'). In this regime, there will be public regulations and social norms regarding the use of ideas. Also, there will still be substantial opportunities for private appropriation of new knowledge thanks to the natural imitation gap. UNDP (1999) emphasises that there are many

---

21 I thank Ron Herring for drawing my attention to 'golden rice' in the first place and Penny Janeway for pointing me to detailed sources on the issue.

alternative approaches to innovation based on 'sharing, open access and communal innovation' (p.73). If abolishing PIPRs sounds dangerous, note that all countries implicitly took this position before the adoption of patent laws. Even after the adoption of the patent system, almost all countries have not accepted PIPRs in certain areas. For example, when they publicly fund certain innovation activities, they usually demand that the resulting knowledge is made a public property.

Another possibility is to replace (at least in certain areas) patents with lump-sum prizes, which will give incentive to people to invest in innovative activities but will do away with the problem of patents blocking further technological progress. This was indeed a popular proposal among the anti-patent campaigners in 19th century Europe, and was famously championed by the magazine, *Economist* (Machlup and Penrose 1950: pp.19-22).[22] The difficulty with this proposal, however, is that we have to either give the same prize to every inventor regardless of the social value of their inventions or have to spend a large amount of resources in order to determine who should get how big a prize.

For a less dramatic, but no less important and certainly a lot more realistic, proposal, we could follow the one made by Scherer (1984). Scherer argues for 'a flexible system of compulsory licensing, under which the patent recipient bears the burden of showing why the patent should not expire or be licensed at modest royalties to all applicants three or five years after its issue' (p.139). He argues that '[w]hen a patent-holding corporation possesses a substantial share of the relevant market and well-established marketing channels ...there would be a presumption in favour of early patent licensing or expiration on the assumption that positive innovation profits could normally be attained without the added inducement of strong patent protection' (p.139).

Scherer acknowledges that there may be some inventions where the uncertainties involved are so overwhelming that only a very strong

---

22 Landes (1969) points out that before the days of cheap mass communication, incentives like medals awarded in expositions motivated potential innovators not only by offering honour but also by offering *de facto* free advertising for their products (p.151).

patent protection will induce the necessary investments. However, he points out that such cases are probably rare and therefore it should be possible to devise policies that treat them as exceptions – in particular, by waiving the presumption in favour of early compulsory licensing or short patent lives (for inventions with high *ex post* private benefit-cost ratios) upon a showing that the patent recipient exhibited exceptional creativity or undertook unusual technical and/or commercial risks in the invention's development (p.140).

The point is that, if what we ultimately want is the widest possible diffusion of technology, we want to 'buy off' the innovators at the minimum possible cost, and there are reasons to doubt that the currently-dominant system of IPRs built around the patent system offers the most cost-efficient way.

Moving more specifically to the case of developing countries, where technology assimilation is a lot more important than the generation of patentable technology, it should be said that the benefits from a national PIPRs regime may be minimal.

The extra innovations generated by stronger PIPRs would be meagre, as economic agents in these countries possess poor innovative capabilities. As even Primo Braga (1996), who is quite sympathetic to TRIPS, admits, there is very little evidence that stronger PIPRs encourage greater R&D in developing countries. Indeed, the recent research on technology issues in developing countries shows that the most important kinds of new knowledge for them are not readily patentable ones. For them, the most important type of knowledge is not knowledge that is truly 'novel' on the world scale, but more tacit and localised knowledge, which is necessary in assimilating advanced technologies (including new organisational knowledge) to the local condition, that cannot be patented, except on the margin.[23]

This is indeed why most countries had to use infant industry protection and other industrial policy measures to encourage this kind of technological development (as was the case with the US and other follower countries in the 19th century). Unfortunately, these measures are now subject to restrictions under the WTO agreement, although

---

23 In order to deal with the difficulty with patenting 'adaptive innovation', Evenson (1990) proposes the use of 'petty patents', which accord shorter protection (4-7 years) without a close examination of originality.

probably not as much as it is widely believed to be (see Akyüz *et al.* 1998; Amsden 2000; and Chang and Cheema 2001).

On the other side of the equation, we must point out that the opportunity costs of establishing and running a strong PIPRs system may be considerable in developing countries, given their lack of technical, administrative, and legal human resources (more on this). Also, given the weak anti-trust law and/or enforcement capability, the developing countries may suffer from the 'monopoly' effect of patents more than do the more advanced countries.

Moreover, when 97% of world patents are held by developed countries (UNDP 1999: p.68), the costs from paying the royalties may significantly outweigh the benefits from (the insignificant) additional knowledge that the system extracts from the nationals of the developing countries.[24] When there is an international system, like TRIPS, that demands compliance (with some adjustment) with the international 'norm', the problems for the developing countries become even bigger – as we shall see in the next section.

4. TRIPS AND THE DEVELOPING COUNTRIES

In the previous section, we examined the role of a domestic IPRs regime in economic development. In this section, we examine the role of an international IPRs regime in economic development, an issue that has been brought into the spotlight following the introduction of TRIPS. In the previous section, we have shown that there is no sound theoretical and empirical support for the argument that a strong protection of private intellectual property rights (PIPRs) is necessary for technological progress and therefore economic development, especially for the developing countries. In this section, we discuss whether stronger PIPRs protection on a world scale will benefit the developing countries through its impact on international generation and transfer of technology.

---

24 Indeed, TRIPS implicitly acknowledges this problem, since it allows exceptions for the least developed countries and to a lesser extent the developing countries.

4.1 The Evolution of the TRIPS Agreement

The issue of TRIPS got incorporated into the WTO agenda mainly for two reasons (see Shell 1998, and Patel 1989 for further details).

First of all, it was a reaction by the advanced countries, mainly the USA, against the attempt by the G77 developing countries to call for the reform of the international IPRs system through the WIPO (World Intellectual Property Organisation) during the 1970s and the early-1980s. At that time, as a part of their push for the New International Economic Order (NIEO), the developing countries sought to generate greater transfer of technology from the advanced countries through the reform of the international IPRs regime. Especially controversial was their push for exclusive compulsory licensing (where the number of licensees is restricted by the government), reduced licensing fees for developing countries, lengthening of the period of 'right of priority' for the developing country inventors, and even allowing the developing countries to revoke licences before the granting of compulsory licensing (and relaxing the condition for revocation) (Shell 1998: pp.120-3). Contrary to the expectation by the G77 countries, these demands galvanised patentees in the developed countries into campaigning for a counter-offensive.

Secondly, the relative decline of US industrial competitiveness prompted a wave of resentment against foreign 'theft' of US PIPRs. Reflecting this mood, the US courts started favouring patentees as never before. Until the early-1980s, and especially during the Black/Douglas Supreme Court (1946-65), the US courts were quite lax in enforcing patentees' rights, but since around 1982-3, they started awarding high damages for infringement of patents and other PIPRs. However, particularly significant was the US realisation that trade threats can be used as a way to enforce the PIPRs of the US corporations onto its trading partners.

In the late-1970s and the early-1980s, the US Trade Representative (USTR) started putting pressure through bilateral trade talks on countries like Hungary, Korea, Mexico, Singapore, and Taiwan, to 'improve' their IPRs regimes. Trade law amendments (especially to the so-called 'Super 301' Section) in 1984 and 1988 made the IPRs issue a key element in the functioning of the USTR. In the meantime, the US realised that the use of trade threats as a means to force changes on its trading partners' IPRs regimes need not be confined to bilateral trade talks, and in April 1986 put forward TRIPS as an item in the agenda for the Uruguay Round of the GATT talks (Shell 1998). The US push for TRIPS became particularly strong from 1988 (Siebeck 1990a).

As is well known, the key features of TRIPS are:

(i)   national treatment
(ii)   mandatory 20-year minimum patent life
(iii) tough restrictions on compulsory licensing (forbidding of exclusive compulsory licensing, toughening of the conditions under which compulsory licensing is accepted)
(iv)   shifting the burden of proof of infringement on process patent from the patentee to the alleged infringer.

There were some concessions to the developing countries, such as the granting of grace periods and acceptance of the non-patentability of 'diagnostic, therapeutic, and surgical methods of human or animal treatment' and of 'plants, animals and their biological processes'.

4.2 The (Alleged) Benefits of TRIPS for the Developing Countries

The defenders of TRIPS argue that, in addition to its positive impact on the innovative activities in developing countries themselves (which we have shown to be minimal), the TRIPS agreement will bring benefit to the developing countries by increasing the availability of advanced technologies to them. This is supposed to happen through, among others, the following mechanisms:

(i)   better protection of the PIPRs of foreign patentees is needed for greater technology transfer, as otherwise advanced country producers may be less willing to reveal their technology;
(ii)   better protection of PIPRs increases FDI flows, as firms are then less worried about the 'theft' of technology by the locals;
(iii) better protection of PIPRs increases inventive activities by developed country firms targeted at developing country markets (e.g., developing drugs for tropical diseases).

As for the argument that a stronger system of international PIPRs protection encourages technology transfer from developed to developing countries, we can say the following. While strengthening the protection of PIPRs in developing countries may in theory increase the willingness of the advanced countries to transfer technology through 'formal' channels, there is actually little evidence of this (see Siebeck 1990b). Moreover, TRIPS will reduce the ability of the developing countries to catch up through imitation and adaptation of advanced technologies through 'informal' channels (e.g., reverse engineering involving minor modifications, developing an alternative process for a patented chemical substance). Indeed, it may be argued that for the developing countries, 'informal' knowledge transfer may be more important than 'formal' transfer (see essays in Fransman and King (eds.) 1984). Therefore, TRIPS may reduce the effectiveness of technology transfer from the developing countries' point of view, especially if we consider both formal and informal channels of such transfer.[25]

How about the argument that a better protection of PIPRs promotes FDI? To begin with, there is little evidence that a stronger protection of PIPRs promotes FDI (Siebeck 1990b). Indeed, a classic article by Vaitsos (1972) argued that patents are often used as substitutes for FDI. Moreover, the IPRs regime is only one of many considerations in FDI decisions, and a minor one at that, so providing a stronger protection of PIPRs is unlikely to have much effect on FDI (Bronckers 1994; Primo Braga 1996). As we mentioned earlier, the historical example of Switzerland also shows that the absence of a patent law was, if anything, a major incentive to invest there (Schiff 1971: pp.102-3). The UNDP (1999) makes similar arguments regarding flows of FDI into Canada and Italy (p.73, Box 2.9). And all of these have to be set against the fact that the impact of FDI is generally ambiguous and highly context-dependent (see Helleiner 1989; Lall

---

25 The past president of the Licensing Executive Society (LES) of Britain and Ireland, Donal O'Connor, admitted that the hypothesis linking increased IPRs protection to technology transfer and investment flows for developing countries 'has not by any means been proven. It is one that we in LES wish to accept because it is one that we consider attractive' (cited in Shell 1998: p.222; the original source is Donal O'Connor, 'TRIPS: Licensing Challenge', *Les Nouvelles* 1995, vol.30, no.1, p.17).

1993; and Chang 1998).

As for the argument that a stronger protection of PIPRs in the developing countries may encourage innovative activities by the advanced country firms targeted at developing country markets, it must be pointed out that the developing country markets are usually marginal for these firms and therefore that the extra profits from them are unlikely to significantly affect their R&D decisions.

The above discussions show that the 'international' benefits for the developing countries of having a stronger regime of PIPRs protection – namely, increased technology transfer, increased FDI, and increased inventive activities by the advanced countries –are likely to be marginal at best.

4.3   The Costs of TRIPS for the Developing Countries

The problem with TRIPS is not only that it does not bring much benefit to developing countries but that it imposes substantial costs on them.

First, the most direct 'international' impact of TRIPS on developing countries is that they would need to increase their royalty payments, which can be a problem, especially in a foreign exchange shortage situation (which most developing countries are in).

Second, a stronger protection of PIPRs in developing countries, following TRIPS, is likely to lead to more widespread monopoly pricing and other restrictive behaviour by the TNCs – as the recent behaviour of some pharmaceutical and agro-chemical TNCs suggests. Given that the developing countries have weak (or sometimes no) anti-trust laws and low law enforcement capacity, it is unlikely that they can successfully restrain the monopolistic behaviour of giant TNCs.

Third, as we have already pointed out, there are the high costs of human resource involved in running a sophisticated IPRs regime in developing countries. Implementing the TRIPS agreement will increase these costs even further. This is not only because the required technical and legal standards for the domestic IPRs regimes will be made higher but also because the disputes in the WTO will require lawyers and others with skills that are not easily available in developing countries.

Fourth, there are costs that developing countries have to pay because TRIPS now allows 'natural' substances and processes that have previously been considered non-patentable, to be patentable (micro-organisms, biological processes, etc.) (for further details, see Ghosh 1999). There are also problems of justice here, because some advanced country producers are able to patent things that are already widely known in developing countries because they are able to 're-package' the products of a 'traditional knowledge system' in a form that is patentable, whereas the developing countries have little such capability. The recent cases of US companies patenting the medicinal use of turmeric (thwarted) or a particular variety of basmati rice under the brand name of, well, 'basmati rice' (granted) are good examples.

Last but not least, with TRIPS, the developing countries are likely to find it difficult to develop their own technological capabilities. With severe restrictions on their opportunities to imitate and make minor improvements – routes that have been so crucial in the development of technological capabilities in the now-advanced countries (see Section 2; also see Fransman and King (eds.) 1984) – the developing countries are likely to have less room for developing their own technological capabilities through engagement in incremental innovation and learning.

5.   CONCLUSION

In this chapter, we have examined the desirability of the currently-dominant form of IPRs regime, and especially the TRIPS regime, from historical, theoretical, and contemporary points of view.

The historical experiences of the now-developed countries when they were developing themselves, which we examined in the second section, show that a 'strong' IPRs regime, in the sense of providing strong protection of private intellectual property rights, was not an essential condition for their economic development. Most of them accorded only very incomplete and weak protection to PIPRs until quite late in their stages of development. Even the most advanced countries, like the UK and the US, established strong PIPRs regimes (except for copyright protection in the US case) only in the mid-19th century, and it was not until much later that such regimes came into being in the less advanced countries.

More importantly for the purpose of the current chapter, all these countries were quite willing to violate other countries' IPRs, even when they had introduced laws protecting IPRs of their own citizens – poaching of skilled workers, smuggling of machinery, industrial espionage, violation of trademark laws, allowance of patenting of imported inventions, or even a flat refusal to adopt the patent system (in the case of the Netherlands and Switzerland). In some cases, countries took what can only be described as a two-faced approach to this matter. The best examples include the US putting pressure on other countries for the 'improvement' of their patent laws in the late-19th century in the build-up to the adoption of the Paris Convention – while flatly refusing to protect foreign copyrights – and the routine violation of British trademarks by German producers in the late-19th century – when the country was putting pressure on Switzerland to introduce a patent law.

I discussed also the problems of the currently dominant regime of IPRs built around the patent system, and the TRIPS agreement as a culmination of it. After pointing out that contrary to the current orthodoxy, a 'good' IPRs regime is not necessarily the one that accords the strongest protection to private IPRs, I examined whether a stronger PIPRs regime, especially the one demanded by TRIPS, is likely to benefit the developing countries. The 'domestic' benefits of a stronger IPRs system – namely, increased knowledge generation by the nationals – are likely to be very small for most developing countries, given that they do little R&D and a lot of the new knowledge that they generate is not patentable. The 'international' benefits of such a regime – greater technology transfer, greater FDI, greater efforts at innovation in the developed countries – are also close to zero, if any. On the other hand, the costs of such a system are likely to be considerable – increased royalty payments, monopolistic abuses, the human (and financial) resource costs of administering an elaborate IPRs system, and so on.

If TRIPS brings at best marginal benefits to developing countries and imposes quite high costs on them, especially from the point of view of promoting long-term technological development, it seems clear that it needs a serious overhaul, if not an outright abolition. The exact form of this reform is difficult to spell out here, as there are still many uncertainties about the exact shape of the TRIPS regime and as different arguments may apply to different industries and to different countries. However, I propose a few principles that I think are useful in designing an alternative to TRIPS.

First of all, I think there should be more sensitivity to the issue of historical justice. By 'historical justice', I do not only mean 'making up for the misdeeds during the imperialist period'. There should be recognition on the part of the developed countries that, when they were developing economies themselves, they were engaged in all kinds of 'illegitimate' practices, including the violation of PIPRs (especially of foreign nationals). This means that they can be legitimately accused of 'pulling up the ladder' by insisting on a tough PIPRs regime for the developing countries. The new TRIPS, if there is going to be one, should start from this recognition.

Secondly, even from a more 'technical' angle, there should be a greater acceptance that the developing countries need fundamentally different IPRs regimes from the ones that the developed countries have. There is some recognition of this in the current TRIPS regime, but this is highly circumscribed possibly except for the 'least developed countries'. There have to be more provisions for the developing countries. Developing countries should be allowed to grant weaker PIPRs (e.g., shorter patent life, easier compulsory licensing[26] and compulsory working, easier parallel imports) and to pay lower licensing royalty rates (probably graduated according to a country's ability to pay).

Third, TRIPS should be reformed in such a way that it does not merely generate greater and cheaper transfer of technologies (which requires a more relaxed attitude towards violation of PIPRs by these countries) but also develops long-term technological capabilities of the developing countries. Developing technological capabilities in developing countries requires 'learning' through increased exposure to advanced technologies, which then leads to incremental innovation. Given that such incremental innovations cannot in general be protected through patent-like schemes, the WTO agreement should be revised in such a way that gives more freedom to developing countries to engage in infant industry protection. We could also institute an

---

26 Levin *et al.* (1987) provide strong evidence showing that compulsory licensing in general does not discourage R&D (p.804).

international tax on patent royalties and use at least parts of it for improving technological capabilities in developing countries.[27]

TRIPS has been imposed on developing countries that did not fully understand its implications. With the accumulation of experience, the developing countries are becoming increasingly aware that the system does not serve their interests (nor the consumers in the developed countries). The historical experiences of the now-developed countries also show how the imposition of this system amounts to 'pulling up the ladder' by these countries against the developing countries. Contemporary evidence also suggests that it is unlikely to bring much direct and indirect benefits to the developing countries, while imposing considerable costs on them in many ways.

Developed countries should also recognise that an international IPRs regime that promotes technological development and growth in developing countries will generate more demands for developed country exports. Therefore, it will benefit them more than a regime that depresses the developing countries in return for some increase in royalty payments and some reduction in export competition for a few industries.

The TRIPS arrangement needs to be radically overhauled. Without an overhaul, it is going to become a major point of contention in the emerging global economic order over the coming years. Without creating a global order that is more just and dynamic than what we have, the world may in the long run descend into chaos, as happened with the first globalisation that started in the late-19th century and came to an 'end' in three decades of wars and the Great Depression.

---

27 TRIPS reform needs to be backed up by other policies to promote technological capabilities in developing countries. The advanced countries could help the developing countries build such capabilities by redirecting aid towards such capability building (e.g., higher education in science and engineering, industrial training). They can also instruct the multilateral financial institutions to minimise cuts in knowledge-related public spending (e.g., education, training, R&D) in their adjustment programmes.

BIBLIOGRAPHY

Akyüz, Y., Chang, H.-J. and Kozul-Wright, R. (1998). 'New Perspectives on East Asian Development', *Journal of Development Studies,* vol.34, no.6, pp.4-36.

Amsden, A. (2000). 'Industrialisation under New WTO Law', a paper for the UNCTAD X meeting, 12-19 February, 2000, Bangkok.

Berg, M. (1980). *The Machinery Question and the Making of Political Economy, 1815-1848.* Cambridge: Cambridge University Press.

Bronckers, M. (1994). 'The Impact of TRIPS: Intellectual Property Protection in Developing Countries', *Common Market Law Review,* vol.31, pp.1245-81.

Bruland, K. (ed.) (1991). *Technology Transfer and Scandinavian Industrialisation.* New York: Berg.

Chang, H.-J. (1998). 'Globalisation, Transnational Corporations and Economic Development', in D. Baker, G. Epstein and R. Pollin (eds.), *Globalisation and Progressive Economic Policy.* Cambridge: Cambridge University Press.

Chang, H.-J. (2002). 'Breaking the Mould – An Institutionalist Political Economy Alternative to the Neo-Liberal Theory of the Market and the State', *Cambridge Journal of Economics,* vol.26, no.5, pp.539-59.

Chang, H.-J. and Cheema, A. (2001). 'Conditions for Effective Technology Policy in Developing Countries – Learning Rents, State Structures, and Institutions', *Journal of Innovation and New Technology,* vol.11, nos.4/5, pp.369-398.

Cipolla, C. (1993). *Before the Industrial Revolution – European Society and Economy, 1000-1700,* 3rd edn. London: Routledge.

Cochran, T. and Miller, W. (1942). *The Age of Enterprise: A Social History of Industrial America.* New York: The Macmillan Company.

Crafts, N. (2000). 'Institutional Quality and European Development before and after the Industrial Revolution', a paper prepared for World Bank Summer Research Workshop on Market Institutions, 17-19 July, 2000, Washington, D.C.

Davids, K. (1995). 'Openness or Secrecy? - Industrial Espionage in the Dutch Republic', *The Journal of European Economic History,* vol.24, no.2, pp.333-348.

Evans, P. (1995). *Embedded Autonomy — States and Industrial Transformation.* Princeton: Princeton University Press.

Evenson, R. (1990). 'Survey of Empirical Studies', in W. Siebeck (ed.), *Strengthening of Intellectual Property Rights in Developing Countries,* Discussion Paper no.112. Washington, D.C.: World Bank.

Fransman, M. (1990). *The Market and Beyond: Information Technology in Japan.* Cambridge: Cambridge University Press.

Fransman, M. and King, K. (eds.) (1984). *Technological Capability in the Third World.* London and Basingstoke: Macmillan.

Ghosh, J. (1999). 'Rules of International Economic Integration and Human Rights', a background paper for *Human Development Report 2000*, Jawaharlal Nehru University.

Harris, J. (1991). 'Movement of Technology between Britain and Europe in the Eighteenth Century', in D. Jeremy (ed.), *International Technology Transfer – Europe, Japan, and the USA, 1700-1914.* Aldershot: Edward Elgar.

Harris, J. (1992). *Essays in Industry and Technology in the Eighteenth Century.* Aldershot: Ashgate.

Harris, J. (1998). *Industrial Espionage and Technology Transfer – Britain and France in the Eighteenth Century.* Aldershot: Ashgate.

Helleiner, G. (1989). 'Transnational Corporations and Direct Foreign Investment', in H. Chenery and T.N. Srinivasan (eds.), *Handbook of Development Economics,* vol.2. Amsterdam: Elsevier.

Jeremy, D. (1977). 'Damming the Flood: British Government Efforts to Check the Outflow of Technicians and Machinery, 1780-1843', *Business History Review,* vol.51, no.1, pp.1-34.

Jeremy, D. (1981). *Transatlantic Industrial Revolution: The Diffusion of Textile Technologies Between Britain and America, 1790-1830s.* Cambridge, MA: The MIT Press.

Kindleberger, C. (1978). 'Germany's Overtaking of England, 1806 to 1914 (chapter 7)', in *Economic Response: Comparative Studies in Trade, Finance, and Growth.* Cambridge, MA: Harvard University Press.

Lall, S. (1993). 'Introduction', in S. Lall (ed.), *Transnational Corporations and Economic Development.* London: Routledge.

Landes, D. (1969). *The Unbound Prometheus – Technological Change and Industrial Development in Western Europe from 1750 to the Present.* Cambridge: Cambridge University Press.

Levin, R., Klevorick, A., Nelson, R. and Winter, S. (1987). 'Appropriating the Returns from Industrial Research and Development', *Brookings Papers on Economic Activity,* 1987, no.3.

Machlup, F. and Penrose, E. (1950). 'The Patent Controversy in the Nineteenth Century', *Journal of Economic History,* vol.10, no.1, pp.1-29.

Mansfield, E. (1986). 'Patents and Innovation: An Empirical Study', *Management Science,* vol.32, pp.173-81.

McLeod, C. (1988). *Inventing the Industrial Revolution: The English Patent System, 1660-1800.* Cambridge: Cambridge University Press.

National Law Centre for Inter-American Free Trade (1997). 'Strong Intellectual Property Protection Benefits the Developing Countries', http://www.natlaw.com/pubs/spmxip11.htm.

Palast, G. (2000). 'Keep Taking Our Tablets (No One Else's)', *The Observer,* Business Section, p.7, 23 July 2000.

Patel, S. (1989). 'Intellectual Property Rights in the Uruguay Round – A Disaster for the South?', *Economic and Political Weekly*, 6 May, pp.978-1057.

Penrose, E. (1951). *The Economics of the International Patent System.* Baltimore: The Johns Hopkins Press.

Peterson, M. (1970). *Thomas Jefferson and the New Nation: A Bibliography.* New York: Oxford University Press.

Primo Braga, C. (1996). 'Trade-related Intellectual Property Issues: The Uruguay Round Agreement and Its Economic Implications', in W. Martin and A. Winters (eds.), *The Uruguay Round and the Developing Countries.* Cambridge: Cambridge University Press.

RAFI (Rural Advancement Foundation International) (2000). *RAFI Communique,* September/October 2000, Issue no.66.

Reinert, E. (1995). 'Competitiveness and Its Predecessors – A 500-year Cross-national Perspective', *Structural Change and Economic Dynamics,* vol.6, pp.23-42.

Scherer, F. 1984. *Innovation and Growth.* Cambridge, MA: The MIT Press.

Scherer, F. and Ross, D. (1990). *Industrial Market Structure and Economic Performance.* Boston: Houghton Mifflin Company.

Schiff, E. (1971). *Industrialisation without National Patents – the Netherlands, 1869-1912 and Switzerland, 1850-1907.* Princeton: Princeton University Press.

Schumpeter, J. (1987). *Capitalism, Socialism, and Democracy,* 6th edn. London: Unwin.

Shell, S. (1998). *Power and Ideas.* Albany: State University of New York Press.

Siebeck, W. (1990a). 'Introduction', in W. Siebeck (ed.), *Strengthening of Intellectual Property Rights in Developing Countries,* Discussion Paper no.112. Washington, D.C.: World Bank.

Siebeck, W. (1990b). 'Conclusions and Recommendations', in W. Siebeck (ed.), *Strengthening of Intellectual Property Rights in Developing Countries,* Discussion Paper no.112. Washington, D.C.: World Bank.

Sokoloff, K. and Khan, B.Z. (2000). 'Intellectual Property Institutions in the United States: Early Development and Comparative Perspective', a paper prepared for World Bank Summer Research Workshop on Market Institutions, 17-19 July, 2000, Washington, D.C.

UNDP (United Nations Development Programme) (1999). *Human Development Report 1999.* New York: Oxford University Press.

Vaitsos, C. (1972). 'Patents Revisited: Their Function in Developing Countries', *Journal of Development Studies,* vol.9, no.1, pp.71-97.

Williams, E. (1896). *Made in Germany.* London: William Heinemann. The 1973 edition with an introduction by Austen Albu. Brighton: The Harvester Press.

Chapter 9

Institutional Foundations for Effective Design and Implementation of Selective Trade and Industrial Policies in the Least Developed Countries: Theory and Evidence

1. INTRODUCTION: THE LINEAGE OF THE DEBATE

THE central issue in the debate on selective industrial and trade policies, namely, the idea that some economic activities are socially more desirable than others and therefore deserve government (or some other form of collective) encouragement, has a long intellectual lineage. It is in fact much longer than what most people realise (Reinert 1995 provides a fascinating summary of this intellectual tradition; Chang 2002a provides evidence on the history of policy practice).

Many people believe that the origin of this idea lies in the works of the late-19th century German economist Friedrich List, the supposed father of infant industry protection. However, List was only developing the ideas that he learned while he was in the United States as a political exile in the early-19th century – ideas developed by now-forgotten American economists like Alexander Hamilton (now only remembered as a politician) and Daniel Raymond, and actively practised up until the early-20th century by successive American governments (Freeman 1989; Reinert 1995; Chang 2002a).[1] The idea, however, goes back even further.

Edward III in 14th century Britain ran what can be described in modern terms as an infant industry promotion programme for the woollen manufacturing industry of his country (Chang 2002a). The early Tudor monarchs, Henry VII (15th century) and Elizabeth I (16th

---

1 From about the mid-19th century to the Second World War, the US was the most protectionist economy in the world. See World Bank (1991: p.97, Box 5.2).

century) in particular, put the idea in practice by promoting the woollen industry by an array of means – imposing import duties for textiles, first imposing export duties for and later banning the export of raw materials, buying up skilled foreign workers (whose migration was often prohibited by their own countries) (Reinert 1995; Chang 2002a)[2].

During the last century or so, with the dominance of neoclassical economics, which denies the very idea that some economic activities can be more socially desirable than others, selective industrial and trade policies have received increasingly less support among the academic economists. However, this does not mean that such policies were not practised in reality. Selective industrial and trade policies were extensively practised in most of the now-developed countries in their early days of development in the late-19th and the early-20th centuries (Chang 2002a). And they persisted in many of these countries well into the latter part of the 20th century – Japan, France, Austria, Finland, and Norway being the most prominent examples (see Cohen 1997, and Hall 1986 for France; see Vartiainen 1995 for Finland and Austria; see Fagerberg *et al*. 1990 for Norway).

Right after the Second World War, the idea that some activities are more desirable than others and therefore deserve government support had become popular in developing countries. There emerged various ideas arguing that the developing countries should now use their newly-acquired policy autonomy in order to discourage primary commodity production and promote manufacturing (for a review, see Chang and Rowthorn 1995a). These ideas were implemented under the (somewhat misleading) banner of 'import substitution industrialisation' (ISI) that used tariffs, quantitative restrictions, regulations, and subsidies in order to promote manufacturing industries (Hirschman 1967 is a classic analysis of this experience; Bruton 1998 is a recent review of it).

The ISI and the ideas associated with it came under severe attack in the 1970s and the early-1980s from the newly resurgent neoclassical development economics, which had fundamental trust in the market

---

2   Britain was a high-tariff economy until the early-19th century. See the same source as above.

mechanism and deep distrust in any government action[3]. However, the tide had turned once again by the late-1980s, when a number of publications on the development of East Asian NICs such as Korea and Taiwan pointed out that these countries did not succeed on the basis of free trade, free market policies as they were supposed to have[4]. Partly drawing on the slightly earlier controversy surrounding the Japanese selective industrial policy in the 1980s[5], these criticisms finally prompted a partial capitulation by the mainstream in the form of the publication of the controversial 'East Asian Miracle Report' by the World Bank (World Bank 1993)[6].

One thing that distinguishes the debate on selective industrial and trade policies generated by the success of the East Asian countries (Japan, Korea, and Taiwan, especially) is that its focus has shifted to the *institutional* prerequisites of policy implementation.

With the debates of the last two decades behind us, their opponents are more willing, and perhaps more obliged, to recognise the theoretical benefits and the (allegedly limited) success in East Asia of selective industrial and trade policies. However, they tend to argue that the success of such policies depends critically on the existence of certain types of institutions which make such interventions feasible, and therefore that these policies cannot be easily transferred to other countries which do not have such institutional prerequisites.

For example, in the earlier phase of the East Asian industrial policy debate, the absence of an elite bureaucracy was singled out as the reason why the Japanese-style industrial policy could not be implemented in the US (e.g., Badaracco and Yoffie 1983; Schultze 1983), while the absence of institutions ensuring the close cooperation between the state and the industrialists made some British commentators sceptical regarding the implementation of selective industrial and trade policies in the modern British context (e.g., Hare 1985).

---

3   Representative works include Balassa *et al.* (1982), Little (1982), and Lal (1983).
4   Seminal works include Jones and Sakong (1980), Evans and Alizadeh (1984), Luedde-Neurath (1986), Toye (1987), Amsden (1989), and Wade (1990). For a summary of this early debate, with a special reference to Korea, see Chang (1993).
5   See Johnson (ed.) (1984) and Chang (1994: Ch. 3).
6   For criticism of the Report, see the special symposium in *World Development* 1994, no.4, Fishlow *et al.* (1994), Singh (1994), Lall (1998), Akyüz *et al.* (1998), and Chang (1999).

Likewise, in the more recent phase of the East Asian industrial policy debate, the absence of a functioning (nevermind it being elite or not) bureaucracy and of the institutions of productive public-private cooperation have again been identified as the obstacles to the adoption of selective industrial and trade policies by other developing countries. The World Bank was most explicit about this in its controversial 'East Asian Miracle Report' (World Bank 1993).

In the report, the Bank argued that the selective trade and industrial policies of the kinds used in Northeast Asia (the report's term for Japan and the four first-tier NICs of Korea, Taiwan, Singapore and Hong Kong), whose benefits it regards as doubtful anyway, require a range of highly developed institutions, and therefore cannot be successfully replicated in other developing economies with poor institutional infrastructure. In contrast, the Miracle Report argued, some Southeast Asian economies, namely, Thailand, Indonesia, and Malaysia, achieved high growth without using very much selective industrial and trade policies, and therefore provide a better role model for other developing economies.

This chapter aims to examine whether there are indeed certain institutional prerequisites that a country should achieve before it can implement selective industrial and trade policies, and if so, what they are, by drawing mainly on the experiences of the East Asian countries but also on the historical experiences of the now-advanced economies of Europe and North America.

In the next section (Section 2), we make some theoretical clarifications on the role of institutions in supporting economic policies and see whether the widespread argument is true that particular types of policies require more institutional 'props'. In the following section (Section 3), we look at certain institutions which have been believed to be important in the success of selective industrial and trade policies – the bureaucracy (Section 3.1), institutions that provide control over resource flows (Section 3.2), and 'intermediate' institutions (Section 3.3). In Section 4, we examine the implications of the recent changes in international institutions, notably the birth of the WTO (World Trade Organisation) regime, for the implementation of selective industrial and trade policies. In the final section (Section 5), we summarise and conclude our discussion and try to draw policy lessons from it.

2. MARKETS, POLICIES, AND INSTITUTIONS: SOME THEORETICAL CLARIFICATIONS

As we have pointed out, it has now become commonplace to argue that, whatever the merits of selective industrial and trade policies, they need certain institutional conditions for them to be successful. At one level, this is a perfectly valid point. Policies do not operate in an institutional vacuum, and therefore it is only natural that the success or otherwise of a particular policy depends on the institutions that enable and/or constrain it. For example, it will be hardly surprising if an incomes policy is easier to implement in a country with a strong, centralised union (that is, as far as the union accepts the spirit of such policy). Thus, it is more than reasonable to say that certain institutions (e.g., a strong centralised union) may be necessary for the success of a particular type of policy (e.g., incomes policy).

However, many of those who talk about the institutional prerequisites for the success of selective industrial and trade policies (henceforth SIT policies for short) tend to mean more than this. In making this argument, they implicitly assume that other types of policies do not need such prerequisites, or at least that whatever institutional prerequisites that other policies need can be relatively easily provided. More specifically, they believe that the more a policy allows the market mechanism to work, the less 'props' it needs in terms of institutions. Hence the assertion that a *laissez-faire* policy regime does not need many institutional prerequisites and therefore can be implemented by any country, whereas the highly interventionist SIT policies of the East Asian economies require an array of sophisticated institutions in order for them to be effective. However, it is not clear whether this is in fact the case.

First of all, well-functioning markets require certain institutional prerequisites as much as well-functioning policies require them. It is well known that well-functioning markets require many institutions, including, among others, stable property right rules, contract law, product liability rules, bankruptcy rules, and well-functioning bureaucratic and court systems to administer the rules. Thus seen, it is not that a successful free market system can operate without institutional 'props'. It may require a set of institutions that are different from the ones required for a successful implementation of SIT policies, but it still needs many institutions.

Moreover, there can be no presumption that the institutions that support more market-oriented policies are simpler than those needed for more 'difficult', selective, policies. For example, a free trade policy may not be as successful as it could be if the country lacks institutions such as contract laws, trade credit facilities, and effective dispute settlement mechanisms. This is because, without these institutions, international trade becomes costly, as it involves long-distance transactions with significant time lags between parties from different social and cultural backgrounds. For another example, a *laissez-faire* industrial policy may produce a lot of 'wastes' in the form of excess capacity and unnecessary bankruptcies (and the scrapping of 'specific' assets), if there are no institutions such as industry associations or cartels that can 'regulate' or 'manage' competition in the industry.

Lastly, it is not clear at all whether establishing the more market-oriented institutions such as good contract law or a functioning court system is easier than setting up the institutions more geared towards selective interventions such as state-funded export credit facilities for some selected industries. Telling from the experiences of various countries, probably the reverse is true. More broadly, the fact that many developing countries have tried during the last half-a-century to build the institutions that are needed to have a well-functioning market economy, often with little success, is testimony to the difficulties involved in constructing the institutions required for a well-functioning market economy.

In short, in order to have a more informed debate on the institutional prerequisites of SIT policies, we need to break away from the unwarranted assumption prevailing in the debate that the less 'market-oriented' a policy is, the more sophisticated institutional 'props' it needs.

3.   INSTITUTIONS FOR SELECTIVE INDUSTRIAL AND TRADE POLICIES: LEARNING FROM PAST EXPERIENCES

In this section, we will examine the experiences of the now-advanced countries in their conduct of SIT policies during the earlier days of their development. We will try to identify those institutions which may have been critical in the success of SIT policies in these countries and see exactly which role they played and, when possible, how they were constructed through conscious government and private sector efforts (if they were).

The focus of the discussion will be on the East Asian countries, although we will draw on the experiences of the European or the North American countries wherever relevant. The concentration on East Asia is at one level motivated by the fact that it was the success of SIT policies in the East Asian countries that generated the recent interest in the role of institutional factors in determining the success of such policies. However, the experiences of the East Asian countries deserve even more attention because many of them were in fact not much more advanced than today's least developed countries until a few decades ago (Chang 1998b).

3.1 The Bureaucracy

As already mentioned in the introductory section, many people have pointed out the high-quality bureaucracy as a factor crucial in explaining the success of SIT policies in East Asia. The same argument has been raised in relation to other countries which have had successes in SIT policies, such as France, whose elite bureaucracy is simultaneously praised and detested for its prominent role in directing the economy through selective intervention. Then is the policy implication, except for those who believe that SIT policies have nothing to contribute, that we should improve the quality of the bureaucracy if we are to conduct SIT policies successfully?

Many commentators, however, will say that this only shows that SIT policies are not relevant for most developing countries. They argue that a high-quality bureaucracy is usually a product of political and cultural tradition, and therefore countries without such tradition cannot just conjure up a high-quality bureaucracy. They point out that the high-quality bureaucracies in the East Asian countries owe their existence to a long Confucian cultural tradition, where the meritocratically-selected elite bureaucracy has dominated the society. Given that very few of the least developed countries can claim a strong bureaucratic tradition (Confucian or not), the case against SIT policies seems sealed. However, a closer look at the past experiences suggests that the story is not so simple.

3.1.1 The Definition of High-Quality Bureaucracy

While not disputing the usefulness of a high-quality economic bureaucracy for the successful design and implementation of SIT policies, we wish to emphasise that what 'high quality' means needs to be defined clearly. The popular perception is that a 'high-quality' economic bureaucracy needs to be staffed with people with advanced training in economics or management. However, the experiences of the successful East Asian countries suggest that this may be a wrong way of looking at the problem.

Most of the elite economic bureaucrats in Japan have been lawyers by training, Korea also has had a high proportion of lawyers running the economic bureaucracy (more so in the earlier days), and in Taiwan the elite economic bureaucrats have been mostly engineers by training. These lawyers and engineers did have some training in economics, but the economics training that they had was often of the 'wrong' kinds – for example, Japanese economics faculties have been until recently dominated by Marxists; Schumpeter and List were widely taught. Above all, the economics training in these countries has not been of such high quality by international standards until recently. The fact that the bureaucracy in India, a country with arguably one of the best economics training in the world, has not been equally success- ful in guiding its economy also suggests that specialised training in economics may not be so crucial in making a 'high-quality' economic bureaucracy[7].

In the end, the competence that is needed for the conduct of a successful SIT policy seems to be, somewhat counter-intuitively, that

---

7   Indeed, if we compare the early Korean five-year plan documents of the 1960s (which employ little more than simple macroeconomic accounting and projection) with the early Indian five-year plan documents of the 1950s and the 1960s (which were based on sophisticated economic models such as the Mahalanobis model), we realise how poor the quality of the Korean bureaucracy's 'economics' was at least in the early days.

of a generalist, rather than that of an economist in the conventional sense, as Johnson (1982) pointed out in his classic work on Japan. This may be because what is most needed for a successful policy, even of the 'selective' kinds, is the ability of the policy makers to make good judgments on main issues, and not specialist knowledge, which can be acquired by consulting experts and also by 'learning-by-doing' on the job. This suggests that the least developed countries intent on developing a good economic bureaucracy should put more emphasis on recruiting people of generally high calibre, rather than looking for specialists in economics and other related subjects.

3.1.2 Political Insulation of the Bureaucracy

It has been frequently pointed out that the bureaucracy conducting SIT policies should not only be highly competent but it should also be insulated from political pressure. This is a natural conclusion, given the nature of SIT policies.

SIT policies, by definition, attempt to change the economic structure over and beyond what the market is able to do by inducing the private sector agents into new activities that they do not have interest in entering under a free-market situation. This means that the SIT policies by definition have no natural supporter groups – a non-existent electronics industry does not have anyone to advance its interests. Therefore, unless the bureaucracy has the political autonomy to go beyond merely responding to private sector demands, the new activities will never get promoted.

Moreover, SIT policies often, although not necessarily, involve a temporary suspension of market incentives. This means that there has to be some force that can discipline the firms receiving protection and subsidies (or more generally other forms of state-created rents). Otherwise, these policies can easily result in 'infant' industries that never grow up or in permanently 'sick' industries – as has so often happened in many developing countries. And if the bureaucracy is to discipline the recipients of state-created rents according to some 'rational' plan, it has to have political independence.

The existence until recently of a highly authoritarian political regime in some of the countries that successfully used SIT policies, such as Korea and Taiwan, has created a widespread belief that bureaucratic insulation is only possible under authoritarianism. However, other countries which successfully practised SIT policies did not have to rely on authoritarianism to ensure the necessary degree of bureaucratic insulation. For example, Japan and France may have had a political system where the executive branch is dominant (and therefore the bureaucracy is not very sensitive to parliamentary demands), but these can, by no stretch of the imagination, be described as authoritarian states. Moreover, Finland, Austria and Norway, the other successful practitioners of SIT policies during the postwar period, had strong parliamentary systems.

The above examples suggest that there is no necessary correlation between a country's bureaucratic insulation and its political system. What seems to be more important than the political system is the existence of a 'Weberian' bureaucracy based on competitive recruitment and well-defined career path that makes politically motivated hiring and dismissal difficult, if not impossible (on the importance of Weberian bureaucracy in the developmental process, see Rauch and Evans 2000).

3.1.3 The Role of 'Pilot Agencies'

Many of the past experiences with SIT policies demonstrate the importance of 'pilot agencies' staffed by elite bureaucrats in increasing the effectiveness of the policies. SIT policies often involve issues that cut across the responsibilities of many different government ministries and agencies, and therefore it is useful to have a pilot agency that has the power and the legitimacy to coordinate activities across different agencies and resolve the potential conflicts between them. In some countries, the pilot agency took the form of powerful planning ministries with formal power to overrule other ministries and agencies (the Economic Planning Board of Korea and the Commissariat General du Plan of France). In others, it assumed the form of a coordinating committee (the Industrial Development Bureau of Taiwan) or even a single ministry (the Ministry of International Trade and Industry of Japan, where the Economic Planning Agency was powerless) with more informal power over other government agencies. However, the underlying principle is the same – you need an agency that has some power to coordinate different interests within and outside the government.

Having a pilot agency also seems to bring the added benefit of increasing the political insulation of the economic bureaucracy that we talked about in the previous sub-section. This is because the pilot agencies in many countries that practised SIT policies were not 'line' ministries and therefore did not have to worry about their 'clients'' interest – this was the case in France, Korea, and Taiwan. However, in Japan, the MITI played the role of the pilot agency very well despite being a line ministry. This goes to show that having a line ministry as a pilot agency is not necessarily bad for political insulation of the elite bureaucracy. Indeed, some may even argue that the tendency of such pilot agencies to become all too powerful, which can sometimes lead to unchecked pursuit of mistaken policy, can be usefully restrained by the presence of other powerful ministries, such as the Ministry of Finance in the Japanese case.

3.1.4 The Role of Bureaucratic Tradition

Many of those who are sceptical about the viability of SIT policies in the least developed countries point out that a good bureaucracy is something that cannot be built overnight. Therefore, they argue, countries without a strong bureaucratic tradition, such as we find in the Confucian countries in East Asia or France, should not attempt SIT policies.

On the surface, this argument seems perfectly sensible. The East Asian countries all have the Confucian cultural heritage dating back many centuries, where meritocratically-recruited bureaucrats have played the leading role. Some European countries which actively used SIT policies, such as France and Austria, can boast some of the oldest and strongest bureaucratic traditions in Europe. It cannot simply be a coincidence that these were the countries which were most willing and able to conduct SIT policies. However, on a closer look, this interpretation becomes less convincing (also see Evans 1995 and 1998).

First of all, it is not clear whether it is really the Confucian tradition that made all the East Asian bureaucracies what they are. For example, in the case of Singapore, it may well be argued that it was really the transplanted British bureaucratic tradition, rather than the Confucian one, that formed the backbone of its current administrative structure. De-emphasising the 'cultural' dimension implies that constructing a new bureaucratic tradition may not be as difficult as some people argue it to be.

Secondly, bureaucratic traditions are quite fragile things which can easily decay and even disappear, and indeed many of the East Asian and the European countries that had successful SIT policies were once good examples of this. For example, the Taiwanese bureaucracy in the 1950s was regarded as lacking in meritocracy and effectiveness – not a very surprising state of affairs considering the infamous corruption and incompetence of the same machinery in mainland China before 1949 (Cheng *et al.* 1998). And all of these despite 2.5 millennia of Confucian bureaucratic tradition. Korea, despite a thousand years of Confucian bureaucratic tradition, was regarded in the 1950s as having an incompetent and non-meritocratic bureaucracy (Cheng *et al.* 1998). The French bureaucracy was regarded as extremely conservative and ineffective for nearly a century before the Second World War, despite its previous tradition of centralised bureaucratic rule (Kuisel 1981). Similar things may be said about the Austrian bureaucracy during the first half of the 20th century, despite hundreds of years of bureaucratic tradition of the Austro-Hungarian empire.

Thirdly, our examples suggest that, while it is easy to squander even millennia-old bureaucratic traditions and end up with a poor bureaucracy, a good bureaucracy is not as hard to construct as it is often believed to be. For example, it was only after the extensive civil service reform during the 1960s and the 1970s that Korea was regarded as having a high-quality bureaucracy – after all, it was sending its bureaucrats to Pakistan and the Philippines for extra training until the late-1960s. The transformation of the French bureaucracy from one of the most conservative to one of the most dynamic in the world after the Second World War also shows how good bureaucracies can be relatively quickly built, if there is a political will and appropriate institutional reforms.

3.2 Institutions that Provide Control over Resource Flows

One common misperception about SIT policies has been that it is all about subsidies and tariff protection. For example, in the early days of recent industrial policy debate, many commentators doubted the very existence of SIT policies in Japan on the ground that the Japanese government did not spend more money on subsidies (as a proportion of GDP) than the majority of the OECD countries. However, SIT policies are much more than subsidies and tariff protection, although these are obviously important instruments.

Many studies have emphasised that one important function of SIT policies is the provision of an 'entrepreneurial vision', which provides 'focal points' around which private sector investment decisions can be (both formally and informally) coordinated (e.g., Renshaw 1986; Chang and Rowthorn 1995b). Provision of such vision can, and to an extent should, involve subsidies and tariff protection, but it also can be done through less costly measures. These include: indicative planning (at national and sectoral levels); encouragement of the formation of private sector cartels and consortia for productivity-enhancement purposes (which may or may not involve price collusion); and the continuation of 'dialogue' with the private sector that will help the relevant actors to forge a common vision. The Japanese state, especially in its encouragement of information technology industries, has been particularly successful in this regard (Renshaw 1986; Okimoto 1989; Fransman 1990), but this applies to the other countries that practised SIT policies actively.

Having emphasised that SIT policies are not all about handing out money to those who are running businesses in favoured industries, it should also be emphasised that the implementation of SIT policies needs to be supported by substantial degrees of control over financial and real resources, if government 'announcements' are to have significant impacts. Two of these stand out – state-owned enterprises and the control over the financial sector.

3.2.1 State-owned Enterprises

Many of the countries which actively practised SIT policies have used state-owned enterprises (henceforth SOEs) extensively. The popular conception is that the larger the SOE sector is, the less efficient and dynamic your economy will be, but the evidence from our East Asian and European examples flies in the face of such an argument[8].

For example, France, Austria, and Norway all had large SOE sectors[9]. Moreover, it is not simply that their SOE sectors are big. They also have been most dynamic, and have led the modernisation of their industries. Taiwan has one of the largest public enterprise sectors in the non-oil-producing world, especially if we include the 'party enterprises' – enterprises owned by the Kuomintang party which are often classified as 'private' enterprises (Fields 1998). The Taiwanese SOEs were mostly in the upstream sectors producing intermediate inputs, and their efficiency has contributed a lot to the competitiveness of the country's downstream industries which use their products as inputs (Amsden 1985; Wade 1990). The Taiwanese government also started off some risky, high-technology SOEs and spun off private sector firms from them – some of the leading semi-conductor firms in the country were created in this way. Korea's SOE sector, while not as large as that of Taiwan, has been as large as that of India, which is often touted as the example of an excessively large state sector, but has been

---

8   The earlier orthodox position on the role of state-owned enterprises in developing countries is well summarised in World Bank (1983). Subsequent criticisms (reviewed in Cook and Kirkpatrick (eds.) 1988, and Chang and Singh 1993) forced the World Bank and its associates to revise its position (World Bank 1995), but even this revised position had a lot of problems (for a critical review, see Chang and Singh 1997). In the case of the developed countries, the orthodox arguments are well summarised in Vickers and Yarrow (1988) and Yarrow (1989). Chang and Singh (1993) also provide some theoretical criticisms of this position.

9   As of the mid-1970s, the share of the public enterprise sector in GDP was 14.5% in Austria and 11.9% in France, when the industrial country average was 9.6%. During the same period, Austria (19.2%) had the highest share of the public enterprise sector in gross fixed capital formation in the industrialised world, and Norway (17.7%) was behind only Australia (18.7%) and the UK (18.6%). See Chang and Singh (1993) for further details.

technologically much more dynamic than the latter[10]. Some of the Korean SOEs are world-renowned firms (e.g., POSCO, the steel producer).

Of course, all these are not to suggest that an effective SIT policy regime requires a large SOE sector. Japan is an important exception to this pattern that proves this point. While its SOE sector is not exceptionally small, it is not very big either, and in manufacturing industries, the role of SOEs in Japan has been minimal. However, it is true that SOEs can provide, and have provided, an important channel through which SIT policies can be implemented. Of course, the problem in many developing countries is that the SOE sector has been a drain on state resources, rather than an effective channel for state control of resources. Therefore ways need to be found in order to improve their performance, including (but by no means exclusively) privatisation – a subject that we do not have the space to go into (see the literature cited in footnote 8; also see Chapter 6 of this volume).

3.2.2 Control over the Financial Sector

Control over the financial sector has been a more important institutional basis than control over SOEs for effective SIT policies. Needless to say, the mechanism through which such control was instituted and maintained has been different across countries, but the government in all countries with successful SIT policy experiences has had strong control over the financial sector in one way or another.

In many countries during much of the time, this took the form of state ownership of banks and other financial institutions. In Korea and Taiwan at some point, all the banks were owned by the government. The bulk of the banking sector is still state-owned in France and Taiwan. The Korean state pulled out of banking ownership in a major way since the 1980s, but still owns a number of key banks. In Norway, at one point the state banks controlled over 50% of bank loans (Fagerberg *et al.* 1990). Japan is an exception here once again, as its

---

10 Of course, in comparing the share of SOEs in two economies (Korea and India, for example), it should be noted that as a rule we have more public ownership in the more industralised economies (here, Korea) due to the ease of nationalising industrial, as opposed to agricultural, assets.

government owned only a relatively limited part of the financial sector, although its famous post office savings scheme allowed it to control a substantial amount of financial flows in the economy.

Direct ownership, however, is only one of the ways in which the governments in these countries maintained their control over the financial sector. The East Asian and the European countries that we are talking about all possessed what is known as bank-led financial systems, where banks are highly exposed to highly-geared corporations (with the exception of Taiwan, where the gearing ratio is low)[11]. This gave the government enormous leverage over the banks, as they had to rely heavily on the state-controlled central banks for their continued survival. Partly because of this, the governments of many of these countries exercised substantial influence on the appointment of top managers in the banks. In Korea, until the recent radical financial liberalisation (1993 onward), the government decided top management appointments in all banks, including the ones which were privatised in the 1980s.

With the outbreak of the Asian crisis in 1997 and the prolonged recession in Japan, state control over the financial sector in the East Asian countries has come under fierce attack. The argument is that, by rationing credits and even guaranteeing repayments according to non-market criteria (dictated by SIT policies), these governments encouraged inefficient investments. It is also pointed out that, in the absence of effective takeover mechanisms through the stock market, and given the continued government support for its 'cronies', it was almost impossible to punish bad investment decisions even after they have happened (for criticisms of the 'crony capitalism' story, see Chang

---

11 Between 1980-91, the average debt-equity ratio in our SIT countries ranged between 270% (Austria) and 555% (Sweden). In between were France (361%), Korea (366%), Japan (369%), Finland (492%), and Norway (538%). Contrast this with the Anglo-Saxon economies, where the ratio ranged between 112% (South Africa) and 179% (USA), with Australia (125%), UK (148%), New Zealand (153%), and Canada (160%) in between. It is interesting to note that the European countries with less active use of SIT policies had debt-equity ratios that were between these two groups of countries, with Switzerland (175%), Belgium (202%), and the Netherlands (216%) having ratios similar to the top-end of the Anglo-Saxon countries (179% for the USA), and Germany (273%), Spain (275%), and Italy (307%) having ratios similar to those of the lower range of the SIT countries (Austria 270%). All data are from Demigruc-Kunt and Maksimovic (1996: p.354).

2000). So the implicit argument is that the state control over the financial sector that we argue to be central to the institutional foundation of SIT policies actually is what bankrupted these countries.

One myth that needs debunking here before we take on the above argument is that the bank-based financial system that has dominated our East Asian and European countries with active SIT policies is somehow a ' deviation' from the 'norm' of the Anglo-American-style capital-market-based financial system. The reality is the reverse. As is well known, bank dominance of the financial system is the norm among developing countries in general, and not just in East Asia, but this is also the case among the developed countries. It is only the US, the UK, and a few other Anglo-Saxon countries that have capital-market-based financial systems, and all the other developed countries have bank-based systems of one type or another (see Zysman 1983, Cox (ed.) 1986, and Dertouzos *et al.* 1989).

It is often argued that the low profitability of the banks and other financial firms in these countries with bank-dominated financial systems proves the inefficiency of their financial systems. However, this assumes that private profitability correctly reflects a firm's social contribution, and therefore that high profitability of the financial institutions means that they are channelling money into the most efficient firms. However, this is an assumption that is unacceptable to everyone except to the most doctrinaire free-marketeers. In our view, the best indicator of a country's financial institutions' ability to mobilise and allocate resources is the country's overall growth performance in the long run, rather than the profitability of its banks and other financial institutions, which does not necessarily reflect their social contribution. And from this point of view, given the superior growth records of the countries concerned during their periods of active SIT policies, we may be able to say that the financial institutions in these countries have performed very well.

The 'cronyism' story is also implausible, even for the economies in crisis like Korea and Japan. In these countries, state favouritism was mostly linked to 'objective' plans, rather than to political connections, as far as it concerned the manufacturing sector (areas like urban planning and defence contracts were another story). Moreover, as the earlier studies repeatedly emphasised, the success of SIT policies in these countries owed a great deal to the willingness and the ability of their governments to discipline the recipients of the state-created rents.

It was in fact due to the weakening of such disciplinary power following financial liberalisation and other deregulatory measures that politically-motivated lending and subsidies increased (Chang 1998a and 2000; Chang *et al.* 1998). Indeed, many observers agree that the recent crisis is largely a product of ill-thought-out financial liberalisation that occurred since the late-1980s, and especially the early-1990s, which encouraged the accumulation of short-term loans and weakened the already weak prudential regulations that existed in these countries[12]. It is also no coincidence that the countries in the region which did not extensively liberalise their state-directed bank-based financial system, namely, China and Taiwan, have survived the crisis the best.

Thus seen, the state control over the financial sector has been critical in ensuring the success of SIT policies, by providing the state with the power to influence private sector investment decisions, and more importantly, by giving it the power to discipline the non-performers. Despite the currently popular attack on state-controlled financial systems, especially of the East Asian variety, there is no evidence that it is the state control over finance that caused the crisis in some of these countries. If anything, the evidence points the other way – in other words, it was the weakening of the state control over the financial sector that allowed the rapid and unsustainable build-up of short-term loans that eventually brought these economies down.

3.3 Intermediate Institutions

Many studies of SIT policies, especially in the East Asian context, have brought out the importance of 'intermediate' institutions that link the state apparatus with individual firms in ensuring the success of SIT policies. The most frequently discussed intermediate institutions are the ones that provide the interface between the bu-

---

12 It is no big surprise that economists and other social scientists who have been sceptical of the orthodox view see things this way – see the essays in the special section in *World Development*, 1998, no. 8, and the special issue of *Cambridge Journal of Economics*, 1998, no.6. However, now even some of the core members of the orthodox group have converged on this view. See, for example, Radelet and Sachs (1998), Feldstein (1998), Corden (1998), Stiglitz (1998 and 2001), and Furman and Stiglitz (1998).

reaucracy executing SIT policies and the firms that are at the receiving end of those policies – such as deliberation councils.

As we emphasised above (Section 3.1.2), political insulation of the bureaucracy is important for the success of SIT policies, but, whatever its benefits are, it is not something that is unambiguously desirable. Above all, a bureaucracy that is overly insulated from external pressures can pursue its aims without external checks. In other words, while some degree of political insulation is needed for the bureaucracy to pursue a long-term, socially 'rational' strategy, feedback from those who are affected by its policies is necessary if it is not to become a power unto itself and pursue its own objectives, rather than serving as an institution through which society can coordinate potentially conflicting interests.

The experiences of countries with successful SIT policies show that indeed their bureaucracies engaged in a dialogue with the private sector, and therefore were able to get detailed feedback on their policies, albeit through different mechanisms depending on the country, and thereby received constant feedback on their policies from those who were affected by them.

For this purpose, Japan used the now-famous deliberation councils, which had representations from both public and private sectors, as well as 'third parties' such as academics, the press, and occasionally other social actors such as consumer groups (World Bank 1993: Chapter 4). Korea used similar institutions, including its own unique monthly export promotion meetings during the 1960s and the 1970s presided by the president and attended by top bureaucrats and top business leaders (Jones and Sakong 1980). However, the decision-making process in the Korean institutions was much more government-dominated than in their Japanese counterparts. Taiwan had to use more informal networks. Its political parameters (such as the ethnic division between the political elite from the mainland and the 'Taiwanese' business elite) dictated that the government discouraged the emergence of large-scale private sector firms, which were the main counterparts to the governments in the deliberation councils in Japan and Korea (Fields 1995). In France, the continued flows back and forth of the top managerial personnel between the public sector and the private sector seem to have ensured a good working relationship between the two, although this has attracted criticisms of 'revolving door' and 'clubbiness' at the top echelon of the French elite.

Once broad policy principles were decided at the national level through deliberation councils and their equivalents, these principles would be translated into concrete action plans and enforced by the industry associations. These associations contributed to the resolution of the 'collective action' problems required for the policy objective (e.g., restraint on competition, contribution to a common marketing scheme) in two ways. First of all, they would share out the overall burden in a manner that is seen as ' fair' (but not necessarily 'equal' in the strict sense) among their members[13]. Secondly, they would devise ways to monitor the compliance by their members with the agreed 'collective action' schemes. This was sometimes done by organising officially-sanctioned formal cartels (most notably in the case of many Japanese industries until the 1980s; see Magaziner and Hout 1980, and Dore 1986 for some more details) but sometimes through informal cartels implicitly backed by the state.

The above-described relationship between the state and the private sector has been captured in the notion of 'embedded autonomy' (the term is due to Evans 1995). Without its embedding in a dense network of public-private interface, it is argued, an autonomous state can easily degenerate into a power unto itself, while without a high degree of autonomy through political insulation, an embedded state will be 'captured' by powerful private sector interest groups[14]. And from this point of view, institutions like deliberation councils and industry associations facilitated the information flows between the bureaucracy and the private sector, on the one hand, and strengthened

---

13 For a fascinating example of how burdens of capacity cuts in the Japanese shipbuilding industry in the late-1970s were shared in what was accepted as a 'fair' manner among different types of firms, see Dore (1986: p.145).

14 However, in some countries, with the growing power of the private sector during the last decade or so, the delicate balance between autonomy and embeddedness seems to have been broken in favour of the latter. This shift was most visible in Korea, where the traditional 'generalistic' relationship between state and big business, where big business was favoured over other sections of the society but only as a group, gave way to a more 'particularistic' relationship, where certain firms were favoured over others – although this is not to suggest that 'cronyism' thus generated was the main, or even an important, cause behind the country's recent crisis (see Chang 1998a, Chang 2000, and Chang et al. 1998).

policy enforcement mechanisms, on the other hand, thus helping the success of SIT policies.

4. CHANGING INTERNATIONAL CONDITIONS FOR THE USE OF SIT POLICIES

During the last decade or so, there has been a marked strengthening of the 'global governance' regime in the direction of greater liberalisation. The conclusion of the WTO (World Trade Organisation) agreement is the most important example, but there have also been other moves such as the attempt to introduce the Multilateral Agreement on Investment (MAI), which aims to restrict industrial and technology policies that discriminate against foreign companies, and bilateral negotiations that are aimed at strengthening the protection of intellectual property rights especially by developing countries.

These attempts have not always been successful. The attempt to push further with the WTO talks in Seattle in late-1999 failed due to strong resistance from developing countries as well as from various pressure groups from developed countries. The talks regarding the MAI initiated by the OECD were also aborted in 1998 by the resistance of many developing countries and some advanced countries. Indeed, quite surprisingly, by late-1999, even the OECD acknowledged the need to introduce a 'code of conduct' for the transnational corporations (TNCs), something that had not been heard of since the 1970s. Bilateral talks to strengthen intellectual property rights in developing countries have been only partially successful.

Despite these setbacks and slowdowns, considerable changes have happened in the international environment for the use of SIT policies, and it is important for the purpose of this chapter to correctly assess the implications of these changes. Below, we focus on the implications of the WTO regime, as it is the centrepiece of the new 'global governance' regime.

The launch of the WTO has prompted many people to argue that, whatever their merits may have been in the past, SIT policies are 'out' now. Is this true? (For further details, see Akyüz et al. 1998, Chang 1999, and Amsden 2000.)

To begin with, it is still not clear how the WTO regime is going to evolve. There are ongoing disputes on what is 'free and fair trade' among the members of the WTO, as best seen in the debates on whether 'lax' labour and environmental standards in developing countries constitute 'unfair competition'. And as far as these disputes reflect genuine differences in values and goals, rather than simple foot-dragging, they are not going to go away easily (on the difficulty of defining the free market, see Chang 1997 and 2002b). Moreover, it is not clear how exactly these disputes will actually be resolved, given the formally 'democratic' decision-making structure of the WTO. Unlike those of the World Bank and the IMF, where the principle of 'one dollar one vote' reigns, or that of the UN, where some countries have formal veto power, the WTO is run on the 'one country one vote' principle and the developing countries seem increasingly more willing to exploit this in their interests (for further details, see Evans 2000).

Second, while it is true that under the WTO, rules on the use of tariffs, subsidies, etc. have become tighter, it is not as if everything was allowed under the old regime. Even under the old GATT regime, there were a lot of restrictions on what countries could do, and countries like Korea often exploited grey areas in implementing their policies. Therefore, it is important not to over-estimate the relative impact of the WTO.

Third, we have to note that, even on paper, the WTO agreement by no means obliges countries to abolish all tariffs and other trade protections, and many developing countries have decided on tariff ceilings that are still considerable (Amsden 2000)[15]. Moreover, the least developed countries have until 2006 to reduce tariffs.

Fourth, infant industry protection is still allowed (up to 8 years), although it must be pointed out that infant industry protection was not the clause invoked by countries like Korea when using protection under the old GATT regime – they usually used the balance-of-payments (BOP) clause that we discuss below.

---

15 Some countries reduced such ceilings substantially – for example, India cut its trade-weighted average tariff from 71% to 32%. However, many countries, including India, have fixed them at relatively high levels – for example, Brazil cut its trade-weighted average tariff from 41% to 27%, Chile from 35% to 25%, Turkey from 25% to 22% (see Amsden 2000: Table 1).

Fifth, there are still provisions for 'emergency' tariff increase ('import surcharge'). This can be done on two grounds. The first is a sudden surge in sectoral imports, which a number of countries have already used (e.g., Argentine tariff on Brazilian cars). The second is the overall BOP problem, for which almost all developing countries qualify and which a number of countries have also used. Since countries have discretion on how much emergency tariffs can be imposed on which commodities, as far as these are on the whole commensurate with the scale of the BOP problem, there is still a lot of room for deliberately creating rents in areas where learning opportunity may be maximised.

Sixth, not all subsidies are 'illegal' for everyone. For example, the least developed countries (roughly below $1,000 income per capita) are allowed to use export subsidies, which other countries cannot. Subsidies for agriculture, regional development, basic R and D, environment-related technology upgrading are still allowed. Moreover, the subsidy restrictions only cover ' trade-related' policies, which means that there are many 'domestic' policies that can be used for the creation of learning rent and other technology policy purposes – examples will include subsidies on equipment investments, support for start-up enterprises, subsidies for investment in particular skills, etc.

Seventh, although the exact future shape of the TRIPS (trade-related intellectual property rights) agreement is still not entirely certain, given the way in which the developed countries, especially the US, are behaving, it is likely to have some important adverse effects on technology transfer to and absorption by developing countries (see Chang 2001 for further details). However, it must be said that the technologies that the least developed countries need to absorb are often the ones that are too old to have patents, hence an overly pessimistic conclusion should not be drawn. Also, they have a longer transition period for the introduction of product patents (until 2006, against 2000 for other developing countries).

Lastly, as for the TRIMs (trade-related investment measures) agreement, it should be noted that it is not as stringent as it is sometimes thought to be. Amsden (2000) points out that developing countries can maintain or even strengthen local-content requirement, which is an important tool for technology upgrading. She also argues that they are still allowed to use export promotion measures, such as 'trade balancing stipulations' (where TNCs are required to export final products whose value equals the imports of parts and components) or export requirements for TNCs in export processing zones. She points out that many countries (e.g., Brazil, Argentina, Chile, India, Indonesia, Mexico, Malaysia, Thailand) have in fact been using these provisions in a number of industries (e.g., automobile, pharmaceutical, various consumer goods industries).

Thus seen, the changing international environment has certainly imposed considerable extra constraints on the conduct of SIT policies by developing countries, but these constraints are by no means overwhelming. The least developed countries also have some extra room for manoeuvre in the form of exemptions (e.g., from ban on export subsidies) and longer transition arrangements (e.g., on tariff reduction and product patents). And many countries have actively sought, and succeeded, to use activist policies without breaching the WTO requirements. And with the increasing demands by the developing countries to forge an international trading and investment order that is less one-sided, backed up for one thing by the 'democratic' structure of the WTO, the scope for SIT policies may even increase in the future.

5. SUMMARY AND CONCLUSION

This chapter has tried to identify the institutions that are important in the effective design and implementation of selective industrial and trade policies, and discussed in exactly what ways these institutions matter and how exactly they should be designed in order to be effective.

We criticised the currently popular view that SIT policies are impractical in most developing countries because they require an exceptional range of 'institutional props' that more market-oriented policies would not require, on the ground that the latter policies would also require their own 'institutional props'. However, we agreed that SIT policies do require certain institutions if they are to be effectively designed and implemented. We identified a number of such institutions – the bureaucracy, state-owned enterprises, controls on financial flows, 'intermediate institutions' such as deliberation councils and industry associations.

We argued that, while these institutions do matter, the ways in which they are supposed to matter are often misunderstood. The most important example is the prevailing view on a 'high-quality bureaucracy', namely, that it means a bureaucracy staffed with economists. We also argued that there is no uniform pattern across countries in the ways in which these institutions matter – the examples included the varying role of state-owned enterprises and the differences in the forms of 'intermediate institutions' that existed in different countries that pursued selective industrial and trade policies. This means that more careful thinking and further empirical research are needed, if we are to draw useful lessons from the experiences of the countries that successfully used SIT policies.

We then confronted the currently popular view that the changes in international institutions, especially the launch of the WTO, have made the use of SIT policies extremely difficult, if not totally impossible. We accepted that there are now more constraints on the use of SIT policies than before, but pointed out that there is still room for manoeuvre and that there are many SIT policies that can be used perfectly legitimately under the WTO regime.

The ultimate question that we face in discussing the institutional foundations of selective industrial and trade policies is the question of replicability. While we realise that transferring institutions across national borders is not a straightforward matter, we also believe that the difficulties involved in it have been far too exaggerated. We have argued, for example, that the high-quality bureaucracies that existed in our 'industrial policy states' that are allegedly the products of unique historical circumstances are in fact products of relatively recent, deliberate attempts to build such institutions.

Thus seen, there are two general lessons that the least developed countries can draw from the experiences of those European and Asian countries that successfully used selective industrial and trade policies. One is that they need to discard the undue optimism that they are encouraged to adopt in relation to 'market reform'. As many developing and transition economies have found out at great cost during the 'market reforms' of the last decade or two, well-functioning markets also require a range of institutions, whose construction is equally, if not more, difficult as the building of institutions helpful for the success of selective industrial and trade policies. The other lesson is that the least developed countries need to discard the undue pessimism about their ability to make institutional changes when it comes to those related to selective industrial and trade policies. As in the case of technological development, there is a lot of scope for imitation and innovation in the area of institutional development. And, as we have tried to argue in this chapter, the very experiences of the 'industrial policy states' of Europe and Asia that we discussed show that these can be achieved in a relatively short period of time, if there is a political will and careful thinking (see Westney 1987, and Evans 1998 for more detailed arguments).

BIBLIOGRAPHY

Akyüz, Y., Chang, H.-J. and Kozul-Wright, R. (1998). 'New Perspectives on East Asian Development', *Journal of Development Studies,* vol.34, no.6.

Amsden, A. (1985). 'The State and Taiwan's Economic Development', in P. Evans, D. Rueschemeyer and T. Skocpol (eds.), *Bringing the State Back In.* Cambridge: Cambridge University Press.

Amsden, A. (1989). *Asia's Next Giant.* New York: Oxford University Press.

Amsden, A. (2000). *Industrialisation under New WTO Law,* a paper presented at the UNCTAD X meeting, 12-19 February, 2000, Bangkok, Thailand.

Badaracco, J. and Yoffie, D. (1983). '"Industrial Policy": It Can't Happen Here', *Harvard Business Review,* November/December.

Balassa, B. (1982). 'Development Strategies and Economic Performance', in B. Balassa *et al., Development Strategies in Semi-Industrial Economies.* Baltimore: The Johns Hopkins University Press.

Balassa, B. *et. al.* (1982). *Development Strategies in Semi-Industrial Economies.* Baltimore: The Johns Hopkins University Press.

Bruton, H. (1998). 'A Reconsideration of Import Substitution', *Journal of Economic Literature,* vol.36, no.2.

Chang, H.-J. (1993). 'The Political Economy of Industrial Policy in Korea', *Cambridge Journal of Economics,* vol.17, no.2.

Chang, H.-J. (1994). *The Political Economy of Industrial Policy.* London and Basingstoke: Macmillan.

Chang, H.-J. (1997). 'The Economics and Politics of Regulation', *Cambridge Journal of Economics,* vol.21, no.6.

Chang, H.-J. (1998a). 'Korea: The Misunderstood Crisis', *World Development,* vol.26, no.8.

Chang, H.-J. (1998b). 'The "Initial Conditions" of Economic Development – Comparing the East Asian and the Sub-Saharan African Experiences', a report prepared for UNCTAD *Trade and Development Report, 1998.*

Chang, H.-J. (1999). *Industrial Policy and East Asia – The Miracle, the Crisis, and the Future,* a paper presented at the World Bank workshop on 'Re-thinking East Asian Miracle', 16-17 February, 1999, San Francisco, USA.

Chang, H.-J. (2000). 'The Hazard of Moral Hazard – Untangling the Asian Crisis', *World Development,* vol.28, no.4.

Chang, H.-J. (2001). 'Intellectual Property Rights and Economic Development – Historical Lessons and Emerging Issues', *Journal of Human Development,* July, 2001.

Chang, H.-J. (2002a). *Kicking Away the Ladder – Development Strategy in Historical Perspective.* London: Anthem Press.

Chang, H.-J. (2002b). 'Breaking the Mould – An Institutionalist Political Economy Alternative to the Neo-Liberal Theory of the Market and the State', *Cambridge Journal of Economics,* vol.26, no.5.

Okimoto, D. (1989). *Between MITI and the Market: Japanese Industrial Policy for High Technology*. Stanford: Stanford University.

Radelet, S. and Sachs, J. (1998). 'The East Asian Financial Crisis: Diagnosis, Remedies and Prospects', *Brookings Paper on Economic Activity*, 1998, no.1.

Rauch, J. and Evans, P. (2000). 'Bureaucratic Structure and Bureaucratic Performance in Less Developed Countries', *Journal of Public Economics*, no.75.

Reinert, E. (1995). 'Competitiveness and Its Predecessors – A 500-year Cross-national Perspective', *Structural Change and Economic Dynamics*, vol.6.

Renshaw, G. (1986). *Adjustment and Economic Performance in Industrialised Countries: A Synthesis*. Geneva: International Labour Office (ILO).

Schultze, C. (1983). 'Industrial Policy: A Dissent', *The Brookings Review*, Fall.

Singh, A. (1994). '"Openness" and the "Market-friendly" Approach to Development: Learning the Right Lessons from Development Experience', *World Development*, vol.22, no.12.

Stiglitz, J. (1998). *Sound Finance and Sustainable Development in Asia*, keynote address to the Asia Development Forum, jointly organised by the World Bank and the Asian Development Bank, 9-12 March, 1998, Manila, the Philippines.

Stiglitz, J. (2001). 'The Role of International Financial Institutions in the Current Global Economy', in H.-J.Chang (ed.), *The Rebel Within: Joseph Stiglitz at the World Bank*. London: Anthem Press.

Toye, J. (1987). *Dilemmas of Development*. Oxford: Blackwell.

Vartiainen, J. (1995). 'State and Structural Change: What Can be Learnt from the Successful Late Industrialisation', in H.-J. Chang and R. Rowthorn (eds.), *Role of the State in Economic Change*. Oxford: Oxford University Press.

Vickers, J. and Yarrow, G. (1988). *Privatisation: An Economic Analysis*. Cambridge, MA: The MIT Press.

Wade, R. (1990). *Governing the Market*. Princeton: Princeton University Press.

Westney, E. (1987). *Imitation and Innovation: The Transfer of Western Organisational Patterns to Meiji Japan*. Cambridge: Cambridge University Press.

World Bank (1983). *World Development Report, 1983*. New York: Oxford University Press.

World Bank (1991). *World Development Report, 1991*. New York: Oxford University Press.

World Bank (1993). *The East Asian Miracle*. New York: Oxford University Press.

World Bank (1995). *Bureaucrats in Business*. New York: Oxford University Press.

Yarrow, G. (1989). 'Does Ownership Matter?', in C. Valjanovski (ed.), *Privatisation and Competition*. London: Institute of Economic Affairs.

Zysman, J. (1983). *Governments, Markets, and Growth*. Oxford: Martin Robertson.